STANDARD METROPOLITAN STATISTICAL AREAS IN OHIO

Political Behavior and Public Issues in Ohio

Political Behavior and Public Issues in Ohio

Edited by John J. Gargan
and James G. Coke
Kent State University

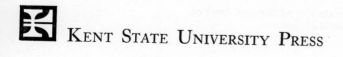

Kent State University Press

Library of Congress Catalog Card Number 72-78408.
ISBN 0-87338-124-6.
Manufactured in the United States of America.
Designed by Harold M. Stevens.
First edition.

Preface

This volume is one product of a project sponsored by the Center for Urban Regionalism, at Kent State University, with the financial support of the Greater Cleveland Associated Foundation. Early in 1969 the center developed a plan for stimulating the interest of the Ohio academic community in studying constitutional change. The time seemed appropriate because a number of activities were underway in preparation for the November, 1972, state-wide vote on the question of convening a convention to revise the Ohio Constitution. The Stephen H. Wilder Foundation had commissioned the Institute of Governmental Research at the University of Cincinnati to undertake a comprehensive study of constitutional issues. The League of Women Voters of Ohio was continuing to make the constitution a state-wide study item. Most important of all, perhaps, was the creation of the Ohio Constitutional Revision Commission by the state legislature in August, 1969. Composed of legislators and public members, the commission was charged with making recommendations on revision to succeeding legislatures throughout the 1970s.

The Center for Urban Regionalism proposed to encourage student and faculty interest through a series of conferences, reports, and grants for research. Student involvement was a primary objective. Following funding of the project in May, 1969, by the Greater Cleveland Associated Foundation, a faculty steering committee was appointed. Overall policy-making authority was vested in this committee, including the approval of individual grant requests. The editors of this volume served the committee in implementing policy and coordinating project activities.

The project began with a conference in November, 1969, attended by faculty members and students from twenty-nine Ohio colleges and universities. Participants were urged to undertake activities at their home campuses and to develop ideas for research and teaching on the subject of constitutional revision. The steering committee reviewed the subsequent applications for support and eventually approved eight requests for funds.

Work on the funded studies was substantially complete by December, 1970, when a second conference was held. Students and faculty members reported on their findings. The papers presented appeared to have general significance for understanding Ohio government and politics, as well as specific relevance for constitutional issues. For this reason, we were encouraged to prepare them for publication, adding some recent research related to the topic, but not financially supported by the project.

Special acknowledgment should be paid to the steering committee, whose judgment was invaluable:

Kathleen, Barber, Political Science Department, John Carroll University

Charles A. Barrell, Political Science Department, Bowling Green State University

Norman Blume, Political Science Department, University of Toledo

Yong Hyo Cho, Center for Urban Studies, University of Akron

Howard Fink, College of Law, Ohio State University

Thomas Flinn, Political Science Department, Cleveland State University

William Harrison, Political Science Department, Ohio State University

Paul Kitchin, Political Science Department, Kent State University

Peter Simmons, College of Law, Ohio State University

Frederick Stocker, College of Administrative Science, Ohio State University

Thomas Ungs, Political Science Department, Kent State University

Herbert Waltzer, Political Science Department, Miami University

To Dr. Eugene Wenninger, Director of the Center for Urban Regionalism, go our thanks for making available time for writing and secretarial resources. Mrs. Carol Toncar, administrative assistant in the center, handled the details of the project with great efficiency and its minor crises with unfailing good humor. Mrs. Janice Crislip expeditiously completed several tedious typing chores.

Finally, we express our gratitude to the Greater Cleveland Associated Foundation for its generous financial assistance and to its staff members, Dr. James A. Norton and Mrs. Barbara Rawson. Dr. Norton's interest, encouragement, and counsel were major factors in the project's achievements.

J. J. G. and J. G. C.
February, 1972

Contributors

KATHLEEN L. BARBER is Assistant Professor of Political Science at John Carroll University.

JOHN H. BOWDEN was a graduate student in political science at Kent State University at the time of this research.

YONG HYO CHO is Associate Professor of Political Science and Urban Studies, and Associate Director of the Center for Urban Studies, University of Akron.

JAMES G. COKE is Professor of Political Science and Senior Research Fellow at the Center for Urban Regionalism, Kent State University.

THOMAS A. FLINN is Professor of Political Science and Chairman of the Department of Political Science, Cleveland State University.

JOHN J. GARGAN is Associate Professor of Political Science and Associate Director of the Center for Urban Regionalism, Kent State University.

JAMES S. GIONOCCHIO was a graduate student in political science at Bowling Green State University at the time of this research. He is presently a candidate for the doctorate in the Department of Political Science, University of Cincinnati.

HOWARD D. HAMILTON is Professor of Political Science, Kent State University.

CARL LIEBERMAN is Assistant Professor of Political Science, University of Akron.

WILLIAM A. SPRATLEY was an undergraduate student at the College of Wooster when he prepared this contribution.

FREDERICK D. STOCKER is Professor of Business Research, Economics, and Public Administration, Ohio State University.

JOSEPH B. TUCKER is Associate Professor in the Department of Government, Ohio University.

Contents

---

*Research funded by the Greater Cleveland Associated Foundation

Introduction

At some future point an enterprising historian may find it useful to describe American political life as a continual search for balance in the capabilities of federal, state, and local governments. He would observe that, over time, the focus of political reform shifted from one level of government to another. There were clearly identifiable periods during which public officials, party leaders, scholars, and civic activists allocated disproportionate amounts of energy to improving the performance of government at one particular level.

Undoubtedly the 1930s and 1940s will be described as the era of national dominance, characterized by the involvement of the national government in new policy areas and by the reordering of governmental machinery in Washington through such prestigious bodies as the Brownlow and Hoover Commissions. The 1950s may have been the decade of local government dominance, when energy and attention were devoted to generating solutions to the development problems of cities and suburbs and the government of metropolitan areas. And in retrospect, the late 1960s might be recalled as the years during which state governments were rediscovered, when fundamental questions were again seriously raised about the role of the states in the federal system and innovative suggestions were brought forth for consideration.

Just as the future historian will record that governmental policy makers were dissatisfied with the performance records of the states during the 1960s, so too will he note dissatisfaction on the part of academic researchers with their methods of analyzing state and local politics. With the notable exception of the works of such scholars as V. O. Key and his followers, much of the pre-1960s literature on state government was concerned with structure and form. In many instances this literature was based upon *a priori* prescriptive assumptions. These assumptions were probably most evident in studies of the defects of state constitutions. But reform biases were also prevalent in discussions of the "irrationality" of "fragmented" administrative structures and of the need for "streamlined" legislatures and courts.

Few subject areas within the discipline of political science have undergone changes so fundamental as those involved in what traditionally has been "state and local government." The revised approach to the study of state and urban politics shifts the focus from "actor defined problems" to "observer defined problems," from developing solutions to governmental problems to answering questions of interest to social scientists. States as well as cities and metropolitan areas have become relevant for study "because of their intrinsic interest as political systems and not primarily because they need a doctor's attention."[1] Terms such as political culture, political development, interest aggregation, and interest articulation are as much a part of the language of the state and local researcher as they are of the language of his colleagues in comparative government.

Accompanying these disciplinary shifts in orientation has been a heightened concern for theory building. If much of the earlier research was normatively based, most of the new is concerned with fundamental questions of empirical theory. For example, a substantial body of recent literature attempts to explain how variations in socio-economic and political factors affect levels of outputs. Or to cite a second example, other studies have drawn upon concepts in role theory and analyzed the perceptions of legislators and judges about their jobs as well as the variables explaining those perceptions.

The growing sophistication of the study of non-national politics is reflected in the methodologies employed. Clearly the comparative approach is a defining characteristic of many contemporary studies. The value of earlier works was limited not only by their normative foundations but also by frequent reliance on the case study. Since the difficulties involved in generalizing from a single case are substantial, scholars have attempted to "compare aspects

---

[1]Wallace S. Sayre and Nelson W. Polsby, "American Political Science and the Study of Urbanization," in Philip M. Hauser and Leo F. Schnore (eds.), *The Study of Urbanization* (New York: John Wiley, 1966), p. 127.

of state and community policy making systems in order to make some general statements about policy systems that will apply to a large number of situations."[2] Moreover, the adoption of a comparative approach, employing a population of fifty states or a large sample of cities, permits the use of a variety of multivariate statistics. The combination of conceptual and statistical rigor has made for dramatic advances in the understanding of state and local political behavior.

Some qualifications are in order. The value placed upon the developments mentioned above is related to the vantage point of the observer. For the academic researcher, whose goal is parsimonious explanations, the values are positive. For the state or urban administrator and interested citizen, the developments may be less valuable. Confronted with frequent crises, the administrator's needs are immediate and pressing; while problems are often particular and specific to his community, the findings of current research are still global and general. Conclusions valid for all states through time may be of little solace to the official worried about a specific state at a specific point in time. Progress in an academic discipline may well result in tension between academicians and public problem solvers, and cries of irrelevancy from both sides.

Considerable effort has been made in this volume to minimize such tensions. All of the research papers have as their primary unit of analysis the State of Ohio or its subdivisions. Although such a focus admittedly limits comparison with other states, the pieces are not "case studies" in the traditional sense. None deal with discrete events simply because of the prominence of the actors or the newsworthiness of the conflict; the studies attempt to demonstrate the relevance of the topic examined to the performance of the larger political system. In a fundamental way the substantive problems dealt with are "real world" problems of taxing and spending, referenda voting, local government reorganization, and so forth. To each of these problems the individual authors have brought an

---

[2]Richard I. Hofferbert and Ira Sharkansky, "The Role of State and Community Political Systems," in Richard J. Hofferbert and Ira Sharkansky (eds.), *State and Urban Politics* (Boston: Little Brown, 1971), pp. 1–2.

awareness of the theoretical and conceptual developments in their disciplines and the methodological skills of the contemporary social scientist. Hopefully, the results will be of value to both the student of and the participant in state and local government and politics.

PART I

An Overview of the Ohio Political System

The Study of Ohio Government and Politics

John J. Gargan and James G. Coke

GIVEN THE SPECIALIZED NATURE OF THE STUDIES CONTAINED IN this volume, an overview of the Ohio political system is in order. This introduction summarizes the major conclusions of the existing body of research on Ohio politics. It also relates the following chapters to the ongoing operations of the state's political institutions.

This introduction is organized in a framework that is by now familiar to most students of state and local government. We present our materials in political system categories, which provide four foci of analysis. We begin with the "political culture," which is an important aspect of the environment that produces political demands and support. Next, we write about the political parties of Ohio, which aggregate and articulate the demands and support that arise out of the political culture. The third focus of analysis is the set of institutions and actors converting demands into policies and programs. Here we describe the legislature, the office of governor, the courts, and local government. Finally, those policies and programs produced—the "outputs" of the political system—are discussed, primarily in terms of expenditure patterns.

Most of the later chapters refer to provisions in the Constitution of Ohio. Because of this underlying theme, we conclude with a discussion of the constitution itself. The order of materials reflects a basic question about constitutional reform: What difference does a constitution make in facilitating or inhibiting a desired set of state and local policies? If judgments are to be made about the usefulness of any constitutional provision, they cannot be isolated from an evaluation of extra-constitutional constraints and their effects. The constitution is a special kind of constraint, but it is only one among many.

I. POLITICAL CULTURE: AN ENVIRONMENTAL FACTOR

Political scientists who discuss "political culture" agree that the concept involves widely shared orientations toward political institutions and political action. Almond and Verba stress the psychological nature of these orientations; that is, the political culture is the political system as internalized through individual cognitions, feelings, and evaluations.[1] Samuel Patterson attaches different labels to the same three components; he calls them empirical beliefs, expressive symbols, and values.[2] Whatever the labels, the internalized orientations to which the terminology refers have an important impact on the political system. The political culture regulates the demands placed upon the system, provides criteria by which citizens judge the legitimacy of political tactics, and gives standards for evaluating the outputs of political action. Furthermore, the political culture helps to determine the ways in which citizens participate in politics. Although the concept of political culture is often elusive, the persistent patterns of behavior that the term connotes seem to be particularly important for understanding Ohio politics.

Those writing about Ohio government and politics frequently find it necessary to explain deviations from expected patterns. Although Ohio has a reputation as a "typical" state, its political

---

[1]Gabriel A. Almond and Sidney Verba, *The Civic Culture* (Boston: Little, Brown and Company, 1963), Chap. 1.

[2]Samuel C. Patterson, "The Political Cultures of the American States," *Journal of Politics,* 30 (February, 1968), 187–209.

system sometimes functions in unexpected ways; some phenomena seem basically at variance with what might be anticipated on the basis of evidence drawn from national studies.

The most synoptic treatments of Ohio politics are found in the writings of Thomas A. Flinn and John H. Fenton. Both have produced basic studies which point out anomalies in Ohio's political patterns. Flinn begins a paper about the 1968 presidential election by asking why the Republicans do so well in a state whose population composition should incline it consistently toward Democratic majorities.[3] In a book about six midwest states, John Fenton discusses Ohio under the title "Issueless Politics in Ohio." Like Flinn, Fenton analyzes voting patterns in this highly industrialized state, which has many union members and urban residents. After World War II, he asserts, Ohioans were generally ignorant of and indifferent toward state politics, and the lower income working classes "failed to associate their economic problems with their votes."[4] Why this occurs is Fenton's primary question. Both Fenton and Flinn find part of their explanations in the political history of Ohio. Through historical analysis, they construct elements of the "political culture" of the state in order to make sense of current patterns.

However suggestive the term "political culture," the application of the concept to all American states has proven difficult. Thus far, the only writer so bold as to categorize all the states according to their political cultures is Daniel Elazar. In *American Federalism: A View From the States,* Elazar describes Ohio and several neighboring states as having a predominantly "individualistic" culture, one which is suspicious of governmental intervention, looks upon the democratic order as another type of marketplace, and sees political participation as one way to secure individual rewards.[5] Ideally, an in-depth discussion of Ohio's political culture

---

[3]Thomas A. Flinn, "State Politics and the 1968 Election in Ohio" (A paper prepared for delivery at the 1971 meeting of the Midwest Political Science Association, Chicago, April 29–May 1, dittoed).

[4]John H. Fenton, *Midwest Politics* (New York: Holt, Rinehart, and Winston, 1966), pp. 117–154, 150.

[5](New York: Thomas Y. Crowell Co., 1966), Ch. 4.

would consider contemporary and historic variations in such factors as basic attitudes of the population, political identification, rates of participation, political styles, and political socialization.[6] But since no scholar has addressed himself specifically to the political culture of Ohio,[7] the most we can do in this introductory essay is to sketch in some persistent orientations towards politics which have derived from the demographic characteristics of Ohio and some aspects of its political history. Some of the more important influences have been patterns of settlement in the state, the ethnic origins of the population, the urbanization process, and the moralistic impulse that nurtured several campaigns for personal and political rectitude.

Settlement Patterns

The movement of settlers into Ohio before 1850 produced sectional patterns of political loyalties that have lasted to the present day. The earliest settlements were the Ohio Company lands centered on Marietta in southeastern Ohio, and the Virginia Military District which lay between the Miami and Scioto Rivers in southwestern Ohio. The Ohio Company was a colonization venture sponsored by New Englanders, while the Military District was a tract reserved by the state of Virginia in order to reward its Revolutionary War veterans. The Yankees around Marietta were strong Whigs. So, too, were the Southerners in the District, most of whom

[6]The variation in these factors as indicators of political culture differences is discussed in Patterson, *op. cit.*

[7]On occasion, however, authors do provide excellent insights into aspects of the political culture. Thus, in discussing how the electorate in Ohio discriminates among candidates for political office, Fenton comments on the basic attitudes of the population: "The first mental screen through which candidates were passed by Ohioans was the 'middle-class' myth. Ohio has been called 'the great middle-class state.' The middle-class myth was a blend of Horatio Alger and the rugged individualist attitudes associated with the frontier. It found concrete expression in a dedication to the homely virtues of honesty, thrift, steadiness, caution, and a distrust of government. Freedom was prized, and restraints tended to be associated almost exclusively with government." Fenton, *op. cit.*, p. 153.

followed the party of Clay rather than the party of Jackson.[8] Both areas moved to the Republican Party during the Civil War[9] and remained a century later the strongest Republican areas in the state. In northeastern Ohio, which was Connecticut's Western Reserve, a similar attachment to the Whigs and Republicans persisted until the early part of the twentieth century, when the immigration of the foreign-born began to shift this highly urbanized industrial area toward Democratic majorities. The remainder of the state tended to attract larger numbers of Scotch-Irish and persons of German origin, either from Germany itself or by way of Pennsylvania. Thus, as Flinn concluded, there was an ethnic-sectional basis for Ohio politics until World War I. "The strongest Whig and Republican counties were Yankee, and many but not all of the strongest Democratic counties had in them strong German elements. . . . This finding plus scattered references in the literature suggest that one of the basic divisions in American politics for many years was this division between Yankee and German."[10]

Ethnicity and the Foreign-born

In many parts of the country, political patterns developed during the early nineteenth century were altered by the influx of the foreign-born and their children. Lacking the experience of such climactic events as the Civil War, and often bringing with them orientations sharply divergent from those of the native stock, the newcomers modified, and in some states virtually transformed, the political cultures of the areas into which they moved.

Despite its location near ports of entry, Ohio was never as strongly affected by immigration as a number of other northeastern and midwestern states. In all census years from 1850 through 1920,

---

[8]Thomas A. Flinn, "Continuity and Change in Ohio Politics," *Journal of Politics,* 24 (August, 1962), 527.

[9]Fenton states that "Ohioans, like lesser mortals in Kentucky and Mississippi were influenced in casting their mid-twentieth-century vote by the battles of Bull Run and Gettysburg." Fenton, *op. cit.,* p. 118.

[10]Flinn, "Continuity and Change in Ohio Politics," *op. cit.,* p. 542.

the percentage of foreign-born whites in the total population was less than 15%. The largest single nationality group throughout the history of the state has been German. In 1850 half the foreign-born were German and another 25% Irish. Approximately one-quarter of both groups were concentrated in Cincinnati alone. Even as late as 1920 the Germans were 16.5% of the state's foreign-born, still the largest single group. The continuing addition of foreign-born Germans to Pennsylvanians and other natives of German stock reinforced the basic political cleavage between Yankees and Germans and was a factor leading to the extraordinary stability of Ohio political party alignments. The voting behavior of rural German groups after 1919, however, produced one of the basic revisions in the traditional pattern. Flinn and Fenton agree that opposition to both world wars, especially the first, shifted the rural counties containing German groups into the Republican column. This is most evident in northwestern Ohio, where there is frequently Democratic voting for governor, but Republican voting for national office.[11]

The foreign-born most frequently associated with allegiance to the Democratic party—the Irish, Italians, and southern Europeans—were attracted primarily to northeastern Ohio, where the heavy industry that sprang up after the Civil War provided many jobs. There were fewer than 2,000 persons born in Poland in the whole state in 1880 and only 17,000 in 1900. By 1920, however, there were 67,000 Poles, 35,000 of whom lived in Cleveland. It was cities like Cleveland, Youngstown, Lorain, and Canton that attracted the Poles and southern Europeans. And as Flinn points out in "The Outline of Ohio Politics," it is the presence of these "Democratic foreign-born" that provides the strongest statistical explanation of voting behavior in the metropolitan counties of Ohio. The influx of the newer ethnic groups was certainly one of the reasons why the Connecticut Western Reserve, traditionally Whig and Republican, became a Democratic stronghold after 1932. The concentration of the Democratic foreign-born in northeastern Ohio

---

[11]*Ibid.*, pp. 535, 539; and Flinn, "The Outline of Ohio Politics," *Western Political Quarterly*, 13 (September, 1960), 709–710.

contributed, in turn, to the persistence of traditional patterns in most other sections of the state.[12]

Urbanization

Urbanization is a modernizing force in the political system. When it is associated with industrialization, as in nineteenth-century America, the cumulative impact is to nurture and sustain new styles of politics. These styles are rational and technocratic, unlike the informal, personal modes of rural politics. The characteristic urban political style has been called "managerial progressivism."[13]

In the United States, rapid urbanization coincided with a great influx of the foreign-born. As most immigrants located in the cities, ethnic diversity was a prominent feature of urban life. Two-thirds of the 1910 population of the eight largest cities was either foreign-born or of the first generation; less than 8% of the rural population in 1910 had been born abroad.

Both newly-emerging urban political styles and the visible ethnicity of city dwellers helped to create an urban-rural division in the politics of several states. The conflict is maintained by

---

[12]This concentration is still evident. According to the 1960 Census, Cuyahoga County (Cleveland) was 33.5% foreign-born or children of foreign-born, and Mahoning County (Youngstown) was 30.1%. The counties containing Cincinnati and Columbus were only 11.4% and 8.7%, respectively. Fenton, *op. cit.*, p. 126.

Thomas Flinn has provided us with a contemporary picture of the self-identification of white, gentile Ohioans in 1968:

Nationality Group	*Percentage*
German	26
English	23
"Other West Europeans"	10
"Just American"	5
Irish	11
Italian	5
Polish	4
"Other East Europeans"	10

Thus only about 30% can be classified as "Democratic nationality groups." See Flinn, "State Politics and the 1968 Election," *op. cit.*, pp. 4–5.

[13]Samuel C. Patterson, *op. cit.*, p. 187.

American political ideology, the anti-urban bias of which has been potent since at least the time of Thomas Jefferson.

In Ohio, population movements between 1860 and 1910 built up the potential for a strong urban-rural split. On the eve of the Civil War, the state had only seven cities of over 8,000 residents, containing 12% of the state's population. For the nation as a whole the group of cities over 8,000 had 16% of the population. By 1910, however, Ohio could boast of fifty-one such cities, with 48% of the population; the comparable figure for the nation was 38%.

Foreign immigration was by no means the major source of urban growth. Native Ohioans moved from the farms to the cities in great numbers. In the decade of the 1880s, there were absolute declines in the population of 755 of 1,316 townships.

Undoubtedly the rapid growth in the size and number of cities was one reason for the strength of progressive reformers in Ohio at the turn of the century. The progressives built their power base in the cities, from which they made occasionally successful sallies against the conservative bastions in state government. Certainly the extent of urbanization gave Ohio's cities an important role in debating a major political question of the 1880–1910 period. Should essential urban services be provided by public or private enterprise?[14]

From another perspective the pattern of urban growth in Ohio may have served, in the long run, to reduce the potential intensity of urban-rural conflict. For one thing, the ethnic differential between city and countryside was slight, except along Lake Erie and in the northeastern counties. For another, the urban population in Ohio was not concentrated in a single metropolis.

One large urban area has historically been the focus of massive urban growth in other industrial states of the midwest; Chicago, Detroit, Milwaukee, and Minneapolis-St. Paul are examples in their respective states. This has not been the pattern in Ohio, where there are a large number of medium-sized cities scattered throughout the state. According to Fenton, "the effect of a diffusion of the (urban) working population, as opposed to their concentration, on

[14]Charles N. Glaab, *The American City: A Documentary History* (Homewood, Illinois: The Dorsey Press, 1963), p. 177.

attitudes and voting behavior was profound."[15] The Ohio working class was inhibited in identifying with working class issues, and this strengthened the tendency of city voters to adopt the political traditions of the surrounding countryside. In short, says Fenton, the urban working class was fragmented and "socially isolated" and therefore unable to associate its economic interests with its vote.

The Moralistic Impulse

Considering the influence of Yankee migration and the frontier nature of early Ohio, one should not be surprised to observe a highly moralistic quality in the state's political history. The Kentucky Revival of 1800 had considerable influence on southern Ohio; it was one of the factors leading to the growth of the more evangelical denominations before 1850.[16] There was a slow growth in Catholic parishes, which did not gain in momentum until the wave of the "new" immigration around 1900. Although the German Reformed and Lutheran churches achieved a relatively important place in Ohio religious organizations, the influence of the Great Revival saw many Lutherans converted to Methodism. By 1850 the Methodists and Baptists had organized over 2,000 churches, while the Presbyterians had 660, and the Lutheran and German Reformed had 330.[17] As these data imply, the activities of Ohio's churches contained a strong aspect of moral regulation. Religious sects with "liberal" creeds were few in number.

The moralistic quality of religious life led to a great concern for "temperance." In the 1850 Constitutional Convention, 300 petitions were received from three-quarters of the counties asking for prohibition of the sale of liquor; the eleven counties that accounted for 139 of the petitions were all located in southern Ohio.[18]

---

[15] Fenton, *op. cit.*, p. 151.

[16] Robert E. Chaddock, *Ohio Before 1850* (New York: Columbia University, 1908), pp. 114–120.

[17] *Ibid.*, p. 128.

[18] *Ibid.*, p. 137. This concern with temperance was to have a considerable impact upon the national scene. Led by a daughter of a former Ohio governor, a group of women met in Cleveland in 1874 to create the Women's Christian Temperance Union. The Anti-Saloon League, which was established in 1893, found a permanent home in the small town of Westerville, Ohio. Its superintendent, Wayne B. Wheeler, was to become one of the most powerful lobbyists in the country.

Moralistic and nativist impulses have also been manifested in such movements as the second Ku Klux Klan, Father Coughlin's National Union, and George Wallace's American Independent Party. Ohio was one of seven states dominated by the Klan in the 1920s. With over 50,000 members in Akron and substantial strength in several other cities, the Klan was able to win local elections in Akron, Toledo, Columbus, and Youngstown. In the Ohio Congressional elections of 1936, thirteen of the candidates who accepted the endorsement of Father Coughlin's National Union were nominated. And in the 1968 George Wallace campaign in Ohio, Klansmen were prominently identified, especially in Cleveland.[19]

Some salient features of Ohio's political culture can be inferred from the discussions of settlement patterns, ethnicity, urbanization, and moralism. Taken together, they portray a foundation of strong and persistent political loyalties. The main divisions are based more on sectional than class lines, and the loyalties are most easily shaken by persuasive evidence that canons of personal morality have been violated. These features of Ohio political culture may account for the unexpected system characteristics that were mentioned at the beginning of this chapter. For a single but very important example, the stability of political loyalties may help to explain the state's low tax effort and its relatively low level of social welfare expenditures, as compared with other urban, industrial states. With the persistent recurrence of traditional patterns and styles, more modern political cleavages are muted, giving Ohio, in Fenton's phrase, "issueless" politics. Flinn also comments on this point in a footnote at the end of one of his articles:

> Observers of Ohio politics are sometimes impressed by the caution with which state politicians treat economic and social issues, a style which seems to contrast with that seen in other states that are similar to Ohio in some respects. An explanation for this fact, if it is a fact, may be that political style reflects the nature of party followings which

---

[19]Seymour Martin Lipset and Earl Raab, *The Politics of Unreason* (New York: Harper and Row, 1970), pp. 119, 169, 354.

in Ohio include not only the usual class and ideological elements but to a more than ordinary degree traditional elements.[20]

II. POLITICAL PARTIES: INTEREST AGGREGATION AND ARTICULATION

The institutions of a political system are affected by, and to a considerable degree are reflections of, the political culture within which they function. At a given point in time, for example, the condition of the political culture will be indicated in the activities and concerns of political parties. During periods of change, developments in the larger society will usually be transmitted to the party system. Such has been the case in Ohio as elsewhere.

For purposes of description, each of Ohio's political parties can be viewed as a "tri-partite system of interactions:"[21] the party in the electorate, the party as organization, and the party in government. The first aspect calls attention to the mass base of party support, the second to the structure of the party and the characteristics of its permanent cadre, and the third to the salience of party membership in determining behavior in policy making centers. The first two aspects are considered in this section. What is known, or not known, about the party in government is discussed in subsequent sections on the legislature, the governor, and the courts.

Parties in the Contemporary Electorate

Interpretation of contemporary patterns of aggregate voting requires a sensitivity to the historic bases of electoral cleavages. While this observation is true for any state political system, it is especially important with regard to Ohio. Thus while major realignments in the American electorate resulted from such major historic events as the reorganization of the party system in 1853, the Civil War, and the depression of 1893, their long range impact on Ohio politics was minimal. Whatever the temporary disloca-

---

[20]Flinn, "Continuity and Change in Ohio Politics," *op. cit.*, p. 544.

[21]The tri-partite concept is taken from Frank J. Sorauf, *Party Politics in America* (Boston: Little, Brown and Company, 1968), p. 10.

tions, the events were followed by a "regeneration of old loyalties to their earlier vigor."[22]

Even the critical election of 1896, which occasioned a major restructuring of electoral groups nationally and in many states, failed to bring about fundamental change in Ohio. According to Thomas Flinn, the major shift in the state's politics came about in 1934, when the metropolitan areas moved firmly into the Democratic camp and the rural Democratic vote declined for the first time below that of the urban areas. Further, after 1934 the majority of Democrats in the legislature came from urban areas.[23] While this pattern of support is clearly "modern," there are, as Flinn demonstrates, certain patterns of electoral behavior that can only be explained by loyalties that "antedate the New Deal."[24]

In terms of contemporary party identification, Ohio is, like the nation, more Democratic than Republican. And at least over the past decade the overall distribution of party identification has been most stable. Fenton cites a 1958 Louis Harris poll of Ohio in which "42 percent of the electorate regarded themselves as Democrats, 31 percent Republicans and 27 percent Independents."[25] For the 1968 election Flinn found precisely the same proportions, 42% Democratic, 31% Republican and 27% Independent.[26] Furthermore, the ratio of strong party identifiers to independents in Ohio is (according to Flinn) about 1.3 to 1. For the national electorate Walter Dean Burnham asserts that the ratio is less than 1 to 1.[27]

According to classification schemes designed to measure the extent of competition within each state, Ohio is invariably classified in the "competitive" or "two-party" category. However, measuring interparty competition and classifying states according to those measurements involves a number of technical questions, among

---

[22]See Flinn, "Continuity and Change in Ohio Politics," *op. cit.*, p. 541.

[23]Flinn, "The Outline of Ohio Politics," *op. cit.*, p. 703. For a discussion of the relationship between urbanization and party competition in Ohio counties, see Heinz Eulau, "The Ecological Basis of Party Systems: The Case of Ohio," *Midwest Journal of Political Science,* 1 (August, 1957), 125–135.

[24]Flinn, "Continuity and Change in Ohio Politics," *op. cit.*, p. 544.

[25]Fenton, *op. cit.*, p. 133.

[26]Flinn, "State Politics and the 1968 Election," *op. cit.*, p. 7.

[27]Walter Dean Burnham, "The End of American Party Politics," *Trans Action,* 7 (December, 1969), 19.

the most basic being which offices to include. Ohio's ranking as a "two-party state" is rather clearly a result of competition for the offices used as indicators by most scholars. The Republican tendencies of the electorate can be seen in a cursory examination of election results, 1940-1970, in contests for a broader range of statewide offices (see Table 1).

TABLE 1

	Number of Elections Won by	
Office	*Democrats*	*Republicans*
President	2	6
U. S. Senator	4	9
Governor	7	6
Lt. Governor	4	9
Attorney General	3	10
Auditor	4	5
Sec. of State	2	11
Treasurer	2	11
TOTALS	28	67

Despite the substantial and stable Democratic majority among the populace, Republican candidates have won 70% of the statewide contests since 1940, and most of the elections for every office but governor.[28] The difficulties confronting the Democrats are evident as well in legislative elections. They have been relegated to an on-going minority status in both the state legislature and in Ohio's delegation in Congress. In recent years the Democrats have controlled both houses of the legislature only twice, following the 1948 and the 1958 elections, and divided seats evenly in the state Senate after the 1964 election. On the basis of the Republican percentage of total vote cast for candidates to the House of Representatives between 1950 and 1970, Ohio has consistently ranked among the

[28]And here the data exaggerate the extent of Democratic Party successes. In nearly half (6 of 13) of gubernatorial elections between 1940 and 1970, the Democratic candidate was Frank J. Lausche who accounts for five of the seven Democratic victories. Lausche also accounts for two of the four Senate victories. While extremely popular with the electorate, Lausche was, by all accounts, more an independent Democrat than a strong, party organization supporter. See Fenton, *op. cit.*, p. 139.

twenty most Republican states in the nation; in six of the eleven elections during the period, Ohio was among the ten most Republican.

With regard to the parties in the electorate, Ohio is "fairly securely Republican but within a two party framework."[29] Numerically, there are more Democratic than Republican identifiers, but the higher participation rate of Republicans has contributed significantly to their party's success.[30] Democrats challenge in nearly every election, and Republicans are usually successful. In brief, it would appear that the state is ranked as two-party competitive because the Democrats frequently almost win.

The impact on a state party system of a series of "almost wins" by one of the parties may be very real. Affected might be public perceptions of the capabilities of the parties as managers of government. As the figures above indicate, even when the Republicans have lost control of the governorship they have managed to retain control of a number of statewide offices as well as the leglature. A consequence of maintaining these lesser offices is to assure the party of a cadre of spokesmen, an ongoing group of officials in positions to make policy, to distribute at least some patronage, and however narrow their empires, to govern. Alternatively, political generations of Democrats come and go, regularly challenging the Republicans, but only infrequently gaining offices and power.

The Parties as Organizations

A factor frequently cited as an explanation of the electoral successes of the Ohio Republican party, despite its numerical disadvantages in registration and party identification, has been that of organization. The Republicans, says Flinn, try harder.[31] Since World War II, and particularly during the tenure of Ray Bliss as chairman, the Republican state organization has been highly centralized. Decisions on nominations, strategy, and the collection and distribution of funds have been strongly influenced by the

[29] *Ibid.*, p. 145.
[30] Flinn, "State Politics and the 1968 Election," *op. cit.*, p. 7.
[31] *Ibid.*, p. 3.

party's statewide leadership.[32] For the Democrats the situation has been much the reverse. Fenton described it thus: "Organizationally, Ohio's Democratic party in the 1960s was more akin to the loosely knit parties of the deep South than the well-organized political machines in most industrial states. There was, in fact, no statewide Democratic party in Ohio."[33]

Political parties are probably less rigid and more susceptible to change than other types of organizations. By the late 1960s and early 1970s there was some evidence, admittedly fragmentary but suggestive, that organizationally the Republicans were neither as strong nor the Democrats as weak as Fenton had described. For one thing, the Republicans have been confronted with some rather bitter intra-party divisions.[34] Whether these divisions are simply temporary deviations from the usual norm of Republican organizational solidarity or manifestations of emerging factionalism within the party remains to be seen.

For the Democrats, the evidence would suggest some amelioration of organization problems. On occasion during the 1960s the party achieved a significant degree of solidarity. The defeat of a 1967 referendum for an Ohio Bond Commission, a measure strongly supported by the Republican governor, resulted from a statewide effort by the Democratic organization in alliance with labor.[35] A

[32]For a statement of Bliss's approach to state politics see Ray C. Bliss, "The Role of the State Chairman," in James M. Cannon (ed.), *Politics U.S.A.* (Garden City: Doubleday and Company, 1960), pp. 159–170.

[33]Fenton, *op. cit.*, p. 137.

[34]The 1970 primary election for the United States Senate, which pitted Governor James Rhodes against Congressman Robert Taft, saw major figures in the Republican party challenging each other in public as had rarely been the case in the past. Moreover, the usual "one for all, all for one" kind of Republicanism so strongly advocated by Bliss was severely hampered in 1970 by reports of alleged improprieties in state loan procedures involving important Republican officials and candidates. Serious disruptions in Republican ranks were evident as groups within the party attempted to persuade candidates to step down in the middle of the campaign.

[35]The alliance of the Democratic party and labor to defeat a statewide referendum had a precedent in their successful 1958 campaign against a proposed "right to work" amendment to the state constitution. The implications of these examples should not be overextended. Complicating the formation of such alliances has been not only the non-ideological orientation of the Ohio labor movement, but also the ideological diversity within the Democratic party.

second example of increased cohesion occurred prior to the 1968 primary, when the Democratic State Executive Committee endorsed John Gilligan for the senatorial nomination. This was an unprecedented move; the party repudiated an incumbent and declared support for a challenger. Finally, the 1970 election of Governor John Gilligan will undoubtedly have an impact on state Democratic politics. Gilligan appears to be significantly more conscious of the importance of maintaining a viable state party organization than were the Democratic governors Michael DiSalle and Frank Lausche.[36] Attempts to overcome the traditionally dispersed power structure of the party[37] seem evident in moves to upgrade the party's organizational cadre and to expand staff facilities at the state level.

Differences between the state organizations have probably been due more to Republican abilities in winning office than to the personal attributes of activists recruited by either party. Flinn and Wirt, in their analysis of the characteristics and attitudes of county party leaders found that, with the exception of religious affiliation (Democratic county leaders being considerably more Catholic than Republicans), the local leaders are very much alike in terms of age, education, and occupation. While Democrats were more supportive of increased federal and state governmental activity than Republicans, the leaders of both parties tended to be in general agreement as to the priorities of governmental action (e.g., slum clearance and public housing, social security benefits, etc.).[38]

Despite the similarities of local leaders, there have been both inter-party and intra-party differences in the level of activities engaged in by the local organizations. Republican party leaders are

[36]See Elsie Reaven, "John J. Gilligan's Campaign for the Senate: A Case Study in Party Responsibility," unpublished M.A. thesis, Kent State University, 1969, for an extended discussion of Ohio politics during the 1960s and a significant amount of material on the political background of John Gilligan.

[37]As noted earlier, the urbanization of Ohio has resulted in a number of medium sized cities, a factor which has complicated Democratic efforts to develop an effective statewide organization. With local bases of power and patronage, Democratic machines in the cities "had little or no interest in statewide elections unless the candidate was from their city." Fenton, *op. cit.*, p. 137.

[38]Thomas A. Flinn and Frederick M. Wirt, "Local Party Leaders: Groups of Like Minded Men," *Midwest Journal of Political Science*, 9 (February, 1965), 86–88, 82–85.

more active in urging candidates to run for the state legislature than their Democratic counterparts.[39] Also, though the differences are slight, Republican leaders apparently have made greater efforts to use available patronage resources in rewarding party workers.[40] Some indication of the intra-party variation in local organizational strength for the Democrats is suggested by Elsie Reaven:

> the degree of organizational strength of the individual county organizations is hard to determine. Only ten counties maintain year-round headquarters. Eighteen maintain newsletters or newspapers that provide a continuous line of communication. Their dispersion, however, over the broad range of the counties without regard for population or percentage of the Democratic vote makes any meaningful analysis impossible. It is clear that the good majority of the year-round headquarters are found in the larger metropolitan communities.[41]

The condition of Ohio's political parties in the 1970s—as parties in the electorate and as organizations—can only be speculated upon. The continuities cited in aggregate voting and party identification might suggest that the future will be much like the past. Yet it is obvious that climactic events or a dramatic expansion of the electoral base to include the previously disfranchised, such as those under twenty-one, could result in significant realignments.[42]

The future condition of the party organizations is equally uncertain. Recent divisions within the Republican ranks may be temporary aberations or indicators of the end of an era of solidarity. Democratic control of the governorship could result in a greater

---

[39]This is pointed out in Thomas Flinn's piece in this volume, "An Evaluation of Legislative Performance: The State Legislature in Ohio."

[40]W. Robert Gump, "The Functions of Patronage in American Party Politics: An Empirical Reappraisal," *Midwest Journal of Political Science*, 15 (February, 1971), 103.

[41]Reaven, *op. cit.*, p. 68.

[42]Indeed, some commentators have argued that a movement of traditional Democratic party supporters (particularly the ethnic blue collar workers) to the more conservative Republican party is already underway. The implications of such a movement for Ohio politics would be far reaching. Kevin P. Phillips, *The Emerging Republican Majority* (Garden City, New York: Doubleday and Company, 1970). On developments in Ohio as interpreted by Phillips, see pp. 330–357.

centralization of party activities. But factors which have in the past worked against Democratic organizational cohesion will undoubtedly continue into the 1970s. The Democratic constituencies are more heterogeneous than the Republican. Fenton notes, "Rural and urban Republicans [have] tended to be conservatives, the 'haves,' and Yankees. The Democrats, on the other hand, [have] included under their generous tent rural conservatives, urban low-income folk, labor unions, liberals, many ethnic groups such as Cleveland's Slovenians, Negroes, and urban political organizations."[43]

Major functions of state political party organizations are the aggregation, modification, and reconciliation of interests generated within the context of the political culture. Whether Ohio's parties perform these functions in an adequate manner is a matter of judgment. Certainly by the criteria of a responsible party model[44] with each party articulating alternative policy positions—they probably do not. It is not without reason that John Fenton grouped Ohio with Indiana and Illinois under the heading of "The Job Oriented States." Parties within these states, says Fenton, use power more to enhance organizational strength than to deal with substantive issues.[45] And as pointed out above, conditions within the Ohio electorate have facilitated and contributed to the maintenance of such a political style.

III. THE STATE LEGISLATURE

Critical writings on state government often give special attention to the state legislature as an institution. Legislatures are regularly attacked as archaic in organization and procedures, unresponsive and generally unable (or unwilling) to cope with the problems of an urbanized, technological society. Along with the whipping boys of lengthy constitutions and fragmented administrative structure, the legislature is a favorite target of reformers.

---

[43]Fenton, *op. cit.*, p. 141.

[44]American Political Science Association Committee on Political Parties, *Toward a More Responsible Two-Party System* (New York: Rinehart, 1950).

[45]Fenton, *op. cit.* Fenton groups Michigan, Wisconsin, and Minnesota as "The Issue Oriented States."

Regardless of the validity of the criticisms, one should appreciate the forces giving rise to them. As policy-making institutions, state legislatures have been confronted in recent years with nearly all the social ills of American society. Not simply the volume but also the complexity of issues has escalated.[46] Decisions made outside the legislature about the legislature (the most dramatic being those of the United States Supreme Court dealing with legislative apportionment) have further complicated its workings. It is the alleged failure of legislatures to cope adequately with these matters that has led to criticism.

Implicit in a number of the most critical studies has been the assumption that there are universal procedural criteria, which by themselves are sufficient measures of the effectiveness of a legislative system. Oftimes these criteria are relatively simple, e.g., number of days the legislature meets, or the salaries received by legislators. Undoubtedly, mandated limits on legislative sessions, low salaries, and a lack of office space do influence the ways in which legislators perceive and perform their jobs. A 1966 survey by the Ohio Legislative Service Commission found that most legislators felt a need for "additional staff services in one or more of the legislative service areas of information and research, bill drafting and clerical and stenographic help."[47] The shortage of office space was considered "a major hindrance to the effective performance of legislative business."

A weakness of many reform-oriented analyses is the assumed, rather than demonstrated, linkage between procedural matters and institutional performance. All too often readily available or easily quantifiable data are employed to measure complex concepts. The number of bills passed during the closing days of a legislative ses-

[46]The Ohio legislature, no less than others, has faced the same problems. The volume of legislative business has dramatically increased over the past decade. During 1957, when sessions were biennial, the Ohio Legislature was in session 87 legislative days, introduced 1,384 bills and enacted 336 measures. During 1967, when the legislature met annually, the House and Senate were in session 131 and 132 legislative days, respectively, introduced 1,447 bills, and enacted 411 measures.

[47]Ohio Legislative Service Commission, *Legislative Services, Facilities, and Procedures.* Staff Report No. 81 (Columbus, 1966), p. 17.

sion, as a familiar case in point, is invariably cited as "proof" of the inadequacy of the existing system. This is not to dismiss such data; used with sophistication they can highlight important aspects of legislative life. John Grumm has generated a legislative professionalism index with only a few variables and, through factor analysis and causal modeling techniques, has analyzed the impact of legislative professionalism on policy outputs.[48] Works such as Grumm's are, however, the exception rather than the rule.

In his essay in this volume, Thomas Flinn has attempted to avoid the problems associated with normative studies of state legislatures. Recognizing the limitations of traditional critiques, Flinn posits six explicit criteria for defining a "strong and healthy legislative system." Using data derived from mail questionnaires and legislative roll calls, he concludes that "the Ohio Legislature gets high marks by the criteria" employed. While some might disagree with the scope of the criteria, the piece nevertheless suggests the kind of work that should precede efforts to reform state legislatures, whether by constitutional revision, statutory amendment, or procedural change.

When attention shifts from the performance of the legislature as an institution to the behavior of individual legislators, students of Ohio politics are in an enviable position. A number of published works provide a basis for comparative and longitudinal analysis. Ohio was one of four states included in the seminal study, *The Legislative System*.[49] Based on interviews conducted in early 1957,

[48]See John Grumm, "The Effects of Legislative Structure on Legislative Performance," in Richard I. Hofferbert and Ira Sharkansky (eds.), *State and Urban Politics: Readings in Comparative Public Policy* (Boston: Little, Brown and Co., 1971). In developing his legislative "Professionalism Index" Grumm uses five variables: (1) "Biennial compensation of legislators," (2) "Expenditures for legislative staff, services, operations, and printing," (3) "Number of bills introduced in 1963–64 sessions," (4) "Length of regular plus extra sessions, in calendar days," (5) "Legislative service score." *Ibid.*, p. 317. On the resulting index of legislative professionalism California, Massachusetts, and New York rank 1, 2, and 3; Ohio ranks 11, immediately behind Wisconsin and Texas. Grumm does find a relationship between professionalism and legislative output; the former, for example, has a significant independent impact on the policy dimension of welfare liberalism.

[49]John Wahlke, Heinz Eulau, William Buchanan, and Leroy C. Ferguson, *The Legislative System* (New York: Wiley, 1962).

the work and the articles which preceded it[50] are a rich source of data ranging from the social-political backgrounds of legislators to their role orientations towards leaders, interest groups, and constituencies. Other scholars have either focused directly on the Ohio legislature, or have included Ohio in multi-state studies.[51]

An important question for students of the legislative process is the basis of conflict within the system. About what kinds of issues do disagreements emerge? What role is played by the governor, legislative leaders, and interest group spokesmen in generating and muting conflict? What explains the voting divisions on those measures which generate disagreement? Is it rural vs. urban constituencies? ideological orientations? party identification?

In their 1957 interviews with Ohio legislators, Wahlke and his colleagues found that significant majorities (79% in the House and 65% in the Senate) felt that urban-rural differences were important sources of opinion conflicts; 61% of the House and 55% of the Senate saw labor issues as bases for conflict; 59% in the Senate, but only 49% in the House, felt that inter-party differences led to substantial conflict.[52] When Wayne Francis in 1963 asked legislators to identify important sources of controversy, he found that Ohio legislators ranked issues in a different way. Issues relating to more versus less spending were selected 50% of the time, business versus labor 41% of the time, and virtually no mention (1 of 22 responses) was made of rural-urban conflict.[53]

[50]John C. Wahlke and Heinz Eulau (eds.), *Legislative Behavior: A Reader in Theory and Research* (Glencoe: The Free Press, 1959).

[51]Among others see Thomas A. Flinn, "Party Responsibility in the States: Some Causal Factors," *American Political Science Review,* 58 (March, 1964), 60–71; Wayne L. Francis, *Legislative Issues in the Fifty States: A Comparative Analysis* (Chicago: Rand McNally, 1967); and Hugh L. LeBlanc, "Voting in State Senates: Party and Constituency Influences," *Midwest Journal of Political Science,* 13 (February, 1969), 33–57.

[52]Wahlke, *et al., op. cit.,* pp. 423–431.

[53]Explaining the differences in perceived legislative conflict between his study, and that of Wahlke, Eulau, Buchanan, and Ferguson, Francis notes: "— six years elapsed between the two studies, and given the fact that the authors report a low crystallization of conflict in 1957, it is reasonable to assume that in Ohio the nature of political conflict has changed, or crystallized." Francis, *op. cit.,* p. 39.

Another discussion of the dimensions of legislative disagreement is found in William Spratley's contribution to this volume. Analyzing voting on constitutional amendment proposals over a thirty-year period, Spratley discovers that the greatest controversy was generated over relatively few issues. Conflict arose over changes in constitutional articles dealing with the legislature, public debt and public works, county and township organization, and apportionment.[54]

Among the more consistent research findings is the salience of party membership as a determining factor in Ohio legislative voting. After examining roll calls over a number of legislative sessions, Thomas Flinn concludes that "party conflict is frequent in the Ohio legislature and . . . the parties obtain high levels of internal unity often enough when in opposition to each other to provide definite alternatives to the voters of the state."[55] Even when constituency similarities are taken into account, the importance of party membership continues to be evident: "It is abundantly clear that members from similar constituencies do not vote in the same way and that differences between the parties are not due to differences in the composition of the legislative parties in terms of constituencies represented."[56] It is interesting to note, however, that legislators themselves do not tend to view inter-party differences as important. Neither Wahlke, *et al.*, nor Francis reported responses indicating that legislators perceived intense partisan conflict.

In explaining variations in levels of party support by legislators of the same party, Flinn has demonstrated that constitu-

---

[54]Ohio's problems with apportionment have perhaps been less intense than those in some other states. At the time of the Court's decisions the Ohio Senate was one of the best apportioned in the nation. However, state constitutional provisions requiring legislative representation for every county did make for malapportionment in the lower house. A number of sophisticated discussions of legislative apportionment in Ohio can be found in Howard D. Hamilton (ed.), *Reapportioning Legislatures: A Consideration of Criteria and Computers* (Columbus: Charles E. Merrill Books, Inc., 1966).

[55]Flinn, "The Outline of Ohio Politics," *op. cit.*, p. 718.

[56]Flinn, "Party Responsibility in the States: Some Causal Factors," *op. cit.*, p. 63.

ency characteristics are important. Legislators from districts most typical of the party are more supportive of party roll-call positions than members from atypical districts. Similar conclusions about the relevance of constituency characteristics—political and socio-economic—for explaining intra-party differences in party support in the Ohio Senate were reached in an analysis by Hugh L. Le-Blanc.[57]

The studies of the legislature cited above are most sophisticated from a conceptual and methodological perspective. These works have made significant contributions to the understanding of legislative role orientations and the determinants of voting behavior within the legislature. Additional research is needed on the role of the legislature as a subsystem within the larger state political system. It might be helpful to have a series of case studies, utilizing a common framework, on policy development in a number of important functional areas. The dynamics of the interaction among legislative leaders, legislative committees, opposing interest groups, and the governor is perceptively described by Myron Hale in his study of the adoption of the 1965 Ohio fair housing law.[58]

IV. THE GOVERNOR

Analysts of state political systems regularly acknowledge the importance of the governor and the executive branch in the policy process.[59] From a historic perspective the governorship has evolved, in William H. Young's phrase, from the "detested minion of Royal power, to stepson of legislative domination, to popular figurehead, to effective executive."[60] In contemporary state politics the governor has become the single most important definer of the political

[57]LeBlanc, *op. cit.*

[58]Myron Q. Hale, "The Ohio Fair Housing Law," in Lynn W. Eley and Thomas W. Casstevens (eds.), *The Politics of Fair Housing Legislation* (San Francisco: Chandler Publishing Company, 1968).

[59]See nearly any text on state government. A useful discussion of the multiple roles of the governor can be found in Thomas R. Dye, *Politics In States and Communities* (Englewood Cliffs: Prentice-Hall, 1969), Chapter 6.

[60]"The Development of the Governorship," *State Government*, 31 (Summer, 1958), 183.

agenda for other decision-making centers. It is within the executive branch that program expertise is found; it is there that fundamental decisions are made about the administration of existing programs and the innovation of new ones.

Despite the growing importance of the state executive, relatively little is written about the behavior of governors and their administrative subordinates. When compared with the conceptual framework and methodological sophistication involved in empirical studies of legislators, voting, and political parties, the literature on governors is primitive.[61] Regarding Duane Lockard's four-fold classification of the resources available to governors for maximizing their leadership potential—personal, party-oriented, publicity, and legal-constitutional[62]—much more is known about the legal-constitutional component than the other three, undoubtedly because the data are more readily available.

From a legal-constitutional perspective, the growth of the gubernatorial office in Ohio has generally paralleled the expansion of executive power elsewhere. From a relatively powerless figure under the 1802 constitution, the Ohio governor has come to occupy a central position. When compared with his counterparts in other states, he is not as constitutionally strong as the very strongest (New York, Illinois, and Hawaii), but is considerably more powerful than most. Within the total set of powers there is some variation; on veto and control over the budget the Ohio governor is

---

[61]Some states are exceptions to these remarks. See Fred Gantt, Jr., *The Chief Executive in Texas: A Study in Gubernatorial Leadership* (Austin: University of Texas Press, 1964); Brett H. Melandy and Benjamin F. Gilbert, *The Governors of California: Peter H. Burnett to Edmund G. Brown* (Georgetown, California: Talisman Press, 1965); James E. Titus, "Kansas Governors: A Resume of Political Leadership," *Western Political Quarterly*, 17 (June, 1964), 356–370; *The Office of Governor: Final Report and Background Papers, Assembly on the Office of Governor* (University of Illinois, Institute of Government and Public Affairs, May, 1963). One classic study of the office of governor is Coleman B. Ransone's *The Office of Governor in the United States* (University, Alabama: University of Alabama Press, 1956). The literature on gubernatorial-administrative politics in Ohio is, in a word, non-existent.

[62]Duane Lockard, *The Politics of State and Local Government* (New York: The Macmillan Company, 1969), Chapter 13.

judged strong, on tenure potential and appointment of administrative personnel slightly less so.[63]

While important, formal powers define only a portion of any executive's total political resources. If a governor has a strong influence with legislative leaders or important clientele groups, even heads of independent agencies may come to follow his policy direction. Similarly, public popularity, mass media support, and leverage through party organizations can at times bring reluctant legislators to support new programs. An example of the role played by the governor in influencing, if not determining, the policies of agencies outside his administrative hierarchy can be found in Joseph Tucker's study of the politics of higher education in Ohio in this volume. General policy making powers, including budgetary recommendations, for public higher education are vested with the Board of Regents, a nine-member body appointed by the governor with Senate confirmation. Despite the formidable powers of the board, the chancellor of the system has noted that "The key person in the development of higher education policy in the state is the governor." As Tucker demonstrates, an ongoing strategy followed by the chancellor is the cultivation of access to the governor. Studies

---

[63]On Joseph A. Schlesinger's "Combined Index of the Formal Powers of the Governors," Ohio receives a total index score of 18 of a possible 20. The index is based upon four items with a potential score of 0 to 5 on each: tenure potential (Ohio, 4), appointive power (Ohio, 4), budget powers (Ohio, 5), veto powers (Ohio, 5). Nine states received scores of 20 or 19, ranking above Ohio. Joseph A. Schlesinger, "The Politics of the Executive," in Herbert Jacob and Kenneth N. Vines (eds.), *Politics in the American States* (Boston: Little, Brown and Company, 1971), 2nd edition, pp. 220–234. For an evaluation of the ways in which governors perceive their formal powers, as well as the constraints on them, see Thad L. Beyle, "The Governor's Formal Powers: A View from the Governor's Chair," *Public Administration Review*, 28 (November/December, 1968). Unfortunately for our purposes, the governor of Ohio did not respond to the Beyle survey. In another evaluation of gubernatorial powers by the Advisory Commission on Intergovernmental Relations, Ohio is rated "medium" on a continuum scaled weak, medium, strong, and very strong. Advisory Commission on Intergovernmental Relations, *Fiscal Balance In The American Federal System, Vol. 1* (Washington: U.S. Government Printing Office, October, 1967), p. 234.

of policy development in other functional areas would undoubtedly reveal that such strategies are not limited to higher education.

Frequently cited as a source of gubernatorial influence is his position within the political party. But mere assumption of office does not guarantee that the governor will be the party leader in anything but name. Even in competitive states, political demography can have a differential impact on the governor's power as party leader. In Illinois, for example, a Republican is usually assured of a preeminent place within his party, while any Democrat must share power with the leader of the Cook County Democratic organization. In Ohio, too, there appear to have been inter-party differences in the ability of governors to be effective party leaders. As noted in our earlier discussion of the political party organizations, Democratic governors have often been unable or unwilling to gain effective control of a party based upon independent urban fiefdoms. On the other hand, the centralized character of the party structure appears to have facilitated control by Republican governors.[64]

V. THE COURTS

Political scientists have only recently begun to look at the judicial apparatus as a subsystem of the state political system. At this point, however, knowledge of Ohio's courts, like that of other state judicial systems, rests primarily upon legal or historical materials. As Vines and Jacob observe, "courts, possibly because they are less visible than other state agencies, have been less systematically investigated than have other aspects of state government.

[64]A governor's influence as party leader is not unlimited and is undoubtedly, to some extent, situational. Thomas Flinn's data (reported below) on the attitudes of Republicans and Democrats in the General Assembly indicate that "neither party . . . is willing to say that it accepts gubernatorial leadership even when the partisan relations are right . . . ." At the same time, Hale's case study of the adoption of fair housing legislation shows rather clearly that Republican party considerations were instrumental in helping Governor Rhodes secure success in the legislature. Hale, *op. cit.*

All too often their conception according to formal, legalistic terms has not emphasized the value allocation functions they share with other state agencies."[65]

There are several reasons for scholarly preoccupation with formal description. The "value allocation functions" performed by the judiciary are simply not as evident as those of other state agencies. Formal codes of ethics and well-accepted norms of judicial conduct mean that conventional lobbying and partisan influences are absent from the court room. Except for reports of unusual decisions, the press devotes little attention to judicial activities. Moreover, the political meaning of the judicial process is frequently obscured by the legal terminology of the proceedings.

Yet the judicial subsystem interfaces with other parts of the political system in several important ways. The appointment of judges, for example, is often related to a governor's political strategies. Because the courts are an important source of patronage, both in number and prestige of positions, political parties have a continuing interest in judgeships and lesser offices. For the same reason, the parties concern themselves with the organization of the courts and especially their geographic distribution. Several studies show that the partisan affiliation of judges is a powerful predictor of appellate judicial decisions.[66]

Descriptive data are available for comparing Ohio's court system with other states. Ohio is one of the twenty-six states closest to the American Bar Association's model of court organization.[67] In addition, Ohio ranks fourteenth on an index of "Legal Professionalism" devised to measure how closely states conform to professional standards of judicial selection, court organization, judicial

---

[65]Kenneth N. Vines and Herbert Jacob, "State Courts," in Herbert Jacob and Kenneth N. Vines (eds.), *Politics in the American States* (Boston: Little, Brown and Company, 1971), 2nd edition, p. 272.

[66]See especially Stuart Nagel, "Political Party Affiliation and Judges' Decisions," *American Political Science Review,* 55 (December, 1961), 843.

[67]Vines and Jacob, *op. cit.,* p. 290. The ABA plan rejects specialized courts. It proposes only four courts in a state: a supreme court, an intermediate appellate court, a trial court of general jurisdiction, and a set of magistrates courts.

administration, tenure systems, and salaries.[68] The index, say Vines and Jacob, is evidence of the relative success of the legal profession in simplifying judicial structure.

The organized bar and allied reform groups have favored appointment over election as the best method of judicial selection. At present twenty-eight states, including Ohio, elect judges of appellate and major trial courts.[69] What the reformers have failed to realize is that their favorite alternatives to election, including the famed Missouri Plan, enhance the governor's control over judicial selection.

Gubernatorial influence is also important in states with elected judges. His influence results from the high frequency of interim appointments. From 1948 to 1967, a majority of supreme court judges in states with an elective judiciary first attained office by appointment.[70] There is some superficial evidence of this phenomenon in Ohio. Of the seven present members of the Ohio supreme court, four attained their office through interim appointment. There also seem to be consistent differences between the elected and appointed groups. While all the elected judges on the supreme court had at some time been members of the Ohio House of Representatives, none of the appointed judges had ever held any elected office. Each of the appointed judges had served on lower courts; three were judges of both common pleas courts and courts of appeals. Only one of the elected judges had prior judicial experience.[71]

Yet, as Kathleen Barber points out in her chapter in this volume, Ohio is an exception to Herndon's generalization about the importance of interim appointments in states that elect judges. Her data show that only 19% of the supreme court judges were ap-

---

[68]*Ibid.*, pp. 291–292.

[69]*State Court Systems* (Lexington, Ky.: Council of State Governments, 1970).

[70]James Herndon, "Appointment as a Means of Initial Accession to Elective State Courts of Last Resort," *North Dakota Law Review*, 38 (1962), 60.

[71]Biographical data from the *Ohio Almanac 1971* (Lorain, Ohio: The Lorain Journal Company, 1971), pp. 46–48.

pointed from 1852 to 1968. In the most recent decade (1960–1968), only 16% of the accessions to the Ohio courts of appeals were by appointment.

Behavioral research on the Ohio judicial system is so rare that one of the very few examples might be described here. In a masters thesis in political science, Larry Baas utilized the Q-technique in order to determine the way in which common pleas and court of appeals judges in Ohio characterize their job and describe the goals they pursue in making decisions. In brief, Baas was attempting to determine the purposive role structure in the Ohio judiciary. Through factor analysis of the Q-sorts of fifty judges, Baas determined that there were five judicial role types, which he called the law interpreter, the adjudicator, the administrator, the trial judge, and the peace keeper.[72] To what extent these role types are correlated with other court processes, or with the decision outputs of the judicial system, is as yet undetermined.

VI. LOCAL GOVERNMENT

Local government often serves as the focal point for many interest-aggregating and articulating groups within a state. As parties usually organize for electoral politics on the basis of counties and large cities, it is at the local level that their day-to-day work is done. Groups interested in the quality and costs of public services are also sensitive to the scope of local activities. Since public services are a mixed state-local responsibility, important political issues arise around the question of which level should administer particular functions. Local tax sources are different from state sources. Therefore, the allocation of a service responsibility implies a decision as to what groups of taxpayers will bear the costs.

Ohio's local government units are typical of the Midwest:

---

[72]Larry Baas, *Role Perceptions of Common Pleas and Court of Appeals Judges in Ohio* (unpublished M.A. Thesis, Department of Political Science, Kent State University, 1970).

TABLE 2
LOCAL GOVERNMENT UNITS IN OHIO
AND NEIGHBORING STATES, 1967

State	*Counties*	*Munici-palities*	*Town-ships*	*Special Districts*	*School Districts*	*Total*
Illinois	102	1256	1432	2313	1350	6453
Minnesota	87	850	1817	148	1282	4184
OHIO	88	933	1324	228	710	3283
Michigan	83	522	1253	110	935	2903
Indiana	92	550	1009	619	399	2669
Wisconsin	72	568	1269	62	519	2490

SOURCE: 1967 Census of Governments, Vol. 1.

counties, townships, municipalities, school districts, and special districts. As can be seen in Table 2, the structure of local government is relatively free of single-purpose special districts, and the numbers of school districts are moderately low. Between 1957 and 1967, the school districts were reduced by 40%.

Compared with other states, the classification of municipalities is quite simple. Each municipal corporation with less than 5,000 population is a village; each with more than 5,000 is a city. Both cities and villages have home rule powers and may draft charters. Very few of the 740 villages have adopted charters, but 136 of the nearly 200 cities had done so by 1970. Although optional forms of municipal government were made available by the legislature in 1913, the vast majority of the non-chartered cities and villages have chosen to operate under the general statutory plan.

As those seeking change regularly discover, governmental form is not politically neutral. Contributing to the political power of local officials is their electoral base. Township officials in Ohio are directly elected; county boards are composed, not of township representatives, but of three county commissioners elected at large. The power of these individual officials is enhanced and consolidated through a variety of statewide associations. Groups such as the Ohio Municipal League, Ohio School Boards Association, the County Commissioners Association of Ohio, and the Ohio Association of Township Trustees and Clerks, work to promote and especially to protect the interests of their constituencies at the state level.[73] The activities of these organizations of public officials contribute to the persistence of local governmental structure. The stability of this structure, in turn, is often a strong constraint on public policy development, especially when proposed policy changes would either alter the state-local mix of service responsibilities or shift responsibilities from one type of local government to another.

On occasion, significant innovations in municipal government have been achieved in Ohio. During the Progressive era, the personalities and programs of Ohio's municipal reform movement were of national repute.[74] Leaders of the movement included such figures as Tom L. Johnson, a millionaire whose conversion to the doctrines of Henry George led him to the mayorality of Cleveland, Sam "Golden Rule" Jones, the Christian Socialist mayor of Toledo, and his successor Brand Whitlock. Their deep interest in substantive programs, as opposed to simple procedural efficiency, was reflected in campaigns for public ownership of public utilities, expanded recreation programs, and more humane welfare standards.[75] The high point of the reform movement came in 1905:

> The real reformist triumph came in the cities. Cleveland re-elected Johnson by an increased majority; Brand Whitlock easily replaced his dead friend and mentor Jones in Toledo; reform mayors won out in Columbus and Dayton; and, most astonishingly of all, in Cincinnati the Cox machine lay in ruins following the victory of Judge Dempsey and the entire Fusion-Democratic municipal, county, and legislative tickets.[76]

---

[73]An observation of Albert H. Rose on "The Place of Civil Township in Ohio's Scheme of Government" illustrates this point: "The Ohio Association of Township Trustees and Clerks, organized in 1928, is a non-partisan association organized as explicitly expressed in its constitution: (1) to safeguard the township from being abolished as a governmental unit; (2) to resist attempts to deprive the township of its present rights and privileges; . . ." Albert Henry Rose, *Ohio Government* (Saint Louis: Educational Publishers, 1953), p. 43.

[74]See Frederick C. Howe, *The Confessions of a Reformer,* 1925 edition (Chicago: Quadrangle Books, 1967).

[75]It was "Golden Rule" Jones's refusal to permit the Toledo police to secure confessions by clubbing that led to his break with the local Republican party and his subsequent election as an independent. Blake McKelvey, *The Urbanization of America 1850–1915* (New Brunswick, New Jersey: Rutgers University Press, 1963), p. 107.

[76]Francis Russell, *The Shadow of Blooming Grove* (New York: McGraw-Hill Book Company, 1968), p. 174.

The municipal reformers turned to political action at the state level when it became clear that the legislature was hostile to "radical" local programs. Their successes in Columbus were limited. Perhaps the greatest achievement was the 1912 Home Rule amendment to the constitution, which allowed as much flexibility and power as the constitution of any other state.

Procedural reforms were to be popular in Ohio cities after 1912. For many years Cincinnati used proportional representation in the election of city councilmen—a rarity in American municipal practice. Six cities over 50,000 population have had long experence with the council-manager plan: Cincinnati, Toledo, Dayton, Springfield, Hamilton, and Middletown. Even today, cities engaged in chartermaking tend to follow the canons of municipal reform. A 1964 survey of charter cities reported that 53% elected all councilmen at large and 82% had nonpartisan elections.[77]

Whether the innovative spirit continues to be as strong as in the past is uncertain. The conditions which might facilitate certain kinds of change do exist. For example, thirty-one of Ohio's eighty-eight counties are within the boundaries of Standard Metropolitan Statistical Areas; one-third of the townships and about half of the remaining types of local governmental units are in these metropolitan counties. However, though there has been considerable interest in metropolitan government in a few areas, such as Cleveland, urban local governments have not proceeded very far in creating viable structures for regional decision making. The council of governments movement is weak in the state, and most county and regional planning commissions have not progressed beyond their classic emphasis on land-use planning.

Additional evidence suggesting a decline in innovation can be found in Thomas Scott's study of the diffusion of the council-manager plan between 1950 and 1960 in suburban communities of California, Illinois, and Ohio.[78] Scott posits four stages in the dif-

[77]John Gotherman, Jr., "Municipal Charters in Ohio," *Ohio Cities and Villages* (October, 1964).

[78]Thomas M. Scott, "The Diffusion of Urban Governmental Forms as a Case of Social Learning," *The Journal of Politics*, 30 (November, 1968), 1091–1108.

fusion process: pre-choice, innovation, emulation, and institutionalization. The study found that while the manager plan became almost universal in California (institutionalization stage) and was adopted at an increasing pace by Illinois suburban communities (emulation), there was no trend toward adoptions in Ohio (innovation). No evidence is provided to account for these differences among the states, but Scott speculates that the state itself provides the environment in which social learning, and therefore diffusion, takes place.

More recent data indicate that Ohio, with respect to manager plan adoptions, is in the diffusion stage that Illinois entered in the 1950s. In 1964, thirty-nine chartered cities had managers; by 1970, this total had grown to fifty-five. Yet during the same six years, twenty-two new charters opted for a mayor-council form.

The evidence from manager adoptions and regional agencies is too limited a base from which to make conclusions about innovative tendencies in Ohio local government. What is clear is that Ohio has relatively strong county government, a substantial tradition of municipal home rule, and a state-local service delivery system that places heavy responsibility on local governments.

VII. OUTPUTS

The outputs of state political systems—what officials decide to do or not to do—are varied, and analysis of them may take many forms. Attention might be given, for example, to policy substance and direction, the regulation of individual behavior, or levels and types of taxation and expenditures. In part because of the availability of comparative data, the most frequently discussed outputs are those related to taxation and expenditures—overall and by major functions.

Discussions of levels of taxing and spending need to be qualified from the outset. These levels are but one type of output, and the quality or effectiveness of a public service can be only partly explained by levels of spending. Aggregate fiscal data do not necessarily tell very much about the outcomes of decisions, which are defined by Jacob and Vines as "the consequences of outputs when they interact with the social and physical environment; they are the results of governmental decisions."[79]

Students of comparative state politics are familiar with Ohio's low ranking in governmental expenditures and tax effort. When state finances alone are considered, rather than the more familiar state-local combination, data generated throughout the 1960s consistently placed Ohio at the bottom, or very near the bottom, in per capita spending and taxing. The position of Ohio relative to other states is not a recent phenomenon. At least since 1903 Ohio has ranked below the United States average in state per capita spending; only in the late 1930s and 1940s did per capita spending exceed the national average.[80] After 1947 the gap between the U.S. average and Ohio widened in magnitudes similar to the 1903-1924 pattern (see Table 3).

TABLE 3
PER CAPITA SPENDING BY STATE GOVERNMENTS

Year	*U.S. Average*	*Ohio*	*Difference*	*Ohio as Percentage of U.S. Average*
1903	$ 2.24	$ 1.65	$ .59	73.7
1913	3.68	2.29	1.39	62.2
1924	9.88	4.85	5.03	49.1
1939	27.34	30.16	−2.82	110.3
1947	63.09	49.53	13.56	78.5
1957	136.64	106.20	30.44	77.7
1965	250.53	149.54	80.99	59.7

SOURCE: Ira Sharkansky, *Spending in the American States* (Chicago: Rand McNally and Company, 1968), p. 41.

A state's overall expenditure level conceals the relative emphasis given to the functions that make up the total. That is to say, state decision makers respond to the pressures for spending with

[79]Herbert Jacob and Kenneth N. Vines, "The Study of State Politics," in Jacob and Vines, *op. cit.*, p. 13.

[80]See also Ira Sharkansky, *Spending in the American States* (Chicago: Rand McNally and Company, 1968), Chapter 3.

varying degrees of generosity. Table 4 suggests Ohio's spending priorities in major functional categories.

TABLE 4
PERCENTAGE OF STATE AND LOCAL GENERAL EXPENDITURES, FROM OWN REVENUE SOURCES, FINANCED BY STATE GOVERNMENTS, 1968–69.

	Total General Expenditures	*Education*	*Highways*	*Public Welfare*	*Health and Hospitals*
U.S. average	50.8%	43.2%	73.1%	74.5%	51.7%
OHIO	41.7	31.2	82.3	65.5	43.6
Number of states ranking below Ohio	1	14	34	12	13

SOURCE: Advisory Commission on Intergovernmental Relations, *1971 Edition-State and Local Finances and Suggested Legislation* (Washington: U.S. Government Printing Office, December 1970), Table 96.

The state's role in financing the public sector shows up rather clearly in these data. On four of the five items, Ohio ranks well below the national average of state government contribution to state-local spending. Only one state, New Jersey, ranked lower than Ohio in total general expenditures. In the expensive functions of education, public welfare, and health and hospitals, Ohio has ranked in or very near the bottom quartile of states.[81] The one function in which the state's expenditures have exceeded the national average is highways. Apparently in Ohio the political appeal of visible improvements, like highways, is much greater than that of the software functions, such as education, welfare, and health.

[81]The data reported are intended only to present an overall view of Ohio state government contribution to state-local spending. They do not consider, for example, total or per capita expenditures by function, nor do they take into account such variables as urbanization, industrialization, etc. Nevertheless, the figures do suggest Ohio's relatively low effort status. And though Ohio does not rank at the very bottom in education, public welfare, and health and hospitals, the states ranking lower are, with some notable exceptions, less urbanized and industrialized than Ohio.

When attention shifts from the expenditure to the revenue side of the financial equation, Ohio's situation remains essentially unchanged. While it is uncertain, in any causal sense, whether low expenditure decisions are a function of the tax structure or, alternatively, whether low taxes result from prior decisions to keep expenditures low,[82] it is abundantly clear that in Ohio taxation is at minimal levels, relative to other states. Revenue-raising effort by Ohio's state and local governments is suggested in Table 5.

TABLE 5
MEASURES OF STATE-LOCAL REVENUE EFFORT, IN OHIO, 1964 AND 1969

	Taxes and Charges as Percent of State Personal Income		*Taxes as a Percent of State Personal Income*	
	1969	*1964*	*1969*	*1964*
U.S. average	14.0	12.7	11.2	10.4
OHIO	11.3	10.9	8.8	8.8
Number of states ranking below Ohio	3	5	0	5

SOURCE: Advisory Commission on Intergovernmental Relations, *1971 Edition-State and Local Finances and Suggested Legislation* (Washington: U.S. Government Printing Office, December 1970), Table 16.

As with expenditures, Ohio is below the national average on state-local revenue efforts. For taxes alone, Ohio ranks last among the states in terms of the percentage of state personal income allocated to the public purse. Again, the phenomena predate the late 1960s. Clara Penniman's analysis of percentage of per capita income devoted to state and local taxes for the years 1932, 1942, 1953, 1962, and 1967 reveals that Ohio was in the lower quartile of states for the latter three years.[83] In brief, the parameters of revenue decisions have been in existence for some time.

Care must be taken not to infer too much from the tax and expenditure data. Ohio residents do, after all, enjoy a variety of public services, much like the citizens of other states. Whether pub-

[82] Clara Penniman, "The Politics of Taxation," in Jacob and Vines, *op. cit.*, 520–521.

[83] *Ibid.*, p. 533.

lic services affect the quality of life as strongly in Ohio as in other states is an empirical question for which data are lacking. Throughout this section attention has been concentrated on outputs rather than outcomes. There is some evidence that Ohio is not viewed as backward or policy stagnant by functional agencies in other states. When state administrators in ten states were asked "if they, or the members of their staffs, ever contacted officials in other states to get advice or information," respondents in four of the ten reported that Ohio was among the states contacted.[84]

Despite these qualifications, the fact remains that in terms of financial outputs, Ohio produces at a lower level than many other urbanized, industrialized states. Some tentative explanations might be suggested. Certainly, as several of the authors in this volume demonstrate, part of the explanation is structural. Constitutional limitations on taxation and debt, and the associated requirements for referenda, have delayed rapid expansion of the public sector and inhibited political elites from even suggesting such expansion. Also involved is the reluctance in any political system to discard long established routines. Ohio's low effort status is not a development of the 1960s; state spending has been consistently low since the early years of the century. Finally, the political culture of Ohio is probably most supportive of a system that minimizes the taxation of one segment of the population to finance services for another. This is not to say that class-oriented issues are never raised for discussion in policy making centers, but that the political styles deemed appropriate by the political culture for electoral success require political leaders to avoid redistributive policies once in office.[85] The mobilization of biases in such a context tends to preserve the *status quo*.

[84]See Jack L. Walker, "Innovation in State Politics," in Jacob and Vines, *op. cit.*, pp. 379 and 382.

[85]Theodore Lowi defines three basic areas of public policy—distributive, regulatory, and redistributive. For the latter, broad categories of the population are affected "approaching social classes. They are, crudely speaking, haves and have-nots, bigness and smallness, bourgeoisie and proletariat. The aim involved is not the use of property but property itself, not equal treatment but equal possession, not behavior but being." Theordore J. Lowi, "American Business, Public Policy, Case-Studies, and Political Theory," *World Politics*, 16 (July, 1964), 677–715.

VIII. THE OHIO CONSTITUTION

The Ohio Constitution is basically the document drafted in 1851 and extensively modified by the Constitutional Convention of 1912. Three-quarters of the 119 delegates to the 1912 convention were considered progressives.[86] These reformers decided to submit a number of amendments to the voters, rather than revise the constitution completely.

The strategy proved effective. Of the forty-one amendments adopted by the convention, thirty-three were approved in the 1912 referendum. Important reform objectives were met in the grant of an item veto to the governor, provision for the initiative and referendum, the requirement for direct primaries, home rule for municipalities, and the institution of a merit system. The irony of the present Ohio Constitution is that many of its provisions reflect the short-lived ascendency of a group of reformers who had little further influence in the state's political system.

In one sense, Ohio was fortunate that no constitutional convention was convened in the last twenty-five years of the nineteenth century. The late 1800s were a period of widespread constitutional revision, and the results were frequently like the architecture of the period—ornate, massive, and rambling. In general, the constitutional products of the period reflected an acute distrust of all public officials and imposed detailed limitations on their powers.

Partially because Ohio was spared the constitutional gingerbread of the late nineteenth century, most authorities agree that its constitution is generally satisfactory. In the post-World War II years, two comprehensive studies, both financially supported by the Stephen H. Wilder Foundation of Cincinnati, have concurred in this judgment.

The first study was prepared by twelve members of the Social Science Section of the Ohio College Association. Published in 1951, it contains ten chapters on the major sections of the constitution.[87] The scholars who contributed to the volume dealt with

[86]Francis Russell, *op. cit.*, p. 223.

[87]Harvey Walker (ed.), *An Analysis and Appraisal of the Ohio State Constitution, 1851–1951,* A Report to The Stephen H. Wilder Foundation, Cincinnati, 1951.

Ohio's basic constitutional problems. They also tended to become involved in the minutiae of constitutional criticism.

The more recent document is a tightly-focused analysis, which concludes with fourteen substantive issues that need attention in constitutional change. The authors state that "Ohio's constitution is in need of revision, not overhaul. Change can be made without scrapping the basic document if the Constitutional Revision Commission concentrates on the substantive problems discussed in this report."[88] Six of Heisel and Hessler's fourteen issues are concerned with state and local finance, four with local government, three with the state executive branch, and one with the selection of judges. By and large, the 1951 study covered the same ground, with similar recommendations, but the sense of priorities was submerged in a great mass of detail about phraseology and obsolete material.[89]

The following are articles identified as troublesome:

1. *State and Local Finance*

   a. Article XVIII, Section 13, is the basis for the judicial doctrine of pre-emption, under which local governments may be prevented from taxing the same source as the state.

   b. Article XII, Section 2, imposes the 10-mill limitation on property taxes (the so-called "inside millage"), and prohibits classification of property by requiring uniform property taxes.[90] The 10-mill limitation creates the necessity for vast numbers of tax levy referenda by municipalities and school districts. The tax uniformity provision prohibits either taxing land and buildings at separate rates or creating tax districts whose residents would pay for different levels of services.

[88]W. Donald Heisel and Iola O. Hessler, *State Government for Our Times* (Cincinnati: The Stephen H. Wilder Foundation, 1970), p. 99.

[89]The relevant chapters of *An Analysis and Appraisal* . . . are Chapter VII, "Finance and Taxation in Ohio," by V. E. Carlson; Chapter VIII, "Home Rule and Local Government in Ohio," by Donovan F. Emch; Chapter IV, "The Executive Department in Ohio," by Harvey Walker; and Chapter V, "The Courts and the Judiciary in Ohio," by Warren Cunningham.

[90]The 10–mill limitation can be exceeded by referendum or home rule charter provision. Counties may set up tax districts if they adopt a home rule charter as authorized by Article X, Section 3.

c. Other sections of Article XII raise the issue of tax earmarking. Section 5a requires all highway user taxes to be used for highways, and Section 9 stipulates that at least 50% of any state income or inheritance tax be returned to the local government of origin, as determined by law.

d. Sections 1 and 2i of Article VIII establish the current state debt. Section 1 limits the total amount of debt to $750,000, but it is in effect nullified by Section 2i, which grants the legislature authority to issue $259,000,000 for certain specified capital improvements and unlimited authority for highway bonds, as long as not more than $500,000,000 is outstanding at any one time. Section 2i, adopted in 1968, is the latest in a long series of special debt authorizations. The additions to Section 2 raise the question of whether constitutional amendments should be necessary whenever bonds are to be issued, as well as the question of whether the state debt limitation should be a fixed dollar amount.

2. *Local Government Structure and Powers*

a. Article X deals with counties. Section 1 provides for a choice of alternative forms of county government, as determined by the legislature. Section 3 authorizes the preparation of county home rule charters and their adoption by referendum. To date, no county has changed its structure by either method. Section 3 places great obstacles in the way of change by requiring four separate voting majorities (three in counties of over 500,000 population) whenever the proposed county charter would confer municipal powers on the county. Section 3 also stipulates that in any conflict over powers between a charter county and a municipality, municipal powers are to prevail.

b. Article XVIII is the municipal government article. Section 2 provides for alternative forms, of which the legislature has given cities a choice of three: a federal plan (mayor-council), a commission plan, and a council-manager plan. Section 7 authorizes the adoption of home rule charters. Section 3 gives home rule powers to all municipalities, charter or non-charter, by allowing them to exercise "all powers of local self-government" and to adopt police, sanitary, and similar regulations that are not in conflict with state laws. In practice, Sections 3 and 7 have required court action to determine the boundaries between state and municipal powers. A leading constitutional issue is whether Article XVIII should be combined with Article X, and home rule redefined for both cities and counties in a single section.

3. *The Executive Branch and the Governor*

Article III names the executive officers to be elected statewide and lists the powers of the governor. Constitutional problems include the extent to which the governor's powers are commensurate with his responsibilities, the role of the lieutenant governor, and the line of succession if the governor's office becomes vacant.

4. *The Judiciary*

Article IV prescribes the court system, including the types of courts and the selection of judges by election. For many years the Ohio State Bar Association has promoted a "Modern Courts Plan," under which Ohio would join a dozen other states in using some variant of the Missouri Plan. The main features of this scheme are gubernatorial appointment of judges from slates of candidates prepared by a nominating commission, and subsequent elections in which the judges selected run on the simple question of whether they should be retained in office.

In writing of the "American reverence for constitutionalism," Duane Lockard observes that

> The formal structure of government seems to fascinate us more than the political methods by which a government operates . . . . Our passion to find the right formula has induced an enormous amount of research, thinking, writing, and pleading about the structure of govern-

> ment . . . . The "right formula" has been sought after like a Holy Grail.[91]

Preoccupation with structural arrangements has had two results. Analysts can frequently be sidetracked by details into a cosmetology of constitutional reform. More importantly, they can overlook the fact that the constitution is a political document. Its provisions work to the advantage of some groups and to the disadvantage of others. The preservation of favored positions is one reason for the difficulty of achieving comprehensive revision.

A central question in the analysis of constitutional provisions is the relative importance of a particular section, in comparison with extra-constitutional constraints on governmental action. Several contributions to this volume are concerned with this question. Stocker assesses the impact of Article XII, Section 9, concerning the return of income tax revenues to local governments. Gionocchio and Hamilton investigate local referenda, most of which are required by the limitations contained in Article XII, Section 2. In his study of the variables that affect tax rates, Cho casts light on the same section. Barber's chapter on the selection of judges is related to the controversy over Article IV. Tucker shows that the failure to mention higher education in Article III has no bearing on the governor's influence over policy for state-supported universities. Bowden and Hamilton demonstrate how the provisions of Article X dictated important strategies for a commission drafting a county charter. Studies like these aid in determining the extent to which, and in what fields, "the political climate of the community is a more persuasive force than its constitutional document."[92]

---

[91]Lockard, *op. cit.*, p. 81.
[92]*Ibid.*, p. 94.

PART II

Taxation and Finance

Editors' Introduction

The general characteristics of public finance in Ohio are similar to those of other states. Nevertheless, there are four distinguishing features that are worthy of note:

1. A state revenue system that was, until 1972, composed almost entirely of sales and excise taxes of various types with a substantial contribution from the profits of state package stores operated by the Department of Liquor Control (see Table 1).

2. A local revenue system that has tended toward a separation of tax sources, with (a) municipalities relying more and more on locally-levied income taxes, (b) school districts using an increasing share of the property tax, and (c) libraries laying claim to almost all of the local-situs intangible property tax, a state-levied, county-collected tax on income from investments (see Table 2)

3. The most frequent use of local tax referenda in the nation, because of a constitutional provision severely restricting the amount of unvoted millage on property.

4. The distribution to local governments of over $100 million in state tax revenues through the Local Government Fund, a form of "revenue sharing' administered by each county.

The chapters in this section relate directly to the first three of these features and indirectly to the fourth. Yong Hyo Cho takes a comprehensive look at municipal taxes and debts in the forty largest cities. Utilizing step-wise regression techniques, he identifies the sets of variables that explain the greatest amount of variation in tax and debt levels and rates. His analysis of recent data shows that income taxes become a substitute for property taxes in municipalities. Cho's findings are supported by other data. The municipal share of statewide property tax collections dropped from 32.2% to 13.6% between 1946 and 1968, the school district share rose from 48.9% to 70.6%, and both the county and township shares (13.6% and 2.3%, respectively, in 1968) remained constant.

TABLE 1
OHIO STATE GOVERNMENT TAX REVENUES, 1970
(Amounts in millions of dollars)

State-Collected Taxes	*Total Collections*	*Distributed to Local Gov'ts*	*Retained for State Use*
1. Retail sales and use	661.1(a)	34.0(b)	627.1
2. Motor vehicle fuel	329.7	79.4	250.3
3. Cigarette	121.7	0.0	121.7
4. Corporation franchise	111.4	0.0	111.4
5. Public utility excise	80.0	0.0	80.0
6. Liquor gallonage and non-spirituous alcoholic beverage	61.3	0.0	61.3
7. Foreign insurance corporations	53.1	0.0	53.1
8. Highway use and operator's license	44.9	0.0	44.9
9. Horse racing	17.1	2.6	14.5
10. State-situs intangible personal property (c)	60.7	55.2(d)	5.5
11. Motor vehicle license	135.5(e)	131.4	4.1
SUBTOTAL	1,676.5	302.6	1,373.9
Liquor sales profits	81.4	0.0	81.4
Inheritance and estate taxes (county collected)	37.5	19.6	17.9
TOTAL	1,795.4	322.2	1,473.2

(a) Does not include $9.1 million collected for 3 counties that levied a ½% "piggy-back" sales tax.
(b) Paid into the Local Government Fund.
(c) A tax on bank deposits, shares of stock, and capital employed by financial institutions and dealers in intangibles.
(d) Paid into the Local Government Fund.
(e) Municipalities that levied an additional $5 motor vehicle license tax.
SOURCE: "State and Local Tax Structure," Staff Report No. 5 to the Tax Reform and Revision Review Committee (The Ohio Municipal League, mimeo., undated).

The growing dependence of municipalities on income taxation is evident in Table 2. The total municipal income tax collection levied by 271 cities and villages was $263.4 million in 1969. But the bulk of the collections ($254.8 million) occurred in only 160 cities; these had an average tax of $41.83 per capita. Property tax collections in the same cities averaged $31.91 per capita. The bedroom

TABLE 2
OHIO LOCAL GOVERNMENT TAX REVENUES, 1969
(Amounts in millions of dollars)

Type of Tax	*Total*	*Counties*	*Twps.*	*Schools*	*Munics.*
1. Real and public utility property					
Amount	1,307.9(a)	171.3	33.2	943.6	158.7
Percent	100.0	13.1	2.5	72.2	12.1
2. Tangible personal property(b)					
Amount	419.0	57.8	7.1	290.2	63.8
Percent	100.0	13.8	1.7	69.3	15.2
3. State-situs intangible property					
Amount	60.7(c)	23.8	3.3	0.0	28.0
Percent	100.0	39.3	5.5	—	46.1
4. Local-situs intangible property(d)					
Amount	53.6(e)	2.4	0.2	0.0	7.7
Percent	100.0	4.6	0.3	—	14.4
5. Municipal income tax					
Amount	263.4	0.0	0.0	0.0	263.4
Percent	100.0	—	—	—	100.0
TOTAL					
Amount	2,104.6	255.3	43.8	1,233.8	521.6
Percent	100.0	12.1	2.1	58.7	24.8

(a) This total includes $1.0 million levied by libraries.
(b) A tax on personal property used in business, such as retail inventory, manufacturing machinery, and furniture and fixtures.
(c) The state retains $5.5 million; the remainder is distributed through the Local Government Fund.
(d) A county-collected tax on income from investments.
(e) $43.0 million (80.2%) goes to the support of libraries.
SOURCES: "State and Local Tax Structure," Staff Report No. 5 to the Tax Reform and Revision Review Committee (The Ohio Municipal League, mimeo., undated). "Income and Property Tax Statistics," Staff Report No. 4 to the Tax Reform and Revision Review Committee (The Ohio Municipal League, mimeo., undated).

suburb is the only type of city in which the property tax brings in more revenue than income taxation.

James Gionocchio and Howard Hamilton provide an empirical investigation of the results of tax referenda and the attitudes of public officials toward this form of "direct democracy." Their data do not lend much support to the "taxpayers revolt" thesis. On the contrary, the electorate appears to be selective in voting on various types of levies.

Frederick Stocker's essay is an example of the sophisticated analysis frequently required when policy makers face a constitutional restriction that appears to limit their alternatives. He shows how the 50% turnback requirement contained in Article XII, Section 9, can be reconciled with fiscal flexibility within the structure of a statewide income tax. He recommends that half of the income tax revenue be returned on a county basis and be applied to the state school aid entitlements of each school district within the county. This course of action would avoid the necessity of amending the constitution.

In essence, Stocker's suggestion was followed in Ohio's first income tax, adopted by the legislature in December, 1971. This ½% to 3½% graduated income tax, which was estimated to produce $380.4 million in its first year, is levied on adjusted gross income, less the income taxable under the intangibles tax. One half of the revenue is returned to the county of origin. The county auditor is directed to pay each school district a specified amount; the remainder of the school aid entitlement is paid as before.

In addition, the state income tax legislation of 1971 changed the source of payments into the Local Government Fund. Instead of $36 million annually from sales tax revenues, the fund is to receive $48 million from income tax receipts. Eleven-twelfths will be distributed to each of the eighty-eight counties according to a two-part formula: 75% on the basis of county municipal tax duplicate and 25% on the basis of county population. The other part of the fund is the state-situs intangibles tax, which is returned to the county of origin. (This was estimated at $56 million in 1971.) Each county then distributes the fund to the local governments of the county (including the county itself) on the basis of "need," as determined by a procedure specified in the law. The county budget commission—composed of the auditor, treasurer, and prosecutor—computes the allocations, which may be used by the recipient governments for any purpose.

Recognizing that the passage of the statewide tax will make it difficult for municipalities to increase their own local income tax rates, the legislature stipulated that one-twelfth ($4 million) would be distributed to each municipality with an income tax on the basis of the ratio of its income tax collections to the total municipal income tax collections in the state.*

*In July, 1972, the legislature gave a "growth dividend" to the Local Government Fund. Instead of a fixed amount from income tax collections, the fund now receives 3.5% of state-collected sales, personal income, and corporate franchise taxes. One-twelfth of the 3.5% is distributed to municipalities with income taxes, according to the method described above.

Tax Structure and Municipal Debt in Large Ohio Cities: The Effect of State Restrictions and Local Politics

Yong Hyo Cho

WE ARE REPEATEDLY WARNED THAT AMERICAN CITIES ARE IN serious trouble. Views concerning the causes of the trouble vary, but most observers would agree that the financial dimension is basic. Indeed, financial anemia epitomizes the public sector in urban America. Funds to finance even the most fundamental governmental activities—education, health, or law enforcement—are in short supply. Tax and bond referenda have become recurrent features in local elections, with more failures than successes. The constant pressure to secure minimally necessary revenues is frustrating to public officials and concerned citizens.

Tax politics is in a deeper crisis at the local level than at the federal or state level. Local governmental costs are rising rapidly due to the increasing demand for governmental services in both old and new functions. Local tax bases are generally less sensitive to economic growth and local taxes less productive than federal or state taxes. Inflation affects governmental costs as everything else. Unionization of local government employees and their in-

The author thanks Professor George Mauer for his valuable comments on the draft of this paper, and to Mr. Sydney Welch for his assistance in collecting the data used.

creasing militancy in demands for pay increases and betterment of working conditions push governmental costs upward. Disapproval of local tax levies or bond issues is one of the few areas where taxpayers feel that they can register dissatisfaction with the Leviathan of government.

The purpose of this study is to examine the tax structure and debt financing of Ohio cities. The cities selected for analysis are the forty largest muncipalities in the state.[1] Since the financing of municipal governments is part of a total state and local financing system, we will first review the state-local financing system in Ohio so as to put the discussion of the tax and debt structure of these municipalities in proper perspective.

I. STATE-LOCAL FINANCING SYSTEM IN OHIO

State and local governments share obligations for providing public services. Therefore, the way in which responsibility for various public functions is divided between state and local governments, and among units of local government, tends also to define the general pattern of financial responsibility. As the state assumes relatively more service obligations, the local obligations and the resulting revenue needs become correspondingly less. If the state raises relatively greater revenues and provides generous financial aid to local governments, local financing requirements will be relatively light, even though local service obligations remain extensive.

Financial patterns at the local level are also affected by state fiscal operations. The extent of local government service responsibilities, the generosity of state financial aid, the specification of jurisdictions benefiting most from that aid, all affect the local fiscal system. For example, when school systems are financed mainly by state aid, the school districts' competition with other governments for a share of the local tax base becomes less intense. If state aids are meager, while state assumption of service responsi-

[1]These forty cities include all the municipalities with a 1960 census population of 25,000 and more.

bility is not particularly extensive, tax competition among local government units becomes stronger.

State Taxes and State Aid to Local Governments

During this century, state governments have expanded their tax bases, first through the sales taxes and then through taxes on personal and corporate incomes. Until 1972, Ohio was one of the few large industrial states which had adopted neither personal nor corporate income taxes. The major sources of tax revenues in Ohio have been limited to general sales, gross receipts, and selective sales taxes. As a result, state tax revenues and tax efforts lagged far behind those of other states. Table 1 compares Ohio state government's tax revenues, tax effort, and tax elasticity to income growth with the average of the fifty states throughout the 1960s.

Ohio's per capita income, an indicator of economic ability to pay taxes, is considerably greater than the national average. Per capita state taxes, however, are markedly lower than the average of all the states, and the gap in tax levels has grown from $11 in 1960 to $65 in 1969. The state tax effort (tax as a percentage of

TABLE 1
TRENDS OF STATE TAXES AND TAX EFFORTS
OHIO VS. FIFTY STATES, 1960–1969

		P.C. Income ($)	*P.C. Taxes* ($)	*Tax Effort* (%)	*Tax Elasticity* (%)
1969	Ohio	3,509	143	4.1	N.A.
	50 States	3,421	208	6.1	N.A.
1967	Ohio	3,056	111	3.6	.77
	50 States	2,963	158	5.3	1.03
1965	Ohio	2,646	101	3.8	N.A.
	50 States	2,566	135	5.3	N.A.
1960	Ohio	1,957	90	4.6	N.A.
	50 States	1,850	101	5.5	N.A.

SOURCES: U.S. Bureau of the Census, *State Government Finances,* Issues of 1969, 1967, 1965, and 1960 (Washington: U.S. Government Printing Office); and Advisory Commission on Intergovernmental Relations, *Sources of Increased State Tax Collections: Economic Growth vs. Political Choice* (Washington: U.S. Government Printing Office, 1969).

income) is also substantially lower than the national average, and the gap in tax effort has grown wider. In 1960, tax collections of the state government accounted for 4.6% of personal income compared with an average of 5.5% for the fifty states. In 1969, the corresponding figure for Ohio was reduced to 4.1%, whereas that for the fifty states was increased to 6.1%. Further, tax elasticity to income growth is about 20% less than the national average. According to the 1967 estimate of the Advisory Commission on Intergovernmental Relations, the increase in state tax revenues in Ohio per 1% increase in income was only 0.77%, compared with a 1.03% average for all states. Ohio's tax elasticity exceeded only Nebraska's (0.70), which had neither income taxes nor sales taxes. All of these measures clearly indicate that Ohio's state tax system was not only far less productive than the national average, but also far less responsive to economic growth. And the gap was growing.

A conservative state tax system sharply limits Ohio's ability to provide financial assistance to local governments. As Table 2 shows, state aid to local governments in Ohio is substantially lower than the national average. In 1965, state aid was $44 per capita, compared with a national average of $61. Five years later, the corresponding figures were $71 and $101. Low state taxes and aid have not created a strong local tax system in Ohio. Rather, per

TABLE 2
TRENDS OF LOCAL TAXES AND STATE AID
OHIO VS. FIFTY STATES, 1965–1969
(in dollars)

		P.C. Total Local Taxes	*P.C. State Aid*[a] *to Local Gov't*
1969	Ohio	162	71
	50 States	172	101
1967	Ohio	138	56
	50 States	148	81
1965	Ohio	124	44
	50 States	130	61

(a) The State aid figure does not include aid for public welfare.
SOURCES: U.S. Bureau of the Census, *Governmental Finances*, Issues of 1968–1969; 1966–1967, and 1964–1965; and *State Government Finances*, issues of 1969, 1967, and 1965.

TABLE 3
PER CAPITA LOCAL EXPENDITURES FOR PUBLIC SCHOOLS AND PER CAPITA STATE AID FOR EDUCATION: OHIO VS. FIFTY STATES, 1960–1969

		P. C. Local Expenditures for Schools ($)	*P. C. State Aid for Education ($)*	*State Aid as a Percent of Local Expenditure*
	Ohio	146	43	29
1969	50 States	166	74	45
	Ohio	128	32	25
1967	50 States	139	60	43
	Ohio	101	21	21
1965	50 States	112	43	38
	Ohio	82	18	22
1960	50 States	84	30	36

SOURCES: U.S. Bureau of the Census, *State Government Finances*, Issues of 1969, 1967, 1965, and 1960; *Governmental Finances*, issues of 1968–1969, 1966–1967 and 1964–1965; and *Statistical Abstract*, 1962.

capita local taxes have been consistently lower than the average of all the states. Although the difference is slight, it increased from $6 in 1965 to $10 in 1969.

Low state aid has the most dramatic effect on local school financing. As Table 3 shows, per capita state aid to local schools is nearly one-half the national average.

In sum, the state financial system of Ohio is characterized by low taxes and low state aid to local governments. But this does not lead to high local taxes. Instead, the overall level of local taxes is below the national average. In education, low state aid results not only in relatively lower levels of spending, but also in considerably greater dependence on local property tax financing. This situation places other local governments, particularly the large cities, under a heavy tax restraint.

Municipal Taxes

The taxing powers of municipalities are largely determined by the state legislature, whose powers are derived from the State Constitution, Article XVIII, Section 13, which states that "Laws may be passed to limit the powers of municipalities to levy taxes and incur debt for local purposes." Until very recently, the state legislature and the state Supreme Court tended to abide by the so-called "pre-emption doctrine" in authorizing municipalities to exercise particular taxing powers. Under constitutional and statutory restrictions, Ohio municipalities were allowed to levy taxes on properties and on earned personal incomes and net business profits.

The state legislature recently enacted legislation which allows counties to adopt a 0.5% piggy-back sales tax and an automobile license tax up to $5 per vehicle. Thirty-seven counties levied the automobile license tax in 1970, and twenty-three had adopted the piggy-back sales tax by the end of 1971.

In the United States, property taxes are the major source of local tax revenues. However, municipal income taxes are gradually gaining popularity, and, in 1971, some 300 Ohio municipalities were levying income taxes in addition to property taxes.[2] In the following paragraphs, we will examine these two principal taxes in the forty largest Ohio cities.

The Ohio State Constitution is unusually restrictive of local powers to levy property taxes without the approval of the electorate. Article XII, Section 2, of the constitution sets the basic limitations as follows:

> No property, taxed according to value, shall be so taxed in excess of one percent of its true value in money for all state and local purposes, but laws may be passed authorizing taxes to be approved by at least a majority of the electors of the taxing district voting on such proposition, or when provided for by the charter of a municipal corporation.

This constitutional provision limiting the maximum unvoted property tax millage to 1% was adopted in 1933. This was a one-

---

[2]There are some 3,500 local governments in the United States with income taxes, of which over 3,100 are local jurisdictions of Pennsylvania. Other local governments using income taxes beside Ohio municipalities and Pennsylvania local governments are large cities in a number of states. See, for details, Advisory Commission on Intergovernmental Relations, *The Commuter and the Municipal Income Tax* (Washington, D.C.: U.S. Government Printing Office, 1970), pp. 2–3.

third reduction from the previous 1.5%, or fifteen-mill limitation. The unvoted millage is allotted to each unit of government by taking two-thirds of the 1929–1933 average levy allotted to the taxing jurisdiction within the fifteen-mill limitation.[3] This is referred to as the "inside" millage. In effect, the unvoted millage of municipal property taxes today is determined by the city's property tax level during the early years of the Depression, unless the city has adopted a charter provision which sets a different rate of unvoted maximum millage. Only a few cities seem to have established a substantially high rate of unvoted millage through charter provisions.[4]

The Ohio State Constitution allows and the state statute requires property taxation at its true value. A recent statutory revision sets the assessment of property value for tax purposes at 50% of the true value of property in money.[5] In practice, however, the assessed valuation varies considerably among the counties, ranging from about 50% to less than 30%. This practice of underassessment of property in effect reduces the unvoted millage to three or five mills, not ten mills, in relation to the property's market value.

Additional property tax levies of individual municipalities beyond these constitutional limitations are subject to voter approval. Local political choice as to the extent of additional property taxes is influenced not only by the community's political progressivism, but also by the lack or presence of local income taxes. Municipal income taxes in Ohio, as elsewhere, are often used as an alternative to an increase in the property tax burden.[6]

The extent of municipal property tax rates for the forty selected cities is measured in three ways: total millage; inside millage, which is the limit, established by the constitution or city charter,

---

[3]*Ohio Revised Code,* 5705. 31D.

[4]Of the forty largest cities, only Akron and Cuyahoga Falls have an unvoted millage exceeding 5 mills; they have 5.95 mills and 11 mills, respectively.

[5]*Ohio Revised Code,* 5715.01.

[6]Elizabeth Deran, "Tax Structure in Cities Using the Income Tax," *National Tax Journal* (June, 1968), pp. 147–152. Deran argues that municipal income taxes are substitutive of property taxes. However, evidence derived from Ohio experience suggests that the effect of income taxes on property taxes is only partially substitutive.

TABLE 4
THE PATTERN OF PROPERTY TAX RATES OF THE FORTY LARGEST OHIO CITIES, 1967

	Total Millage	*Statutory Millage*	*Voted Millage*
Highest	19.90	11.00	15.45
Lowest	3.14	2.00	.00
Mean	7.88	3.83	4.06
Standard deviation	4.03	1.35	3.83
Coefficient of variation	51.1	35.2	94.3

SOURCES: Ohio Department of Taxation, *Tax Rates Inside and Outside the Ten Mill or Charter Limitation* (Columbus, Ohio, 1968).

that the municipality can levy without voter approval; and outside millage, which is the extent of the levy that the voters have authorized beyond the ten mill or charter limits.

Table 4 shows the pattern of variation in these three measures of property tax rates among the forty cities.[7] Total millage ranged from a high of 19.90 mills to a low of 3.14 mills, with an average of 7.88 mills. The statutory inside millage ranged from 11 mills to 2 mills, while the voted outside millage ranged from 15.45 mills to zero. Five of the cities had no voted outside millage.[8] As shown

TABLE 5
THE PATTERN OF PROPERTY TAX REVENUES OF THE FORTY LARGEST OHIO CITIES, 1968

	Property Taxes (Per Capita $)
Highest	61.38
Lowest	9.24
Mean	26.33
Standard deviation	13.50
Coefficient of variation	51.03

SOURCE: Auditor of State, *Financial Report and Public Debt Statement, Ohio Cities, 1968* (Columbus, undated).

[7]See Appendix 1 for the tax rates for each of the forty cities.
[8]The five cities are Canton, Columbus, Lancaster, Lima, and Zanesville.

by the coefficient of variation, the outside millage varies the most, while the inside millage varies the least.

Table 5 summarizes the pattern of variation in per capita property tax revenues among the forty cities.[9] Like tax rates, the levels of property tax revenues vary widely among the cities. Per capita total property taxes range from a high of $61.38 to a low of only $9.24, with an average of $26.33.

The pre-emption doctrine, highly restrictive property taxes, and the political difficulties in passing additional property taxes by voter approval, have all contributed to the adoption of municipal income taxes. Toledo led the way by first adopting the tax in 1946. By 1955, 17 cities had adopted the tax.[10] The income tax cities increased to 77 in 1963, to 95 in 1965, to 261 in 1969, and to 298 in 1970.

The state statute governing municipal income taxes is the Uniform Municipal Income Tax Law of 1957.[11] This statute specifies that the income tax must be levied at a uniform rate not to exceed 1.0% on wages and salaries earned by the residents, wages and salaries earned within the city by non-residents, and business net profits earned within the city by both residents and non-residents. Rates in excess of 1.0% can be adopted by the city for a specific purpose, subject to voter approval. Since 1968 the requirements for approval are 50% of the voters in a general election or 55% in a special or primary election. These requirements for passage were more rigid before 1968; i.e., 55% in general elections and 60% in special or primary elections.

All but two of the forty cities had incomes taxes in 1968. The income tax rates of the thirty-eight cities ranged from a high of 1.5% in Toledo and Youngstown to a low of .50% in five cities.

---

[9]See Appendix 1 for the property tax levels of individual cities.

[10]It is evident that increasing difficulty in raising additional property taxes has been instrumental in the adoption of income taxes. During the period 1951–1954, 51.8% of all municipal property tax levy issues failed. See Ohio Legislative Service Commission, *Local Government Financing Problems in Ohio* (Columbus, 1959), p. 11.

[11]*Ohio Revised Code.* 718.01–718.03.

TABLE 6
PER CAPITA INCOME TAX REVENUES OF THE FORTY LARGEST CITIES IN OHIO, 1968

	Per Capita ($)
Highest	57.98
Lowest	.00
Mean	28.30
Standard deviation	15.71
Coefficient of variation	55.50

SOURCES: Ohio Expenditure Council, Service Letter, "Municipal Income Taxes in Ohio, 1964–1968," Columbus, Ohio, 1968.

The rates for other cities were 1.00% in twenty-one, .75% in eight, .70% in one, and .60% in the remaining city.[12]

Although detailed information is not available, the rate structure has changed since 1968. For example, at least four cities in 1970 had a rate exceeding 1.0%, including Toledo and Youngstown. The others are Akron (1.3%), and Canton (1.5%). Between 1967 and 1969, several cities in the Cleveland metropolitan area, including Cleveland Heights, Euclid, Parma, and Lorain, increased their income tax rates from .50% to 1.0%.[13]

Table 6 summarizes the inter-city variation pattern of per capita tax revenues in 1968. The average of the forty cities was $28.30. This figure is slightly higher than the average property tax collection, which was $26.33. Per capita income tax revenues ranged from $57.98 in Dayton to zero in Elyria and Upper Arlington, the only cities of the group without income taxes. The standard deviation and the coefficient of variation indicate that the inter-city variation is slightly higher than that of property tax revenues.

Table 7 presents the inter-city variation pattern of per capita total tax revenues of the forty cities in 1968. The average was

[12]This information is provided by the Ohio Municipal League. The rates for some cities are adjusted. For example, a city levying .50% in the first half of 1968 and 1.00% in the remainder is regarded as having a rate of .75% throughout the year.

[13]ACIR, *The Commuter and the Municipal Income Tax, op. cit.*, p. 4.

TABLE 7
PER CAPITA TOTAL TAX REVENUES OF THE FORTY LARGEST OHIO CITIES, 1968

	Per Capita (\$)
Highest	97.54
Lowest	21.73
Mean	55.16
Standard deviation	18.26
Coefficient of variation	33.10

SOURCE: Auditor of State, *Financial Report and Public Debt Statement, Ohio Cities, 1968* (Columbus, undated).

\$55.16, ranging from \$97.54 in Dayton to \$21.73 in Upper Arlington.[14] Inter-city variation of total taxes is substantially smaller than that of either property or income taxes, as the coefficient of variation indicates.

Municipal Debt

Borrowing is the primary means through which municipal governments raise revenues to finance capital improvements of long-term consequence. Long a major component of the municipal financing system, debt financing is likely to become more important.[15] All municipalities face increasing demand for the replacement of obsolescent facilities or for the construction of new facilities, or both. At the same time, current revenues from local taxes that have heretofore made sizable contributions to municipal capital

[14]Tax revenues from other than property and income taxes are negligible. For example, Cincinnati collected \$228,000 from public utilities and \$223,000 from unspecified sources of selective sales taxes in 1968–1969. See U.S. Bureau of the Census, *City Government Finances in 1968–69* (Washington, D.C.: U.S. Government Printing Office, 1970), p. 50.

[15]During the four-year period from fiscal 1964 to fiscal 1968, net long-term outstanding debt of the forty-three largest cities in the United States grew \$2,250 million, from \$13,812 million to \$16,062 million. In comparison, tax revenues during the same period grew \$1,551 million, from \$4,984 million to \$6,535 million. See U.S. Bureau of the Census, *City Government Finances, 1964–65* and the volume in the same series for 1968–69.

investment funds are tending to diminish. Although there is strong support for the "pay-as-you-go" approach to capital improvements, the fact is that current revenues are becoming increasingly inadequate even to meet the financial requirements for current operating purposes.

The state restricts local debt to keep local governments financially solvent and responsible. Three specific forms of state restrictions are most often used to regulate the borrowing and indebtedness of local governments. These include limits on the amount of outstanding local government debt in relation to the property tax base; limits on property tax rates that can be levied for debt service requirements, or for various purposes including debt service; and requirements for specific referendum approval of proposed bond issues. Provisions limiting the amount of debt in relation to the property tax base (assessed valuation) are found in thirty-four state constitutions. Only a few states apply limits to local tax rates for debt service. However, nearly all states use the referendum device to regulate local debt issuance, but the referendum provisions differ in their potential restrictiveness among states and often within a single state.[16]

There is some evidence that long-term local debt is somewhat lower in those states with specific constitutional limitations than in states without them. Long-term general debt of local governments per $1,000 of personal income in the fourteen states without specific constitutional limitations was $82.28 in 1957, as compared with $71.06 in the thirty-four states with specific constitutional limitations. Full faith and credit debt of local governments per $1,000 personal income in the former states was $63.16 as compared with $51.22 in the latter.[17]

This aggregate comparison is useful to show that the existence of state constitutional restrictions may make a difference in local

[16]Advisory Commission on Intergovernmental Relations, *State Constitutional and Statutory Restrictions on Local Government Debt* (Washington, D.C.: U.S. Government Printing Office, 1961) pp. 27, 28–32.

[17]James A. Maxwell, *Financing State and Local Governments* (Washington, D.C.: The Brookings Institution, 1965), pp. 198–199.

government indebtedness. However, it is unclear from such evidence how constitutional limitations affect the debt financing behavior of particular localities, for each state imposes local debt limits differently. More importantly, since the decision to adopt a particular level of debt, within the limits imposed by the state, is a local one, the relationship between debt financing behavior and community characteristics must be examined.

While the Constitution of the State of Ohio does not provide specific limitations on local debt, it authorizes the legislature to regulate local debt by law. Thus, the Uniform Bond Law of 1927 created a class of debt subject to state restrictions called "statutory debt." The statutory debt is defined as the total outstanding debt "less the amount held in sinking funds or other bond retirement funds and less bonds or notes issued in anticipation of collection of special assessments or current revenues and public utility mortgages or revenue bonds."[18] State restrictions are in effect applied to full faith and credit long-term debt for non-revenue producing purposes.

The limits on statutory debt are specified in two ways: total limits and limits that can be incurred without voter approval. Both are defined in relation to the assessed valuation of taxable property. The total limit of statutory debt was 7% of assessed valuation until 1969, when it was raised to 10%. Until 1968, the statutory debt which could be incurred without voter approval was 2.5% of assessed valuation for charter cities and 1.5% for cities without charters (statutory cities). In 1968, the unvoted debt limits were increased to 3.5% and 2.5% respectively, for each class of city.*

As noted, state restrictions on local debt were devised to keep local governments financially solvent and responsible. In this regard, Ohio has applied only partial control by leaving debts for special assessment projects, public utility mortgages and revenue

---

[18]Seymour Sacks, *et al.*, *Financing Government in a Metropolitan Area* (Glencoe: Free Press of Glencoe, 1961), p. 279.

*By the end of 1971, the debt limits had been changed. The unvoted debt limit was 4% for non-chartered cities and 5.5% for chartered cities with appropriate language in their charters. The overall limit was 10.5%. (Editors' Note)

bonds unrestricted. This is not to argue that revenue bonds or public utility mortgages should be regulated in the same way as statutory debt, but that the existing system of control lacks logical consistency, in view of the original rationale for state restrictions on local debt.

Limits on statutory debt are tied to the property tax base. This was perfectly logical when municipal revenues were mainly derived from property taxes. However, the municipal tax base is shifting and property taxes are declining in importance. For example, in 1967, the forty largest cities in Ohio raised only 55.9% of their tax revenues from property taxes and the remaining 44.1% mostly from municipal income taxes.[19] The property tax base (assessed valuation of taxable property) alone can no longer be considered an appropriate measure of municipal debt capacity. Since municipal income taxes are as important as property taxes, personal income levels should be recognized as another measure of fiscal capacity for municipal debt control purposes, if such control is meaningful at all. It should be noted that assessed value of taxable property and personal income are not equivalent indicators of community economic capacity. The correlation coefficient between the two is only .476 among these forty cities.

Even though assessed valuation is not an entirely appropriate measure of fiscal capacity, it is presently the criterion used for municipal debt control purposes. For this study, two measures of debt rate have been developed, a statutory debt index and a total debt index. The statutory debt index was devised to measure existing statutory debt in relation to the state imposed debt ceiling. The 1967 statutory debt of each of the municipalities was computed as a percentage of seven times the assessed valuation of taxable property. (The statutory debt ceiling was 7% of assessed valuation in 1967.) If the statutory debt in a particular municipality reached the allowable maximum, the index so computed equals 1.00; the index value becomes lower as the gap between statutory debt and

[19]It is evident that the share of property tax contribution to total municipal tax revenues will continue to decline. Since 1967, four more of the forty cities included in this study adopted municipal income taxes, and a few others increased their income tax rates.

the debt limit widens. The total debt index is a measure which expresses the total outstanding debt in 1967 as a percentage of assessed valuation. This measure represents the burden of all debt, statutory and otherwise, in relation to assessed valuation.

Table 8 summarizes inter-city variation on the two debt indices. As shown in column 1, none of these cities reached the debt limit. The most indebted city (Middletown) reached 86% of the debt limit, while the least indebted (Lancaster and Lima) incurred only 4% of the debt limit. The mean of .32 shows that, on the average, the statutory debts of the cities were only 32% of the state-imposed limit.

State law sets the limit of unvoted debt at 2.5% of assessed valuation in charter cities and 1.5% in statutory cities.* In order to examine which cities have incurred statutory debts beyond the unvoted debt limit, the value of the unvoted limit was computed in terms of the statutory debt index for the two categories of cities. If a charter city incurred statutory debt to the unvoted limit and no more, the statutory debt index of the city would be .36, while that for a statutory city would be .21.

Of the twenty-six charter cities, statutory debt exceeded the unvoted debt limit in fourteen, while it remained below in twelve. Of the fourteen statutory cities, statutory debt exceeded the unvoted limit in three, was equal to the limit in one, and remained below

TABLE 8
PATTERN OF DEBT RATES OF THE FORTY LARGEST OHIO CITIES, 1967

	Statutory Debt Index	*Total Debt Index*
Highest	.86	13.72
Lowest	.04	.86
Mean	.32	4.83
Standard deviation	.24	2.98
Coefficient of variation	75.00	61.70

SOURCE: Ohio Municipal Advisory Council, *Compendium of Municipal Debt in the State of Ohio as of January 1, 1967* (Cleveland, 1967).

*See Editors' Note on p. 68.

the limit in ten cities. The statutory debt index of the twenty-six charter cities averaged .38, slightly above the unvoted debt limit, while that of statutory cities averaged .16, considerably below even the unvoted debt limit.

Two characteristics of the 1967 statutory debt of these largest Ohio cities can be noted. First, the statutory debt outstanding varies markedly from city to city. Second, all statutory debts are below the state imposed total debt limit. In fact, more than half (twenty-two) of the forty cities had not even reached the unvoted debt limit in 1967. None reached the overall limit.

Column 2 of Table 8 shows the pattern of inter-city variation in the total debt index. The index ranges from a high of 13.72 in Cincinnati to a low of .86 in Norwood, with an average of 4.83 for all the cities. The coefficients of variation for the two indices demonstrate that the inter-city variation in statutory debt (c.v. = 75.0) exceeds that of total outstanding debt (c.v. = 61.7).

As another way of measuring municipal debts, 1967 per capita statutory and total outstanding debts were computed for each of the forty cities. The resulting data are summarized in Table 9. Both per capita statutory debt and total outstanding debts vary sharply from city to city. Per capita statutory debt ranges from a high of \$338.47 in Middletown to a low of only \$7.03 in Lima; the forty-city average was \$73.39. Per capita total outstanding debt ranges

TABLE 9
PATTERN OF MUNICIPAL DEBT LEVELS OF THE FORTY LARGEST CITIES IN OHIO, 1967
(in dollars per capita)

	Per Capita Statutory Debt	*Per Capita Total Outstanding Debt*
Highest	\$338.47	\$566.43
Lowest	7.03	25.04
Mean	73.39	153.01
Standard deviation	65.08	109.61
Coefficient of variation	88.20	71.60

SOURCE: **Ohio Municipal Advisory Council, *Compendium of Municipal Debt in the State of Ohio as of January 1, 1967* (Cleveland, 1967).**

from $566.43 in Middletown to $25.04 in East Cleveland, with an average of $153.01. As the coefficient of variation indicates, per capita statutory debt varies relatively more than per capita total outstanding debt.

II. RELATIONSHIPS OF MUNICIPAL TAX AND DEBT STRUCTURE TO COMMUNITY CHARACTERISTICS

The great variation in the tax and debt structures of Ohio cities reflects differences in local political decisions on fiscal policies. Under the general constraint of state regulations, there is substantial latitude for individual communities to adopt particular tax and debt structures of their own.

In view of the chronic fiscal plight of the cities, it is useful to understand the bases of inter-city variations in local fiscal policies. To be more specific, it is useful to understand which community factors are associated with particular fiscal decisions. As a means of investigating this question, we examined the relationships of twenty selected variables representing socio-economic and political-governmental characteristics to the tax and debt structure of the forty Ohio cities.

The Design for Analysis

The tax and debt structure of Ohio municipalities, as those of other cities, has developed into the present pattern over a long period of time. Likewise, the socio-economic and political characteristics of the municipalities have also experienced change during their existence. We believe it is conceptually valid to assume that the current pattern of tax or debt structure can be explained by the current characteristics of the community, assuming that the tax or debt structure is mainly a deliberate choice of the community. However, we also consider that a deliberate choice does not necessarily exclude the possibility that such choice may be influenced by situational factors such as fortuitous events or the miscalculations of decision makers, which do not necessarily reflect the characteristics of the community.

A municipality's tax and debt structure is a complex phenomenon, and no single measure can describe it adequately. Therefore, eleven measures are used to describe various aspects of the tax and debt structure. These eleven measures are regarded as dependent variables.

Tax and Debt Structure Variables

1. Total millage of property taxes, 1967
2. Inside millage of property taxes, 1967
3. Outside millage of property taxes, 1967
4. Income tax rates, 1968
5. Per capita property tax revenues, 1968
6. Per capita income tax revenues, 1968
7. Per capita total tax revenues, 1968
8. Statutory debt index, 1967
9. Total debt index, 1967
10. Per capita statutory debt, 1967
11. Per capita total debt outstanding, 1967

The twenty community characteristics are regarded as independent variables. They include six population variables, three economic variables, two geographic location variables, and nine political-governmental variables.

Community Characteristics Variables

A. Population Characteristics
1. Total population, 1965
2. Population density, 1965
3. Percentage of population change, 1960-1965
4. Median school years completed, 1960
5. Percentage of white collar workers, 1960
6. Percentage of nonwhite in the population, 1960

B. Economic Characteristics
7. Median family income, 1960
8. Per capita total assessed valuation, 1967
9. Percentage of home ownership, 1960

C. Geographic Characteristics

10. Central city dummy
11. Non-central city dummy

D. Political-Governmental Characteristics

12. Percentage of voter turnout for the 1962 gubernatorial election
13. Total school tax millage, 1967
14. Number of years income tax in effect as of 1968 (Income tax duration)
15. Per capita intergovernmental revenues, 1967
16. Number of years city charter in effect as of 1968 (Charter duration)
17. Charter city dummy
18. Non-charter city dummy
19. Council-manager city dummy
20. Mayor-council city dummy

We here attempt to assess relationships between variables representing municipal tax and debt structure and those socio-economic and political variables characterizing municipalities. Though it has been a general practice in earlier studies to use a number of common independent variables to account for the variation in the dependent variables,[20] we depart from this earlier approach. We assume that when dependent variables measure different things—property tax revenue levels, income tax revenue levels, debt rates, or debt levels—the particular combination of independent variables explaining these dependent variables changes from one dependent variable to the next. Under this assumption, we have identified the six most influential independent variables among the twenty through stepwise multiple regression analysis.[21] Since the stepwise regression does not compute partial correlation coefficients, we reran the regression equation with the six selected independent

---

[20]Studies using a number of common independent variables to explain selected dependent variables are numerous. For example, see Thomas R. Dye, *Politics, Economics, and the Public: Policy Outcomes in the American States* (Chicago: Rand McNally, 1966).

[21]The computer program used for this operation is BMDO-Stepwise Regression-Revised June 26, 1969, Health Sciences Computing Facility, UCLA. This type of analytic approach was used by Ira Sharkansky in *Regionalism in American Politics* (Indianapolis: The Bobbs-Merrill Co., 1970), pp. 145–160.

variables for each dependent variable in the regular multiple regression program.[22]

Findings

Tables 10, 11, 12, and 13 report the relationships between tax and debt structure and community characteristic variables.[23] For each dependent variable, four statistical relationships are reported; the simple correlation coefficient; the last order partial correlation coefficient; the regression coefficient that can be used in the estimating equation for predicting the dependent variable; and finally, the change (ΔR^2) in the coefficient of multiple determination (R^2) attributable to each independent variable. In addition, shown in the last two columns are the multiple correlation coefficient (R), coefficient of multiple determination (R^2), and the constant.

Table 10 shows the relationships of the three property tax rates and the income tax rate to the six most powerful explanatory variables. The four sets of independent variables identified for each of the tax rate measures display a somewhat different combination of community characteristics. However, those variables most commonly included in the four equations are dummy for charter city, income tax duration, population size, and population change. The six variables together account for 70.6% of the total millage variance, 26.5% of the inside millage variance, 65.6% of the outside millage variance, and 55.4% of the income tax rate variance.

It is not surprising to find that variations in inside millage are not significantly related to community characteristics. The cities share of the ten-mill limit was determined in the 1930s. The change in the city portion of the ten-mill limit brought about by municipal charter amendments or the adopton of a new charter is illustrated by the strong relations between charter city dummy and all three tween the charter city dummy and property tax rates indicates that the political autonomy accorded charter cities actually tends measures of property tax rates. In addition, the relationship be-

[22]The computer program used for this operation is General Statistics Program -04- Multiple Regression Analysis by G. L. Simmons.

[23]The simple correlation coefficients of the twenty community characteristic variables with each of the tax and debt measures are shown in Appendix B.

TABLE 10

RELATIONSHIPS OF MUNICIPAL TAX RATES TO SELECTED INDEPENDENT VARIABLES: FORTY LARGEST OHIO CITIES

Tax Rates	*Statistical Relationships*	*Charter City Dummy*	*Income Tax Duration*	*Total Pop. 1965*	*Pct. Pop. Growth 1960–65*	*Council Manager City Dummy*	*Population Density 1965*	*R (R^2)*	*Constant*
Total millage of property taxes, 1967	Simple r	.497	−.492	.359	−.051	−.011	.337	.840	
	Partial r	.553	−.693	.427	−.382	−.294	.BDR	(.706)	7.289
	Regression coeff.	3.771	−.346	.008	−.175	−1.773	.0003		
	Δ R^2	.247	.185	.155	.063	.036	.019		
		Council Manager Dummy	*Charter City Dummy*	*Pct. Pop. Change 1960–65*	*P.C. Assessed Total Valuation 1967*	*Median School Year 1960*	*Central City Dummy*	*R (R^2)*	*Constant*
Inside millage of property taxes, 1967	Simple r	−.252	.121	−.132	−.197	.076	.148	.515	
	Partial r	−.396	.293	−.320	−.238	.197	.058	(.265)	1.471
	Regression coeff.	−1.265	.929	−.084	−.0005	.361	.174		
	Δ R^2	.063	.084	.055	.029	.032	.003		
		Charter City Dummy	*Income Tax Duration*	*Total Pop. 1965*	*Pop. Density 1965*	*P.C. Inter-gov'tal Revenue 1967*	*P.C. Total Assessed Valua-tion, 1967*	*R (R^2)*	*Constant*
Outside millage of property taxes, 1967	Simple r	.481	−.438	.372	.340	.131	.138	.803	
	Partial r	.411	−.657	.347	.439	.346	.188	(.646)	−1.716
	Regression coeff.	2.282	−.314	.006	.0005	.056	.0006		
	Δ R^2	.231	.143	.156	.053	.051	.013		
		Income Tax Duration	*Total School Millage, 1967*	*Pct. Home Ownership 1960*	*Pct. Voter Turnout 1962*	*Pct. Pop. Change 1960–65*	*Charter Duration*	*R (R^2)*	*Constant*
Income tax rate, 1968	Simple r	.638	−.439	−.152	−.317	−.263	.110	.744	
	Partial r	.529	−.402	.420	−.283	−.240	.200	(.544)	2.260
	Regression coeff.	.022	−.024	.012	−.024	−.010	.002		
	[illegible]	[illegible]	[illegible]	[illegible]	[illegible]	[illegible]	[illegible]		

to strengthen political efficacy in determining property tax policies.

Income tax duration is inversely related to property tax rates, but shows a positive relation to income tax rates. The inverse relationship with property tax rates indicates a significant degree of substitutive effect on property taxes.[24] The positive relationship with income tax rate suggests that extended experience with income taxes leads to community acceptance and thus to further increases.

The positive correlations of population size and population density indicate that property tax rates are generally responsive to the needs of the communities' public services. By contrast, the inverse correlation of population change with total property millage and income tax rate suggests that the response of tax structure generally lags behind population growth, particularly in suburbs.

The significant positive correlation of intergovernmental revenues to the outside millage of property taxes is particularly noteworthy. First, it relates to the long standing debate whether state and federal aids to local government have a stimulative, additive, or substitutive effect on local taxes. On the basis of the correlation, state and federal aids to Ohio municipalities evidently tend to stimulate municipal property tax efforts. Second, the amount of aid a municipal government secures from state and federal governments may be an indicator of the successful grantsmanship of the governmental leaders of the community. If this assumption is valid, the skills of effective grantsmanship in intergovernmental fiscal relations may be the same as those required to persuade the voters to adopt a local property tax package.

Those variables closely associated with the income tax rate illuminate local tax politics in several ways. The positive correlation with home ownership suggests that home owners prefer income taxes to the additional burden of property taxes. The inverse relation of voter turnout may reflect the impact of a citizen tax rebellion. The more participatory the electorate, the more effectively does the taxpayer's rebellion seem to be channelled into curbing the rise of income taxes, even when the issue is not directly voted upon. The inverse correlation with school tax millage indicates

[24]A further analysis shows that a $1.00 increase in income taxes reduces 45¢ of property taxes in the forty Ohio cities.

that those communities with high school taxes are inclined to hold down municipal taxes by repudiating income tax increases. This finding affirms the earlier discussion of the effect of inter-local tax competition on municipal taxes. It further suggests that education is a high priority in the electorate's choice of public services.

In summary, these findings indicate that the structure of municipal tax rates is mainly explained by governmental system (charter status of the city, form of city government, and intergovernmental relations with state and federal governments and with schools) and population characteristics, not by economic factors.

Table 11 presents the relationships of per capita total taxes, property taxes, and income taxes to the six selected variables. All six variables account for variances of 76.6% of per capita income tax, 70.1% of property tax, and 69.6% of total tax.

Most of the variables selected for the three tax level equations are the same as for the tax rate equations, and the direction of influence is also identical. The new variables appearing in the tax level equations include per capita total assessed valuation, percent nonwhite, percent white collar workers, and median family income.

Assessed valuation is strongly and positively correlated with all measures of tax level. This finding indicates that tax bases are important in determining tax productivity, unlike tax rates. However, the fact that property valuation is positively correlated with income tax revenues, while median family income is correlated inversely with the tax, is interesting and requires elaboration. First, this apparently contradictory relationship does not seem to be the result of multi-collinearity of property valuation and income, considering the sufficiently low correlation between the two (.476). Second, since property taxes and municipal income taxes are both regressive, property valuation in effect tends to serve as the indicator of tax bases for both property and income taxes.[25] According to

[25]For the estimate of tax burdens of each type of tax at each level of government, see Tax Foundation, Inc., *Tax Burdens and Benefits of Governmental Expenditures By Income Class, 1961 and 1965* (New York, 1967). Although most municipalities in Ohio and most local governments in Pennsylvania are using local income taxes, they are only allowed to use a flat rate and to tax earned incomes. Thus, the local income taxes tend to be as regressive as other local taxes.

RELATIONSHIPS OF PER CAPITA MUNICIPAL TAX REVENUES TO SELECTED VARIABLES: FORTY LARGEST OHIO CITIES, 1968

Tax Variables	*Statistical Relations*	*Independent Variables*						*R (R^2)*	*Constant*
		P.C. Total Assessed Valuation 1967	*Pct. Nonwhite 1960*	*Pct. Voter turnout, Gubernatorial Elect. 1962*	*P.C. Intergv'tl Revenues 1967*	*Pct. White Collar Workers, 1960*	*Charter City Dummy*		
Per capita total taxes	Simple r	.590	.488	−.463	.385	−.258	.158	.834	110.26
	Partial r	.727	.058	−.407	.235	−.331	.308	(.696)	
	Coeff.	.016	.124	−1.351	.169	−.442	8.377		
	ΔR^2	.348	.211	.066	.027	.012	.032		
		P.C. Total Assessed Valuation 1967	*Income Tax Duration*	*Charter City Dummy*	*P.C. Intergv'tl Revenues 1967*	*Pct. Voter Turnout Gub. Elec. 1962*	*Total Pop. 1960*	*R (R^2)*	*Constant*
Per capita property taxes	Simple r	.483	−.428	.418	.218	−.096	.222	.837	
	Partial r	.622	−.691	.410	.410	−.361	.190	(.701)	59.14
	Coeff.	.009	−1.191	7.365	.230	−.850	.010		
	ΔR^2	.233	.180	.126	.090	.060	.020		
		Income Tax Duration	*P.C. Total Assessed Valuation 1967*	*Median Family Income*	*Pop. Density 1965*	*Pct. Home Ownership 1960*	*Pct. Pop. Change 1960–65*	*R (R^2)*	*Constant*
Per capita income taxes	Simple r	.772	.253	−.419	.135	−.387	−.379	.875	
	Partial r	.734	.624	−.508	.286	.250	−.140	(.766)	−12.37
	Coeff.	1.405	.011	−.004	.001	.226	−.213		
	ΔR^2	.596	.068	.074	.011	.013	.005		

the Ohio Tax Study Commission's estimate, real and intangible property taxes take 11.38% of income of the under $2,000 annual income group and only 2.60% of income of the over $10,000 annual income group, with a regressive burden between the two extremes. Likewise, municipal income taxes in Ohio take .62% of income of the lower income group, but only .38% of income of the higher income group.[26] The regressiveness of municipal income taxes is due to the fact that incomes other than salary, wage, and business net profits are not subject to the taxes and the tax rates are uniform. Third, when the home ownership variable is considerable in relation to the income variable, the meaning of the inverse correlation between median family income and income tax revenues becomes clearer. Communities with a high rate of home ownership tend to support income taxes to reduce tax burdens on residential properties, while communities with high median family income tend to repudiate income taxes to protect take-home pay.

The presence of a high proportion of nonwhite population in a community is strongly correlated with high total taxes. This relationship may mean two things: it may indicate the responsiveness of tax policies to needs, since the nonwhite are likely to be poor and the poor require more municipal services; and it may affirm the Wilson-Banfield findings that nonwhite groups are more supportive of public expenditure measures than others.[27]

The percentage of white collar workers in the labor force is inversely correlated with total taxes. This may mean that white collar workers prefer to finance education rather than municipal services. The correlation .595 between the percentage of white collar workers and school tax millage tends to support this.

As in the case of tax rates, income tax duration is inversely correlated with property taxes and positively correlated with income taxes. This finding reaffirms the substitutive effect of income with property taxes. The positive effect on income tax revenues suggests

---

[26]Ohio Tax Study Commission, *The State and Local Tax Structure of Ohio* (Columbus, 1967), pp. 35, 34–35.

[27]James Q. Wilson and Edward C. Banfield, "Public-Regardingness as a Value Premise in Voting Behavior," *American Political Science Review,* 58 (December, 1964), 876–887.

that the cities with a longer experience with income taxes not only have higher income tax rates, but also more effective administration for income tax collection.

In summary, the level of tax revenues is closely associated with economic and social variables, though governmental variables are not unimportant.

Table 12 reports the relationships of statutory and total debt indices to the six explanatory variables. The sets of variables explain 61.6% of statutory debt index variance and 59.0% of total debt index variance. The most influential variables explaining the statutory debt index include four governmental and two economic variables, while the six selected for the total debt index include two governmental, two social, and one each of the locational and economic variables.

Those cities older in charter experience, receiving larger federal and state aids, and having higher assessed valuation tend to have higher statutory debt rates. By contrast, those with the council-manager form of government, longer duration of income tax, and higher median family income tend to have lower statutory debt rates. As noted earlier, the state constitution provides a more lenient limit for unvoted statutory debt in charter cities. The high correlation (simple as well as partial) indicates that such leniency in state control does make a difference in the actual statutory debt rates of the charter cities.

The inverse correlation of income tax duration seems to describe an important role of the income tax for municipal capital investment. Those cities with income taxes usually earmark a proportion of the revenues for capital investment, thereby reducing the pressure or need for borrowing.

The total debt index is positively related to the percentage of nonwhite, charter city dummy, central city dummy, and percentage of white collar workers. It is negatively related to median family income and the council-manager form of government. The positive correlation of the percentage of nonwhite with the total

---

[28]*Ibid.*

TABLE 12

RELATIONSHIPS OF DEBT RATE INDICES TO SELECTED MEASURES OF COMMUNITY CHARACTERISTICS FOR THE FORTY LARGEST OHIO CITIES, 1967

Debt Rate Index	*Statistical Relations*	*Independent Variables*							
		Charter Duration	*P.C. Intergov'tal Revenues*	*Council-Manager City*	*P.C. Total Assessed Valuation*	*Income Tax Duration*	*Median Family Income*	*R* (R^2)	*Constant*
Statutory debt index	Simple r	.522	.461	.065	.254	.003	.006	.785	.027
	Partial r	.678	.444	−.446	.396	−.341	−.264	(.616)	
	Regression	.007	.005	−.201	.00011	−.009	−.00003		
	ΔR^2	.273	.151	.089	.046	.028	.029		
		Percent Nonwhite	*Charter City*	*Central City*	*Median Family Income*	*Council-Manager City*	*Percent White Collar*	*R* (R^2)	*Constant*
Total debt index	Simple r	.650	.372	.600	−.330	.108	−.282	.768	3.546
	Partial r	.308	.405	.283	−.336	−.259	.229	(.590)	
	Regression r	.148	2.343	1.808	−.00085	−1.305	.090		
	ΔR^2	.423	.068	.029	.028	.020	.023		

debt index again supports the Wilson and Banfield finding that nonwhite voters tend to approve bond issues and expenditure measures in referenda elections.[28] The finding that central cities tend to have a higher total debt index indicates that central cities require more capital investment through debt financing in order to maintain extensive overhead capital facilities. It is interesting to note that median family income is inversely correlated with both statutory and total debt indices. This finding is contrary to earlier studies, which consistently report that income level is positively associated with governmental spending, taxation, or borrowing.

Table 13 summarizes the relationships of per capita statutory and total debt to the six community characteristic variables. The variance accounted for by the six variables is 70.1% for per capita statutory debt and 64.4% for total debt. The six variables included in the per capita statutory debt equation are identical with those included in the statutory debt index equation, and the direction of association is also the same. The cities with more affluent property tax bases (property valuation), longer experience with municipal charters, and more effective intergovernmental grantsmanship tend to have a higher level of statutory debt. Those cities with a council-manager form of government, high income, and an extended experience with income taxes tend to have a lower level of statutory debt.

The total debt outstanding is positively related to percentage of nonwhite, assessed valuation, charter city, and education. It is inversely related to median family income and population density.

III. SUMMARY

Ohio municipal governments are responsible for financing local services needs largely from their own local revenue sources. State aids to municipal governments are generally insignificant. The Ohio State Constitution and statutes place a number of restrictions on municipal powers for taxation and borrowing: e.g., the ten-mill limit of unvoted property taxes, the one percent limit for unvoted municipal income taxes, unvoted and total limits on statutory debts,

TABLE 13

RELATIONSHIPS OF P.C. DEBT TO SELECTED MEASURES OF COMMUNITY CHARACTERISTICS FOR THE FORTY LARGEST OHIO CITIES, 1967

Debt Level Index	*Statistical Relationships*	*Independent Variables*							
		P.C. Total Assessed Valuation	*Charter Duration*	*P.C. Intergov'tal Revenues*	*Council-Manager City*	*Median Family Income*	*Income Tax Duration*	*R (R^2)*	*Constant*
Per capita statutory debt	Simple r	.545	.471	.395	.135	.081	.013	.837	−69.66
	Partial r	.715	.660	.359	−.353	−.425	−.385	(.701)	
	Regression coeff.	.065	1.706	.894	−36.994	−.014	−2.516		
	ΔR^2	.297	.198	.088	.037	.030	.052		
		Percent Nonwhite	*P.C. Total Assessed Valuation*	*Charter City*	*Median Family Income*	*Education*	*Pop. Density*	*R (R^2)*	*Constant*
Per capita total debt outstanding	Simple r	.613	.369	.324	−.196	−.268	−.078	.802	−234.62
	Partial r	.457	.589	.456	−.417	.210	−.201	(.644)	
	Regression coeff.	6.440	.090	80.392	−.039	27.147	−.006		
	ΔR^2	.376	1.116	.046	.072	.021	.015		

and referendum requirements for taxes and borrowing beyond specified limits.

Under these general state constraints, local political decisions primarily determine the particular local tax and debt structure of individual municipalities. To what extent a municipal government will tax property, whether the municipal government will adopt an income tax, or, if it does, at what rate, and how much of the municipal financing will be done through borrowing, are all subject to local political choice. The marked variation that we observed in the tax rates, tax revenues, debt rates, and debts outstanding among these Ohio cities reflects the differences in municipal fiscal policy choices associated with variations in localities.

An examination of the relationships of the twenty variables representing the socio-economic and governmental-political characteristics of the communities to the eleven municipal tax and debt structure variables reveals a number of interesting patterns. The property tax millage within the constitutional limitation does not display close relationships to current community characteristics. This lack of a significant relationship reaffirms the arbitrary nature of the constitutional limitation imposed upon local taxing powers nearly four decades ago. However, the other ten measures are significantly responsive to the governmental system and socio-economic environment of the communities.

Table 14 summarizes the findings reported in Tables 10 through 13. In the governmental-political dimension, charter cities and cities attracting a larger amount of intergovernmental aid tend to have higher rates and levels of municipal taxes and debts. Income taxes tend not only to substitute for property taxes, but also to repress debt financing.

On the socio-economic dimension, cities with stronger property tax bases, larger population, higher population density, greater proportion of nonwhite population, and locations in metropolitan core areas tend to have higher taxes and/or debts. Cities with higher family income tend to have lower debt rates and debt levels, and cities with more rapid population change tend to have lower taxes.

TABLE 14.
RELATIONSHIPS OF MUNICIPAL TAX AND DEBT STRUCTURE TO COMMUNITY CHARACTERISTICS: SUMMARY

	Municipal Tax Rates				*Per Capital Tax Revenues*			*Debt Rates*		*Per Capital Debts*		*Frequency of Independent Variables*		
	Total Millage	*Inside Millage*	*Outside Millage*	*Income Tax Rate*	*P.C. Total Tax Rev.*	*P.C. Property Tax Rev.*	*P.C. Income Tax Rev.*	*Stat-utory Debt Index*	*Total Debt Index*	*P.C. Stat-utory Debt*	*P.C. Total Out-standing*	*Total*	*+*	*−*
Charter city dummy	+	+	+		+	+			+		+	7	7	0
Charter duration				+				+		+		3	3	0
Council-manager dummy	−	−						−	−	−		5	0	5
Income tax duration	−		−	+		−	+	−		−		7	2	5
School tax millage				−								1	0	1
P.C. intergovernmental revenues			+		+	+		+		+		5	5	0
% Voter turnout				−	−	−						3	0	3
P.C. total assessed valuation		−	+		+	+	+	+		+	+	8	7	1
Median family income		+					−	−	−	−	−	6	1	5
% home ownership				+			+					2	2	0
Total population	+		+			+						3	3	0
Population change	−	−		−			−					4	0	4
Population density	+		+				+				−	4	3	1
% Non-white					+				+		+	3	3	0
% White collar workers					−				+			2	1	1
Education											+	1	1	0
Central city dummy		+							+			2	2	0

NOTE: + sign indicates positive relationship and − sign indicates inverse relationship. This direction of association is based on regression coefficients presented in Tables 10 through 13.

APPENDIX I. MUNICIPAL TAX, DEBT, SOCIO-ECONOMIC, AND POLITICAL-GOVERNMENTAL VARIABLES OF THE LARGEST OHIO CITIES

Ohio Cities Over 25,000	*A-1. Tax Rates* 1	2	3	4	*A-2. Tax Levels* 5	6
Akron	10.39	5.95	4.44	1.00	63.77	23.19
Alliance	4.4	4.0	.4	.60	36.46	15.86
Barberton	4.3	3.5	.8	1.00	61.91	17.06
Canton	3.4	3.4	.00	1.00	53.67	9.24
Cincinnati	12.82	3.52	9.3	1.00	92.43	49.52
Cleveland	19.90	4.45	15.45	.75	75.40	49.62
Cleveland Heights	9.8	3.72	6.08	.75	33.88	22.46
Columbus	3.14	3.14	.00	1.00	47.12	9.38
Cuyahoga Falls	11.94	11.0	.94	1.00	50.45	30.62
Dayton	10.0	3.82	6.18	1.00	97.54	39.48
East Cleveland	10.90	3.72	7.18	.50	43.87	29.08
Elyria	9.23	4.2	5.03	0	48.54	43.18
Euclid	12.5	3.88	8.62	.75	93.25	61.38
Findlay	5.9	2.9	3.0	1.00	61.25	23.54
Garfield Heights	10.0	3.64	6.36	.75	33.75	23.59
Hamilton	5.62	3.81	1.81	1.00	42.07	12.74
Kettering	7.4	2.5	4.90	1.00	48.28	30.09
Lakewood	16.2	3.47	12.73	.50	52.86	43.67
Lancaster	3.3	3.3	.00	.50	28.14	10.03
Lima	3.9	3.9	.00	1.00	48.73	14.92
Lorain	6.7	4.96	1.74	.50	53.56	35.78
Mansfield	4.57	3.47	1.10	1.00	70.45	17.47
Maple Heights	12.5	3.2	9.3	.75	52.78	34.12
Marion	4.8	4.2	.6	.70	42.97	18.00
Massillon	4.0	3.7	.3	1.00	45.59	13.12
Middletown	6.41	2.92	3.49	1.00	93.25	35.63
Newark	4.7	3.7	1.0	1.00	41.91	13.27
Norwood	4.02	3.4	.62	1.00	71.03	18.86
Parma	8.7	3.39	5.31	.75	47.53	28.46
Portsmouth	13.27	4.06	9.21	.50	48.91	34.87
Sandusky	8.65	4.25	4.40	1.00	56.38	30.68
Shaker Heights	11.0	4.5	6.5	.75	74.07	58.01
South Euclid	11.2	4.05	7.15	.75	35.51	25.42
Springfield	3.9	3.27	.63	1.00	46.18	11.18
Steubenville	9.9	3.2	6.7	1.00	51.18	27.04
Toledo	4.4	2.5	1.9	1.50	73.06	16.12
Upper Arlington	5.1	2.0	3.1	.00	21.73	21.73
Warren	3.9	3.4	.5	1.00	52.38	14.56
Youngstown	9.1	3.7	5.4	1.5	73.44	28.77
Zanesville	3.4	3.4	.00	1.00	41.03	11.60

Variable Description: 1=Total millage of property taxes, 1967; 2=Inside millage, 1967; 3=Outside millage, 1967; and 4=Income tax rates, 1968. 5=Per capita total tax revenues, 1968; 6=Per capita property tax revenues, 1968; 7=Per capita income tax revenues, 1968.

A-3. *Municipal Debt Rates and Debt Levels B. Population Characteristics*

7	*8*	*9*	*10*	*11*	*12*	*13*	*14*	*15*
40.59	.57	5.85	123.37	179.51	298	5448	2.63	10.8
20.61	.21	3.79	43.02	111.20	28	5167	−1.27	11.0
44.85	.14	1.73	33.66	59.77	35	4695	3.53	10.5
44.43	.09	2.20	17.78	67.66	110	7946	−3.19	9.9
42.46	.80	13.72	184.18	452.22	495	6569	−1.50	9.7
25.31	.66	8.41	158.72	287.50	855	11542	−2.40	9.6
10.68	.49	3.51	110.22	114.42	62	7631	.30	12.5
37.70	.71	12.27	138.84	340.62	540	5430	14.57	11.2
19.81	.26	4.99	46.00	124.50	51	5916	6.42	12.4
57.98	.46	6.26	109.05	224.35	260	7693	−.88	10.4
14.73	.13	.91	23.64	25.04	40	12255	5.28	11.4
.00	.39	6.94	93.36	206.02	50	3105	14.20	11.3
29.32	.44	4.17	136.56	182.01	70	5888	11.11	11.9
37.63	.10	3.98	23.00	126.56	33	3372	8.75	12.0
10.15	.39	3.34	58.54	73.59	43	5341	11.81	10.9
29.32	.10	7.34	18.59	188.06	73	5980	.89	9.9
18.19	.19	1.29	40.72	41.33	65	3223	19.34	12.4
9.20	.84	7.15	154.06	187.57	71	12028	7.32	12.2
17.79	.04	2.70	8.82	75.27	31	4603	3.62	10.8
33.70	.04	9.36	7.03	239.24	56	6224	9.72	10.9
12.50	.34	3.52	84.29	125.30	76	3572	10.25	10.3
52.85	.17	4.79	41.53	172.02	49	9859	3.53	10.9
16.44	.50	3.98	107.47	124.19	35	6209	10.52	11.4
24.29	.07	1.37	13.86	137.02	38	6285	2.48	10.8
32.44	.13	2.59	22.55	66.27	32	4338	2.44	10.3
57.63	.86	10.07	338.47	566.43	43	2552	2.10	10.6
28.65	.13	4.83	23.16	129.43	44	3370	5.28	10.9
52.16	.07	.86	18.20	33.97	34	11527	−1.67	9.7
18.45	.30	2.38	64.46	74.86	91	4163	9.84	11.9
14.04	.27	5.60	45.91	135.92	32	3058	−4.86	9.4
25.70	.41	5.64	85.65	167.07	34	4570	6.28	10.7
15.29	.21	1.76	73.06	85.79	37	5787	1.48	13.2
10.00	.26	2.54	51.28	72.13	30	5993	8.81	12.2
35.00	.16	3.81	28.94	103.45	83	5552	.33	10.6
23.80	.37	5.36	89.73	185.18	35	5603	7.70	9.9
56.94	.20	3.53	46.26	120.18	354	6517	11.31	10.4
.00	.19	1.84	54.77	75.30	33	3700	15.84	14.0
37.82	.11	6.65	25.41	208.36	63	5423	5.61	10.9
44.70	.76	6.95	161.74	212.14	162	4961	−2.81	10.0
28.94	.19	5.25	29.67	119.09	38	5142	−2.75	10.0

Variable Description: 8=Statutory debt index; 9=Total debt index; 10=Per capita statutory debt; 11=Per capita total debt; 12=Total Population (in thousands), 1965 estimate; 13=Density, 1965; 14=Percent population change, 1960–1965; 15=Median school years completed, 1960; 16=Percent white collar workers, 1960; 17=Percent nonwhite, 1960; 18=Median family income, 1959; 19=Per capita total assessed valuation, 1967; 20=Percent home ownership, 1960.

	16	17	18	C. Economic Characteristics 19	20	D. Geographical Characteristics 21	22
Akron	40.4	13.1	6466	3067.12	67.1	1	0
Alliance	42.3	10.1	5924	2931.49	67.4	0	1
Barberton	36.2	4.5	6204	3442.87	67.8	0	1
Canton	36.9	9.8	5736	3063.65	62.5	1	0
Cincinnati	42.0	21.8	5701	3294.57	40.4	1	0
Cleveland	32.9	28.9	5935	3416.91	44.9	1	0
Cleveland Heights	71.3	.7	8623	3253.36	70.0	0	1
Columbus	46.0	16.6	5982	2774.00	51.7	1	0
Cuyahoga Falls	60.0	.1	7738	2492.11	85.2	0	1
Dayton	39.6	21.9	6266	3579.35	55.1	1	0
East Cleveland	53.0	2.4	6844	2742.08	37.5	0	1
Elyria	37.6	9.2	6486	3467.33	70.5	1	0
Euclid	51.2	.2	7739	4355.71	73.3	0	1
Findlay	46.1	.6	6077	3099.82	68.0	0	1
Garfield Heights	43.8	.7	7454	2200.26	89.1	0	1
Hamilton	39.4	6.1	6232	2560.70	64.6	1	0
Kettering	61.2	.2	8441	3240.72	80.0	0	1
Lakewood	63.5	.2	7533	2619.78	50.9	0	1
Lancaster	39.7	.5	5873	2784.77	65.0	0	1
Lima	42.3	10.5	5637	2555.66	62.5	1	0
Lorain	32.4	6.5	5908	3550.22	67.8	1	0
Mansfield	41.6	9.2	6492	3585.08	62.3	1	0
Maple Heights	43.3	.9	7516	3113.45	93.0	0	1
Marion	42.0	2.5	5854	2699.87	67.4	0	1
Massillon	38.3	8.8	5954	2557.45	72.6	0	1
Middletown	41.9	11.3	7146	5619.34	63.6	1	0
Newark	40.8	2.4	5877	2678.53	69.3	0	1
Norwood	38.1	.2	6235	3930.61	47.2	0	1
Parma	49.6	.3	7849	3134.96	87.6	0	1
Portsmouth	45.3	4.8	5123	2424.06	59.4	0	1
Sandusky	39.6	10.3	6064	2660.03	63.2	0	1
Shaker Heights	78.8	1.0	13933	4860.69	64.1	0	1
South Euclid	65.4	.1	8939	2828.84	89.7	0	1
Springfield	41.6	14.4	5673	2708.56	56.6	1	0
Steubenville	39.5	11.3	6162	3451.43	52.1	1	0
Toledo	42.6	12.7	6299	3395.67	63.9	1	0
Upper Arlington	84.7	.2	11915	4082.74	85.6	0	1
Warren	36.2	11.6	6562	3125.74	65.6	1	0
Youngstown	35.6	19.1	5749	3049.66	66.0	1	0
Zanesville	39.1	7.5	5218	2268.03	63.5	0	1

Variable Description: 21=Central city dummy; 22=Non-central city dummy.

E. Political-Governmental Characteristics

23	*24*	*25*	*26*	*27*	*28*	*29*	*30*	*31*
75.0	26.10	6	23.81	51	1	0	0	1
72.6	27.7	11	14.28	0	0	1	0	1
72.0	29.75	15	16.69	0	0	1	0	1
73.0	29.9	14	15.82	0	0	1	0	1
67.0	23.6	15	64.96	52	1	0	1	0
67.0	26.0	2	25.91	56	1	0	0	1
72.0	36.0	2	11.89	57	1	0	1	0
68.0	27.86	21	21.61	55	1	0	0	1
77.0	35.85	2	12.27	10	1	0	0	1
65.0	35.85	20	27.35	56	1	0	1	0
62.0	34.4	2	4.70	53	1	0	1	0
75.5	32.1	0	17.84	4	1	0	0	1
71.0	28.0	2	12.84	18	1	0	0	1
74.0	27.9	2	14.70	0	0	1	0	1
74.5	31.4	2	12.55	13	1	0	0	1
73.0	31.55	9	18.34	43	1	0	1	0
71.0	28.2	1	10.77	14	1	0	1	0
69.0	34.5	2	12.99	56	1	0	0	1
75.7	29.3	5	14.13	0	0	1	0	1
67.0	27.23	10	15.85	49	1	0	0	1
73.0	27.15	2	70.34	0	0	1	0	1
68.6	35.6	9	17.63	0	0	1	0	1
75.1	31.4	2	13.29	38	1	0	0	1
69.4	27.7	10	10.92	0	0	1	0	1
73.0	29.5	9	15.16	0	0	1	0	1
70.2	27.5	11	24.26	56	1	0	1	0
75.7	27.05	10	20.00	0	0	1	0	1
67.6	19.8	15	11.76	0	0	1	0	1
75.0	32.7	2	12.49	0	0	1	0	1
76.0	36.04	4	32.50	41	1	0	1	0
73.0	27.75	1	13.47	55	1	0	1	0
73.7	36.8	2	12.35	38	1	0	0	1
77.9	37.1	2	12.80	16	1	0	0	1
72.0	31.1	21	15.03	56	1	0	1	0
71.9	20.75	7	19.46	0	0	1	0	1
73.0	26.5	23	25.53	55	1	0	1	0
81.7	34.8	0	9.94	50	1	0	1	0
68.0	28.1	19	17.98	0	0	1	0	1
70.0	22.9	20	93.02	46	1	0	0	1
69.2	26.9	10	14.34	54	1	0	1	0

Variable Description: 23= Percent voter turnout for 1962 Gubernatorial election; 24=Total school millage of property taxes, 1967; 25=No. of years income tax in effect as of 1968; 26=Per capita intergovernmental revenues, 1967; and 27=No. of years city charter has been in effect as of 1968; 28=Dummy for Charter City; 29=Dummy for Non-Charter City; 30=Dummy for Council-Manager City; and 31=Dummy for Mayor-Council City.

APPENDIX II.
SIMPLE CORRELATIONS BETWEEN TAX AND DEBT MEASURES AND COMMUNITY CHARACTERISTICS VARIABLES

A. Simple Correlation: Tax Rates and Community Characteristics

	Total Millage	*Inside Millage*	*Outside Millage*	*Income Taxes*
Population				
Total pop.	.359	.017	.372	.217
Pop. density	.337	.043	.340	.035
Pop. change	−.051	−.132	.007	−.263
Schooling	.109	.076	.088	−.412
Pct. white collar	.238	.039	.236	−.372
Pct. nonwhite	.111	−.045	.133	.371
Economic				
M. F. I.	.216	.009	.227	−.339
Assessed valuation	.016	−.197	.138	−.065
Home ownership	−.076	.148	−.132	−.152
Location				
Central city	−.085	−.055	−.070	.320
Non-central city	.085	.055	.070	−.320
Politics-Government				
Election participation	−.051	.160	−.109	−.317
School millage	.232	.201	.174	−.439
Income tax duration	−.492	−.226	−.438	.638
Intergovernmental revenues	.136	.036	.131	.275
Duration of				
City charter	.335	−.096	.386	.110
Charter city	.497	.121	.481	−.039
Non-charter city	−.497	−.121	−.481	.039
Council-manager city	−.011	−.252	.077	.048
Mayor-council city	.011	.252	−.077	−.048

B. Simple Correlation Per Capita Tax Revenues and Community Characteristics

	Per Capita Total Taxes	*Per Capita Property Taxes*	*Per Capita Income Taxes*
Population			
Total pop.	.399	.222	.279
Pop. density	.192	.120	.135
Pop. change	−.260	.061	−.379
Schooling	−.290	.207	−.519
Pct. white collar	−.258	.259	−.511
Pct. nonwhite	.488	.074	.510
Economic			
M. F. I.	−.072	.388	−.419
Assessed valuation	.590	.483	.253
Home ownership	−.388	−.088	−.387
Location			
Central city	.407	−.037	.494
Non-central city	−.407	.037	−.494
Politics-Government			
Election participation	−.463	−.096	−.467
School millage	−.261	.145	−.428
Income tax duration	.325	−.428	.772
Intergovernmental revenues	.385	.218	.241
Charter duration	.228	.226	.088
Charter city	.158	.418	−.176
Non-charter city	−.158	−.418	.176
Council-manager city	.064	.011	.081
Mayor-council city	−.064	−.011	−.081

C. Simple Correlation Debt Rates and Community Characteristics

	Statutory Debt Index	*Total Debt Index*
Population		
Total pop.	.501	.554
Pop. density	.094	−.032
Pop. change	−.029	−.102
Schooling	−.055	−.323
Pct. white collar	.009	−.282
Pct. non-white	.434	.650
Economic		
M. F. I.	.006	−.330
Assessed valuation	.254	.011
Home ownership	−.187	−.391
Location		
Central city	.600	.330
Non-Central city	−.600	−.330
Politics-Government		
Election participation	−.186	−.325
School millage	−.121	−.247
Income tax duration	.003	.293
Intergovernmental revenues	.461	.421
Charter duration	.522	.466
Charter city	.489	.372
Non-charter city	−.489	−.372
Council-manager city	.065	.108
Mayor-council city	−.065	−.108

D. Simple Correlation Per Capita Debts and Community Characteristics

	P. C. Statutory Debt	P. C. Total Debt
Population Ch.		
Total pop.	.399	.485
Pop. density	−.013	−.078
Pop. change	−.050	−.116
Schooling	−.040	−.268
Pct. white collar	.006	−.237
Pct. nonwhite	.402	.613
Economic Ch.		
M. F. I.	.081	−.196
Assessed valuation	.545	.369
Home ownership	−.171	−.358
Location		
Central city	.330	.597
Non-central city	−.330	−.597
Political-Governmental		
Election participation	−.182	−.321
School millage	−.144	−.259
Income tax duration	.013	.263
Intergovernmental revenues	.395	.400
Charter duration	.471	.436
Charter city	.423	.324
Non-charter city	−.423	−.324
Council-manager city	.135	.169
Mayor-council city	−.135	−.169

Fiscal Policy Making by Plebiscite: Local Tax and Bond Referenda in Ohio

James S. Gionocchio and Howard D. Hamilton

A 1929 AMENDMENT TO THE OHIO CONSTITUTION ESTABLISHED A comprehensive property tax limitation of fifteen mills, which was made more stringent by a 1933 amendment setting the limit at ten mills. That provision authorizes two important exceptions: home rule cities may specify an alternative limit in their charters, and any local unit may impose levies beyond the constitutional limit for periods of three to five years if the levy is approved in a referendum. Bond issues to be financed by property tax revenue also must be approved in a referendum. The ten-mill ceiling proved to be unrealistic—the average tax rate in the state today is approximately forty mills; and one of the most conspicuous features of the Ohio political system is the "tax levy election." Annually there are between one and two thousand referenda in the state, and Ohio has become the leading practitioner of direct democracy.

The principal consequences of the ten-mill limit were not the intended ones of constricting tax rates and public expenditures; its principal effect was a profound transformation of the political system, transferring authority for local government fiscal policy making from local officials to the electorate of each community. The purpose of this research is to investigate the consequences of this system of fiscal policy making by plebiscite and to appraise it.

Six dimensions of this system of popular policy making will be studied:

1. Voting behavior. What are the trends in referenda results? What are the success rates of different classes of local government? Are the success rates different for bonds and operating levies, for new and renewal levies? Do voters have distinct functional preferences? Do scheduling and voter turnout make a difference?

2. Strategies of local officials in tax and bond "elections."

3. Effect on public finance. To what extent has it depressed expenditures? Does it have different consequences for schools, cities, or counties; rural or metropolitan communities? Has it distorted financial structures?

4. Impact on the policy making process and administration. Does it generate uncertainty, instability, feast and famine? In what ways does it handicap local officials?

5. The views of local officials by location and type of jurisdiction: schools, cities, counties, metropolitan, and rural areas.

6. Appraisal. How does the Ohio system compare with the legal provisions of other states which have tax and/or debt limitations? What are the credits and debits of the system? What are the alternatives?

I. THE SYSTEM

The history of "tax elections" in Ohio is a curious one; it seems that Ohio arrived at its present system more by accident than by design. It was an unintended by-product of the efforts beginning in the Progressive era to tax intangibles and utilities; the referendum for bonds occurred entirely inadvertently. A statute in 1910 prescribed an aggregate property tax limit of fifteen mills and inaugurated the referendum system for the presumably rare occasions when a community might choose to exceed that limit. Subsequently the rate limit was changed several times. From 1911 to 1919 the absolute limit was fifteen mills, but that experiment with a rigid property tax limit proved to be catastrophic for local governments and was abandoned.

An obstacle to selective taxation of intangibles was the venerable uniformity provision of the constitution. In 1929 an effort to repeal the uniformity section culminated in an amendment with three components: repeal of the uniformity section, substitution of a clause requiring uniform taxation of land, and a fifteen-mill tax limit except for levies approved by referenda. In 1933, the figure was reduced to ten mills by an amendment "popularly initiated" by property interests.

The final phase of the evolution of Ohio's fiscal referendum system was a 1935 court ruling that the tax limitation is implicitly also a debt limitation for local governments. The court arrived at that judgment by coupling Sections 2 and 11 of Article XII (the tax limit) with the section which requires every bond enactment simultaneously to impose a tax for amortization.[1] Thereby local governments became subject to a peculiar species of debt limitation, not merely the usual one of a ratio of assessed valuation, but also the requirement of a referendum. Thus Ohio arrived by inadvertence at its comprehensive system of local fiscal policy making by plebiscite.

The constitutional requirement of a referendum for any levy in excess of the ten-mill limit is comprehensive with only one significant exception. A home rule city may substitute a different limit in its charter. Hence referenda are less important for cities than counties and school districts for that reason, and also because cities are less dependent on property taxes.

All subdivisions may conduct extra millage referenda and, with rare exceptions, for any amount. There are, however, three procedural requirements which to some indeterminate extent inhibit proposals: supramajorities for some referenda, time limitations on levies, and the requirement that a proposition may be placed on the ballot only by a two-thirds majority vote of the local board.

Passage of a levy is by simple majority for referenda coincident with general elections or primaries in even numbered years, but 55% of the vote at "special elections" or in odd-year primaries.[2]

---

[1]*State v. Kountz,* 129 O.S. 272 (1935).
[2]*Ohio Revised Code,* sec. 5705.20.

The supramajority requirement is because of the notoriously lower turnout of voters for primaries and "specials." The requirement obviously tilts the scales, occasionally producing instances of minority rule. Hence a 1967 act stipulating a simple majority vote for all school referenda was a significant modification of the system.[3]

An important procedural feature is whether a levy may be for an indefinite period, as in Michigan, or for only a few years. The general statutory rule is that extra millage levies may not exceed five years. Hence the most significant modification of the system since 1933 was a 1959 statute authorizing school districts to levy up to ten mills for an indefinite period and other levies for periods of ten years.[4]

A levy may be presented to the electorate thrice in a year: at the primary and general election and at a special election more than thirty days preceding or following an election. Hence most "specials" occur in June or December as second efforts of defeated proposals.

In Ohio all referenda are called "tax elections." The proposition ballot must state the amount to be levied in terms of mills, the number of years of the levy, and the purpose. Characteristically the purpose is expressed as a specific function, e.g., "for operating the schools," or "to construct a county home," but occasionally it is for "current expenses." Even a bond referendum is simultaneously a tax referendum, because the millage for amortization must be specified on the ballot. This ballot arrangement, where the voter is informed of the cost to him in mills of the proposed project, is unusual (said to be unique) and may be viewed as optimal for rational voting—and optimal for inhibiting expenditure.

The statutory regulations of bond issues are prolix.[5] The most significant provisions are that a city may incur indebtedness equal to 3.5% of its assessed valuation without a referendum,* a county

---

[3] *Laws of Ohio,* vol. 133, p. 2812.

[4] *Ibid.,* vol. 128, p. 574.

[5] *Ohio Revised Code,* sec. 133.

*By the end of 1971, the debt limits had been changed. The unvoted debt limit was 4% for non-chartered cities and 5.5% for chartered cities with appropriate language in their charters. The overall limit was 10.5%. (Editors' Note).

up to 1%, and a school district up to .10%. School districts have far greater capital outlays than the other units of local government. Manifestly, rather little capital expenditure for school purposes occurs *sans* plebiscite. School district bonds require only a simple majority and may be submitted at any election. Generally other units may submit bonds only at general elections, and if at a primary or special election, a 60% majority is required.

The tax referendum was intended to afford flexibility to the constitutional and statutory limitations which exist in numerous states by permitting local units occasionally to exceed the legal limit.[6] The system may operate that way in states with specific limits for classes of local governments, but the effect of the Ohio overall type limit, coupled with unrestricted authority for referenda, is to make the referendum a routine procedure in which the judgments of local officials require endorsement by the electorate.

Ohio exemplifies the variations that may exist in a federal system. Bond referenda occur to varying extents in most states.[7] Some states have no tax referenda, others have them occasionally in some classes of local units, while a few states have them very extensively. Thus neighboring Indiana has no fiscal referenda, but bond and "extramillage" elections are frequent in Michigan. No state approaches the volume of Ohio fiscal referenda, and the institution apparently has its greater importance in Ohio local government.

II. VOTING PATTERNS

Ohio tax elections recently have acquired some national publicity by the drama of school closings (only brief suspensions),

---

[6]A recent survey by the Advisory Commission on Intergovernmental Relations reports that forty-three states limit local property taxes to some degree, but some of those states do not have referenda. *State Constitutional and Statutory Restrictions on Local Taxing Powers,* report A-14 (October, 1962). Hereafter cited as ACIR, *Tax Limitations.*

[7]Advisory Commission on Intergovernmental Relations, *State Constitutional and Statutory Restrictions on Local Government Debt,* report A-10 (September, 1961). Hereafter cited as ACIR, *Debt Limitations.*

and there has been widespread talk of a "taxpayers' revolt." To analyze voting patterns, we have classified referenda results for 1958 and 1968 in seven metropolitan and four "rural" counties[8] (see Table 1).

There are conspicuous differences in the volume of categories of referenda in 1958 and a decade later. The volume of bond issues was much less in 1968, but that decline was more than offset by the increase in referenda on operating levies. Evidently officials recently have been giving priority to the acquisition of operating revenue. Change was slight in the sampled rural counties, but in the metropolitan counties the frequency of school levies doubled and those of other units were up by one-fourth.

TABLE 1
VOLUME OF FISCAL REFERENDA IN SEVEN METROPOLITAN AND FOUR RURAL COUNTIES

	1958		*1968*	
	Number	*Percent Passed*	*Number*	*Percent Passed*
School Districts—Levies				
Metro counties	82	89	162	73
Rural counties	29	83	36	70
Other Units—Levies				
Metro counties	102	66	125	77
Rural counties	15	54	11	100
New School Levies				
Metro counties	31	71	97	60
Rural counties	10	70	18	50
Bond Issues				
Schools	87	69	47	77
Other units	39	56	26	54
TOTAL				
Metro counties	293		356	
Rural counties	61		51	

SOURCE: *Ohio Election Statistics, 1958,* and data in archives of the Secretary of State.

[8]Cuyahoga, Franklin, Hamilton, Lucas, Montgomery, Stark, and Summit; Hancock, Lawrence, Sandusky, and Wood.

Do voters display any preference patterns? Examining referenda results in Cuyahoga County between 1949 and 1959, James Norton found some evidence of voter selectivity. The Cuyahoga voters approved thirteen of fourteen welfare proposals but displayed a propensity for "no" voting on other types of issues.[9] Our data are consistent with Norton's observation. The most distinct pattern is the electorate's preference for operating expenditures over capital outlays. And voters display a marked discrimination between objects of construction; they prefer to "buy" schools more than the capital items of other units of government.

In 1958 schools were more successful than the other local units in winning operating levies, but not a decade later. The 1968 passage rate of levies for all other functions except parks and roads equalled or exceeded that of schools as shown in Table 2. In this context, however, one must remember that school levies typically are substantially larger than nonschool levies.

TABLE 2
FUNCTIONAL CLASSIFICATION OF REFERENDA ON OPERATING LEVIES IN ELEVEN COUNTIES

	1958		*1968*	
Function	*Number*	*Percent Passed*	*Number*	*Percent Passed*
Current expense	56	57	30	77
Child welfare and retarded persons	3	67	8	87
Fire protection	22	95	44	91
Hospitals	5	60	4	100
Police protection	3	100	17	71
Parks	2	0	6	33
Road maintenance	14	50	8	50
Recreation	6	50	11	73
Miscellaneous	6	67	8	68
SUBTOTAL	117	64	136	79
Schools	111	87	198	73
TOTAL	228	76	334	75

[9]James A. Norton, "Referenda Voting in a Metropolitan Area," *Western Political Quarterly*, 16 (March, 1963), 195–213.

Not surprisingly, fire department levies are the most successful, but police department levies are less certain of passage. One might expect hospital and welfare levies, few and small, also to be sure winners, and they were in 1968 but not in 1958. The functions with the least electoral appeal are roads and parks—but recreation programs fare better.

The comparative data on approval rates do not portray a taxpayers' revolt. In both years three-fourths of the operating levies were approved; school bonds were more successful in 1968, as were the operating levies of all units but schools. The only category which fared worse in 1968 than in 1958 was school operating levies. Two circumstances may have contributed to the success of measures in 1968: prosperity and the high voter turnout for a presidential election. These data indicate that opposition to property taxes is not of uniform intensity in all functions, and that the principal effects of taxpayer resistance are a substantial decline in the passage of *new* school levies, and a reduction by inhibition—rather than defeat—of capital proposals.

These data and interviews with officials indicate that direct democracy has significant effects on substantive policy relative to capital expenditures. It delays capital expenditures, constricts the volume to a significant extent, and subtly modifies the functional allocation of the pie, to the sharp detriment of some functions and to the general disadvantage of city and county officials. The requisites for success are that a function or capital item have "box office" appeal and/or backing by formidable interest groups (or be picayune). Some critical capital needs have none of the requisites for ballot success. Direct democracy does not appear to be a mechanism for the optimal allocation of capital goods.

Renewals

Renewals are rarely defeated. The passage rate is 98% for schools and over 90% for other jurisdictions, indicating a consensus that prevailing budgets and tax rates should not be reduced. There is no such consensus on new levies for noneducational functions. In the 1950s there was a consensus in favor of more school taxes, but since then it has eroded. The voters' reflex to endorse renewals manifests popular thinking about public finance. The "proper" amounts of public expenditures and tax rates are the existing ones, whatever they may be.

The recent authorization of school levies without an expiration date eliminates superfluous referenda. Since the other jurisdictions also win renewals about as routinely as the schools, should not the same authority be extended to them?

School Referenda

Referenda are of crucial importance for schools in Ohio, where a larger proportion of school revenue is raised locally than in many states (69% in the late 1960s). Two-thirds of the new tax levies and more than half of all fiscal referenda are school district proposals. In dollars, about 80% of the expenditure decisions made by the voters concern school revenue. The Ohio referendum system is predominantly the school finance system.

In light of the hallowed status of public education in American ideology and the dependence of the schools on property tax revenue, one might expect an extraordinary success rate for school measures. That was true in the 1950s, but the fortunes of schools changed in the 1960s, as is shown in Table 3. The passage rate of new levies dropped below 90% in 1960 and slumped to 44% in the general election of 1969. The greatest change has been with respect to school bonds. In 1954, the voters approved 245 bond issues, but only 35 in 1969 with an approval rate of only 33%.

Schoolmen offer a variety of explanations. A majority of those interviewed stated that property owners feel they are carrying too much of the burden, a belief especially prevalent among officials in rural areas. Some metropolitan officials believe they confront an additional difficulty; they assert that a significant percentage of white voters are saying "no" to black demands for curriculum revision, busing, and changes in society as a whole by voting against levies.

Another explanation is suggested by the data of Table 3. Apparently voters feel that the schools "have enough." They endorse

TABLE 3
DECLINING SUCCESS OF SCHOOL PROPOSALS
(Percent passed)

General Election	*Operating Levies* *New**	*Renewal*	*Bond Issues*
1954	99	99	91
1958	94	99	70
1960	87	99	86
1962	76	97	71
1964	68	99	65
1965	43	98	42
1966	34	100	60
1967	64	98	64
1968	62	99	55
1969	44	97	33

***Excludes combinations of New and Renewals.**

the prevailing levels of expenditures and taxation but resist increases, and they are particularly skeptical of capital outlays.

One of the most prominent trends is the larger size of school levies. Is that a wise strategy for the school boards in a period of rising voter resistance? The data of Table 4 show that, contrary to conventional wisdom, in recent years large levies have been as successful as small ones.

With respect to bonds, Byron Marlowe, research director of

TABLE 4
SIZE, VOLUME, AND OUTCOMES OF NEW SCHOOL OPERATING LEVIES*

Year	*Number* *Below 5 mills*	*Over 5 mills*	*Percent Passed* *Below 5 mills*	*Over 5 mills*
1964	260	43	71	51
1965	165	22	41	59
1966	185	43	51	58
1967	172	57	60	47
1968	175	129	68	59
1969	146	146	42	42

*** Omits special elections and combinations of new and renewal.**

TABLE 5
RESULTS OF BOND REFERENDA BY SIZE PER A.D.M., 1967
(Percent passed)

Type of District	*Size of Bond/A. D. M.* $50	*$50–100*	*$100 up*
City	80	100	100
Rural	76	60	50
Statewide	76	73	60

A. D. M. = Average daily membership.
SOURCE: Marlowe, "Voting Behavior."

the Ohio Educational Association, observes "that voters in urban and rural areas have very different perceptions about what are appropriate amounts."[10] There is a consistent association of size and outcome in rural districts but not in urban ones (see Table 5).

One would expect that the higher a district's tax rate the greater would be the resistance to new levies, but Marlowe states that:

> In nearly every year the highest rates of approval of new issues occur in districts which have tax rates at both extremes of the existing property tax scale. Districts with average millage consistently have the most difficulty. In the case of bond issues the opposite of the common sense assumption is true—voter approval tends to increase with total millage.[11]

Levies should be more successful in those districts with the

TABLE 6
ASSESSED VALUATION PER PUPIL AND RESULTS OF LEVIES, 1966
(Percent passed)

Type of District	*$10,000 or Less*	*$10,000 or More*	*$20,000 or More*
City	50	52	62
Rural	51	53	54
Statewide	51	53	56

SOURCE: Marlowe, "Voting Behavior."

[10]Byron H Marlowe, "Voting Behavior in School Bond and Tax Elections in Ohio, 1946–1969." This chapter draws extensively on this unpublished memorandum.

[11]*Ibid.*

most taxable wealth. Table 6 shows that is distinctly true in city districts only. Perhaps the slight association in rural districts reflects the influence of educational standards, particularly when mandated by statute.

During the halcyon 1950s, support for new levies was strongest in those districts spending the least per pupil, but since 1964 rural and city districts exhibit contrasting behavior. The plausible negative relationship of passage rate and per pupil expenditures continues in rural districts, but in city districts there is the opposite pattern.[12]

A survey by the Office of Education of referenda in a national sample of school districts reports an inverse relationship between turnout rate and the passage of propositions.[13] Those findings are consistent with one of the well-known theories of political alienation, but they are at variance with the judgments of Ohio officials and the data of Table 7. The types of elections are listed in order of increasing turnout; presidential voting attracts about 70% of adults, primaries about 30%, and specials often less than that. The data are unambiguous. In Ohio the *general* relationship between turnout and outcomes is positive.

Illustrative of the turnout-outcome relationship were the 1960 referenda in Cuyahoga County. Six levies failed at the May pri-

TABLE 7
PASSAGE RATES OF SCHOOL ISSUES BY TYPE OF ELECTION

Type of Election	*Levies*	*Bonds*
Special elections, 6 years*	34%	36%
Primaries, 1954–1970	66%	51%
Local elections, 1955–1969	87%	62%
State & cong., 1954–1966	92%	73%
Presidential, 1956–1964	93%	81%

***Tax levies for the years 1964 to 1969; bonds for the years 1962 to 1967.**

[12] *Ibid.*

[13] Richard F. Carter and William Savard, *Influence of Voter Turnout on School Bond and Tax Elections* (U.S. Office of Education, 1963).

mary, but all won by landslides in November. With respect to taxation and expenditure for schools, the composition of the electorate may be profoundly different in May and November—and even more so at special elections.

III. EFFECTS ON PUBLIC ADMINISTRATION

Property tax limitations have been widely criticized for allegedly harmful effects on public administration. For example, the national Advisory Commission on Intergovernmental Relations made this appraisal:

> Tax rate limitations serve no useful purpose and have great potential for mischief. They have aggravated the proliferation of special districts, necessitated recourse to short-term borrowing, encouraged long-term borrowing for activities which might have been financed from current revenues, necessitated quantities of special legislation, impaired the ability of local officials to budget effectively, and are incompatible with responsible local government.[14]

Is the ACIR indictment apropos to Ohio, where the referendum is available to overcome constitutional and statutory limits? The recent wave of school closings demonstrates one of the most deleterious effects of the Ohio system, and interviews with local officials indicated others, notably inadequate revenue and underpaid employees.

A case study documents the ACIR indictment. On the basis of observations in Toledo, Norman Blume states that the system fosters fiscal and political irresponsibility, weakens control of the administrative apparatus by elective officials, and confounds rather than strengthens control by the voters, who react to the frequent fiscal referenda by negative voting. Elected officials, he observes, for fear of being identified with higher taxes, shirk their responsibility by allowing administrative agencies and allied interest groups to

[14] ACIR, *Tax Limitations*, 4–6.

wage referendum campaigns. The agencies seek earmarked levies to gain fiscal autonomy. Administrators become professional campaigners with their own campaign organizations. Some levy and bond proposals are misrepresented to the electorate. To avoid the consequences of defeat, governments resort to dubious financial expedients—special assessments, fees and service charges, short-term borrowing, and the use of utility funds for general operating expenses. "To expect apathetic voters to control this growing political anarchy is unrealistic. To bring some degree of political responsibility to local government," the referendum system should be abolished, "forcing elected officials to assume their fiscal responsibilities."[15]

Instability of revenue and hence of the level of public services is one of the most serious disadvantages of the fiscal plebiscite system. Fiscal planning is inherently handicapped by the uncertainty of prospective levy elections, and actual defeats occasionally necessitate drastic retrenchment and curtailment of services. Erratic administration is always a hazard of the plebiscite system, and it occurs with disconcerting frequency. The plebiscite tends to produce a feast or famine system.

A case in point was the Lucas County financial crisis of 1965, a serious defeat with effects still visible in 1970. Because of an unusual chain of circumstances, a renewal levy fell slightly short of the required 55% majority. The loss of $2 million in revenue necessitated drastic retrenchment: cessation of capital improvements, cancellation of a promised pay increase for employees, and wholesale layoffs followed by the resignations of some of the most able professional staff. In 1970 the county was still experiencing difficulty in recruiting some types of skilled personnel.

Sometimes similar effects occur less dramatically. According to Cincinnati officials, their city suffered from the ill effects of the referendum system for several years. "We were slowly strangling" until the electorate finally approved an increase in the payroll tax.

---

[15]Norman Blume, "Tax Limitations," *National Civic Review*, 58 (January, 1969), 15–19.

IV. THE VIEWS OF LOCAL OFFICIALDOM

What are the perceptions and attitudes of local officials? To tap that reservoir of experience and informed judgment, structured interviews were conducted in 1970 with thirty-nine officials. The interviews were designed to provide a sample of metropolitan and non-metropolitan communities and of three classes of local units: counties, cities, and school districts.

There is a consensus among local officials that the referendum system is a serious obstacle to effective planning, curtails public expenditures, and results in understaffing and underpaying employees. Nearly all city and county officials regard their bailiwicks as inadequately financed and the referendum as one contributor to that condition.[16] However, some qualify their replies. "Inadequately financed," they note, is a subjective judgment, and the proper amount of revenue is a decision to be made by the electorate. Thus officials adhere to populist democracy even when its results are at variance with their own judgments and handicap their official roles.

County officials have more intense views, pro and con, than city officials. Although all county officials agree that the system causes difficulties, and occasionally even crises, a majority favor the system on the populist premise that "the people" should decide (directly) how much money their government spends. Several officials believe that a referendum is a type of public debate, in which the most persuasive argument receives the larger vote. It follows that inadequate revenue is the result of a poor selling job by the political elite.

Those who favor the abolition of the referendum are certain that the populist rationale is fallacious. They say that the communications problem is at the receiving end. The media, mailed brochures, and open hearings provide objective information, but the predispositions of voters screen out rational argument. Critics stress the complexity and technical nature of budgetary decisions. The average citizen, they assert, has neither the time nor the in-

[16]Apropos was a comment of a county commissioner: "We haven't increased welfare assistance since 1966. I just don't see how those people can afford to eat."

clination to study issues in depth. Also, referenda voting may be affected by considerations having little to do with the substance of the issue. Critics believe that many people who feel that federal or aggregate taxation is too high are voting on the basis of that diffuse attitude rather than on the merits of the particular levy or bond proposal. Might elimination of referenda lead to excessive spending? The critics are confident that the power to "vote the rascals out" is a sufficient guarantee.

Officials agree that the system seriously handicaps planning, but only a minority saw in their own jurisdictions examples of Blume's theses that the system fosters fragmentation of the fiscal system, encourages dubious financial expedients, and weakens control of administrative agencies by elected officials. These effects were perceived as present and consequential by officials in two of the five cities and in one county where a large agency has its "own" special levy. "Without the power of the purse, we cannot control them."

A strong majority of local officialdom approve of bond referenda, although several officials say that the present system should be relaxed by authorizing a larger amount of indebtedness without a referendum. City officials were provided more discretion by a 1969 statute which elevated the municipal debt ceiling from 1.5 to 3.5%.* "We just take a poll and find out which issues will win and which will lose. Those we think will win we put on the ballot. Those we think will lose we pass in council." The other jurisdictions without a generous margin for unvoted bonds obviously cannot employ this strategy. However, ingenuity may take many forms: a county in our sample acquired a computer by embedding it in a bond proposal for equipment for a regional police network. One aspect of the referendum system is occasional subterfuge.[17]

One of the most distinct fruits of the system, in the judgment of local officials, is a reservoir of capital needs. Officials in every

---

*See Editors' Note on p. 68.

[17]Another ploy was this phrasing of a levy ballot: "— County will levy one mill for operating expenses including those of the Childrens Home and the Home for the Aged." The revenue was for the county general fund.

city and county enumerated capital items which they deem critical, but beyond their reach because the projects lack electoral appeal. Nevertheless, they endorse the system. This anomaly attests to the prevalence of populist ideology.

The referendum is least popular among school officials; for many of them it is a *bête noire.* Four-fifths of the interviewed school officials (board members and administrators) favor abolition of the referendum for operating levies, but a majority would retain it for bonds. They observe that the system has its most adverse effect on schools during periods of inflation, when costs increase more rapidly than property tax revenues and school boards must seek new levies to maintain existing levels of service. Schoolmen do not view the referendum as the only cause of their financial difficulties. Like city and county officials, they regard the property tax as an inadequate revenue source. The referendum and tax source problems are inextricably bound together in their minds.

Several arguments for abolition of the referendum requirement are advanced by schoolmen. Because intelligent fiscal decisions require considerable knowledge of educational standards, methods, and budgetary details, they doubt the competence of the public to make informed decisions. Referenda may fail because of "emotional

TABLE 8
ATTITUDES OF INTERVIEWED OFFICIALS
TOWARD THE REFERENDUM SYSTEM

Policy View	*Operating Levy Referendum*					*Bond Referendum*		
	City	*County*	*School*	*Elected*	*Appointed*	*City*	*County*	*School*
Approves status quo	2	8	1	11	0	8	13	6
Favors less stringent limit	7	2	0	9	0	3	1	4
Discontinue the referendum	5	5	8	8	10	3	1	0
Has no viewpoint	0	0	1	0	1	3	1	0
TOTAL	14	15	10	28	11	14	15	10

issues," e.g., "voting race." An aversion to levy campaigning was another reason evident in the interviews.

School officials are more pessimistic than other officials about the implications of a levy defeat. "If the city loses a levy, they can cut expenses on garbage pickups, street maintenance, and things of that nature. If we lose, we have to close the schools." Some city and county officials feel they are providing an array of important but not necessarily indispensable services and that their constituents as customers have the right to determine how much service they will buy. To school officials, the educational function is a necessity which must never be short-changed; they are not populists.

Surprisingly, the idea of bond referenda was supported more by schoolmen than by other officials. All approve of bond referenda in principle, and most regard the public as competent for making decisions on school capital outlays. They would like more authority, however, to borrow without referenda in order to expedite repairs, renovation, and emergency needs.

The viewpoints of the officials interviewed are classified in Table 8. "Discontinue" means repeal of the constitutional provision, restoring authority to local boards to levy property taxes or issue bonds as they see fit. Those in the "Favors less stringent limit" category regard the ten-mill ceiling as unrealistic and in need of upward revision. To give greater discretion to local officials (and reduce the number of referenda) any new legal ceiling would have to approximate prevailing property tax rates, which ranged from twenty-nine to sixty-two mills in 1969.

If the system were revised to conform to the modal views of each type, the operating levy referendum would be discontinued for school districts, the legal limit would be revised upward for municipalities, and the system would continue unchanged for counties. Something of the sort could be done, and in fact exists in several states, but not on the basis of a single overall tax limit.

V. APPRAISAL OF THE SYSTEM

Evaluating this system of fiscal policy making by plebiscite is not a simple matter. Although one can identify the entries for each side of the balance sheet, most cannot be quantified with any precision, and the weights to be attached to some are highly subjective. Thus, one of the most significant effects of the system is that it depresses the level of public expenditures to some unknown extent. The system acts as a depressant because it is a one-way system; referenda can only reduce the budgetary decisions of local officials. Overall and statewide, its inhibition of public expenditures is not tremendous. The level of property taxes and local public expenditures in Ohio are not profoundly different from those in comparable states without the referendum, and the constitutional provision's failure to check property taxes reminds one of King Canute. At first blush, the referendum appears to be a mighty restraint of educational expenditures in Ohio, but there are other factors; compare the expenditures of Michigan, another referendum state. (See Table 9.) The effect of the Ohio system may be principally to delay rather than reduce expenditures. Viewed in this perspective, is the amount of economy worth the candle even if one cherishes economy?

But there is another perspective. The short-run and localized effect in numerous instances is to inhibit specific operating levies and capital projects—indeed, more frequently than the number of levy and bond defeats would suggest. Officials do not recklessly court defeat if they think it probable. Manifestly, the natural indisposition of electorates to self-impose taxes does block or defer some potential capital outlays, does compel some local units to operate on austerity budgets, does occasionally compel retrenchment, does occasionally close schools. There are some economies from the standpoint of local property owners, at least in the short

TABLE 9

EXPENDITURES FOR PUBLIC SCHOOLS, 1969–70

	U.S.	*Ohio*	*Ind.*	*Mich.*	*N.Y.*
Average teacher salary	$8840	8599	9574	10125	10200
Expenditure per pupil	$ 926	804	847	1019	1420
Expenditure/personal income	% 5.5	4.6	5.3	5.9	5.9

SOURCE: Office of Education, *Digest of Educational Statistics, 1970.*

run. This brings us to two conundrums. What is "economy"? And what are the merits of these forms of it? On which side of the balance sheet does this entry, the inhibition of public expenditures in some unknown amount, belong?

In the perspective of political philosophy, the system has the virtues of direct democracy, participation, and responsibility. It is about the only substantial practice of direct democracy left in the American political system. (Ohio does not have town meetings.) It is the only opportunity for all adults to participate in deciding public policies, and the policies are not trivial. It also is a useful instrument of public education and official responsibility. A levy campaign is the occasion for an extraordinary amount of public reporting by officials. These are nebulous values, but who would say they are insignificant?

In the perspective of public finance, the central question is the efficacy of the system for allocating resources. Does direct democracy allocate resources as well as representative democracy? We have noted evidence that the system probably does not allow the optimal allocation of capital expenditures. A larger question is whether it makes optimal the apportionment of resources between public expenditures and private expenditures. An intelligent answer involves more than a reflex reaction from one's value system; it also requires appraisal of the character of the specific economies that the system produces.

It might be said that the referendum is the best way to make an optimal allocation of our resources between private and public expenditures, because "the people decide how much public service they wish to buy." The validity of that proposition is very dubious for two reasons. The actual referendum electorate is only a minor fraction of "the people," sometimes a very small fraction, and the preceding data show that at low turnout elections in Ohio, it is likely to be decidedly unrepresentative. In addition, an optimizing decision entails a judgment as to whether the community benefit from a proposed levy is worth the increment of expenditure. The task is to weigh the cost against the benefits with respect to the commonweal. Does the referendum voter engage in that cost-benefit calculus, or does he substitute his personal cost and benefit?

To the extent that the latter occurs, the referendum system is hardly an optimizing institution. How many voters even have the information for weighing community benefit and cost? Are voters better situated to do that task than the city council or school board?

Sheer logic suggests that representative democracy is a more efficacious decision making process than plebiscites. A locally elected board has the intrinsic merits of a legislature. Being representative in composition, its members are sensitive to the interests, mores, and currents of opinion in the community. Groups and individuals have both formal and informal access to the local board for the expression of viewpoints and other information. The board has considerable knowledge of the technical details of the functions in its charge. It scrutinizes operating reports, financial statements, and the details of budget requests. And it arrives at decisions by protracted discussion and deliberation. Legislating is a deliberative process. The referendum transfers the decisional authority from the local board—which has examined extensive information, weighed arguments and pressures, and deliberated at length—to the voters, most of whom have not participated in the deliberative process at all. This is a curious way of making "sound" decisions.

There are other disadvantages of the system. In various ways, it is inimical to effective public administration. Local officials agree that it obstructs planning and may handicap the recruitment of able personnel due to low salaries. It may produce chronic fiscal malnutrition or the erratic feast and famine effects. The most catastrophic effect is the occasional crisis when a levy defeat causes drastic retrenchment or the suspension of functions. The referendum system fosters fragmentation of the fiscal system, handicapping comprehensive budgeting and control by elective boards of administrative agencies which have their "own" fees, earmarked levies, or the autonomy of a special district.[18] In the eyes of some observers, the combined effects devitalize local government and vitiate the responsibility of elected officials. Thus the ACIR characterizes the system as "incompatible with responsible local government."

---

[18]The fragmentation effects were perceived as serious by only a minority of officials interviewed.

The participatory benefits of referenda campaigns have some immediate costs. Considerable time may be expended in campaigns; the time and emotional burden of some officials is substantial. Occasionally there is an intangible cost, when the strategy involves some bending of the truth. The most serious intangible cost is the by-product of community conflict. Some fiscal referenda generate intense community conflict.

Both logic and limited empirical evidence suggest that the fiscal plebiscite is inferior to representative democracy as a decisional process or as a mechanism for optimizing the allocation of resources. It follows that the case for the fiscal referendum system must rest on a value judgment that its disadvantages are outweighed either by the inhibition of public expenditures and/or by the values of participatory democracy.

VI. ALTERNATIVES

Between the poles of retention of the Ohio system and the ACIR's recommendation of the abolition of fiscal referenda are a host of alternatives. The system might function better with some minor statutory changes. The ceiling for indebtedness without referenda might be raised for counties and school districts. Abolition of the supramajority requirement for nonschool tax levies would eliminate the possibility of minority rule.[19] Authorizing all local units to enact levies without an expiration date would eliminate largely superfluous renewal referenda. These modifications would diminish the hazards for local officials, fostering more revenue stability and opportunity for planning.

The system could be adapted in various ways by amendment of the constitution. Patently it is ridiculous to hold referenda for any aggregate rate above ten mills when state law requires school districts to levy seventeen and a half mills to qualify for the state

[19]The supramajority may be inconsistent with the equal protection standard of the U.S. Constitution. That was the recent decision of the West Virginia supreme court.

foundation grant. A more appropriate constitutional figure would be the present median aggregate rate—approximately forty mills. However, a constitutional aggregate rate ceiling probably is the most unfeasible system of regulation. Many states have set legal limitations for classes of local units. The present anomaly suggests the unwiseness of embalming any tax limitation formula in a state constitution. Any system should be more workable if it is established exclusively by statute.

There are several alternatives to the system of referenda on all bonds: reversion to the pre-1935 arrangement of no state regulation, review and approval of bonds by a state agency (such as the Michigan Municipal Finance Commission), or requiring referenda for issuance of bonds above a specified net interest rate or in excess of some ratio of debt to assessed valuation. The latter standard is the conventional form of debt limitation, but the market mechanism is an alternative standard.

Referenda on operating levies might be discontinued for school districts only. A novel variation of that idea is a recent proposal by a Michigan study commission. The efforts of school officials in Michigan to abolish levy referenda led to a proposal by a Governor's Commission on Educational Reform that local school taxes be supplanted by a uniform state property tax imposed by the legislature and collected by the state. The state equalization grant would become the exclusive source of local school funds, except to the extent that some districts might exercise the option of funding "enrichment programs" by a local property tax. That is a proposal for thorough equalization of both tax rates and expenditures per pupil, which would stabilize the revenues of schools and largely or entirely end the referendum system.[20] In view of the comparability of Michigan and Ohio experience, such an innovative proposal merits consideration.

The Advisory Commission on Intergovernmental Relations, the body established by Congress for continuous study of our federal system, recommends that states entirely discontinue consti-

---

[20]*Report of the Governor's Commission on Educational Reform* (1969), p. 4.

tutional and statutory limitations of local property taxes and debt.[21] It views such liberation as essential for the revitalization of local government. A *sine qua non* for responsive and responsible local government, the commission asserts, is that local legislative bodies possess unfettered discretion. The logic is that any external limitation designed to prevent error by local officials inherently dilutes responsibility and vitiates their capacity for doing good. The commission would agree with the aphorism of Harold Laski that "in any political system, trust must reside somewhere."

[21]For the full exposition of the commission's reasoning, see its documents *Tax Restrictions*, pp. 65–85, and *Debt Limitations*, pp. 1–9.

The Effect of Ohio Constitutional Provisions on the Distribution of Revenue from a State Personal Income Tax

Frederick D. Stocker

DURING THE DECADE OF THE 1960S, DISCUSSION THROUGHOUT OHIO of a possible enactment of state taxes on personal and corporate income grew from furtive whispers to the point where in 1970, both major parties' candidates for governor openly espoused income taxation as the key to tax reform. The Thatcher study of 1967,[1] the Report of the Ohio Tax Study Commission in 1967,[2] and the report of the Sealy Committee in 1969[3] all pointed toward the necessity for Ohio to adopt personal and corporate income taxes, not only for the revenue they might produce but also to improve the equity and other structural features of Ohio's state-local tax system. Finally in early 1971, the Citizens Task Force on Tax Reform recommended to Governor Gilligan a tax reform program centered on income taxation, and the governor in March 1971 presented essentially that same program to the General Assembly as his tax program.*

---

[1] *Tax Revision Alternatives for the Tax System of Ohio,* George W. Thatcher, Director, Columbus, Ohio, 1962.

[2] *Report of the Ohio Tax Study Commission,* Columbus, Ohio, 1967.

[3] *Report of the Select Committee on Local Government Tax Revision,* Albert H. Sealy, Jr., Chairman, Columbus, Ohio, November, 1969.

*For a brief description of the tax bill enacted in December, 1971, see the Editors' Introduction to this section.

Through all this discussion and debate there has lurked in the background a crucial constitutional question that must be faced if Ohio is to adopt state taxes on income. The question concerns the meaning of, and the possible problems created by, that part of Art. XII, Sec. 9, of the State Constitution, which reads as follows:

> Not less than fifty per centum of the income and inheritance taxes that may be collected by the state shall be returned to the county, school district, city, village, or township in which said income or inheritance tax originates, or to any of the same, as may be provided by law.

The effect of any source-based distribution of revenue from a state tax is of course to favor those communities which have a high ratio of tax base to population and to disfavor those with low. In the case of a personal income tax, for example, it would give the richest community the highest per capita distribution and leave the poorer ones with relatively little. The Battelle Memorial Institute, in research done for the Sealy Committee, estimated that a flat rate tax on personal income, with no exemptions, would produce seven times as great a return per capita in the richest Ohio county as in the poorest.[4] If the smaller units of government were chosen to share in the source-based distribution, the disparities would be still greater. Use of graduated rates and personal exemptions would also magnify the disparities.

Some have argued that Art. XII, Sec. 9, would need to be repealed or revised to make way for a genuine state income tax. Oddly enough, some of those who see Art. XII, Sec. 9, as an insuperable obstacle to adoption of a *state* personal income tax of the sort found in more than forty other states argue that Ohio should instead resort to a mandatory *county* income tax. Under this plan the General Assembly would place the county commissioners in each of the state's 88 counties under a legislative mandate to enact a county income tax, presumably of a uniform type prescribed by the legislature. The entire revenue from such a tax, rather than only 50%, would remain in the county of origin. It seems obvious

---

[4]John H. Bowman and others, *Local Government Tax Revision in Ohio,* Battelle Memorial Institute, Columbus, Ohio, 1968, p. 30.

that this approach, far from avoiding the problem inherent in the 50% turnback requirement, would magnify it.

This study assesses the nature and magnitude of the problem posed by Art. XII, Sec. 9, considers how serious a barrier it poses to the adoption of state income taxes on personal and corporate income, and explores methods of complying with this constitutional provision. It attempts to answer the question whether repeal or revision of Art. XII, Sec. 9, is a necessary precondition to adoption of a conventional form of income taxation in Ohio.

I. CORPORATE INCOME TAX

The problem of disparities in per capita distributions of income tax revenue is especially apparent under a business net income tax. The Battelle Memorial Institute, in its 1968 study of local government tax revision, estimated that a tax of 7% on the net income of both incorporated and unincorporated business would produce a statewide average of $34.43 per capita in 1969, with individual county figures ranging from $83.02 in Monroe County to $4.64 in Adams County.[5] A 50% turnback would of course result in per capita payments just half as large.

It would appear that the application of the 50% turnback to a corporate income tax could be avoided by framing the tax as a franchise tax imposed on the privilege of doing business and establishing net income as the *measure* of the tax. The distinction between *subject* and *measure* of the tax is one that is well established in tax law. Hellerstein defines the subject of a tax as: (1) the property taxed in the case of a property tax; (2) the activity, event, privilege, or specific property right taxed in the case of an excise tax; (3) the income received or accrued in the case of an income tax.

The *measure* of the tax, however, is "the yardstick or base to which the tax rate is applied." Thus in the case of a sales tax, which is an excise tax, the subject of the tax is the making of a sale, while the measure is the sales price of the goods. In income taxes the

[5]*Ibid.*, pp. 22–23.

subject of the tax and the measure of the tax are the same. The receipt or accrual of income is the subject, and the same income is the measure to which the tax is applied.[6]

This distinction has been recognized by the Ohio courts in decisions concerning the present Ohio corporation franchise tax. This tax is imposed on the value of the use of the corporate franchise. The courts have held it to be an excise on the privilege of doing business. The privilege is thus the *subject* of the tax. The *measure* of the tax is essentially the net worth of the corporation (in case of an interstate corporation, that portion of net worth apportioned to Ohio).[7]

It would seem clearly consistent with past court decisions that substitution of net income for net worth as the *measure* of the tax would not alter the nature of the tax as an excise on the privilege of doing business and would not mean that the income itself is being taxed. This conception is consistent also with court interpretations of the Ohio intangible personal property tax, under which income-producing intangible assets are taxed according to their income yield. The courts have held that use of *income* as the measure of value of the asset does not alter the fact that the tax is a property tax, not an income tax.[8]

The obvious conclusion is that a corporate franchise tax that employs net income as the measure of value of the franchise would not be subject to the turnback required of income taxes by Art. XII, Sec. 9.

II. PERSONAL INCOME TAX

In the case of a personal income tax the subject-measure distinction has no application. As noted above, the subject and mea-

---

[6]Jerome R. Hellerstein, *State and Local Taxation* (New York: Prentice-Hall, 1952), p. 19.

[7]*The Southern Gum Company v. Laylin,* 66 Ohio St. 578, (1902); *Aluminum Co. of America v. Evatt,* 140 Ohio St. 385 (1942); *International Harvester Co. v. Evatt,* 146 Ohio St. 58 (1945), 329 U.S. 416 (1947).

[8]*Bennett v. Evatt,* 145 Ohio St. 587 (1945).

sure are the same. There appears to be no legal precedent by which a personal income tax can be interpreted as other than a tax on the income itself. As such it would be subject to the requirement set forth in Art. XII, Sec. 9.

It may be useful first to consider the intent that appears to lie behind this constitutional provision. As originally adopted in 1912 this provision was worded as follows: "not less than fifty per centum of the income and inheritance taxes that may be collected by the state shall be returned to the city, village, or township in which said income or inheritance tax originates." This wording, in calling for distribution to these three specified classes of governmental units, would return income tax revenue to the *smallest* units of local government that would (in combination) completely blanket the state.

In 1930 this section was amended to add the county and school district to the list of eligible recipient units, and to add the words "or to any of the same as may be provided by law." It seems evident that the intent of this amendment was to free the legislature to distribute income tax revenues to these two other classes of local government, both of which also blanket the state.

The adoption of Art. XII, Sec. 9, probably reflects the understandable and legitimate concern of the people of Ohio at that time for avoiding excessive centralization of financial power in the hands of the state government. Yet it is interesting that even then, in a day when economic and social conditions were such that decentralized financing of government made far more sense than it does today, the people of Ohio were willing to require only that half the revenue be reserved for local use.

The changes that have occurred in the past forty years—vastly improved transportation and communication, the increased mobility of our population, the geographic expansion of markets, the process of urbanization and the burgeoning of the suburbs, and the concentration of people and wealth in a few areas of the state and the relative economic decline of other portions—all tend to make this 50% turnback an anachronistic requirement. As noted earlier, the inherent tendency of a source-based distribution of revenue from a state imposed tax is to pour revenue into the wealthier areas of the state, while doing little for the poorer areas. The problem is identical to (but only half as troublesome as) the problem of a county income tax, where *all* the revenue would go to the local area of origin.

It is significant to note that Art. XII, Sec. 9, was written at a time when very little state money flowed to local governments. Over the years, the same concern for maintaining the fiscal viability of local government that impelled the adoption of this provision has produced a vast expansion in state aid to local governments. In 1968–1969 the state government turned over more than $700 million in state-collected revenues to be spent at the local level. Included here are state payments to local school districts and to the Local Government Fund, as well as highway aids and many other state aid programs. It may fairly be said that the state, through the development of these programs of aid to local governments from state revenue sources, has already accomplished the purposes of Art. XII, Sec. 9.

It is significant also that the constitution does not require that all the enumerated classes of local governments share in the distribution. The words "or to any of the same, as may be provided by law" make this clear, as does the precedent in the statutory distribution of inheritance tax collections, which go to the cities, villages, and townships.[9] Counties or school districts do not share in this distribution.

When these two points are recognized, it becomes evident that there are ways in which the state could readily comply with both the spirit and the letter of the turnback requirement, while avoiding its inherent disequalizing tendencies and without necessarily increasing payments to local governments above their present level. For example, the state might provide that the 50% of the revenue that must be returned on the basis of origin be paid to "county school fiscal districts," created for this purpose. These would have as their major or sole purpose the receiving of state income tax monies and would be required in turn to apportion them among operating school districts that lie wholly or partly within the

[9]Sec. 5731.53, Ohio Revised Code.

county[10] in proportion to their entitlement under the basic school foundation program. This distribution would be credited toward their foundation entitlement. The full amount of the foundation payment would then be made up by a supplemental state distribution from nonearmarked funds, such as the other 50% of income tax collections or other state general fund revenues.

To suggest this possibility is not meant to imply any judgment on whether, or by how much, state aid to schools and other units of local government should be increased, but only to point out that the proper amount and distribution of state aid can be a separate issue to be dealt with entirely on its own merits, irrespective of what form a state income tax might take. This approach does not force any particular decision regarding the total amount of state aid to schools or other local units. It assumes only that a school foundation program will continue in effect and that the total amount of money will be at least as large as at present. Additional distributions to other units of local government, for example through the local government fund, would also be fully compatible with this approach.

Whether such an approach could be implemented depends on the amount of revenue a personal income tax would generate in each of Ohio's eighty-eight counties, and whether these amounts could be absorbed into the school foundation program without exceeding the formula amount in any county. The following section examines this problem.

Income Tax Yield—Estimating Procedure

Estimation of the revenue obtainable from a personal income tax is a difficult task. Definition of taxable income and determina-

[10]For school districts that overlap county lines, the simplest procedure would be to apportion their foundation entitlement between or among the counties in accordance with residence of their pupils. The piece of the district that lies in each county would then be figured in that county's calculation of the aid to be distributed, and the district's total payment would be the sum of the payments it receives in each county.

tion of the amount taxable within the state are complex problems. These are severe enough under a flat-rate tax. When graduated rates and personal exemptions or credits are involved, the difficulties are compounded. They are almost insurmountable when the task becomes that of estimating the yield on a county-by-county basis. The most difficult part of the present study has been estimating the revenue that would be generated in each of Ohio's eighty-eight counties under alternative forms of personal income tax.

Three estimates were made of income tax yield in each of Ohio's eighty-eight counties. The first was based on an assumed flat-rate tax of 2% on adjusted gross income as defined in the federal Internal Revenue Code. The second (Graduated Rate A) was based on the graduated rate structure proposed by Governor Gilligan on March 15, 1971:

On the first $3,000 of adjusted gross income	1%
On AGI between $3,000 and $6,000	1½%
On AGI between $6,000 and $10,000	2%
On AGI between $10,000 and $15,000	3%
On AGI between $15,000 and $20,000	4%
On AGI between $20,000 and $25,000	5%
On AGI between $25,000 and $35,000	6%
On AGI between $35,000 and $50,000	7%
On AGI above $50,000	8%

In lieu of personal exemptions the plan would allow a credit of $10 for the taxpayer, spouse, and each dependent allowed under the Internal Revenue Code.

The third (Graduated Rate B) assumed a $1,500 personal exemption for a single person and a $3,000 exemption for families, and a rate structure on the remainder as follows:

On the first $7,500 of taxable income	1%
On taxable income between $7,500 and $15,000	2%
On taxable income above $15,000	3%

The basic statistical information on which all the estimates rest are estimates by the Center for Business and Economic Research, Ohio State University, of Ohio personal income by county by source of income. These estimates (the latest year available at time of writing was 1967) were adjusted in two ways: (1) by subtracting nonmoney income and transfer payments, both of which are ordinarily nontaxable; and (2) by adding the net excess of residents' earnings from out-of-county employment over nonresidents' earnings within the county. The latter adjustment essentially localizes income in the county of residence rather than the county of employment.[11] Each county estimate was further adjusted downward by 11% so as to conform the county totals to the state total adjusted gross income as reported for 1967 by the U.S. Internal Revenue Service, and was then increased by 23%, which is the estimated percentage increase in Ohio personal income between 1967 and 1971–1972. The resulting estimates of AGI are shown in Column 1 of Table 1.

Estimation of the revenue yield from a 2% flat rate tax (no exemptions, deductions, or credits) simply involved multiplying the estimated AGI for each county by the 2% rate. The results are shown in Table 2.

For the graduated rate structure, a far more complex procedure was necessary. Because county-level data on taxpaying units by income-size class and by size of family were not available, county revenue yield estimates had to be constructed from statewide relationships.

Each county was assumed to have the same percentage of state taxpaying units as it has of state population. The total number of taxpaying units in each county was estimated by applying these percentages to the total number of federal tax returns filed from Ohio. These were then apportioned into fourteen income segments by applying the statewide distribution of taxpaying units among the fourteen income classes (as reported in the *Statistics of Income*) to the total returns for the county. The basic assumption in this procedure was that the configuration of income distribution within each county is similar to that of the state at large, but shifted upward or downward in proportion to differences between county average income and state average income. Thus, if the lowest statewide income class (as reported in the SOI) contains 9.5% of the

[11]The method followed is similar to that explained in *Local Government Tax Revision in Ohio*, *op. cit.*, pp. 32–37.

taxpaying units, then 9.5% are assumed to fall in the lowest income segment in each county, although the limits of the lowest income bracket for the county may be either higher or lower than those of the lowest bracket for the state.

For each county, the average income within each income segment was estimated on the assumption that the average income in each segment bears the same relationship to the overall county average as the corresponding state bracket average bears to the overall state average income; this assumption was implemented by applying to each county's average AGI per taxpaying unit the statewide ratios of average AGI in each of the fourteen income brackets to the overall statewide average AGI. Thus, for example, because the statewide ratio of average income in the lowest bracket to statewide average income is 0.071, the lowest income segment in each county is assumed to have an average income that is 7.1% of the overall average income for that county.

Next, the statewide average effective rates under the state income tax were calculated for each of the fourteen specific income classes or brackets. (The "effective rates" simply are tax liabilities expressed as percentages of AGI.) These statewide average effective rates (which reflect the credits for the weighted-average household size for each income class) were applied to the average AGI per taxpaying unit in each of the fourteen county income brackets.

The calculations just described produced estimates of the average tax liability per taxpaying unit for each of fourteen income classes in each of the eighty-eight counties. It was possible to estimate the aggregate tax liability for each county by multiplying the number of taxpayers in each bracket by the respective bracket average liabilities, and then summing across brackets to arrive at county totals. From the county tax estimates, of course, derivation of the state total tax yield was a matter of simple addition. The results for rate structures A and B are shown in Tables 3 and 4 respectively.

The application of statewide effective rates implicitly assumes that the composition of each income class, by size of family, is not greatly dissimilar among Ohio's eighty-eight counties; this assumption seems reasonable. Further, a check on the possible validity of this assumption with the 1960 Census data on family size and income size failed to show any systematic variation in family size among counties of widely different average incomes, thereby tending to support the reasonableness of the assumption, or at least failing to suggest an alternative to it.

Income Tax Yield—Results

The statewide total annual tax liabilities from the first two rate structures turn out (by coincidence) to be almost identical, thus facilitating direct comparison. Some striking contrasts are evident. Graduated rate structure A affects the pattern of tax distribution among counties in such a way as to produce lower per capita liabilities and a smaller percentage of the state total than the flat rate structure in all but three counties. These three—all well above the state average in per capita AGI—are Cuyahoga, Hamilton, and Montgomery. Graduated rate structure B, involving only three rate brackets, produces smaller total and per capita yields in every county. In comparison with the flat rate tax, structure B produces greater percentages of state total in four relatively high income counties—the three just mentioned plus Summit County. Lucas County would generate the same percentage under both taxes.

Under the flat rate tax, liabilities would range from a low of \$27 per capita in Pike County to a high of \$98 in Hamilton County —a ratio of high-to-low of about 3.5:1. Graduated rate structure A would give a range from \$11 to \$123 per capita (11:1), these same two counties representing the extremes, and rate structure B a ratio of 9:1.

III. SCHOOL FOUNDATION AID

Can the 50% return of income tax revenue required by Article XII, Sec 9, of the Ohio State Constitution be absorbed into the school foundation program? To answer this question, it is necessary not only to estimate the amount that would be returned from alternative income tax structures (as explained in the preceding section) but also the amount of state aid flowing to school districts in each county.

This calculation is not as simple as it seems. A large proportion of Ohio's school districts overlap county boundaries. Only one county (Ashtabula) has all its school districts lying entirely within its boundaries. As a result it was necessary to apportion the foundation program entitlement of intercounty school districts among the counties in which they exist. This apportionment was made in accordance with the county residence of pupils enrolled in the district.

The resulting foundation aid figures then represent the total funds attributable to districts or portions of districts lying within the geographic boundaries of each county. The calculations shown in Table 5 are based on an assumed foundation payment of $635 per pupil in average daily attendance.

It appears that either the flat rate personal income tax with a 2% rate or the graduated rate structure with rates from 1% to 8% would produce a 50% turnback greater than the amount of foundation aid, calculated at $635 per pupil, in two counties—Cuyahoga and Hamilton. The lower graduated rate structure, with rates from 1% to 3%, however, would not produce an excessive turnback in any county. Alternatively, a school foundation program based on an allocation of $680 per pupil (with additional payments channeled into districts with high concentrations of ADC pupils) would fully absorb the 50% income tax turnback in all of Ohio's counties.

For any given total revenue yield, a graduated rate structure, because it concentrates a larger part of its revenue in the richer counties such as Cuyahoga and Hamilton, is more likely than a flat rate tax to produce an excess of revenue over what the school foundation program would absorb. Likewise, a foundation program that makes sizable payments to districts with high ADC concentration will increase payments in counties such as Cuyahoga and Hamilton, easing the problem of absorbing the 50% turnback.

The general conclusion seems warranted that the 50% turnback requirement can readily be met by applying income tax revenues toward the school foundation entitlement, so long as the personal income tax is of modest total productivity and the school foundation program entails sizable aid distributions. This solution would effectively neutralize the disequalizing tendency inherent in a source-based distribution.

If in the future income tax revenues should grow to the point where the 50% turnback exceeds the amount of school foundation aid, the state might still avert the necessity for a constitutional amendment in any of several ways. One would be to finance state payments into the local government fund as well as into the school foundation program from the 50% of income tax revenue earmarked for turnback. At present a statutory amount of sales tax revenue plus the revenue from the state-situs intangibles tax is paid into the local government fund, which is then distributed among the counties. Each county share is in turn divided among local governments within the county. There appears to be no constitutional reason why income tax revenue could not be substituted by statute for the revenues from sources now designated.

Another way of increasing the capacity of the school foundation program to absorb revenue from the income tax turnback would be to enlarge school districts. Many Ohio school districts now extend across county lines and some school districts are larger in geographic size than some counties. The continuing process of consolidation is bringing about a gradual enlargement of school district size. There would appear to be no constitutional bar to accelerating this process to the point of designing multi-county districts able to absorb the income tax turnback within the formula-determined foundation payment. Alternatively, if it should be considered desirable to avoid school administrative units as large as might be necessary to accomplish the desired fiscal objective, it would presumably be possible to establish multi-county "fiscal" school districts (as described earlier) with functions limited to receiving and distributing revenues from the 50% turnback.

Thus a variety of approaches seems to be available whereby the constitutionally required distribution can be accomplished, while avoiding the undesirable fiscal result normally associated with distribution of income tax revenue to the point of origin. If the process of amending the state constitution were totally costless, it

TABLE 1
ESTIMATED PERSONAL INCOME TAX BASE (BEFORE EXEMPTIONS) AND POPULATION, BY COUNTY

County	*Adjusted Gross Personal Income 1971–72 ($ Million)*	*Population, 1970*
Total	37,891.2	10,652,057
Adams	28.9	18,957
Allen	343.8	111,144
Ashland	123.6	43,303
Ashtabula	272.5	98,237
Athens	102.5	54,889
Auglaize	115.2	38,602
Belmont	180.7	80,917
Brown	48.5	26,635
Butler	705.5	226,207
Carroll	48.1	21,579
Champaign	84.3	30,491
Clark	458.9	157,115
Clermont	224.3	95,725
Clinton	79.4	31,464
Columbiana	274.1	108,310
Coshocton	102.3	33,486
Crawford	162.8	50,364
Cuyahoga	8,214.6	1,721,300
Darke	119.2	49,141
Defiance	122.1	36,949
Delaware	107.8	42,908
Erie	256.6	75,909
Fairfield	194.8	73,301
Fayette	66.1	25,461
Franklin	2,945.1	833,249
Fulton	84.5	33,071
Gallia	41.2	25,239
Geauga	173.4	62,977
Greene	176.1	125,057
Guernsey	87.6	37,665
Hamilton	4,504.6	924,018
Hancock	198.9	61,127
Hardin	75.7	30,813
Harrison	49.3	17,013
Henry	73.5	27,058
Highland	60.4	28,996
Hocking	51.1	20,332
Holmes	45.4	23,024
Huron	157.9	49,587
Jackson	57.2	27,124
Jefferson	258.0	96,193
Knox	114.5	41,795

County	Adjusted Gross Personal Income 1971–72 ($ Million)	Population, 1970
Lake	630.2	197,200
Lawrence	83.9	56,868
Licking	329.0	107,799
Logan	85.0	35,072
Lorain	768.4	256,843
Lucas	1,904.5	484,370
Madison	62.2	28,318
Mahoning	961.3	303,424
Marion	191.9	64,724
Medina	212.5	82,717
Meigs	30.6	19,799
Mercer	103.4	35,265
Miami	270.8	84,342
Monroe	52.8	15,739
Montgomery	2,689.7	606,148
Morgan	28.9	12,375
Morrow	52.7	21,348
Muskingum	189.5	77,826
Noble	23.9	10,428
Ottawa	80.6	37,099
Paulding	36.5	19,329
Perry	54.9	27,434
Pickaway	88.9	40,071
Pike	25.3	19,114
Portage	304.5	125,868
Preble	72.5	34,719
Putnam	74.5	31,134
Richland	441.4	129,997
Ross	165.2	61,211
Sandusky	177.7	60,983
Scioto	174.9	76,951
Seneca	191.8	60,696
Shelby	123.5	37,748
Stark	1,234.5	372,210
Summit	2,166.5	553,371
Trumbull	810.6	232,579
Tuscarawas	235.7	77,211
Union	66.6	23,786
Van Wert	74.2	29,194
Vinton	15.5	9,420
Warren	178.0	84,925
Washington	149.4	57,160
Wayne	251.7	87,123
Williams	103.6	33,669
Wood	269.1	89,722
Wyandot	56.7	21,826

SOURCE: Income estimated as described in text. Population from 1970 Census.

TABLE 2

ESTIMATED REVENUE YIELD, FLAT RATE TAX OF 2% ON PERSONAL INCOME, BY COUNTY, 1971–72

County	*Amount ($000)*	*Per Capita ($)*	*Percentage of State Total*
Total	757,824	71	100.00
Adams	578	30	.08
Allen	6,876	62	.91
Ashland	2,472	57	.33
Ashtabula	5,450	55	.72
Athens	2,050	37	.27
Auglaize	2,304	60	.30
Belmont	3,614	45	.48
Brown	970	36	.13
Butler	14,110	62	1.86
Carroll	962	45	.13
Champaign	1,686	55	.22
Clark	9,172	58	1.21
Clermont	4,486	47	.59
Clinton	1,588	50	.20
Columbiana	5,482	51	.72
Coshocton	2,046	61	.27
Crawford	3,256	65	.43
Cuyahoga	164,292	95	21.69
Darke	2,384	49	.31
Defiance	2,442	66	.32
Delaware	2,155	50	.28
Erie	5,131	68	.68
Fairfield	3,897	53	.51
Fayette	1,322	52	.17
Franklin	58,903	71	7.78
Fulton	1,890	57	.25
Gallia	823	33	.11
Geauga	3,468	55	.46
Greene	3,522	28	.47
Guernsey	1,751	47	.23
Hamilton	90,093	98	11.89
Hancock	3,977	65	.52
Hardin	1,515	49	.20
Harrison	986	58	.13
Henry	1,471	54	.19
Highland	1,208	42	.16
Hocking	1,023	50	.14
Holmes	908	39	.12
Huron	3,159	64	.42
Jackson	1,147	42	.15
Jefferson	5,161	54	.68
Knox	2,290	55	.30

County	Amount ($000)	Per Capita ($)	Percentage of State Total
Lake	12,603	64	1.66
Lawrence	1,678	30	.22
Licking	6,580	61	.87
Logan	1,700	49	.22
Lorain	15,367	60	2.03
Lucas	38,090	79	5.03
Madison	1,244	44	.16
Mahoning	19,225	63	2.54
Marion	3,838	59	.50
Medina	4,250	51	.56
Meigs	611	31	.08
Mercer	2,068	59	.27
Miami	5,416	64	.72
Monroe	1,057	67	.14
Montgomery	53,793	89	7.10
Morgan	577	47	.08
Morrow	1,055	49	.14
Muskingum	3,789	49	.50
Noble	477	46	.06
Ottawa	1,612	44	.21
Paulding	731	38	.10
Perry	1,098	40	.15
Pickaway	1,778	44	.23
Pike	506	27	.07
Portage	6,091	48	.80
Preble	1,449	42	.19
Putnam	1,490	48	.20
Richland	8,828	68	1.17
Ross	3,212	53	.42
Sandusky	3,553	58	.47
Scioto	3,497	45	.46
Seneca	3,836	63	.51
Shelby	2,469	65	.33
Stark	24,690	66	3.26
Summit	43,331	78	5.72
Trumbull	16,212	70	2.14
Tuscarawas	4,715	61	.62
Union	1,332	56	.18
Van Wert	1,483	51	.20
Vinton	309	33	.04
Warren	3,561	42	.47
Washington	2,988	52	.39
Wayne	5,034	58	.66
Williams	2,073	62	.27
Wood	5,382	60	.71
Wyandot	1,135	52	.15

SOURCE: Calculations based on Table 1.

TABLE 3
ESTIMATED REVENUE YIELD OF PERSONAL INCOME TAX
GRADUATED RATE STRUCTURE A,[1] BY COUNTY, 1971–1972

County	*Amount ($000)*	*Per Capita ($)*	*Percentage of State Total*
Total	755,651	71	100.00
Adams	281	15	.04
Allen	6,152	55	.81
Ashland	2,155	50	.29
Ashtabula	4,737	48	.63
Athens	1,266	23	.17
Auglaize	2,021	52	.27
Belmont	2,434	30	.32
Brown	597	22	.08
Butler	12,629	56	1.67
Carroll	647	30	.09
Champaign	1,465	48	.19
Clark	8,020	51	1.06
Clermont	3,045	32	.40
Clinton	1,201	38	.16
Columbiana	4,150	38	.55
Coshocton	1,818	54	.24
Crawford	2,914	58	.39
Cuyahoga	196,330	114	25.98
Darke	1,795	37	.24
Defiance	2,185	59	.29
Delaware	1,631	38	.22
Erie	4,592	61	.61
Fairfield	2,973	41	.39
Fayette	1,006	40	.13
Franklin	54,274	65	7.18
Fulton	1,647	50	.22
Gallia	430	17	.06
Geauga	3,014	48	.40
Greene	1,580	13	.21
Guernsey	1,188	32	.16
Hamilton	113,311	123	15.00
Hancock	3,559	58	.47
Hardin	1,140	37	.15
Harrison	862	51	.11
Henry	1,271	47	.17
Highland	781	27	.10

County	Amount ($000)	Per Capita ($)	Percentage of State Total
Hocking	774	38	.10
Holmes	579	25	.08
Huron	2,827	57	.37
Jackson	740	27	.10
Jefferson	3,957	41	.52
Knox	1,990	48	.26
Lake	11,280	57	1.49
Lawrence	808	14	.11
Licking	5,850	54	.77
Logan	1,241	35	.16
Lorain	13,545	53	1.79
Lucas	35,980	74	4.76
Madison	837	30	.11
Mahoning	17,207	57	2.28
Marion	3,367	52	.45
Medina	3,218	39	.43
Meigs	300	15	.04
Mercer	1,808	51	.24
Miami	4,848	58	.64
Monroe	945	60	.13
Montgomery	57,610	95	7.62
Morgan	391	32	.05
Morrow	793	37	.10
Muskingum	2,852	37	.38
Noble	324	31	.04
Ottawa	1,082	29	.14
Paulding	462	24	.06
Perry	704	26	.09
Pickaway	1,196	30	.16
Pike	213	11	.03
Portage	4,449	35	.59
Preble	936	27	.12
Putnam	1,020	33	.13
Richland	7,901	61	1.05
Ross	2,451	40	.32
Sandusky	3,106	51	.41
Scioto	2,355	31	.31
Seneca	3,433	57	.45
Shelby	2,210	59	.29
Stark	22,098	59	2.92

County	*Amount ($000)*	*Per Capita ($)*	*Percentage of State Total*
Summit	40,931	74	5.42
Trumbull	14,848	64	1.96
Tuscarawas	4,191	54	.55
Union	1,161	49	.15
Van Wert	1,123	39	.15
Vinton	162	17	.02
Warren	2,302	27	.30
Washington	2,280	40	.30
Wayne	4,401	51	.58
Williams	1,854	55	.25
Wood	4,744	53	.63
Wyandot	864	40	.11

[1]On the first $3,000 of adjusted gross income	1%
On AGI between $3,000 and $6,000	1½%
On AGI between $6,000 and $10,000	2%
On AGI between $10,000 and $15,000	3%
On AGI between $15,000 and $20,000	4%
On AGI between $20,000 and $25,000	5%
On AGI between $25,000 and $35,000	6%
On AGI between $35,000 and $50,000	7%
On AGI over $50,000	8%
$10 credit for each allowable dependent	

TABLE 4
ESTIMATED REVENUE YIELD OF PERSONAL INCOME TAX
GRADUATED RATE STRUCTURE B,[1] BY COUNTY, 1971–1972

County	*Amount ($000)*	*Per Capita ($)*	*Percentage of State Total*
Total	431,042	40	100.00
Adams	173	9	.04
Allen	3,530	32	.82
Ashland	1,153	27	.27
Ashtabula	2,543	26	.59
Athens		13	.17
Auglaize	1,172	30	.27
Belmont	1,416	18	.33
Brown	338	13	.08
Butler	7,246	32	1.68
Carroll	376	17	.09
Champaign	786	26	.18
Clark	4,308	27	1.00
Clermont	1,767	18	.41
Clinton	667	21	.15
Columbiana	2,317	21	.54
Coshocton	1,044	31	.24
Crawford	1,791	36	.42
Cuyahoga	110,545	64	25.65
Darke	968	20	.22
Defiance	1,347	36	.31
Delaware	906	21	.21
Erie	2,855	38	.66
Fairfield	1,663	23	.39
Fayette	558	22	.13
Franklin	33,056	40	7.67
Fulton	884	27	.21
Gallia	264	10	.06
Geauga	1,610	26	.37
Greene	975	8	.23
Guernsey	690	18	.16
Hamilton	60,690	66	14.08
Hancock	2,188	36	.51
Hardin	636	21	.15
Harrison	463	27	.11
Henry	653	24	.15
Highland	443	15	.10

County	*Amount ($000)*	*Per Capita ($)*	*Percentage of State Total*
Hocking	430	21	.10
Holmes	326	14	.08
Huron	1,629	33	.38
Jackson	420	15	.10
Jefferson	2,293	24	.53
Knox	1,017	24	.24
Lake	6,499	33	1.51
Lawrence	478	8	.11
Licking	3,359	31	.78
Logan	690	20	.16
Lorain	7,821	30	1.81
Lucas	21,698	45	5.03
Madison	483	17	.11
Mahoning	9,872	33	2.29
Marion	1,809	28	.42
Medina	1,796	22	.42
Meigs	184	9	.04
Mercer	971	28	.23
Miami	2,980	35	.69
Monroe	586	37	.14
Montgomery	31,728	52	7.36
Morgan	227	18	.05
Morrow	443	21	.10
Muskingum	1,538	20	.36
Noble	188	18	.04
Ottawa	626	17	.15
Paulding	257	13	.06
Perry	394	14	.09
Pickaway	696	17	.16
Pike	138	7	.03
Portage	2,474	20	.57
Preble	531	15	.12
Putnam	605	19	.14
Richland	4,954	38	1.15
Ross	1,365	22	.32
Sandusky	1,669	27	.39
Scioto	1,378	18	.32
Seneca	1,970	32	.46
Shelby	1,363	36	.32
Stark	13,667	37	3.17

County	Amount ($000)	Per Capita ($)	Percentage of State Total
Summit	24,683	45	5.73
Trumbull	9,098	39	2.11
Tuscarawas	2,407	31	.56
Union	621	26	.14
Van Wert	627	21	.15
Vinton	99	11	.02
Warren	1,307	15	.30
Washington	1,270	22	.29
Wayne	2,364	27	.55
Williams	1,064	32	.25
Wood	2,739	31	.64
Wyandot	482	22	.11

[1]On the first $7,500 of taxable income **1%**
On taxable income between $7,500 and $15,000 **2%**
On taxable income above $15,000 **3%**
$1,500 exemption for a single taxpayer
$3,000 exemption for a family

TABLE 5
SCHOOL FOUNDATION AID AND LOCAL SHARE OF STATE INCOME TAX REVENUE, BY COUNTY 1971–1972
(Thousand dollars)

	50% of Revenue from Income Tax			
County	*2% Flat Rate*	*Graduated Rate A*	*Graduated Rate B*	*School Foundation Aid ($635 per pupil)*
Adams	$ 289	$ 141	$ 87	$ 2,224
Allen	3,438	3,076	1,765	6,963
Ashland	1,236	1,078	577	3,444
Ashtabula	2,725	2,369	1,271	7,428
Athens	1,025	633	357	3,499
Auglaize	1,152	1,011	586	3,036
Belmont	1,807	1,217	708	5,183
Brown	485	299	169	3,024
Butler	7,055	6,315	3,622	16,478
Carroll	481	324	188	1,862
Champaign	843	733	393	2,995
Clark	4,586	4,010	2,154	13,183
Clermont	2,243	1,523	884	12,939
Clinton	794	601	333	3,412
Columbiana	2,741	2,075	1,158	10,446
Coshocton	1,023	909	522	1,852
Crawford	1,628	1,457	896	3,036
Cuyahoga	82,146	98,165	55,272	76,556
Darke	1,192	898	484	4,537
Defiance	1,221	1,093	674	2,771
Delaware	1,078	816	452	3,504
Erie	2,566	2,296	1,427	3,858
Fairfield	1,948	1,397	831	6,670
Fayette	661	503	279	1,586
Franklin	29,451	27,137	16,528	62,809
Fulton	945	824	442	2,518
Gallia	412	215	132	2,437
Geauga	1,734	1,507	805	5,915
Greene	1,761	790	487	12,924
Guernsey	876	594	345	2,502
Hamilton	45,046	56,656	30,345	41,004
Hancock	1,989	1,780	1,094	3,711
Hardin	757	570	318	2,070
Harrison	493	431	232	837
Henry	735	636	326	1,491

County	*50% of Revenue from Income Tax* 2% Flat Rate	Graduated Rate A	Graduated Rate B	*School Foundation Aid ($635 per pupil)*
Highland	604	391	222	2,883
Hocking	511	387	215	1,847
Holmes	454	290	163	1,634
Huron	1,579	1,414	814	3,969
Jackson	572	370	210	3,199
Jefferson	2,580	1,979	1,146	3,633
Knox	1,145	995	508	3,065
Lake	6,302	5,640	3,249	13,172
Lawrence	839	404	239	6,933
Licking	3,290	2,925	1,679	9,664
Logan	850	621	345	3,271
Lorain	7,684	6,773	3,910	21,042
Lucas	19,045	17,990	10,849	28,125
Madison	622	419	241	2,008
Mahoning	9,613	8,604	4,936	17,406
Marion	1,919	1,684	904	4,520
Medina	2,125	1,609	898	9,075
Meigs	306	150	92	2,791
Mercer	1,034	904	485	3,208
Miami	2,708	2,424	1,490	7,172
Monroe	528	473	293	766
Montgomery	26,897	28,805	15,864	39,660
Morgan	289	196	114	1,138
Morrow	527	397	221	2,353
Muskingum	1,895	1,426	769	6,125
Noble	239	162	94	1,003
Ottawa	806	541	313	2,404
Paulding	365	231	129	1,751
Perry	549	352	197	3,006
Pickaway	889	598	348	2,422
Pike	253	107	2,225	1,237
Portage	3,045	2,225	1,237	11,638
Preble	725	468	266	3,725
Putnam	745	510	302	2,702
Richland	4,414	3,951	2,477	9,288
Ross	1,652	1,226	683	5,261
Sandusky	1,777	1,553	834	4,113
Scioto	1,749	1,178	689	8,381
Seneca	1,918	1,717	985	3,058

County	50% of Revenue from Income Tax 2% Flat Rate	Graduated Rate A	Graduated Rate B	School Foundation Aid ($635 per pupil)
Shelby	1,235	1,105	681	2,177
Stark	12,345	11,049	6,833	25,320
Summit	21,665	20,466	12,341	37,997
Trumbull	8,106	7,424	4,549	14,410
Tuscarawas	2,357	2,096	1,203	6,141
Union	666	581	310	1,822
Van Wert	742	562	313	1,355
Vinton	155	81	50	1,096
Warren	1,780	1,151	654	9,684
Washington	1,494	1,140	635	3,896
Wayne	2,517	2,201	1,182	6,758
Williams	1,036	927	532	2,106
Wood	2,691	2,372	1,369	5,087
Wyandot	567	432	241	1,396
TOTAL	$378,912	$377,826	$215,521	$718,286

would be my judgment that Art. XII, Sec. 9, should be repealed. But even relatively simple and noncontroversial amendments require expenditure of time, effort, and money if they are to succeed. In matters involving taxation, the problems are especially great and the outcome especially in doubt. Under these circumstances it seems to me that retention of Art. XII, Sec. 9, of the Ohio Constitution poses no serious difficulties to designing a modern state personal income tax.

PART III

Institutional Analysis

Editors' Introduction

For the student of state politics, comparison of an organizational chart of Ohio government with those from other states would reveal little that is surprising. Indeed, Ohio is quite typical; by the criteria used to evaluate structure and form, it occupies a modal position. Ohio governors are adjudged relatively powerful; the legislature ranks among the more professional in the nation; and the court system is closer to the American Bar Association model than those of most states. Ohio's administrative structure is neither as orderly as some nor as fragmented as others. And there is evidence of recent efforts to rationalize the system. In 1950 Ohio had 122 administrative agencies, compared to a national average of 91; in 1967 there were 60 agencies, fewer than the national average of 67.

Recognizing that institutional structure has an impact on policy making, many reformers have given substantial attention to a search for the most appropriate structure of state government. If one were to criticize their efforts, it would not be because of the focus of the search, but because of its intensity. Undue concern with structure and form can lead to a slighting of more fundamental matters. It can also contribute to the growth and uncritical acceptance of a conventional wisdom about state government. For example, included in a list of conventional wisdom items might be the following:

a. The weakest branch of state government is the legislative. The legislature impedes progress and change because of its archaic organization, its unrepresentative character, and its domination by conservative coalitions, usually rural-based.
b. The quality of justice will be enhanced by the recruitment of "better men" to the state judiciary. Such is best accomplished by non-partisan methods, which keep politics out of the judicial selection process.
c. Because the lives and futures of society's young people are involved, higher education and politics should not be mixed. Education policy making should be structurally separated from the day-to-day passions of state politics. Every effort must be made to protect the integrity of the public universities, perhaps by special constitutional provisions.

Each of the contributions to this section deals with an important institution of state government. While the topics analyzed are somewhat diverse—legislative performance, higher education politics, and judicial selection—one unifying theme is the refutation of conventional wisdom.

In the first study, Thomas Flinn assesses legislative performance in Ohio. After considering the unfavorable criticisms which have been leveled against state legislatures as institutions, Flinn suggests that some criticisms may result from inappropriate standards of evaluation. Positing alternative criteria of legislative performance, and evaluating them with a variety of data, he concludes that the Ohio legislature receives high marks on his criteria.

A detailed analysis of the Ohio judicial recruitment process is contained in Kathleen Barber's study. She finds that the existing system of selecting appellate judges—partisan primaries and non-partisan elections—tends to produce very real partisan results. Because of greater interest and high participation by Republican party identifiers in judicial elections, Republicans dominate the judicial system. Professor Barber argues that alternative selection plans—such as gubernatorial appointment of judges from a list submitted by a nominating commission—would not necessarily maximize goals of political visibility and judicial responsibility. Such plans do not eliminate politics from the selection process, but merely shift the loci of political decision making to private groups. A more appropriate means, suggests Barber, would be gubernatorial appointment of judges with confirmation by the state senate.

The relationship between state politics and higher education is traced out in the final chapter by Joseph Tucker. Throughout his analysis, Tucker nicely delineates the inevitability of political tensions—whether they result from competition among institutions attempting to maximize their individual appropriations, or between institutions seeking to maintain autonomy and the Board of Regents working for a coordinated system. As Tucker demonstrates, structural independence in the educational function does not result in political independence. Whatever its formal powers, the Board of Regents, and particularly its chancellor, is dependent upon the governor for promotion of educational interests. Finally, Tucker notes that on the basis of experience in other states, the benefits of constitutional status for public universities would probably be marginal at best. Any constitutional protection of the universities' status would be more symbolic than real.

An Evaluation of Legislative Performance: The State Legislature in Ohio

Thomas A. Flinn

I. INTRODUCTION

The state legislature is to me one of the most interesting of all political arenas. I am impressed by the integrity of the members, their own respect for the legislative institution, the parliamentary and political skills of the leaders, and the clash of groups within the context of rules, written and unwritten, which tend to preserve friendships and the dignity of the participating legislators. There is a lack of publicity, with the consequence that a legislator's fulfillment in doing a good job is the recognition of his fellow legislators and self-fulfillment. In a time of images and image-making which may or may not correspond to reality, this too has an appeal.

But praise for state legislatures is not heard often. Much more common are remarks like this: "The legislatures are the bawdy houses of state government. Without exception, legislatures, as a whole, are a shambles of mediocrity, incompetence, hooliganism,

The research on which this paper is based was supported by research funds granted to me by Oberlin College and by the Ohio Center for Education in Politics. Their support is acknowledged gratefully.

and venality."[1] That statement is by journalist Robert S. Allen in his introduction to a set of essays on the politics of various states, including Ohio. The essay on Ohio is by a Cleveland journalist, Richard L. Maher. His attitude toward Ohio government is summarized by his opening sentence, "Ohio, fourth state in population and third in industrial wealth, boasts an oxcart-model government in an atomic age."[2] Maher's attitude toward the legislature is suggested, if not precisely summarized, by this rhetorical question and answer, "The question is frequently raised in Ohio, 'Who runs the Legislature?' Certainly it is not the people."[3]

A less flamboyant survey of the scene is presented by the journalists who cooperated with James Reichley, but their conclusions are fairly dark.[4] Reichley's title for the "epilogue" is "States in Crisis." The problems of the states, he says, are constitutional obsolescence, lack of financial resources, and possible loss of political legitimacy.[5] He goes on to say that

> Perhaps most fundamental of all the problems confronting the states is that of political legitimacy. Do the states, after all, have any real basis for continued existence? Do they inspire loyalty and respect in the hearts of their citizens? Are they political anachronisms, like the Turkish and Austro-Hungarian Empires in the years immediately preceding World War I, or are they vitally related to the social and economic realities of the present day?[6]

The indictment is of state governments generally and not state legislatures in particular; but hardly anyone would doubt that the legislatures are either the most important center of state government or, at least, that state legislatures retain within their sphere something like the importance ascribed generally to legislatures in democracies not too many years ago. So the state legislature must

---

[1]Robert S. Allen (ed.), *Our Sovereign State* (New York: The Vanguard Press, Inc., 1949), p. xxi.

[2]*Ibid.*, p. 166.

[3]*Ibid.*, p. 172.

[4]James Reichley, *States in Crisis: Politics in Ten American States, 1950–1962* (Chapel Hill: The University of North Carolina Press, 1964).

[5]*Ibid.*, p. 257.

[6]*Ibid.*, p. 261.

be no less than one of the parties in the indictment. Several surveys by academic observers, not so much given to condemnation, are different in style, but still not much more flattering. A committee of the American Political Science Association issued a study a few years ago which included the following summary statement:

> Present-day legislative responsibilities are of such complexity, such magnitude, that they cannot be met adequately by the old-fashioned, time-consuming legislative procedures, antiquated organization, inadequate and incompetent staff services. Committee systems are archaic, not having been changed in most states in any important respect for fifty or a hundred years—or more. Rules of procedures that antedate the invention of the printing press still prevail in many jurisdictions.[7]

The last of these statements is scarcely believable, or else the product of unusually diligent historical research, but the central content of the charge is unmistakable: failure to modernize. And not much has happened since the issuance of the report although those who join it can point to signs of "progress" here and there.

The Eighth American Assembly considered the work of the states.[8] It was restrained in its criticism, but let he who wishes try to find commendation or even happy acceptance. Of course, it may be said that the assignment of participants was to find ways for advance and not to strike balanced judgments. Even so, it may be noted that their suggestions for improvement seem based on abstract or "outside" criteria and not on the idea of proceeding from existing practice and from appreciation of existing systems except insofar as such compromises were politically required or expedient.

It would seem that the weight of opinion is against the favorable views with which I began. Actually, other friendly statements could be collected if that would advance the inquiry; however, all that would do is increase the list of authorities, greater or lesser,

---

[7]Belle Zeller (ed.), *American State Legislatures, Report of the Committee on American State Legislatures of the American Political Science Association* (New York: Thomas Y. Crowell Co., 1954), p. 3.

[8]The American Assembly, *The Forty-eight States: Their Tasks as Policy Makers and Administrators* (New York: The American Assembly, Graduate School of Business, Columbia University, 1955).

on either side of the argument. The issue is the quality of state legislative performance and to settle it one needs agreement on criteria, and then application.

II. CRITERIA OF LEGISLATIVE PERFORMANCE

One way to lay down criteria for evaluation of legislative performance is to search the literature in order to find what seem to be agreed upon criteria, but the fact is that such a search would be largely futile. In the writing on congresses, parliaments, and state legislatures, there is little in the way of explicit criteria for judgment. To be sure, one may find demands that procedures be "streamlined" and that more staff be supplied for legislators; but what criteria and judgments lead to even these routine suggestions are not really clear.

The only course open seems to be the assertion of some criteria without the support of authority. Let two things be emphasized here: criteria will be asserted and not extensively defended, and only some of the possible criteria will be named. With regard to the fact that criteria will be asserted and not much defended, it is hoped that they will be reasonably acceptable on their face.

I would suggest *first* that one test of a legislature is to be found in the process by which its members are recruited. This is not legislative performance itself, but the recruitment process is very likely to strongly condition performance. I would assert that persons winning legislative nominations should have experience in and commitment to continuing political organizations. There may be surrogates for this experience and commitment, but the demand seems reasonable. Perhaps the best quick defense for alleging reasonableness is to imagine a legislative body which recruits members who are without experience in or commitment to continuing political organizations. It seems likely that they would have difficulty selecting leaders, achieving an effective division of labor, and forming stable coalitions necessary for doing legislative business. It might also be that this would be a truly venal legislature.

With regard to this first criterion, it should be noted that it is stated in general terms. In order to apply it, the criterion needs to be made operational. The way in which this is done will appear as findings are reported. There will be no special defense of the way in which criteria are made operational even though this step may be a crucial one.

A *second* criterion for legislative performance is that members have organized political attitudes so that as issues arise they may be recognized and fitted into a system of experiences and preferences. The legislator is then able to use the knowledge and sets of values he has accumulated through time and probably with some pain. Again, it may be pointed out that what is being asserted is not a test of legislative performance itself but a condition which is likely to influence behavior strongly. As before, a good quick defense of the asserted criterion may be to imagine a legislature which does not meet it, that is, a group of legislators for whom most issues have a high degree of novelty. Decisions are likely to be difficult, unpredictable, subject to mood and emotion, and influenced by events in the lives of the legislators that have no proper relation to the issues at hand. Public opinion seems to take on this character when issues arise for which members of the public have no available attitude structure.

These attitude structures should also be common, that is, shared by members of the legislature. It is easy to see that discussion and decision become very difficult when participants are treating issues within different frames of reference. Furthermore, I have the impression from looking at legislatures that funny things happen when members do not have attitude structures for issues at hand. It is then, I think, that revolts of the rank-and-file against the leadership, unexpected voting alignments, and seeming indifference to pertinent evidence happen. Frequent occurrence of these events would be demoralizing and ultimately chaotic.

The *third* criterion is that there be a bloc structure in the legislature and that not too many legislators be isolated from it. Without a bloc structure and with numerous "isolates," it would seem likely that the task of the majority-builders would be difficult if not impossible and the psychological state of other members precarious.

The *fourth* criterion has to do with roles, a concept that has been elaborated very carefully in some social and political analyses. All that is meant here is the expectation a legislator has about the ways in which he, as well as other legislators, should behave. The criterion is that some roles should urge a measure of deference for the facilitators, arrangers, or majority-builders in the legislature. Criterion four recognizes that in the legislative divison of labor there must be a supported effort to get on with the job somehow, and preferably with as much mutual satisfaction as possible.

The *fifth* criterion is that legislators have memberships in groups which support their activities as legislators. Two prime possibilities are legislative social groups and friendship groups outside the legislature.

The *sixth* and last criterion for a strong and healthy legislative system is that it be based on majority rule. Its internal procedures should be subject to control by majorities, and blocs within the legislature should win or lose majority status depending on the number of voters who support them in elections. It seems likely that, within the context of democratic politics, a legislature which one way or another denies majority rule will lack public respect and support and even the respect and support of some of its members.

In summary, these posited criteria represent hypotheses concerning legislative performance. They are that experience in and commitment to continuing political organizations by legislators, the existence of common political attitude structures, the appearance of bloc structures, etc., contribute to the good working of a legislative body. I do not know that these hypotheses are true, but I assume that they are. Having made that assumption, it is possible to evaluate legislative performance by checking for the conditions which contribute to good operation. If they are present, the legislature gets high marks. If they are absent, the legislature gets low marks.

III. DATA ANALYSIS

Does the Ohio legislature meet the criteria that have been set out above? The first of these criteria had to do with experience in and commitment to continuing political organizations, in particular, political parties. Some data I collected in 1963, by sending questionnaires to members of the legislature, relate to it.[9] Included was one set of three questions asking members about the relation of their party organization to their nomination in 1962 and when they first ran, if 1962 was not their first try. The questions are as follows:

1. Did the organization of your party (the officers acting singly or as a group) suggest that you file for the legislature last year?
2. If 1962 was not your first race for the legislature, did the organization of your party (officers acting singly or as a group) suggest that you file when you first ran?
3. Can you say that your candidacy received "clearance" last year from your party organization before the primary?

A limited number of responses were offered as alternatives from which the respondent could choose. They were: Yes, No, and Not Relevant.

The only question that might need some explanation is the third, which employs the notion of "clearance." I had discovered earlier by some conversations with county party officers that parties in Ohio may have an effect on legislative and other nominations without much formal decision making and even without much apparent activity. In some instances, nearly everyone in the party organization and their cohorts will understand that one or more candidates for nomination would be acceptable nominees, that they

---

[9]Responses were received from 100 of the 170 members, a return of 59%. The proportion of Republicans and of Democrats replying was almost exactly the same. Respondents are probably representative of the whole legislature. My reason for thinking so is that I found after careful checking that a sample of county political party officers in Ohio obtained by a mailed questionnaire was representative. See Thomas A. Flinn and Frederick M. Wirt, "Local Party Leaders: Groups of Like Minded Men," *Midwest Journal of Political Science*, 9 (February, 1965), 77–98, esp. 97–98. Another recent study also supports the representativeness of samples collected by mailed questionnaires: Edward C. McDonagh and A. Leon Rosenblum, "A Comparison of Mailed Questionnaires and Subsequent Structured Interviews," *Public Opinion Quarterly*, 29 (Spring, 1965), 131–136. I should add that Fred Wirt assisted in gathering data for the 1963 study and that almost none of the 1963 data has been published before.

are not to be "vetoed" assuming the party could if it tried, and that these candidates are in a sense "cleared."

Responses to this set of three questions are set out in Table 1.

TABLE 1
POLITICAL PARTIES AND LEGISLATIVE NOMINATIONS, OHIO GENERAL ASSEMBLY, 1962 ELECTIONS
Percent by Party

(Dem. N=35; Rep. N=65)

	Question #1		*Question #2*		*Question #3*	
Response	*Dem.*	*Rep.*	*Dem.*	*Rep.*	*Dem.*	*Rep.*
Yes	23	55	14	48	54	62
No	74	43	69	22	23	15
Not relevant	—	—	11	20	23	23
No answer	3	2	6	11	—	—
TOTAL	100	100	100	101	100	100

***Percentages are rounded to the nearest whole percentage point. Failure of totals to equal 100 is due to rounding.**

With regard to these answers, the response "not relevant" was not given for question 1. It appears with question 2, and the obvious explanation is that a significant number of respondents were making their first race in 1962. The "not relevant" response to question 3 may mean that the term "clearance" did not mean anything to some legislators.

Insofar as inferences are concerned, "yes" answers suggest experience in and the possibility of commitment to the organized parties. Taking first the Republicans, who were the majority, it may be seen that more than half of them said that they had been asked by some leader of their party to run in 1962. One should not conclude this was the reason for their decision to run, but it does show a closeness to party. About two-thirds of the Republicans who answered the second question said that officers of their party had asked them to run when they made their first race, and 62% of all Republican respondents said that their candidacy had been "cleared" before the 1962 primary. Only 15% said they did not have clearance. All this suggests that the Republicans as a group are fairly close to their regular organization.

The Democrats are different. Nearly three-fourths reported that they had not been asked by party officers to run in 1962, and of those who answered the second question more than 80% said that the party had not asked them to make their first try for the legislature. On the other hand, more than half did say that they had been "cleared" before the 1962 primary, and only 23% said they did not have clearance. In general, the Republicans seem to be much closer to their party organization than the Democrats, although the Democrats are not, on the basis of these questions, entirely removed from their party either.

Three other questions in the questionnaire relate to the first criterion of legislative performance, i.e. experience in and commitment to party. The questions,[10] available responses, and the frequency of each response by party is shown below:

4. Have you ever held an office in your party (precinct committeeman, county chairman, etc.)?

Dem. Yes 63%	Dem. No 37%
Rep. Yes 48%	Rep. No 47%

(3% of the Republicans did not answer the question.)

5. During the time you have been in the General Assembly, did the officers of your county party (as a group or as individuals) tell you about their views on legislative issues?

Democrats

Often 0%	Never 29%
Sometimes 23%	No Ans. 8%
Seldom 40%	

Republicans

Often 3%	Never 26%
Sometimes 15%	No Ans. 20%
Seldom 35%	

6. During the time you have been in the General Assembly, do you think your votes were consistent with the views of the officers of your county party organization?

[10]The numbering of the questions is for convenient reference. For instance, the question above numbered 4 may be referred to as question 4, 1963.

Democrats

Yes 46%	No 11%
Don't Know 3%	No Ans. 40%

Republicans

Yes 51%	No 5%
Don't Know 8%	No Ans. 35%

With regard to these answers, the relatively large number of respondents not answering should be kept in mind since it qualifies whatever inferences may be made from these data.

It appears that almost two-thirds of the Democrats and almost half of the Republicans have held an office in their own party organization. There is rather little communication between party officers and legislators concerning legislative issues; but about half of both the Democratic and Republican legislative groups think, nonetheless, that they are doing about what the leaders of their party would do also. Few believe that their stands conflict with the views of their party leaders, and even fewer profess not to know.

Holding party office is certainly experience in a political party, and as noted it is fairly common. Limited communication between legislators and party officers might suggest that the two groups are distant from one another, but the probably better interpretation is that much communication is not necessary. Agreement is widely assumed, and nothing happens to contradict that assumption. Thus this bit of the 1963 evidence suggests that legislators do have experience in and commitment to continuing political organizations, that is, their own political parties.

During 1966 I made a much more extensive investigation of nominations for the state legislature, and some of that information is of use in the present discussion.[11] For the purpose of the analysis which follows, respondents were divided into twelve groups depending on party, whether they were incumbents or former members on the one hand or new candidates on the other, and whether

[11]Questionnaires were mailed to all 522 candidates for seats in the House or Senate. Replies were received from 265, a response of 51%. Almost exactly equal proportions of Republicans and Democrats replied. For reasons indicated before, I am willing to believe that the sample is reasonably representative.

or not they were unopposed or winners or losers in primary contests. So there is, for example, a group of fifty-one candidates for Democratic nominations who were new candidates and who failed in their bid for nomination; and there is, for example, another group composed of nineteen Republicans who were incumbents or former members and who were nominated without opposition.

Candidates were asked why they had decided to run in 1966. More precisely, they were given a list of seven statements, which might fit a decision to run; and they were requested to select the statement that best fitted their decision and then the statement that next best fitted their decision to be a candidate.[12] Incumbents and former members, almost to a man, chose the alternative that said in effect that they liked their job and were expected to run again. Their reply was as anticipated and not very informative. They were asked, however, to select the statement which best fitted or next best fitted their decision to run when they first won a seat in the General Assembly.

Table 2 summarizes the reported "best fit" reasons given by new candidates for their decision to run in 1966 and "best fit" reasons given by incumbents and former members for their decision to run when they first won. The designation "NC" means new candidate, and the designation "OC" means literally old candidate, actually incumbent or former member. The decisions to run which can be considered "pro-party" are shown separately, and all "non-party" decisions are listed under "other." References to victory or defeat (sub-grouping) have to do with 1966 primary results.

As was stated, "pro-party" responses have been listed separately and "non-party" responses grouped. It may cause some surprise to find that an insurgent attitude is counted as "pro-party" and, hence, listed separately. The explanation is that an insurgent,

---

[12]Interpreting replies was not always easy. One problem which affects what follows is that some respondents named only the statement that next best fitted their decision to run. It is possible that they may only have got the number of the statement best fitting their decision in the wrong space, but I decided that those respondents should not be considered careless. What they may have meant was that none of the available statements fitted precisely their decision to run but that there was a second best statement.

TABLE 2
REASONS FOR DECISION TO RUN, 1966, OR WHEN FIRST ELECTED, OHIO GENERAL ASSEMBLY

Reason to Run		*Group 1* (*N*=32) %	*Group 2* (*N*=105) %	*Group 3* (*N*=31) %	*Group 4* (*N*=97) %
1. "Meat filler"	A	3	1	0	0
	B	3	1	0	0
	C	0	3	0	2
	T	6	5	0	2
2. "Recruited"	A	9	5	6	6
	B	3	0	6	3
	C	6	1	6	4
	T	18	6	18	13
3. "Party worker"	A	6	18	3	14
	B	6	18	3	21
	C	22	8	35	8
	T	34	44	41	43
4. "Insurgent"	A	6	0	0	0
	B	3	8	0	4
	C	3	2	0	1
	T	12	10	0	5
5. Other	A	9	3	0	4
	B	3	19	3	22
	C	12	6	10	1
	T	24	28	13	27
6. No answer	A	0	5	10	3
	B	0	3	6	5
	C	3	1	10	1
	T	3	9	26	9
TOTAL*		97	102	98	99

***Failure to equal 100 is due to rounding.**
Legend:
Group 1. OC Democrats
2. NC Democrats
3. OC Republicans
4. NC Republicans
Sub-Group A. Winners
B. Losers
C. Unopposed
Reason 1. "Meat Filler": "There is little chance for a member of my party to win in this district unless something unusual happens, but responsible people in my party . . . appealed to me. . . ."
Reason 2. "Recruited": "It would be best to say that I was recruited. Some of the officers of my party or persons close to them suggested that I . . . run. . . ."

even though not in love with the existing local organization of his party, is strongly enough committed to his party to make a considerable effort to improve it. Such a commitment may be stronger than that arising from the sense of gratitude which may be felt by a candidate recruited for a race which offers a good chance for success.

It is interesting to note that only 5% of the New Republican candidates were insurgents and nearly all of them lost in the primary. "Insurgency" is not rampant in the Democratic Party either, but does affect about 10% of the new Democratic candidates. It may also be noted that it does not pay to run as an outsider in the primaries of either party. On the other hand, chances for success are very good, although not perfect, if a candidate can arrange to be "recruited."

Insofar as criterion one is concerned (experience in and commitment to continuing party organizations), data in Table 2 seem to be positive. Only about one-fourth of the candidates in any of the four groups could be counted outsiders; and if the new candidates are considered (groups 2 and 4), then it may be added that very few of them win nominations. In contrast, 34% to 44% of the candidates describe themselves as having been party workers when first elected, or party workers before 1966 if that was the year of their first attempt to win a nomination. Further, 18% of Republican and Democratic incumbents or former members say that they were asked to run in the year when they were first elected. Without belaboring the point, the evidence is that candidates for the General Assembly and particularly the successful ones are reasonably close to their party organizations.

Other questions put to the primary candidates in 1966 would provide additional evidence concerning criterion one, but enough

---

Reason 3. "Party Worker": "I have been active in the affairs of my party . . . helping it and party candidates . . . Now . . . there is an opportunity for me to seek a seat in the legislature. . . ."
Reason 4. "Insurgent": "Frankly, the organization of my party in this district is not what it should be. I hope that my campaign for the legislature will encourage new people to get into politics and help create a new attitude among members of my party in this area. . . ."
Reason 5. "Other": The term "Outsider" could be substituted, and it is used in the following discussion. (a) "I have not been active in politics before, but I thought running for the legislature would be an interesting experience. It's a free country. . . ." (b) "I have been interested in politics for a number of years although I have not been associated closely with the leaders of either political party in my district. . . ."

has been said so that only one bit of additional evidence will be cited. Candidates were asked to indicate by a check whether they were strong, weak, or independent Democrats or Republicans, as the case might be. The results are as follows: 59% Strong Democrats; 64% Strong Republicans; 1% Weak Democrats; 1% Weak Republicans; 37% Independent Democrats; 31% Independent Republicans. Two percent of the Democratic respondents did not answer the question, nor did 4% of the Republican respondents. (Failure of percentages for Democratic groups plus Democrats not answering to equal 100 is due to rounding.) Very few candidates described their party position as "weak," and the explanation may be that the adjective is an opprobrious one.

The number of candidates describing their party position as "independent" is surprisingly high in view of the preceding discussion, but a further breakdown of the replies removes the surprise (see Table 3).

TABLE 3
PARTY POSITION OF CANDIDATES FOR THE OHIO GENERAL ASSEMBLY ACCORDING TO SUCCESS OR FAILURE, 1966

Party Position	*Dem. Winners* (N=80) %*	*Dem. Losers (N=57) %*	*Rep. Winners* (N=69) %*	*Rep. Losers (N=59) %*
Strong	66	49	68	59
Weak	0	4	0	2
Ind.	30	47	29	34
No answer	4	0	3	5
TOTAL	100	100	100	100

***Successful in a primary contest or unopposed.**

The proportion of strong party identifiers rises to over two-thirds among winners, and the proportion of independent party men falls to 30% or less. With regard to criterion one, the conclusion here and in general is that the nominating process tends very clearly to select candidates who have had experience in their party organization and who are committed to it.

One way to discover whether members of a group have a common attitude structure on some subject (criterion two) is to ask them about a series of issues that seem to relate to the subject. Then issues may be arranged in order from least to greatest popularity.[13] It may be found at this point that every member or virtually every member of the group, once having given an affirmative reply on some issue, will proceed to give an affirmative reply to every following and more popular issue. This is evidence of common attitude structure. But such a result may be prevented by a few items in the list which may be accepted or rejected without much reference to whether more or less popular issues are accepted or rejected. These items may be thrown out as non-scale items, the usual explanation being that the issues do not relate to the same subject as others in the list. The appearance of a common attitude structure may be prevented also when a few members of the group accept one or more less popular issues and reject some of the more popular issues. These "non-conformists" may be rejected as non-scale, and providing they do not constitute more than 10% of the group, the convention is that one may still claim that there is a common attitude structure.

In the 1963 study, legislators were asked to state their preferences with regard to a series of ten issues involving regulation of the economy, welfare, and taxes.[14] Members were asked whether they thought government support for the issue should increase, decrease, or remain the same.[15] A sample of the analysis involving Republican members is shown in Diagram 1. An *X* indicates either an "increase" or a "remain the same" response. Thus, Republican

---

[13]The procedure will be recognized immediately by those who work with this sort of problem as Guttman scale analysis. For a good description of the technique, see Lee F. Anderson, *et al.*, *Legislative Roll-Call Analysis* (Evanston: Northwestern University Press, 1966), Ch. 6.

[14]These issues appeared in 1963 to be the more salient of those which McClosky had used a few years earlier. See Herbert McClosky, *et al.*, "Issue Conflict and Consensus Among Party Leaders and Followers," *American Political Science Review* 54 (June, 1960), 406–427.

[15]In order to make a Guttman scale analysis, it was necessary to dichotomize the replies; and for technical reasons replies of Republicans and Democrats could not be dichotomized in the same way. So it was necessary to analyze the two groups separately.

DIAGRAM 1
ATTITUDE STRUCTURE OF REPUBLICAN LEGISLATORS,
1963 OHIO GENERAL ASSEMBLY, FIVE SELECTED MEMBERS

Issue	*Legislator* *A*	*B*	*C*	*D*	*E*
1. Gov't Reg. of Business	X				
2. Level of Farm Price Supports	X				
3. Tax on Business	X	X			
4. Corp. Inc. Tax	X	X			
5. Tax on Large Incomes	X		X		
6. Fed. Aid to Ed.	X	X	X		
7. Reg. of Public Utilities	X	X	X	X	
8. Soc. Security Benefits	X	X	X	X	X
9. Minimum Wages	X	X	X	X	X
10. Enforcement of Anti-Monopoly Laws	X	X	X	X	X

member *C* thought that government support for the four least popular issues should decrease but that government support for the six more popular issues should remain the same or increase. It may be noted also that member *B* had one non-scale response: he thought, contrary to expectations, that taxes on large incomes should decrease. But this level of dissent does not require that he be classified as outside the common attitude structure. Insofar as the whole Republican legislative delegation was concerned, it was found that there was a common attitude structure which involved generally matters of government action.

Analysis of attitudes of Democratic legislators was similar in procedure and results. Issues were ranked in the same order from least to most popular. The only item which came close to being non-scale was federal aid to education. The conclusion is that there was a common attitude structure among Democratic legislators concerning government action.[16]

A further inference is justified: Republicans and Democrats shared a common attitude structure on matters of government action. This is not to say they agreed with each other; they did not.

[16]For those familiar with Guttman scaling, the Guttman scale for both legislative groups had an Index of Reproducibility of 92.

The Republican position was considerably more conservative than that of the Democrats, but this difference is another matter. Persons or groups may share an attitude structure without being in agreement on specifics. What they agree upon is that some things go together and that there is an order to them.[17]

Criterion three is that there be a bloc structure in the legislature. One way to test for its appearance is to examine roll-call voting, and I have done that for most of the sessions from the end of the second World War to the present. A possibility investigated is that the legislature divided into urban and rural groups. The finding was clearly negative: urban-rural blocs and urban-rural factionalism do not exist in the Ohio legislature.[18] Conversations with experienced legislators confirm what the statistics show. Furthermore, some legislators add that the big city delegations can get pretty much what they want without serious controversy when they are in agreement.

What one does find is party blocs and party competition, as the following data from the 1959 session show beyond dispute.[19] Every roll call in the House of Representatives was inspected. The reason for choosing the House was that it was much larger than the Senate (139 to 33), and consequently its bloc structure is less likely to reflect the idiosyncrasy of a few members. Each roll call on which the minority was 10% or more of the majority was selected for

---

[17]Members of the 1963 legislature were asked also to give their opinions on a set of specifically state issues. Results are similar to those reported above.

[18]I have reported these studies before, and will not repeat myself here in order to save space for other things. See "The Outline of Ohio Politics," *Western Political Quarterly,* 13 (September, 1960), 702–721, esp. 715–718, and "The Election System and the Party System," in Howard D. Hamilton, *Reapportioning Legislatures* (Columbus: Charles E. Merrill Books, Inc., 1966), pp. 59–72.

[19]The 1959 session is unusual since it was one of the two sessions since World War II in which there was a Democrat majority; the other was 1949. The number of controversial roll calls in these sessions was much higher than usual. Choosing one of them for the purpose of analyzing roll calls has the advantage that they are sessions in which latent divisions in the legislature come to the surface, i.e. the floor. And as between 1949 and 1959, the latter has the advantage of being a session in which there was an ambitious gubernatorial legislative program (that of Michael DiSalle), which probably also has the effect of bringing out latent divisions.

further examination. They were called controversial roll calls, and the reason for concentrating on them was that unanimous or nearly unanimous roll calls would reveal nothing about bloc structure. The behavior of Republicans and Democrats on every controversial roll call was compared. When a majority of one party opposed the majority of the other, the vote was considered to be a "party vote," and the number of these was counted. Indices of likeness were also computed for every roll call.[20] The index expresses in a single number the degree to which two voting groups (in this case, parties) are alike or unlike. Indices of likeness may range from 0 to 100. An index of 100 indicates that they reacted to the issue in the same way, such as each voting 80-20 in favor, 60-40 against, or being evenly divided. An index as high as 50 indicates the groups being compared are behaving rather differently since it may be produced by a roll call on which one group votes 75-25 against.

In the 1959 session there were 414 controversial roll calls, and 241 (58%) of them were party votes. Indices of likeness for all 241

TABLE 4
INDICES OF LIKENESS FOR PARTY VOTES, 1959 SESSION, OHIO HOUSE OF REPRESENTATIVES

Range	*Votes* %	*(N)*	*Range*	*Votes* %	*(N)*
100–90	1	(2)	49–40	17	(40)
89–80	1	(2)	39–30	13	(32)
79–70	5	(13)	29–20	15	(36)
69–60	11	(26)	19–10	10	(23)
59–50	10	(25)	9–0	17	(42)
TOTAL	28	(68)		72	(173)

party votes are shown in Table 4. What this table says, for example, is that 10% of the party votes, or 25 out of 241, had indices of likeness between 50 and 59 and that 17% of the party votes, or 42 out

[20]A description of the index of likeness is provided by Lee Anderson, *et al., op. cit.*, pp. 44–45. Indices for the 1959 session were calculated with a computer using the ACCUM and CORR programs furnished by Anderson, *et al.*, pp. 176–191.

of 241, had indices between 0 and 9. The groups being compared are, of course, Republicans and Democrats.

It appears that party votes are common and that nearly three-fourths of them (72%) yield low indices of likeness, i.e. below 50. Furthermore, some 27% of the party votes yield very low indices of likeness, i.e. below 20. There is no escaping the existence of party voting blocs. There may be other blocs too, but all that is required to satisfy criterion three is that there be some bloc structure. And there is certainly that.

The fourth criterion is that some roles urge a measure of deference for the facilitators, arrangers, or majority-builders in the legislature. Since the bloc structure is partisan, at least to an important degree, the question is one of attitudes toward partisan leaders and partisan majorities. Three items in the 1963 study are pertinent:

7. A legislator should support the plans and programs of a governor belonging to his own party whether or not the governor can impose rewards and punishments.
8. A legislator should vote with the majority of his own party in the legislature whenever the majority of one party opposes the majority of another, and he should do this as a matter of principle and not merely as a matter of self-interest.
9. To get ahead in the legislature, a member must support the stands taken by a majority of his own party.

Members were asked to answer according to the following scheme: 1 — agree; 2 — tend to agree; 3 — undecided; 4 — tend to disagree; 5 — disagree. The assumption implicit in item 7, that the governor is a partisan leader, should surprise no one. Items 7 and 8 may be considered self-perceptions of role and item 9 perception of role by others. Results by party are set forth in Table 5.

Thus, 38% of the Republicans (12% + 26%) think that they should help a Republican governor whether or not he can hurt or help them. The percentage of Democrats sharing this view is almost exactly the same (14% + 23% = 37%). The proportion of Republicans who think they should go along with a majority of their own party as a matter of proper behavior is 58%, and for the Democrats the proportion is rather different, 37%. A large party difference is revealed as well, when the question is conformity to party

TABLE 5
ROLES RELATING TO GUBERNATORIAL LEADERSHIP AND SUPPORT FOR PARTY MAJORITIES, 1963 SESSION, OHIO GENERAL ASSEMBLY

Item		*Answers* (%)						
		1	**2**	**3**	**4**	**5**	**NA**	**T****
7.	R*	12	26	2	17	35	8	100
	D*	14	23	0	17	43	3	100
8.	R	26	32	5	11	20	7	101
	D	20	17	9	11	40	3	100
9.	R	22	37	2	14	17	10	102
	D	29	14	0	17	37	3	100

***Rep. N=65; Dem. N=35.**
****Failure of totals to equal 100 is due to rounding.**

position and success, or non-conformity and possibly lack of success. The Republicans are about two to one of the opinion that conformity to party position is the price of success, but more Democrats than not think it unnecessary to conform to party positions to get ahead. The difference between the Republican and Democratic response on item 9 is perhaps related to the fact that the Republicans are the usual majority and the Democrats the usual minority. If such is the case, the conclusion is that majority party members tend to conform to majority party positions and minority party members need to decide whether supporting the minority leadership or playing along with the majority party leadership is the best way to have some effect.

But the unexpected must be set forth separately. Neither party in the legislature is willing to say that it accepts gubernatorial leadership even when the partisan relations are right, and there is no appreciable difference between Republicans and Democrats on this score. This is more than a little odd since most observers think that each party supports its own governors when they have a program. The assumed loyalty is not absolute, but it is thought to be a major fact of legislative life. Hence, it seems that legislators do not necessarily see themselves as troops for gubernatorial armies; but that something intervenes. Perhaps it is the influence of those in the party who do accept gubernatorial leadership, and perhaps it is the legislative leadership which acts for its executive partner.

Insofar as the criterion is concerned (roles supporting partisan positions), the answer is not clear. Gubernatorial leadership is subject to scrutiny. Conformity to party positions is not to be presumed either. Success in the legislature is thought by a substantial number to be related to loyalty to their partisan leaders, but the idea is much less than universal. What seems to be a fair conclusion is that there is enough support for gubernatorial leadership and party positions to give both governors and partisan leaders a good chance of success, if they can support a presumption in their favor.

The fifth criterion for a well functioning legislature is that members have some personal associations which support their position in the legislative system. Since their position tends strongly to be a partisan one, the following are appropriate questions: (a) are a legislator's friendships outside the legislature consistent with his party membership; that is, are his non-legislative friends members of his party? and (b) are a legislator's friendships with other legislators consistent with his party membership; that is, are his legislative friends members of his party?

Data collected in my 1963 study are again relevant. Specifically, legislators were asked these two questions:

10. In general, how many of your closest friends identify themselves with your party?
    All ______ Most ______ Some ______
    Few ______ None ______ Don't Know ______
11. How many of your closest friends in the *legislature* belong to your party?
    All ______ Most ______ Some ______
    Few ______ None ______ Don't Know ______

Replies are summarized in Table 6.

It may be seen that nearly two-thirds of the Republicans (62%) report that all or most of their friends are also Republicans; and none of them confess that they have few or no Republicans among their closest friends. On the other hand, only about one-third of the Democrats say that all or most of their closest friends are

TABLE 6
FRIENDSHIP OF LEGISLATORS OUTSIDE AND INSIDE THE LEGISLATURE, MEMBERS OF 1963 OHIO GENERAL ASSEMBLY

Answer	*Question 10*		*Question 11*	
	Dem. (*N=35*) (%)	*Rep.* (*N=65*) (%)	*Dem.* (*N=35*) (%)	*Rep.* (*N=65*) (%)
All	3	2	3	3
Most	31	60	34	51
Some	43	31	26	9
Few	17	0	0	2
None	3	0	6	3
Don't know	3	6	9	5
No answer	0	2	23	28
TOTAL*	100	101	101	101

***Failure of totals to equal 100 is due to rounding.**

Democrats; and one-fifth admit that there are few or no Democrats among their closest friends. It may be inferred that the partisan identity of Republican legislators is re-enforced by their social relationships but that Democratic legislators tend not to receive the same re-enforcement.

With regard to friendships among legislators, it must be pointed out that there is a fairly large number of "no answers" and also some "don't knows," which is scarcely believable. If respondents in these categories are eliminated, 80% of the Republicans say that all or most of their closest friends in the legislature are Republicans and only 7% say that there are few or no Republicans among their closest legislative friends. Again, replies from Democrats are contrasting. Just over half of them (54%) say that all or most of their closest friends in the legislature are Democrats, but only 8% report that there are few or no Democrats among their closest friends. It may be inferred (cautiously because of the large number of "no answers") that Republicans find their identity as Republicans re-enforced by their friendships in the legislature, but that Democrats tend not to receive the same re-enforcement. However, the contrast between the two parties is less great than when the point of comparison is friendships outside the legislature.

The difference in the friendship patterns of Republicans and Democrats is intriguing. In the course of a study of county party leaders in Ohio, of which I was a co-author, the same difference was observed.[21] An explanation which came to mind, although we did not report it, was that Republican and Democratic county leaders had about the same social and economic characteristics and that their social status was relatively high. Hence, both moved on a level more populated by Republicans than Democrats; so it would not be surprising if Democratic leaders associated more with Republicans than vice versa. But the same explanation will not do with regard to differences in friendship patterns in the legislature. The consequence is that the explanation just made in terms of social status is weakened, and the mystery somewhat deepened.

The sixth and last criterion to be applied in this discussion is that a legislature existing within a generally democratic system apply the principle of majority rule. The principle may be frustrated by the internal processes of the legislature or by an election system which does not produce a majority for an actual, existing legislative bloc when it gets a majority of the votes cast for legislative candidates. Insofar as internal processes in the Ohio legislature are concerned, they are majoritarian. Dilatory tactics are not very effective on the floor, and the committee system responds to the wishes of the leaders of the majority party. To be sure, the partisan leadership per se does not have an opinion on many matters; and a committee chairman backed by a majority of his committee may go his own way on "policy" matters, that is, matters on which the leadership has taken a definitive position.

The election system as it has operated in recent years has over-represented rural counties[22] in the House. They have usually cast about one-third of the votes and have won about one-half the seats. But what criterion six requires is that the election system provide legislative majorities for existing, not hypothetical, legislative blocs;

[21] Flinn and Wirt, *op. cit.*, pp. 90–92.

[22] The definition of rural is non-metropolitan, and metropolitan counties are those classified as standard metropolitan areas or as parts of SMSAs by the Census Bureau.

and urban and rural blocs are not present or not particularly important. It is party blocs which are obvious and important. The test then is this: Does the election system give the Republicans or Democrats a majority when they deserve it on the principle of majority rule? Examination of every House election from and including 1948 through 1964 shows that the party winning the support of a majority of the voters has won a legislative majority with the exception of 1964 when the Democrats had a popular but not a legislative majority.[23] Hence, it is not possible to write-off the election system as a total failure according to the criterion employed here. In any event, it has been scrapped as a result of court action; and a system using districts of approximately equal population went into effect in 1966.

IV. CONCLUSIONS

First, the Ohio legislature gets high marks by the criteria I have used. The Republican legislative party by these criteria appears to be somewhat stronger than the Democratic, but the difference is not great. I do not mean to say that the legislature necessarily does what I would like it to do, but that is not an objective test, anyway.

Second, I am willing to be tentative about the substantive conclusion that the Ohio General Assembly appears to be a very successful legislative system. My hypotheses concerning the good functioning of legislatures could be incorrect or, more likely, my list may not include some other important and perhaps more important hypotheses. There could be trouble with some operational statements, and the evidence could be less than decisive.

But I am not willing to be tentative about the approach that has been taken. Evaluation of legislative performance requires clear and explicit statement of the conditions or characteristics of successful legislative operation. Whether these conditions or characteristics

[23]A much fuller report of this analysis is given in two studies cited before: "The Outline of Ohio Politics" and "The Election System and The Party System."

are present or absent, then, needs to be established by some process of controlled observation.

Finally, I am not willing to be tentative about my belief that proper evaluation and a fair understanding should precede legislative reform. Too often, it seems that the prescriptions of legislative mechanics do not arise from a just appreciation of the state legislative institution, which is to me an impressive one. And that takes me back to where I began.

Selection of Ohio Appellate Judges: A Case Study in Invisible Politics

Kathleen L. Barber

AMID A WELTER OF PROPOSALS FOR CONSTITUTIONAL CHANGE IN Ohio is an articulate and well-organized campaign by the Ohio Bar Association, backed by the American Judicature Society, to alter the judicial article by submitting a so-called Missouri Plan type of selection of judges for the present elective system. The arguments made by the proponents of change are cast in terms of getting better judges and taking the judges out of politics.[1] A survey of the literature has revealed no contemporary defenders of the present system outside of the legislature, although at least one bar association, the Cuyahoga County Bar, is committed by its constitution to the elective judiciary.[2]

A plan similar to the Ohio Bar Association's current proposal was defeated by the voters of Ohio, by a two-to-one margin, in 1938;

My thanks go to Professor Sheldon Gawiser and Fr. Paul Woefl, S. J., of John Carroll University, for valuable criticism and assistance, and to Vincent d'Alessandro, for collection of judicial election statistics. Any errors are, of course, my own.

[1]Glenn R. Winters, "The Merit Plan for Judicial Selection and Tenure—Its Historical Development," *Duquesne Law Review,* 7 (1968–1969), 77–78.

[2]H. G. Binns and C. K. Clark, "Pro and Con Commentary on Proposal for Selection and Tenure of Judges," *Ohio Bar,* 30 (1957), 920–921.

two years before it was adopted in Missouri and thence became known as the Missouri Plan. In 1967, the Ohio House of Representatives eliminated this judicial selection feature from the Modern Courts Amendment before it was presented to the people for approval, and in March 1970, the Ohio House defeated a proposed constitutional amendment embodying the same features.

The Constitution of Ohio provides for the election of judges of the supreme court, the court of appeals, and the courts of common pleas for terms of not less than six years (Art. IV, sec. 6). Under the election laws of Ohio, these judges are nominated in partisan primaries and elected on nonpartisan ballots at the regular state election in November of the even-numbered years.[3] Vacancies are filled by gubernatorial appointment, but the appointee must run for the unexpired term at the next general election.[4]

The Ohio Bar Association proposes to replace this method of selection with a combination of appointment and election. As the proposal is presently drawn up, the governor would appoint judges to vacancies on the supreme court and the courts of appeals from panels of nominees submitted to him by a judicial nominating commission. This commission, whose size, selection, compensation, qualifications, and terms are to be determined by law, would be constitutionally limited to not more than one-half from the same political party, and not less than one-half members of the bar of Ohio. After service for five or six years (the original term expiring in the odd-numbered year), such judges would submit their names to the electorate for a referendum on the question of continuation in office. A majority of those voting on the question would retain or reject a judge. If a judge is rejected, his position on the bench is filled by gubernatorial appointment from another nominating

[3]Ohio Stat. 3513.01 (4785-67). Independent nominations by petition are permitted, Ohio Stat. 3513.28 (4785-91a), but this method has not been used in recent years. Ohio Stat. 3505.04.

[4]Ohio Constitution, Art. IV, sec. 13. If the appointment occurs less than forty days before the next general election, the appointment does not expire until the following general election. If the vacancy occurs in a term which has less than a year from the date of the next general election to run, the appointee finishes the term without facing the electorate.

commission panel.[5] The three key features, in summary, are: the nominating commission, gubernatorial appointment, and the popular referendum in which the judge runs on his record. This plan, with minor variations, is known as the Missouri Plan, the Merit Plan, and the Nonpartisan Court Plan. Thirteen states have adopted some form of this plan for supreme court judges, five states use it for the intermediate appellate courts, and in sixteen states some trial courts or courts of limited and special jurisdiction are staffed by this method.[6]

The present study has been undertaken because of two serious deficiencies in the framework of debate about judicial selection. First, the theoretical premises of alternative means of judicial selection have not been subjected to rigorous analysis; and second, the debate has been conducted in a factual vacuum. The empirical results of partisan nomination and nonpartisan election have not been examined. The Ohio Bar implies, by campaigning so ardently for change in method to "improve the quality" of the judiciary, that the judges in the state are unqualified for their positions. The bar has not produced evidence of corruption nor standards by which incompetence should be measured. No analysis of the appellate decisions of Ohio judges and Missouri judges, for example, has been made available to the public to demonstrate the inferiority of elected judges. The legal profession has not provided a definition of the "politics" it seeks to eliminate from the selection of the judiciary. If we assume that, by "politics," partisan behavior is meant, again systematic evidence is lacking.

Few political scientists have plowed the field of state judicial selection. Judicial behavioralism has suffered from an over-concentration on the United States Supreme Court, although the power and visibility of that bench at the pinnacle of the political system make such a preoccupation understandable. In recent years a growing body of single-state judicial studies has been developing, largely

[5]Ohio House of Representatives, H. J. R. No. 27, 108th General Assembly, Regular Session (1969–1970).

[6]American Judicature Society, Report No. 18, "The Extent of Adoption of the Non-Partisan, Appointive-Elective Plan for the Selection of Judges" (Chicago: American Judicature Society, 1969), mimeo., 4 pp.

directed toward analysis of judicial output and collegial behavior. Hypotheses relating these variables to the method of judicial selection are few; for the most part, investigators have built on the conventional wisdom about judicial nominations, elections, and appointments. Those few cross-state studies which have been done suffer from the variety in methods of state judicial selection and from the differences in political culture which diminish comparability.

The purpose, then, of the present study is two-fold: first, to provide an analytical framework for debate within which a dialogue between the legal profession and political scientists about the premises which underlie alternative methods of judicial selection can develop; and second, to test some of the folklore about judicial selection by analysis of empirical data drawn from the universe of Ohio judicial elections for appellate court positions from 1960 to 1968.

I. ANALYTICAL FRAMEWORK

The most common analytical dichotomy regarding judicial selection is made between executive appointment, the method used in the original states as a continuation of colonial practice, and popular election, an alternative which swept much of the country in the middle of the nineteenth century as a component of Jacksonian democracy. Each of these categories is then subdivided. Elective states are sorted out by partisan and nonpartisan ballot; appointive states by simple appointment, with confirmation by another body as in the federal judiciary, and some variation of the Missouri Plan.

The central conceptual argument of this paper is that such a dichotomy is false because it ignores the central political features of all four types of selection. The meaningful choices are to be found in "visible" methods of selection on the one hand, and "invisible" methods on the other. "Visible" is used here to mean that the relevant public (those who are interested in the work of the courts) can see, know, or understand how judges are selected and can therefore hold them (or those who select them) accountable for their activities, if they wish to do so. "Invisible" refers to methods of selection which confuse or keep in ignorance the relevant public, so that neither direct nor indirect accountability of judges is possible. The most common methods of judicial selection must then be reassembled under different headings: Partisan election and simple executive appointment with confirmation by another agency of state government are both "visible" methods of selection. Nonpartisan election and variations of the Missouri Plan are both "invisible" methods. A fifth method of state judicial selection is omitted from this analysis: legislative election, a method used by Connecticut, Rhode Island, South Carolina, and Virginia. This method, which partakes of both visible and invisible features, is a special case, not currently relevant to Ohio.

This changed framework of analysis obviously raises more questions than it settles. The concept of accountability is made the crucial standard of differentiation, a concept derived from democratic theory. Yet in America, from the elite notions of Alexander Hamilton through de Tocqueville's analysis to the present day, the judiciary has been regarded as a separate kind of governmental structure designed to protect the people from the evils of democracy (self-rule) and, therefore, insulated from accountability.

De Tocqueville's trenchant observations of American life were made in the 1830s when the elective judiciary was a popular item on reformers' lists. He gravely feared that this innovation would destroy first judicial independence and then "the democratic republic itself." For it would reduce the influence of the lawyers, the only aristocratic element in society capable of saving the people from themselves. The extraordinary political powers of lawyers and judges were "mitigations of the tyranny of the majority." Theodore Becker makes a modern restatement of this notion suggesting that the judiciary fills our need for "a bevy of Platonic guardians to guard the ramparts from mob-rule-acting-as-and-through-legislature."[7]

[7]Alexis de Tocqueville, *Democracy in America* (New York: Vintage Books, 1954), Vol. I, pp. 288–289; Theodore L. Becker, "On Science, Political Science, and Law," *American Behavioral Scientist*, 7 (1963), 12.

The notion of the courts as apolitical instrumentalities is as old as the blindfolded Astraea, holding her scales of justice. The high priests of the ancients examined the entrails of birds to find signals of justice from the gods. Blackstone, whose impact on the American legal tradition was profound, insisted that judges "found" the law and did not make it, a view expressed in classic terms by Justice Roberts:

> It is sometimes said that the court assumes a power to overrule or control the action of the people's representatives. This is a misconception . . . . When an act of Congress is appropriately challenged in the courts as not conforming to the constitutional mandate the judicial branch of the Government has only one duty,—to lay the article of the Constitution which is invoked beside the statute which is challegend and to decide whether the latter squares with the former. All the court does, or can do, is to announce its considered judgment upon the question . . . . This court neither approves nor condemns any legislative policy. [*United States v. Butler,* 297 U.S. 1 (1936).]

This concept of judicial function is known as the "phonographic" or "mechanical"[8] theory of justice.

A contrasting legal philosophy is found in common law tradition, the law *made* and not discovered by judges.[9] The courts deal daily with factual situations for which there is no pre-existing rule; as rapidly as the judges develop new rules, conditions in society change, creating the need for incremental modification of the new judicial wisdom. Holmes' introduction to *The Common Law* bears repeating:

> The life of the law has not been logic; it has been experience. The felt necessities of the time, the prevalent moral and political theories, intuitions of public policy, avowed or unconscious, even the prejudices which judges share with their fellow men, have had a good deal more

[8]Morris R. Cohen, *Law and the Social Order* (New York: Harcourt, Brace, 1933), p. 113; Charles G. Haines, "General Observations on the Effects of Personal, Political and Economic Influences in the Decisions of Judges," *Illinois Law Review,* 17 (1922), 96.

[9]"The whole of the rules of equity and nine-tenths of the rules of common law have in fact been made by the judges," L. J. Mellish in *Allen v. Jackson,* 1 Ch.D. 399 (1875), at 405, quoted in Haines, *op. cit.,* p. 100.

> to do than the syllogism in determining the rules by which men should be governed.[10]

Called by Haines the "free legal decision" theory,[11] this concept accommodates the creative policy making function of the judiciary. Building on this notion, the judicial behavioralists of the 1950s began to collect bits and pieces of empirical evidence from which a political theory of the judicial system could be developed. The collection of data for such an effort has not been unimpeded. The normative assumption that judicial decision making is a process of logical deduction from legal premises has led to the suppression of factual inquiry.

For example, from 1914 to 1916, a public statistician in the court system of New York City kept records on the individual magistrates. Comparative tables of rates of conviction were published for these three years, but the rates varied so widely among the judges within classes of similar cases that the city discontinued not only publishing but even keeping such records. It was better for the public, and for the city government itself, not to know the degree to which the individual value preferences influenced the allocation of justice.[12]

This fear of public knowledge of personal influence on justice persists. Theodore Becker warns us that to destroy popular faith in the objectivity of the courts may undermine the political system: "Is it not possible that the 'myth' of the 'objectivity' of the Court and courts is quite functional for this or for any society? What if it is a ***key*** function for stability and/or equilibrium?" Becker argues that if the "legitimizing and checking functions" of the judiciary play a vital role in maintaining the political system, then for political scientists to prove and popularize their proof that judges are policy-makers "could be positively disastrous."[13]

By 1970, however, the political concept of the judicial function

---

[10]O. W. Holmes, Jr., *The Common Law* (Boston: Little, Brown & Co., 1881), p. 1.

[11]Haines, *op. cit.*, p. 96.

[12]*Ibid.*, pp. 105–106.

[13]Becker, *op. cit.*, p. 12.

is well-established among most political scientists, if not among lawyers or judges.[14] Legal decisions are recognized as "social events with social causes and consequences,"[15] and adjudication is recognized as an alternative to legislative policy making or violence as a means for settling conflict in a political system. Demands are made on the judicial system in the form of litigation, and conversion of those demands occurs in the decision making process. The judges are actors charged with special responsibilities, and their decisions, the outputs of the judicial system, allocate values in society such as opportunity, liberty, money, protection, or representation in other types of decision making. Like other political decision making, this allocation of values is differential; that is, some individuals and groups are favored and others are disadvantaged. These policy outputs are called "justice," but this justice is neither final nor irrevocable because, like other political decisions, judicial determinations of policy can be overturned or modified by other actors and institutions in the system: higher courts, legislatures, executives (for example, by pardons or by non-enforcement), and administrators. The consequences of the decisions both for the immediate parties and for society become "feedback;" the outputs of the courts increase or decrease the demands made on the political system generally and the support generated for it.[16]

The political nature of the judicial role is apparent not only in the settlement of individual disputes, but also in the extraordi-

---

[14]In a cross-state study based on interviews with state supreme court judges, Vines identified judicial role perceptions as "ritualist," "adjudicator," "policy-maker," and "administrator." Fifty-eight percent of the judges interviewed saw their role as "ritualist," i.e., following precedent, interpreting law by impartial and pre-existent norms, avoiding policy commitments on problems. In contrast, only 31% viewed their role in policy-making terms. Kenneth N. Vines, "The Judicial Role in the American States," in Joel B. Grossman and Joseph Tannenhaus, *Frontiers of Judicial Research* (New York: John Wiley & Sons, 1969), pp. 468–469.

[15]Louis Mayo and Ernest Jones, "Legal-Policy Decision Process: Alternative Thinking and the Predictive Function," *George Washington Law Review,* 33 (1964), 318.

[16]For further discussion of a systems model of the judiciary, see Glendon Schubert, *Judicial Policy-Making* (Chicago: Scott, Foresman & Co., 1965), pp. 3–4.

nary power of judicial review. Recent elections in Wisconsin and California[17] have been fought in the context of hostile public reaction to the policy content of state court decisions. In these elections, supporters of the judges seeking to retain office defended not their decisions but the institutional norms of the judiciary, specifically the independence of the courts.

This defense, successful in Wisconsin but unsuccessful in California, illuminates the special nature of the judicial role. While judicial decision making must be understood in a political context, the courts differ from other political institutions in significant ways. Respect for legal precedent diminishes the decision making latitude of judges; that is, policy innovations must be rationalized by former decisions in similar situations. The concept of judicial role restricts the freedom of judges to make policy in two ways. Externally, judicial discretion is limited by public expectations that the actions of courts are "law-oriented," that is, based on objective principles. Internally, judicial discretion is limited by the socialization process of legal training which teaches potential judges that they ought to be guided by impartial principles. Professional norms as well as legal training emphasize the special restrictions on judicial role. The American Bar Association's Canons of Judicial Ethics prohibit judges from engaging in political activity and specifically forbid revealing opinions about a case before the decision is announced.

Becker makes a useful distinction between the impartiality and the independence required of a judge: "As the judge is dependent upon the law (bound to interpret and apply it), he is impartial; as he would resist those in other positions (or those who support

---

[17]Jack Ladinsky and Allen Silver, "Popular Democracy and Judicial Independence: Electorate and Elite Reactions to Two Wisconsin Supreme Court Elections," *Wisconsin Law Review* (1967), p. 129; Mark A. Sullivan, "Appointment of Judges, The Key to a Qualified and Independent Judiciary," *New Jersey Law Journal*, 90 (February 9, 1967), 87. A majority of the California Supreme Court justices were defeated on a yes/no ballot after declaring Proposition 14 (invalidating California's open housing law) unconstitutional. In the 1970 June primary, Judge Gitelson, who had ordered the integration of Los Angeles schools, was forced into a run-off election by a challenger named Kennedy who attacked the integration decision. In November, Kennedy defeated Judge Gitelson. *New York Times*, November 8, 1970.

them) who would have him violate this dependency, he is independent."[18] Although placing adjudication in the conversion process of the political system, Easton recognizes its special characteristics that cut "conflict down to a minimum; the adversary proceeding is limited to the actual parties to a dispute; the parties believe that the rules by which their dispute is to be settled already exist, have something to do with justice, and have been sanctioned by the community."[19]

Finally, there are structural protections of the independence of the judiciary that tend to reinforce the concept of judicial isolation from political pressures. Tenure tends to be for longer terms than other public officials enjoy, sometimes for life, and salaries are protected from legislative retaliation.

Judges, then, are policy makers of a special sort, participants in the political process but restricted by the expectations of their relevant publics and by the legal and professional norms which define their role. Not all judicial roles are alike, however. The level of the court is significantly associated with the degree of difference between judicial and other political decision making. The trial judge and the appellate judge differ in role, tasks, working procedures, and prestige, sometimes called judicial majesty. Trial courts dispose of particular controversies, while appellate courts deal more often with questions which involve developing new law. It is the difficult and ambiguous cases, in which precedent is less likely to be clearly applicable, that are appealed and enable or even require the higher bench to shape the law. The appellate court, says Mayers,

> is in effect presenting a commentary or gloss on some traditional doctrine, or on some statutory provision, amplifying it, refining it, distinguishing it from some related rule. Thus our legal rules, both traditional and statutory, are subjected to a ceaseless process of re-evaluation and minor modification, sometimes of erosion, sometimes of accretion. The name by which a rule is known may remain unchanged for

---

[18]Theodore Becker, *Comparative Judicial Politics* (Chicago: Rand, McNally and Co., 1970), p. 145.

[19]David Easton, *A Systems Analysis of Political Life* (New York: John Wiley & Sons, 1965), pp. 265–266.

decades, but meanwhile its content may, by almost imperceptible steps, have been materially changed.[20]

Trial courts differ from appellate courts not only in exercising a lesser degree of policy making responsibility, but also in having a quantitatively greater impact on the political system. Because more individuals come into contact with the trial courts, and more disputes are settled there, the quality of justice dispensed at the lower levels of the judiciary may have more bearing on the legitimacy of the judicial process than that provided in the upper courts.[21] The particularistic nature of the judicial proceedings at the trial level creates multiple favors which the judge may dispense, and judicial patronage, in the form of selection of auxiliary court personnel, is most available in the courts of the first instance. The potential for partiality and personality is greater in the trial courts and may require the consideration of different standards for judicial selection. Mayers, a legal scholar opposed to the partisan election of judges, suggests that partisan selection for state appellate judges is "less serious" than for trial judges. He emphasizes that in the appellate courts the judges are subject to fewer pressures for political favors, in fact have fewer favors to dispense, make collegial decisions so that one judge cannot control the outcome of a case, and tend to be insulated from politics by the "aura of power, dignity and remoteness" of the appellate environment.[22] Dolbeare, a political scientist, concluded more strongly that the policy orientation of the upper courts should lead to programmatic evaluation of judicial candidates. Staffing the trial courts, he found, brought into play the *extractive* characteristics of local pol-

[20]Mayers, *op. cit.*, p. 348.

[21]In an excellent study of trial courts in a New York county of over one million population, Dolbeare found that only 7% of the total case load was eventually resolved in a manner different from the decision of the trial court, although 23% of all cases were appealed. Kenneth M. Dolbeare, *Trial Courts in Urban Politics* (New York: John Wiley & Sons, 1967), p. 82. On the question of legitimacy, Stafford emphasizes the importance of the trial court level: "For all practical purposes, the court of limited jurisdiction is not only the court of last resort, *it is the court of lasting impression.*" Charles F. Stafford, "Public's View of the Judicial Role," *Judicature*, 52 (August–September, 1968), 73.

[22]Mayers, *op. cit.*, pp. 387, 395.

itics generally, based on concern for jobs, contracts, power, and patronage, characteristics unrelated to the making of policy.[23]

The Ohio Bar Association plan reverses this order of priorities, providing a new method of selection for the appellate courts in an attempt to remove what we have shown to be the more policy-oriented judges from "politics," and leaving to the discretion of the legislature inclusion of the common pleas judges in the plan.[24] Because of this restriction in the Ohio Bar proposal, and because of time limitations for the collection of data, this investigation concentrates, from this point forward, on the selection of the appellate judges who exercise a qualitatively greater influence on the political system as policy making groups, developing and shaping the law as they deal with the small but significant proportion of controversies that reach them. This research decision postpones but does not obviate the need for a comprehensive inquiry, both conceptual and factual, into the variables associated with the selection of trial judges in Ohio.

II. EXPLANATION OF JUDICIAL BEHAVIOR

Since judges, deciding cases in the same legal-institutional framework, with access to the same body of legal precedent, according to the same collegial rules of the game, can and often do arrive at conflicting opinions, the student of judicial selection is compelled to ask if there are ways of predicting judicial propensities. Are there characteristics of personality, social background, or political affiliation of potential judges that would enable those who staff the bench (whether voters or appointing agencies) to influence the outputs of the courts?

The search for the wellsprings of judicial behavior has been underway at least since the publication of Cardozo's *Nature of the*

---

[23]Dolbeare, *op. cit.*, p. 124. See also Wallace S. Sayre and Herbert Kaufman, *Governing New York City: Politics in the Metropolis* (New York: Russell Sage Foundation, 1960), pp. 538ff. for patronage aspects of the local judiciary.

[24]Ohio House of Representatives, H.J.R. No. 27, 108th General Assembly, Regular Session, 1969–1970.

Judicial Process.[25] The attempt to identify the influence of personality factors on judges' opinions has yielded unsatisfactory results.[26] Few propositions are testable by means available to students of the problem, since judges are understandably reluctant to submit to psychoanalysis.[27] Interviewing judges as an alternative method of investigating personality factors[28] is limited by the kinds of conclusions that can be drawn from the responses. The judge's personality is filtered through his own perceptions and willingness to make revelations to curious investigators. If a judge is unaware of a given attitude, or if he is aware of it and it conflicts with judicial norms so that he is unable or unwilling to admit that it is related to his decision making, interviewing cannot reach important influences on behavior.

Scattered findings about the use of social background factors as predictors of judicial behavior have also yielded somewhat limited results. Investigators in this field recognize the inferential quality of conclusions, and do not assert a cause and effect relationship between background factors and judicial voting behavior.[29] But the

[25]New Haven: Yale University Press, 1921. See also the simple but heuristic model of judicial behavior in Haines, *op. cit.*, p. 116.

[26]Glendon Schubert claims to have demonstrated the influence of a personality factor which he calls "pragmatism/dogmatism" in judicial decision making. See his *Judicial Mind* (Evanston, Ill.: Northwestern University Press, 1965), p. 259. For a critical discussion of his conclusions, see Martin Shapiro, "Political Jurisprudence," *Kentucky Law Journal,* 52 (1964), 329.

[27]Jerome Frank discusses this problem in *Law and the Modern Mind* (New York: Coward-McCann, 1930). See also his *Courts on Trial* (Princeton: Princeton University Press, 1949) for the recommendation that judges be psychoanalyzed before being permitted to take on judicial duties. David J. Danelski has analyzed United States chief justices according to the personality types identified by Karen Horney (compliant, aggressive, and detached), but the findings relate more to the process of leadership in a particular small group than to judicial opinion formation. *Journal of Conflict Resolution,* 11 (1967), 71–86.

[28]Theodore L. Becker, "A Survey Study of Hawaiian Judges: The Effect on Decisions of Judicial Role Variation," *American Political Science Review,* 60 (1966), 677–680.

[29]Joel Grossman, "Social Backgrounds and Judicial Decisions: Notes for a Theory," *Journal of Politics,* 29 (1967), 335. The first major work in this area was John Schmidhauser, *The Supreme Court: Its Politics, Personalities and Procedures* (New York: Holt, Rinehart and Winston, 1960). See also Robert Heiberg, "Social Backgrounds of the Minnesota Supreme Court Justices, 1858–1968," *Minnesota Law Review,* 53 (April, 1969), 901–937.

attempt is made to identify the decisional propensities of judges by their socio-economic, religious, and ethnic identity. Religious affiliation and national origin were found to be significantly associated with the type of litigant favored in decision making by state and federal supreme court judges, but a replication of this study with federal courts of appeals judges and their decisions in the same type of cases failed to substantiate the pattern of behavior.[30]

The one variable which has turned up significant findings in a number of different judicial situations is political party affiliation. An exception to this generalization must be made for the United States Supreme Court, for reasons related to its special institutional norms. A crude but useful measure, party label appears to have an "organizing quality," to be an "effective 'net result' of many judges' hierarchies of values."[31] Party has been identified as a significant predictor of behavior in economic issues by federal courts of appeals judges,[32] and on many types of cases decided in the highest state appeals courts. In Nagel's study, the most comprehensive of its kind to date, Democratic judges on state supreme courts tended to favor: 1) the defense in criminal cases, 2) the administrative agency in business regulation cases, 3) the claimant in unemployment compensation cases, 4) a finding of constitutional violation in criminal-constitutional cases, 5) the government in tax cases, 6) the tenant in landlord-tenant cases, 7) the consumer in sales of goods cases, 8) the injured party in motor vehicle accident

---

[30]Stuart S. Nagel, "Testing Relations Between Judicial Characteristics and Judicial Decision-Making," *Western Political Quarterly,* 15 (1962), 425–437; and "Ethnic Affiliations and Judicial Propensities," *Journal of Politics,* 24 (1962), 92–110; Sheldon Goldman, "Voting Behavior on the United States Court of Appeals, 1961–1964," *American Political Science Review,* 60 (1966), 382.

[31]Sheldon Goldman, "Politics, Judges and the Administration of Justice," Unpublished Ph.D. Dissertation, Harvard University (1965), p. 267, quoted in Grossman, *op. cit.,* p. 346. A recent cross-national study of elite attitudes found that "background factors with the widest scope . . . were again associated with adult socialization experiences—especially occupation and party affiliation." Lewis J. Edinger and Donald D. Searing, "Social Background in Elite Analysis: A Methodological Inquiry," *American Political Science Review,* 61 (1967), 436.

[32]Goldman, "Voting Behavior on the United States Courts of Appeals, 1961–1964," *op. cit.*

cases, and 9) the employee in employee injury cases. Republican judges tend to favor the opposite party. It is not suggested that the party affiliation determines the vote of a judge in a particular case, but that personal values lead a judge both to his party affiliation and to his decisional propensities. However, party affiliation may have an indirect effect as "a feedback reinforcement on his value system" which in turn affects decision making.[33]

Generalizing from the identity of the favored parties in the nine significant types of cases, Nagel argues that Democratic judges' decisions tend to favor a "viewpoint associated with interests of lower or less privileged economic or social groups in one's society and (to a less extent) with acceptance of long-range social change," while Republican judges' decisions reflect the "viewpoint associated with the interests of the upper or dominant groups and with resistance to long-range social change."[34] In these decision making propensities, judges resemble their fellow-partisans in the public at large, in Congress, and in the executive, as shown in other studies.

The power of party affiliation as a predictor of judicial voting behavior has been noted in analyses of Michigan Supreme Court decisions, in which Democratic judges were found to be more favorably inclined toward workmen's compensation claims and unemployment compensation claims[35] than Republican judges. In the course of judicial response to reapportionment controversies in Ohio and Michigan, 82% of the federal district judges and state supreme court justices who participated in legislative reapportionment decisions consistently voted to support the plan which was to the advantage of their political party.[36]

---

[33]Stuart S. Nagel, "Political Party Affiliation and Judges' Decisions," *American Political Science Review*, 55 (1961), 845, 847. See also Stuart S. Nagel, "Judicial Backgrounds and Criminal Cases," *Journal of Criminal Law, Criminology and Police Science*, 53 (1962), 333–339.

[34]*Ibid.*, p. 847.

[35]Glendon Schubert, *Quantitative Analysis of Judicial Behavior* (New York: Free Press of Glencoe, 1959), pp. 129–142; Sidney Ulmer, "The Political Party Variable in the Michigan Supreme Court," *Journal of Public Law*, 11 (1962), 352–362.

[36]Kathleen L. Barber, "Partisan Values in the Lower Courts: Reapportionment in Ohio and Michigan," *Case Western Reserve Law Review*, 22 (1969), 406.

The proposition that judicial voting behavior can be predicted by partisan affiliation has been subjected to rigorous critical analysis. Goldman, who found partisan affiliation a significant predictor of judicial voting on economic disputes, failed to find a corresponding factor in cases involving accused criminals or civil liberties.[37] Howard argues the importance of group interaction in the process of collegial decision making. Socialization to the bench, group strategy of conserving institutional power, and changes in personal perception of judges, may all intervene "between attitude and action and (qualify) both."[38] Although noting that "party identification and the socializing process of party activism may impart issue orientations which affect the decisions made by officeholders, including judges," Adamany notes factors which may diminish the importance of the party variable on the bench. Party becomes an "improper consideration" under the judicial rules of the game; the judge becomes concerned with different reference groups than those relevant to other public officeholding, particularly the legal profession and the newspapers, which also consider partisan influence improper in the courts. A certain degree of isolation from former associates occurs in the life of most judges, and the expectations of colleagues on the bench tend to shape a new judge's attitudes. Finally, the complexity of the particularistic controversies which reach appeals courts tends to reduce the applicability of party policy.[39]

Adamany's most significant contribution is the replication of the Michigan studies of Schubert and Ulmer with Wisconsin data. Workmen's compensation and unemployment compensation are economic issues which clearly suggest partisan conflict; Michigan and Wisconsin offer similar systems for investigation. Both states have strong, competitive, issue-oriented parties, financed by groups with coherent and opposed interests. In both states judges are elected in

---

[37]Goldman, "Voting Behavior on the U.S. Courts of Appeals, 1961–1964," *op. cit.*, p. 381.

[38]J. Woodford Howard, Jr., "On the Fluidity of Judicial Choice," *American Political Science Review*, 62 (1968), 43–46.

[39]David W. Adamany, "The Party Variable in Judges' Voting," *American Political Science Review*, 63 (1969), 59, 60.

the spring on a nonpartisan ballot, and the governor is empowered to fill vacancies. In both states the supreme court changed gradually during the period of the studies (1957–1966) from a Republican to a Democratic majority. The analysis of Wisconsin supreme court cases, however, shows no evidence of bloc party voting on the particular issues selected, and no increase in dissenting along party lines on the total caseload as the court became more Democratic.[40]

Adamany accounts for these divergent findings in Michigan and Wisconsin by three important differences. First, in Michigan judges are nominated by party conventions and in Wisconsin in nonpartisan primaries. This structural difference leads to the second factor, the effect of constituency. In Michigan, constituencies are highly partisan in their orientation to judicial elections, while in Wisconsin bipartisan groups support opposing judicial candidates. Thirdly, Wisconsin has a resident supreme court, whose members live in the state capital and work in adjacent offices where a high degree of informal interaction occurs. Michigan, on the other hand, has a non-resident court whose members live in different parts of the state and circulate their opinions in writing. Under the procedure used by the Michigan supreme court, the majority opinion becomes known only when every member has signed an opinion.[41] In Wisconsin, the processes of on-the-bench socialization are facilitated, while in Michigan, the potentiality for dissension is increased by procedure. The fact that the dissension falls along party lines in Michigan is related back to the partisan nomination of judges and to the partisan political culture.

Both conceptual and methodological problems persist in the exploration of the significance of party affiliation in judicial behavior. Contrasting findings from different states suggest the importance of diverse political cultures in arriving at normative conclusions about the "best method" of judicial selection. If party label is an accurate predictor of judicial voting, then it could be argued that voters are entitled to the knowledge of that label in elective systems. If judges make policy, it could be argued that

---

[40] Adamany, *op. cit.*, pp. 62, 65–68.
[41] *Ibid.*, pp. 62, 69, 72.

judges should be selected by means that enable the people for whom they make policy to hold them accountable.

Very little effort has been made to measure public attitudes toward the selection of judges or toward the judicial role in society. The fragmentary evidence available suggests popular ambivalence and inconsistency. A recent study showed that in response to the statement, "judges should be free from political pressure to insure that their decisions are impartial," 98.5% of the respondents agreed as to federal and state judges, and 97.6% agreed as to city and county judges, an extremely high consensus in favor of impartiality, reflecting a lack of perception of a representational role for judges. However, a majority of respondents also indicated that judges should be accountable for their actions. In response to the statement, "in a democracy judges should be accountable to the people for their official actions," 65.2–66.2% agreed with respect to the different levels of the judiciary.[42]

This popular ambivalence should not be surprising. The special case of judicial decision making, which involves limited political output, creates a systemic problem. Inevitably the conflict between judicial norms and political reality produces a state of tension between independence and responsiveness. In fact, for the judiciary to fulfill its complex function, this state of tension may be necessary. Hence the central normative question about methods of judicial selection is not, How do we take the courts out of politics? but What method of selection best accommodates the delicate balance between accountability and independence?

III. OHIO APPELLATE JUDGES AND THE ELECTORAL PROCESS

From 1802 until 1851, the judges of Ohio were selected by the legislature, a body believed to be singularly well-equipped to make the choices because of its proximity to the people. Advocates of

---

[42]Carl D. McMurray and Malcolm B. Parsons, "Public Attitudes Toward the Representational Roles of Legislators and Judges," *Midwest Journal of Political Science*, 9 (1965), 170, 171.

change at the constitutional convention in 1851 argued that the courts had become "undemocratic," because party service had become the indispensable qualification to win a judgeship. To restore the courts to the people, the new constitution provided for nomination of judges in party conventions and election on a partisan ballot, a structural feature widely adopted in the states in the afterglow of Jacksonian democracy. By the end of the century, the state courts were once again viewed as captives of the parties, and structural changes were sought to make them more democratic. The concepts of the Progressive movement at this time equated "more democratic" with eliminating politics from governing processes. The anti-party thrust of the Progressive philosophy led to the passage of the Nonpartisan Judiciary Act of 1911, the express purpose of which was to take "the judges out of politics."[43] The act required nonpartisan ballots for the election of judges, and rotation of judicial candidates' names on the ballot. The following year, a constitutional convention, to which a majority of Progressives had been elected by the people of Ohio, drew up a new judiciary section which required direct primary nomination of all elected officers, including judges except those nominated by petition [Ohio Constitution (1912), Art. V, Sec. 7]. With this change, the sixty-year tradition of a party judicial convention disappeared.

Like the structural changes which preceded them, primary nomination and the nonpartisan ballot were soon subjected to severe criticism. It was widely noted that "ability to get publicity rather than judicial fitness" had become the pathway to the Ohio bench.[44] Dean Dunmore of Western Reserve Law School noted that "when judicial candidates were selected in party conventions, much was left to be desired, but such conventions at their worst would not have selected some of the men who select themselves for the primaries and who sometimes gain sufficient publicity to secure nom-

[43]Francis R. Aumann, "Selection of Judges in Ohio," *University of Cincinnati Law Review,* 5 (1931), 409, 412. This article is the basis of this summary of the history of Ohio judicial selection.
[44]Aumann, *op. cit.*, p. 414.

ination and election."[45] The cycle of growing dissatisfaction with the quality of the judiciary and impetus for reform was repeated, this time culminating in the 1938 popular defeat of a constitutional amendment to substitute the appointive-elective method of selection which came to be known as the Missouri Plan. Contemporary analysis of the 1938 defeat of judicial reform has not been located. A search of the legal and political literature has turned up no systematic study of the qualifications or background characteristics of the judges of Ohio. In the absence of agreed-upon and measurable characteristics to ascertain the "quality" of judiciary chosen by different methods, reformers have continued to operate in the realm of speculation. Sketchy empirical evidence is available from other states that different selection systems create "varying informal requirements for office, give access to different groups, and grant special advantages to some aspirants."[46]

One of the most common assumptions about elective judiciaries is that the "normal" means of access to the bench is appointment to fill an unexpired term, followed by election due to the appointee's advantage of incumbency. Ohio, along with Arizona, Maryland, and Michigan, combines partisan nomination with nonpartisan election, a combination classified by Herndon as "semi-partisan" in a cross-state study based on judges of state supreme courts from 1948 to 1957. Although Herndon found that 56% of all elective state supreme court judges were initially appointed, in this period the proportion of appointments in individual states ranged from 12.5% in Alabama to 100% in Maryland, South Dakota, and Wyoming. When the states were classified as partisan, semi-partisan, and nonpartisan, he found that appointment increased as a means of initial access as the method decreased in degree of partisanship.[47] The high proportion of appointive judges reported in Herndon's study has

---

[45]Walter T. Dunmore, "Cleveland Bar's Influence in Judicial Elections," *Journal of the American Judicature Society,* 12 (1929), 178.

[46]Herbert Jacob, "The Effect of Institutional Differences in the Recruitment Process: The Case of State Judges," *Journal of Public Law,* 13 (1964), 106.

[47]James Herndon, "Appointment as a Means of Initial Access to Elective State Courts of Last Resort," *North Dakota Law Review,* 38 (1962), 67, 63.

been used by advocates of the Ohio Bar Association plan to support the elimination of elections for the Ohio judiciary.[48]

To test Herndon's proposition about the "normal" path to the bench, a tabulation was made of means of initial access of members of the Ohio supreme court from 1852 through 1968. Far from showing a majority of appointees who were subsequently elected, we find that in the entire history of the elective judiciary in Ohio, 18.6% of the supreme court judges were appointed (34 of the total of 183 accessions to the supreme court). Of the twenty-six appointees who stood for election for the remainder of the term, more than half were defeated by the people. A further finding is that the party of the appointing governor is significantly associated with an appointee's chances for subsequent election. Twelve of the

TABLE 1
OHIO SUPREME COURT APPOINTEES WHO RAN FOR ELECTION TO THE UNEXPIRED TERM, 1852–1968

Party of Appointing Governor	*Outcome of Election for the Unexpired Term*		
	Defeated	*Elected*	*Total*
Republican	3	9	12
Democratic	12	2	14
TOTAL	15	11	26

SOURCE: Tabulated from Ohio, *Official Roster of Federal, State, County Officers* (Columbus, O.: Secretary of State, 1970), pp. 106–112.

fourteen supreme court judges appointed by Democratic governors were defeated; only three of the twelve appointed by Republican governors suffered this fate. Table 1 shows supreme court appointees by party electoral success subsequent to appointment.

Current trends support the findings from the historical data. Of twenty-six total accessions to the Ohio supreme court from 1960 through 1968, four were by appointment (15.3%). Three of these four appointees had run for election to the unexpired term by 1968, and all three were defeated by the voters of Ohio. Significantly, all three were Democrats, appointed by Governor DiSalle.

[48]W. Donald Heisel and Iola O. Hessler, *State Government for Our Times* (Cincinnati, O.: Stephen H. Wilder Foundation, 1970), p. 92.

The fourth, a Republican appointed by Governor Rhodes, was endorsed by the electorate in 1970.[49]

Herndon's theory of the "normal" path to the bench is further disconfirmed with respect to Ohio by data on all appellate judges appointed in the years 1960–1968. Of a total of eighty-seven accessions to the Ohio courts of appeals in this period, fourteen (16.1%) were by appointment. The supreme court accessions added to those in the courts of appeals total to a summary tabulation of Ohio appellate judges, as shown in Table 2.

Fifteen of the eighteen appointees in this period ran for election to the unexpired term. Table 3 shows the voters' response to their candidacies. In contrast to the fate of a majority of supreme court justices for the historical period (1852–1968), a slight majority (53.3%) of the appellate judicial appointees in the 1960s were subsequently elected. However, the partisan pattern of voting in these contests is more pronounced, with 85.7% of the Democratic appointees defeated, and only 12.5% of the Republican appointees defeated.

It is clearly not the case in Ohio, as asserted by Heisel and Hessler, that "more than half of the judges serving on the supreme court and courts of appeals were originally made judges through appointment by the governor."[50] The appellate judiciary of Ohio is overwhelmingly elective in practice as well as in theory. The minority of appellate judges who gain access to the bench by appointment tend to be elected if they are Republican and are likely to face defeat if they are Democratic. In view of the nonpartisan ballot for the election of judges in Ohio, the fate of judicial appointees shows discrimination on the part of the voters which is not recognized in the conventional wisdom about judicial elections.

During the period of this study, a "gross shift" in partisan control, as defined in Herndon's study, occurred in Ohio when the

[49]Judge John W. Peck was actually appointed by Governor DiSalle in 1959, but has been included in this analysis because he ran for election to the unexpired term in 1960, the first of the five elections tabulated. Robert M. Duncan, the Ohio Supreme Court's first Negro justice, ran unopposed for the unexpired term.

[50]Heisel and Hessler, *op. cit.*, p. 92.

TABLE 2
OHIO APPELLATE JUDGES, BY MEANS OF ACCESSION, 1960–1968

	Elected	*Appointed*	*Total*
Supreme Court	15	4	19
Courts of Appeals	73	14	87
Total Number	88	18	106
Percent	83%	17%	100%

SOURCE: Calculated from Ted W. Brown, Secretary of State, *Ohio Election Statistics*, published as follows: 1959–1960 (Columbus, O.: F. J. Heer Printing Co., 1961), 1961–1962 (Columbus, O.: F. J. Heer Printing Co., 1963), 1963–1964 (Columbus, O.: Columbus Blank Book Co., 1965), 1965–1966 (Columbus, O.: Columbus Blank Book Co., 1967), 1967–1968 (Columbus, O.: National Graphics Corp., 1969).

Republican party won the governor's chair with 58.9% of the two-party vote in 1962. Herndon argues that the greater the shift in partisan control in a state, the smaller the percentage of appointed judges. The partisan shift in electoral sentiment in Ohio in 1962 may help to account for the voters' rejection of the defeated governor's appointees to the bench in 1960 and 1964, but the proportion of appointees (17% of total accessions) still falls far below the 62.1% Herndon reports in his cross-state sample of semi-partisan and nonpartisan elective judiciaries where gross shifts in partisan control had occurred.[51]

To explore further the relationship between gross shifts in partisan control, and the proportion of appointments in an elective judiciary, we will take the supreme court judges only, a limitation corresponding to Herndon's data, and will extend the time period to cover Ohio's elective judiciary (1852–1968). It was noted earlier that 18.6% of supreme court judges in Ohio gained initial access to the bench by appointment in this 116-year period. During this time span, there were seventeen shifts in partisan control in Ohio, out of a total of fifty-five gubernatorial elections. In only four of

[51]States were classified as "stable," meaning no shift in party control of the gubernatorial office; "proximate shift," referring to displacement of the party in office by the opposing party winning 50.1–54.9% of the vote; and "gross shift," measured by partisan displacement when the displacing party wins more than 55% of the statewide two-party vote. Herndon, *op. cit.*, pp. 69–70, Table 8, p. 71.

TABLE 3
OHIO APPELLATE COURT APPOINTEES WHO RAN FOR ELECTION TO THE UNEXPIRED TERM, 1960–1968

Party of Judge	*Outcome of Election for the Unexpired Term* Defeated	Elected	Total
Republican	1	7	8
Democratic	6	1	7
TOTAL	7	8	15

SOURCE: Tabulated from Ohio Election Statistics, *op. cit.*
Chi Square=7.84 p<.01

those did the displacing party's gubernatorial candidate win more than 55% of the vote.[52] It appears that the explanation of the low proportion of appointments in the elective judiciary of Ohio, supported in the sixties according to the hypothesis of gross shifts in partisan control, does not hold up over time.

IV. PARTICIPATION IN OHIO JUDICIAL ELECTIONS

Herndon's "normal" pattern of appointive access to the bench in elective judiciaries is posited on the assumption of an apathetic electorate, at least indifferent with respect to judicial elections. Hence the next proposition to be tested relates to participation. The conventional wisdom concerning judicial elections suggests that voters participate at significantly lower rates in judicial elections than in elections for executive and legislative office. Little measurement has been done of participation in judicial elections. For example, in a study of the Texas judicial system, Henderson and Sinclair note at the outset that since 50% of the state's appellate judges attained their position initially by appointment, the state has "primarily an appointive system."[53] The authors proceed to ignore

[52]Calculated from *Ohio Election Statistics*, 1967–1968, *op. cit.*, pp. 225–235.
[53]Bancroft C. Henderson and T. C. Sinclair, *Judicial Selection in Texas* (Houston: Public Affairs Research Center, University of Houston, 1964), p. 20.

the elected half of the judges, as well as the voters that chose them, and devote the rest of the study to the politics of appointment, the governor and the bar.

To test the hypothesis that participation in judicial electoral politics is significantly lower than in executive or legislative politics, data were collected on participation in both primary and general elections for the top partisan candidate on the Ohio ballot (excluding the Presidency) and for the judicial candidates. Due to the four-year gubernatorial term, instituted in Ohio in 1958, the top state race in 1960 was that for state auditor. The gubernatorial candidates headed the ballot in 1962 and 1966; the senatorial candidates in 1964 and 1968.

Unopposed judicial races, which constituted one of the fifteen supreme court races and 37% of the races in the courts of appeals, have been eliminated from the analysis. "Participation" is measured by the percent voting in the judicial race of the total voting in the top partisan race. By this measure, primary participation in opposed supreme court races was significantly lower than in executive or legislative races, with the exception of the 1960 Republican primary, in which the top partisan office was uncontested. Table 4 shows the extent of statewide primary participation. Although the 1960 primary data are distorted by the absence of a contest for the top partisan office, this fact in itself is significant. If the absence of contests or low participation rates are reasons to eliminate judicial primaries, then the justification for other primaries is also called into question, since these factors also characterize the selection process for many executive and legislative offices.

Table 4 also shows generally lower rates of participation in Democratic judicial primary contests than in Republican ones, a factor of considerable significance, as will be seen in later analysis.

Participation in opposed courts of appeals races shows a similar pattern. Because these races occurred in ten districts from 1960 to 1966, and in eleven districts in 1968, no statewide totals are presented. The unit of measure used is the participation rate by county. The number of counties with opposed courts of appeals races have been aggregated for the five elections used in the analysis. Three levels of participation have been defined: "low" participation oc-

TABLE 4
STATEWIDE PRIMARY PARTICIPATION IN OPPOSED SUPREME COURT RACES, AS PERCENT OF VOTE FOR TOP PARTISAN OFFICE, 1960–1968

Year	*Republican Primary*	*Democratic Primary*
1960	103.7%	(a)
1962	84.9	65.7%
1964	74.1	69.5
1966	(a)	83.8
1968	(a)	(a)

SOURCE: Calculated from Ohio Election Statistics, *op. cit.*
[a]All supreme court races unopposed.

curs when less than 70% of those voting in executive and legislative races vote in contested courts of appeals races. "Moderate" participation occurs when 70–99% of those voting in the top partisan race vote in contested courts of appeals races; and "high" participation is found when more voters participate in appeals judge contests than in the top partisan races. Table 5 presents the data by number and percent distribution of counties in each category of participation.

It is clearly the case that participation in judicial primary courts of appeals contests tends to be lower than participation in primary voting for the top partisan office. In a surprising number of instances, however, participation in judicial races exceeded that

TABLE 5
DISTRIBUTION OF PARTICIPATION IN OPPOSED COURTS OF APPEALS PRIMARY RACES, AS PERCENT OF VOTER FOR TOP PARTISAN OFFICE, BY COUNTY, 1960–1968

	Republican Primary		*Democratic Primary*	
Participation	*No. of Counties*	*Percent*	*No. of Counties*	*Percent*
Low (under 70%)	6	3.1	19	24.4
Moderate (70–99%)	161	84.3	56	71.8
High (100% and over)	24	12.6	3	3.8
TOTAL	191	100.0	78	100.0

SOURCE: Calculated from *Ohio Election Statistics, op. cit.*
Chi Square=32.28 $p<.001$

in the top partisan race.[54] As in the supreme court contests, Republican activism in the arena of judicial selection is greater than Democratic activity. Not only are there fewer counties with low participation rates in Republican primaries, but also there is a significantly higher number of counties in which seats on the appeals bench are contested by Republican aspirants. Almost two and a half times as many counties had contested judicial races for the courts of appeals in Republican primaries from 1960 through 1968 as in Democratic primaries in the same period. This imbalance between parties is reduced, however, when the competition is measured by judicial seats instead of by counties. In Republican primaries, 21.4% of the courts of appeals races were contested, in contrast to 15.7% of the races in the Democratic primaries of this period. At the statewide level, in primaries for seats on the supreme court, the difference in number of contested seats disappears. In both party primaries, 20%, or three of the fifteen, total races for the supreme court were contested.

Contests in judicial elections occur more frequently than in the primaries. For the supreme court, 93.3%, or fourteen of the fifteen total races from 1960 to 1968, were contested (see Appendix).

TABLE 6
PARTY COMPOSITION OF THE OHIO SUPREME COURT, 1959–1968

Party	*April, 1959– Dec. 1960*	*Jan. 1961– Nov. 1964*	*Nov. 1964– Dec. 1968*
Republican	3	4	6
Democratic	4	3	1

SOURCE: Ohio, *Official Roster, op. cit.*, pp. 111–112.

[54]The extremely high participation rate in the data is found in Mahoning County in the 1964 Democratic primary when 163% of those voting in the Young-Glenn Senate race voted in a contested court of appeals race. The lowest participation rates in judicial contests were found in the 1968 Democratic primary when unusually high participation was induced by the Lausche-Gilligan contest for the Senate. This illustrates the care with which these data must be interpreted, since the fluctuation in voting patterns in this instance was due to an exciting partisan contest at the top of the ballot, not to unusual apathy in the judicial contest.

The party composition of the supreme court changed as a result of these contests. Table 6 shows the partisan division on the supreme court for this period.[55]

The conditions of judicial voting in the general elections must be taken into consideration in interpreting participation rates. The nonpartisan judicial ballot is on a separate piece of paper from the partisan ballot and from the issues ballot. Yet participation in contested supreme court races, shown in Table 7, was at least "moderate," as defined above. In no case, however, did participation rates surpass those in partisan races.

General election participation rates for supreme court justice appear relatively constant in the five elections. The two top races were the third seat in 1960, pitting appointed incumbent John Peck against popular former Governor C. William O'Neill for the unexpired term; and the 1962 race for Chief Justice, in which Repub-

TABLE 7
PARTICIPATION RATES IN GENERAL ELECTION CONTESTS FOR THE OHIO SUPREME COURT, 1960–1968, AS PERCENT VOTING FOR JUSTICE OF THE TOTAL VOTING FOR TOP PARTISAN OFFICE

	Supreme Court Races			
Year	(1)	(2)	(3)	(4)
1960	84.7%	83.5%	87.7%	
1962	85.4	79.2	79.7	
1964	78.5	81.2	75.4	76.6%
1966	81.1	80.2		
1968	82.8	75.5		

SOURCE: Calculated from *Ohio Election Statistics, op. cit.*

[55]With the death in 1969 of Justice Zimmerman, the only remaining Democrat on the court, and Governor Rhodes's appointment of Judge J. J. P. Corrigan to the unexpired term, the court became solidly Republican and remained so through 1970. C. J. Kingsley Taft died in 1970; Justice O'Neill was elevated by Governor Rhodes to Chief Justice; Republican Judge Leonard J. Stern of the 10th District Court of Appeals was appointed to O'Neill's seat. When Justice Matthias resigned between the 1970 primary, in which he had been unopposed, and the November election, Governor Rhodes elevated another Republican judge from the 10th District Court of Appeals, Robert E. Leach, to the state's high bench.

TABLE 8
DISTRIBUTION OF PERCENT VOTING IN OPPOSED COURTS OF APPEALS RACES, AS PERCENT OF VOTE FOR TOP PARTISAN OFFICE, BY COUNTY, 1960–1968

Participation	*1960*	*1962*	*1964*	*1966*	*1968*
Low (under 70%)	3	7	13	10	14
Moderate (70–99%)	56	51	59	51	61
High (100% and over)	0	0	0	0	0

SOURCE: Tabulated from *Ohio Election Statistics, op. cit.*

lican incumbent Kingsley Taft challenged Chief Justice Weygandt, a Democrat who was first elected as chief justice in 1932.

In general elections for the courts of appeals, forty-six of seventy-three races, or 63% of the total, were contested between 1960 and 1968. Participation by county in these contests differs from primary participation chiefly in that no races attracted more voters than the top partisan race. In most counties, the participation in contested courts of appeals races was "moderate" as defined earlier. The number of counties in each category of participation is shown in Table 8.

In summary, participation in appellate judicial partisan primaries and nonpartisan elections tends to be lower than participation in primaries and elections for legislative and executive offices. However, few judicial races register participation below 70% of participants in other races, and some judicial races even draw out a higher proportion of the electorate than other state races. If low voter participation supports the elimination of judicial primaries and elections, it also raises serious questions about some executive and legislative primaries and elections.

V. OHIO'S REPUBLICAN JUDICIARY

The combination of partisan primaries and nonpartisan elections in Ohio's system of judicial selection has led to the label, "semi-partisan." An analysis of party affiliation of successful can-

TABLE 9
ACCESSIONS OF OHIO APPELLATE JUDGES, BY LEVEL OF COURT AND BY PARTY AFFILIATION, 1960–1968

Level of Court	*Elected*			*Appointed*			*Total*		
	Rep.	*Dem.*	*Total*	*Rep.*	*Dem.*	*Total*	*Rep.*	*Dem.*	*Total*
Supreme Court	13	2	15	1	3	4	14	5	19
Court of Appeals	53	20	73	10	4	14	63	24	87
TOTAL	66	22	88	11	7	18	77	29	106
Percent, by Party	75	25	100	61.1	38.9	100	72.7	27.3	100.0

SOURCE: Tabulated from *Ohio Election Statistics, op. cit.*

didates suggests that the system is partisan in results, since one of the most striking characteristics of Ohio's elective judiciary is the Republican affiliation of a large majority of the state's appellate judges. This fact is demonstrated in Table 9.[56]

Numerous studies have shown the tendency of non-partisan electoral systems to provide advantages to upper-income, better-educated voters, who tend to identify with the Republican party.[57] There are two major dimensions of political behavior involved in this phenomenon. People in upper socio-economic groups tend to vote Republican, a dimension of political preference. Persons of generally high socio-economic status are also the most highly edu-

[56]In the cases of three appeals judges who ran in the general election without nomination in partisan primaries, the party affiliation of the winner was confirmed by a letter from State Republican Party Chairman John S. Andrews, dated July 30, 1970. The three, appointees of Governor Rhodes who ran for the unexpired terms to which they had been appointed, were Donald J. Morrisroe, Robert E. Leach, and John W. Potter, all registered Republicans. No appellate judicial appointment has been made across party lines by an Ohio governor since 1953 when Governor Lausche (D) appointed James Collier (R) to the 4th District Court of Appeals.

[57]See Charles R. Adrian, "Some General Characteristics of Nonpartisan Elections," *American Political Science Review,* 46 (1952), 766–776; Eugene Lee, *The Politics of Nonpartisanship* (Berkeley, Calif.: University of California Press, 1960), pp. 139–140; Hugh A. Bone and Austin Ranney, *Politics and Voters,* 2nd ed. (New York: McGraw-Hill, 1967), pp. 111–113.

cated members of the political system, and education levels are associated with activity, a dimension of participation. Thus those who tend to vote Republican are the most likely to vote, the most likely to talk about politics, and thus to become "opinion leaders," and the most likely to be psychologically capable of conceptualizing political events.[58]

The high proportion of organizational memberships among these upper-income, politically active voters, provides them with more cues which enable them to cope with the directionless, nonpartisan judicial ballot. In contrast, lower-income, less-educated voters, who tend to vote Democratic and to vote less regularly, are more likely to be bewildered by the unlabeled names on a nonpartisan ballot. Responding to this bewilderment, Democratic voters are more likely to withdraw from making a selection (the familiar phenomenon of the "fall-off" from the partisan to the nonpartisan ballot), or to vote for a familiar name, reassured in those rare cases by the warmth of recognition that they can do their civic duty (vote) in a not altogether meaningless way. Since judges have less opportunity to develop a political personality of which the voter may become aware, judicial nonpartisan choices are even more remote from the lower-income, less-educated voter than are other nonpartisan elections, such as local councilmen.

The data on participation have shown higher participation in judicial primaries by Republicans (Tables 4 and 5) and significant success for Republican judicial candidates in Ohio (Table 9). The missing link in the analysis is the behavior of the voter in casting his nonpartisan ballot for judges.

Opinion research on public attitudes toward judicial candidates and elections is scanty. A search of the literature has turned up such investigation only in Wisconsin, where judicial elections, although nonpartisan as in Ohio, are held in April, separated in time as well as in character from races for executive and legislative posts. Ladinsky and Silver have provided us with a preliminary sketch of the judicial electorate in that state. In 1964–1965, 46% of the total electorate knew that Wisconsin judges were elected; 30% could

[58] Bone and Ranney, *op. cit.*, pp. 27–28.

tell which of the two candidates for a supreme court seat was an incumbent; and 15% could identify the political parties with which the candidates had been associated.[59]

In connection with the last item on the survey, it is significant to note that Wisconsin judges, unlike those in Ohio, are nominated in nonpartisan primaries. With these levels of familiarity, 30% of the eligible voters had participated in a hotly-contested, policy-oriented election for a supreme court seat in that state.

Another Wisconsin opinion survey showed that participation in the judicial system as litigants, jurors, or witnesses in the five years prior to a judicial election and media attention toward the work of the courts created no significant differences in evaluation of the judiciary ("Judges are doing a 'good' job"), attitude toward method of selection ("Judges should be elected"), or actual participation in a judicial election.[60]

Public opinion research is beyond the scope of the present study but should be undertaken to provide data for testing hypotheses about inadequacies of the present election system. In the absence of such data, election statistics were analyzed to explore the linkage between participation rates and electoral results.

Republican candidates for appellate judicial posts in Ohio are not only more likely to win than Democratic candidates, but also are more likely to win in runaway contests, that is, by more than 60% of the vote. Table 10 shows the margin of victory in contested appellate judicial races in Ohio from 1960 through 1968.

The great disparity between parties in intensity of the vote is seen at the extremes; only 19.6% of Republican appellate judges in Ohio won in "close" contests, compared to 35.7% of Democratic winners; 54.3% of successful Republican judicial candidates won in "runaway" contests, while only 21.4% of Democratic appellate judges experienced such success.

---

[59]Jack Ladinsky and Allen Silver, "Popular Democracy and Judicial Independence; Electorate and Elite Reactions to Two Wisconsin Supreme Court Elections," *Wisconsin Law Review* (1967), p. 161.

[60]Herbert Jacob, "Judicial Insulation—Elections, Direct Participation, and Public Attention to the Courts in Wisconsin," *Wisconsin Law Review* (1966), p. 818.

TABLE 10
"INTENSITY" OF THE VOTE, CONTESTED RACES FOR THE OHIO APPELLATE JUDICIARY, 1960–1968

Margin of Victory	*Republican* *Number*	*Percent*	*Democratic* *Number*	*Percent*	*Total* *Number*	*Percent*
50.1–55%	9	19.6	5	35.7	14	23.3
55.1–60%	12	26.1	6	42.9	18	30.0
Over 60%	25	54.3	3	21.4	28	46.7
TOTAL	46	100.0	14	100.0	60	100.0

SOURCE: Calculated from *Ohio Election Statistics, op. cit.* Classification scheme, with the extremes of "close" and "runaway" elections, is borrowed from Herbert Jacob, "Judicial Insulation—Elections, Direct Participation, and Public Attention to the Courts in Wisconsin," *op. cit.*, p. 807.

The political fate of judicial candidates in Ohio is not as closely tied to their parties' fortunes as that of judges elected on a partisan ballot, as in West Virginia. In his study of the West Virginia judiciary, Davis calculated an average vote, measured by percent Democratic, for six top state executive offices in eight elections from 1928 through 1956, and found that the vote for supreme court judge in each of those elections deviated from the party vote by less than one percent.[61] In contrast, in Ohio wide fluctuations occur in the statewide percent of the party vote for top partisan office and for judicial candidates on the nonpartisan ballot. Table 11 shows statewide differences in voting patterns.

Table 11 shows that in ten of the fourteen contested supreme court races, the Democratic candidate received a lesser share of the statewide vote than the Democratic candidate for the top partisan office. In the four cases where the reverse was true, the advantage of the Democratic candidate on the nonpartisan ballot can be explained by the familiar characteristics of long-term incumbency and famous name.

Because statewide election statistics may obscure variations in patterns of partisan support, the percent Democratic of the two-

[61]Claude J. Davis, *Judicial Selection in West Virginia* (Morgantown, W. Va.: Bureau for Government Research, University of West Virginia, 1959), pp. 26–27.

TABLE 11
PERCENT DEMOCRATIC OF THE VOTE FOR TOP STATE PARTISAN OFFICE AND FOR CONTESTED SEATS ON THE SUPREME COURT, WITH DIFFERENCES, 1960–1968

Year	*Top State Race Pct. Democratic*	*Sup. Ct. #1 Pct. Dem.*	*Diff.*	*Sup. Ct. #2 Pct. Dem.*	*Diff.*	*Sup. Ct. #3 Pct. Dem.*	*Diff.*	*Sup. Ct. #4 Pct. Dem.*	*Diff.*
1960	40.8	54.5	13.7[a]	37.7	−3.1	38.4	−2.4	—	—
1962	41.1	49.97	8.9[a]	36.6	−4.5	34.4	−6.7	—	—
1964	50.2	59.4	9.2[a]	32.4	−17.8	48.4	−1.8	33.7	−16.5
1966	37.8	43.7	5.9[b]	31.6	−6.2	—	—	—	—
1968	48.5	38.5	−10.0	28.7	−19.8	—	—	—	—

[a]Long-time Democratic incumbents ran for re-election.
[b]A Democrat named Brown (Clifford) ran for the supreme court.
SOURCE: Calculated from *Ohio Election Statistics*, *op. cit.*

party vote by county was calculated for these supreme court races and the top partisan races. A matrix of correlation coefficients for the five partisan and fourteen nonpartisan races shows significant relationships. First, as shown in Table 12, it appears that the pattern of support for partisan candidates in Ohio remained relatively constant through the nine-year period covered by the study.

Although shifts in partisan strength in the counties of Ohio have occurred, either through population mobility or changes in partisan attachments, such shifts have been incremental and relatively steady over time. This suggests that the inability to measure

TABLE 12
CORRELATION COEFFICIENT[a] MATRIX, TOP PARTISAN RACES, 1960–1968

	Auditor 1960	*Gov. 1962*	*Sen. 1964*	*Gov. 1966*	*Sen. 1968*
1960, Auditor	1.0				
1962, Governor	.89	1.0			
1964, Senator	.86	.86	1.0		
1966, Governor	.77	.84	.82	1.0	
1968, Senator	.69	.76	.78	.85	1.0

[a]Pearson product-moment correlation coefficient.

TABLE 13
CORRELATION COEFFICIENT[a] MATRIX, TOP PARTISAN RACES AND CONTESTED SUPREME COURT RACES, BY COUNTY, 1960–1968

Top Partisan Office	*Supreme Court Races* #1	#2	#3	#4
1960, Auditor	.51	.81	.29	
1962, Governor	.68	.38	.49	
1964, Senator	.44	.61	.43	.52
1966, Governor	.39	.63		
1968, Senator	.50	.41		

[a]Although these coefficients are not derived from a sample population, note that all correlation coefficients are significant at .001, 86 df, except 1960 Aud./Supreme Court #3, which is significant at .01.

the vote for the same top partisan office in each election is not a serious defect in the data.

Table 13 shows the correlation coefficients for the percent voting Democratic for the top partisan office and the percent voting for the Democratic candidate in contested supreme court races, by county. The race with the least significance in party voting (r=.29) was that of former Governor O'Neill against John Peck, appointee of Governor DiSalle, in 1960. This somewhat deviant case suggests the influence a political personality and a well-known name may have on electoral response. Given the nonpartisan ballot, a number of Democrats may have been attracted by the name O'Neill to elevate to the bench a popular former governor whom DiSalle had defeated just two years earlier. The second least partisan judicial race is revealed in the correlation of percent Democratic voting for governor in 1962, and supreme court race #2 (r=.38). The successful judicial candidate was the Republican nominee, John M. Matthias, an incumbent since 1954 when he defeated the Democrat whom Governor Lausche had appointed to the bench at the death of Matthias' father in 1953. Since Edward S. Matthias was first elected in 1914, and re-elected six times, the name Matthias had been on the nonpartisan judicial ballot for forty-eight years when the voters went to the polls in 1962. It is reasonable to infer a signficant Democratic crossover on the nonpartisan judicial ballot to support so traditional a judicial name.

The third lowest correlation coefficient relates the Democratic voting in the 1966 governor's race to a supreme court race (r=.39), in which Democrat Clifford Brown ran against incumbent Republican Louis Schneider. It could be hypothesized that Republicans, who are accustomed to voting for candidates named Brown, crossed over significantly, although not in large enough numbers to elect the Democrat Brown. On the same ballot was Republican Paul Brown, who defeated Democratic candidate Bryan for the supreme court, in a more highly partisan vote (r=.63).

The influence of well-known names on judicial voting is reflected also in the judicial races in which Democratic candidates received a larger share of the two-party vote than the top partisan Democratic candidate. The statewide differences were shown in

TABLE 14
DIFFERENCE OF MEANS,[a] PERCENT DEMOCRATIC OF THE VOTE FOR TOP PARTISAN OFFICE AND SUPREME COURT RACES BY COUNTY, 1960–1968

Year and S.C. Race		*Republican Candidate*	*Democratic Candidate*	*Mean Difference*	*T Value*	*Level of Significance*
1960	(1)	Hoover	*Bell	−15.6	−24.022	.001
	(2)	*K. Taft	Ellison	.001	.002	ns
	(3)	*O'Neill	Peck	2.0	2.192	.05
1962	(1-CJ)	*K. Taft	Weygandt	−7.0	−11.859	.001
	(2)	*Matthias	Mayer	−1.9	−2.515	.05
	(3)	*P. Herbert	Cole	2.8	4.046	.001
1964	(1)	Douglas	*Zimmerman	−9.4	−13.522	.001
	(2)	*O'Neill	Bryan	15.1	29.023	.001
	(3)	*Schneider	Griffith	−4.2	−5.146	.001
	(4)	*P. Brown	Gibson	17.1	28.118	.001
1966	(1)	*Schneider	C. Brown	−12.5	−17.943	.001
	(2)	*P. Brown	Bryan	6.8	14.685	.001
1968	(1-CJ)	*K. Taft	Duffy	8.0	11.328	.001
	(2)	*T. Herbert	Brothers	15.3	20.531	.001

***Denotes winner.**
[a]Difference of means test, t test at 87 df. At .001, t=3.421; at .01, t=2.638; at .05, t=1.991.

Table 11.[62] The data by county have been analyzed by a difference of means test to investigate whether these differences were distributed statewide. Table 14 presents the results.

From Table 13 it is apparent that the most partisan judicial race of this period was the K. Taft-Ellison contest in 1960 ($r=.81$). The high correlation in Democratic voting in this race on the partisan and nonpartisan ballots is reflected in Table 14, where this race stands out as the only contested supreme court contest in which there is no significant difference in the mean Democratic vote in the counties of Ohio for auditor and for supreme court seat. All the other contests show significant *t* values in the difference of means test.

In six races, negative *t* values show that the Democratic judicial candidate garnered a larger share of the vote than the Democratic partisan candidate. These races involved long-term Democratic incumbents (Bell, Weygandt, and Zimmerman), a Democrat named Clifford Brown, and two races in which relatively unknown Democratic candidates (Mayer and Griffith) ran strongly ahead in many rural counties but fell behind in the populous urban counties.

In seven races, the significant *t* value is positive, indicating that the top Democratic partisan candidates ran significantly ahead of the Democratic judicial candidates in the Ohio counties. These are the races in which the familiar-name syndrome operated in favor of Republican judicial candidates with "good political names" such as O'Neill, Brown (Paul), Taft (Kingsley), and Herbert (both Paul and Thomas).

A final characteristic of judicial voting in Ohio is the insulation from state and national partisan trends, which may be attributed to the effect of the separate, non-partisan ballot. A strong Republican tide in 1962 and 1966 in Ohio politics and a strong national Democratic trend in 1964 do not appear to have had a significant effect on judicial voting in the state. In all three of these tidal years, the politics of judicial elections exhibited their normal characterstics: high levels of support for Republican candidates, with Democratic strength shown only by candidates with names of high famil-

[62] *Ibid.*, p. 31.

iarity to the voters. This insulation of judicial from other politics was confirmed in 1970 when, in the face of a gross shift to the Democrats in executive and legislative offices in Ohio, Supreme Court Chief Justice O'Neill won re-election with 68.9% of the vote and a Republican Corrigan (J.J.P.) defeated a Democratic Brown (Allen) with 55.7% of the vote.[63]

To summarize the empirical findings about Ohio's appellate judges:

1) The appellate judiciary of Ohio is largely elective, in practice as well as in theory.
2) The minority of appellate judges who gain access to the bench by gubernatorial appointment tend to be defeated subsequently by the electorate if they are Democratic and elected if they are Republican.
3) The appellate judiciary of Ohio, elected on a nonpartisan ballot, is overwhelmingly Republican in partisan affiliation.
   a) Higher participation in Republican than in Democratic judicial primaries suggests a higher level of interest in and concern about the judiciary among Republicans than Democratic voters, an interest which may be carried over to the election.
   b) The "intensity" of support for Republican judicial candidates in the general election races, as measured by the margin of victory of winning candidates, suggests a higher level of participation by Republican-oriented voters on the nonpartisan judicial ballot. Republican advantage on the nonpartisan ballot has been confirmed in other studies of nonpartisan elections, and may be explained by the following propositions:
      (1) Better-educated, higher-income voters, who tend to be Republicans, are more likely to have organizational affiliations and to use access to channels of communication that inform them about judicial candidates. They feel more motivated to vote the judicial ballot, both due

[63]Calculated from unofficial results published in *The Plain Dealer*, November 5, 1970.

to a sense of civic duty fostered by their education and to the higher level of access to relevant information.

(2) Lower-income, less-educated voters, who tend to be Democrats, are less likely to vote the judicial ballot because they are confused by the lack of a cognitive map supplied on the partisan ballot by the party label, are less motivated by an education-oriented sense of civic duty to vote the judicial ballot, have less information about judicial candidates, and, lacking knowledge or direction, are likely to vote only when they recognize a familiar name.

These are inferential propositions which suggest some important lines of inquiry for public opinion research on response to judicial elections.

VI. LAWYERS AND JUDGES

A final phase of the empirical investigation conducted for the present study is a small-scale inquiry into bar association recommendations for judicial posts. As a pilot project to explore what kinds of data would be relevant to an evaluation of bar participation in judicial politics, the endorsements for Ohio Supreme Court seats and the Eighth Circuit Court of Appeals bench by the Cleveland Bar Association and the Cuyahoga County Bar Association were collected. Interviews with the executive secretary of the Cleveland Bar Association, the past president of the Cuyahoga County Bar Association, and the chairman of the latter's Committee on Judicial Endorsements were conducted to inquire into the conditions of endorsement and the differences, if any, between the two groups.

The Ohio Bar Association Plan, like its model, the Missouri Plan, is based on the assumption that judges are "a special type of public official for which the Bar has a unique responsibility." In fact, lawyers profess "a special competence in evaluating which of their brethren should ascend to the bench."[64] The literature on lawyers' political participation, especially with respect to selection of judges, suggests several hypotheses about apathy, favoritism toward incumbents, conservativism, and potential representation of opposing interests in society.

1) *In bar polls for endorsements of judicial candidates, a minority of those eligible to vote do so.* This first hypothesis is suggested by scattered evidence from judicial selection plans in which lawyers participate formally or informally. In Missouri, for example, 31% of the lawyers eligible to vote for bar representatives on the judicial nominating commissions from 1946 to 1951 actually did so. In advisory bar polls in Texas, lawyers have been "more apathetic than the public"; in six bar polls in the 1950s, less than 50% of the lawyers eligible to vote picked up a ballot to mark a preference.[65]

A more basic question is raised in the treatment of the organized bar as representative of American lawyers. Less than half of all lawyers are members of the American Bar Association,[66] suggesting that its role as "voice" of the American legal profession is self-assumed.

In a study of A.B.A. influence in federal judicial appointments, a cross section survey of American lawyers revealed that 89.2% had "never been asked" for their evaluation either of judicial candidates or of A.B.A. Committee members who would subsequently recommend judicial candidates.[67] During the Eisenhower administration, when the A.B.A. Standing Committee on the Federal Judiciary was most visible both to the profession and to the public, only 10% of a cross section of American lawyers and 13% of A.B.A. members could name either the committee member from their judicial circuit, or the chairman of the committee. State and

---

[64]Richard A. Watson and Rondal G. Downing, *The Politics of the Bench and the Bar* (New York: John Wiley & Sons, 1969), p. 330.

[65]George G. Moran, "Counter-'Missouri Plan' for Method of Selecting Judges," *Florida Bar Journal,* 32 (1958), 473; Robert W. Calvert, "Selection of Appellate Judges," *Texas Bar Journal,* 26 (1963), 152.

[66]Joel B. Grossman, *Lawyers and Judges: The ABA and the Politics of Judicial Selection* (New York: John Wiley & Sons, 1965), p. 81.

[67]*Ibid.*, p. 111.

local bar membership figures are not generally available and vary widely with the existence of the organized bar. Oligarchical rule appears to be as characteristic of lawyers' associations, whether national, state, or local, as it is of other organized professions and trade unions.[68] Oligarchy is an organizational condition which reinforces and is reinforced by low membership participation in association activities.

A 1959 analysis of Cleveland Bar Association advisory polls, which have been taken since 1933, estimates that the lawyer response has ranged from 40 to 60% of those polled.[69] The percentage of ballots returned in Cleveland Bar Association polls from 1960 to 1968, based on estimates of the number of ballots distributed in those years, is shown in Table 15.

It should be noted that the Cleveland Bar Association sends ballots to all members of the bar in Cuyahoga County, whether or not they are members of the association. No tabulation is kept of returns from members as distinct from non-members. It appears that participation in bar polls is sustained by a minority of lawyers

TABLE 15
LAWYER PARTICIPATION IN CLEVELAND BAR ASSOCIATION JUDICIAL POLLS, 1960–1968

Year		*Estimated Percent of Ballots Returned*
1960		48.35
1962		45.03
1964		45.51
1966		41.14
1968	Primary[a]	32.45
	General Election	35.68

[a]1968 was the first year in which the Cleveland Bar Association made judicial endorsements in the primaries.
SOURCE: Calculated from estimates provided by Peter P. Roper, Executive Director, in a letter dated August 20, 1970.

[68]Jack Ladinsky and Joel B. Grossman, "Organizational Consequences of Professional Consensus," *Administrative Science Quarterly*, 11 (1966), 96, 104.
[69]Marc D. Gleisser, "Judicial Candidates: The Bar's Endorsement Role," *Cleveland Bar Association Journal*, 30 (1959), 167–168.

who are eligible to vote, and that with the exception of a slight upturn in 1964, participation has decreased through the 1960s. The Cuyahoga County Bar Association was unable to furnish participation data for bar polls of the same period.

2) Those lawyers who participate in bar polls tend to endorse incumbent judges. Since lawyers tend to consider judicial experience an important qualification for the appellate bench, it should not be surprising that bar polls would tend to favor incumbents.[70] However, bar groups seeking special access to the judicial selection process criticize voters for their alleged tendency to favor incumbents. As with participation, little data can be found on the variable of incumbency in endorsements. A 1946 evaluation of fourteen years of Cleveland Bar Association polls noted generally that "with few exceptions," incumbents were endorsed.[71] The hypothesis is tentatively confirmed by data on judicial endorsements of both the Cuyahoga County Bar Association and the Cleveland Bar Association from 1960 to 1968, as shown in Table 16. It is clear that a large majority of endorsements go to incumbents in the polls of both local bar associations.

A third hypothesis relates both to partisanship and to a conservative bias believed to characterize the legal profession. 3)

TABLE 16
INCUMBENCY AS A VARIABLE IN APPELLATE JUDICIAL ENDORSEMENTS BY LOCAL BAR ASSOCIATIONS, 1960–1968

	Percent of Total Endorsements	
Organization	*Incumbents*	*Non-incumbents*
Cleveland Bar Assoc.	82.8	17.2
Cuyahoga Co. Bar Assoc.	82.4	17.6

SOURCE: **Calculated from lists of judicial endorsements, 1960–1968, supplied by Roper, *op. cit.*, and Arnold, *op. cit.***

[70]In a small questionnaire sent to a cross section of American lawyers, "trial experience" and "judicial experience" were ranked first and second as standards of qualifications deemed desirable for the judiciary. Ladinsky and Grossman, *op. cit.*, p. 91.

[71]Edward T. Butler, Jr., "The Cleveland Bar Association's Plan for Judicial Campaigns," *Journal of the American Judicature Society*, 30 (1946), 44.

Among both incumbent judges and challengers, Republican candidates are more likely to be endorsed by bar groups than Democratic candidates for the judiciary. The traditional exponent of the hypothesis that lawyers represent and favor conservative, upper-status interests in American society is Alexis de Tocqueville, who observed in 1835 that the lawyers in the United States formed the "highest political class," a natural aristocracy which served "as the most powerful, if not the only, counterpoise to the democratic element," capable of neutralizing "the vices inherent in popular government."[72] This view of the legal profession was sustained in 1878 by the motivating force which led to establishment of the American Bar Association, namely concern about a trend in judicial decision making toward legitimation of public control of private enterprise. "Committed to the growing industrial empire, the bar leaders saw the judiciary as the last bastion of defense against encroachments on the entrepreneurial prerogative, and intensified their efforts to assure the recruitment of judges who shared their own views of society."[73]

The alleged conservatism of lawyers has been attributed to legal education, to the methods of legal procedure, and to the business-oriented clientele of the legal profession, such as banks, corporations, realtors, and insurance companies.[74] Because these latter interests tend to support the Republican Party in Ohio politics, bar endorsements of Republican judicial candidates would be anticipated. No tabulation of partisan affiliation of judicial candidates endorsed by bar associations has been found in the literature. From the list of endorsements provided by the two local bar associations, however, it appears that Republican candidates indeed fare better than Democratic candidates. The partisan division of endorsements from 1960 to 1968 is shown in Table 17.

---

[72]De Tocqueville, *op. cit.*

[73]Grossman, *Lawyers and Judges, op. cit.*, p. 52. *Munn v. Illinois*, 94 U.S. 113 (1876), is the decision cited by Grossman as illustrative of the judicial trend which prompted lawyers to form a national organization.

[74]Heinz Eulau and John D. Sprague, *Lawyers in Politics* (Indianapolis: Bobbs Merrill, 1964), pp. 22–27. See also Ralph Nader, "Law Schools and Law Firms," *The New Republic*, 151 (October 11, 1969), 20–23.

TABLE 17
PARTISAN AFFILIATION AS A VARIABLE IN APPELLATE JUDICIAL ENDORSEMENTS BY LOCAL BAR ASSOCIATIONS, 1960–1968

	Percent of Total Endorsements	
Organization	*Republicans*	*Democrats*
Cleveland Bar Assoc.	65.5	34.5
Cuyahoga Co. Bar Assoc.	70.6	29.4

SOURCE: Calculated from lists of judicial endorsements, 1960–1968, supplied by Roper, *op. cit.* and Arnold, *op. cit.*

Rival bar associations are known to exist in Toledo and Cincinnati as well as in Cleveland, reputedly reflecting a similar cleavage between plaintiffs' and defendants' lawyers. Further investigation of the organized bar in Ohio metropolitan areas should be conducted to test the hypotheses about participation, incumbency, and partisanship. If the Cleveland bar is representative of lawyers elsewhere in Ohio, it appears that the state's lawyers, much like the state's voters, tend not to participate in judicial politics, and those who do participate tend to favor incumbents and/or Republicans.

TABLE 18
IDEOLOGICAL CLEAVAGES AND INCOME DISTRIBUTION AMONG OHIO LEGISLATORS, 1957

Ideology	*Lawyers*	*Non-Lawyers*
Liberal	31%	24%
Moderate	25	24
Conservative	44	52
TOTAL	100%	100%
(N)	(59)	(102)
Income		
$5–10,000	21%	53%
$10–20,000	51	33
Over $20,000	25	11
Not ascertained	3	3
TOTAL	100%	100%
(N)	(59)	(103)

SOURCE: Eulau and Sprague, *op. cit.*, pp. 26, 37.

The weakness of the evidence about conservatism among lawyers has led some investigators to suggest a model of the legal profession based on plural representation of interests. Eulau and Sprague argue that lawyers serve labor unions, humanitarian causes, and reform as well as powerful and conservative economic interests that seek the preservation of the status quo. An inquiry into the ideology of a sample of lawyer and non-lawyer legislators in four states showed a higher proportion of liberal lawyer legislators than of liberal non-lawyer legislators. Although usually categorized as middle class, lawyer legislators were found to have a "highly heterogeneous" class position.[75] (See Table 18 for Ohio data.) These considerable differences in income could provide a basis for class politics within the legal profession. A survey published in 1954 revealed that 68% of American lawyers in private practice were solo practitioners, 27% were partners in law firms, and 5% were associates in law firms.[76]

Diversity and cleavage within the legal profession, however, may or may not be reflected in professional organizations. In the most comprehensive study of state judicial selection done to date, Watson and Downing identified a virtual two-party system working in the metropolitan bar associations of Missouri. A significant socio-economic cleavage in the bar is reflected there in competing organizations. In both Kansas City and St. Louis, rival bar associations represent plaintiffs' lawyers and criminal attorneys in one organization and in the other, defendants' lawyers and corporation attorneys. The members of the "plaintiffs' lawyers" groups

---

[75]Eulau and Sprague, *op. cit.*, pp. 25, 26, 37. Eulau and Sprague argue that the model of the lawyer as a captive of business and financial interests has been "kept alive by such crude analyses" as C. Wright Mills's *White Collar: The American Middle Classes* (New York: Oxford University Press, 1951), pp. 121–129. Lawyers are, if captive, also subservient to the interests of labor unions, government bureaucracies, and other countervailing institutions. See also Talcott Parsons, "The Distribution of Power in American Society," in *Structure and Process in Modern Societies* (New York: The Free Press of Glencoe, 1960), p. 219.

[76]Albert P. Blaustein and Charles O. Porter, *The American Lawyer: A Summary of the Survey of the Legal Profession* (Chicago: University of Chicago Press, 1954), p. 8. See also the discussion of class diversity among lawyers, pp. 58–63.

were characterized by solo practice or small firm arrangements, lower median income, Democratic party affiliation, and legal education at a local law school. The members of the "defendants' lawyers" groups, on the other hand, tended to practice in firms with six or more members, had a higher median income, tended to affiliate with the Republican party, and a significantly higher proportion had received their legal education at prestige law schools out of state.[77]

This organized cleavage in the metropolitan Missouri legal profession has been relevant to the selection of judges since the Missouri Plan was first proposed. The defendants' lawyers associations supported the plan, while plaintiffs' attorneys groups opposed it. This rivalry shifted to operate within the new selection system, once the state had adopted it, and the competing groups sponsor opposing candidates for the lawyers' seats on the nominating commission. What are the stakes for the lawyers who compete for the nominating commission posts? Both plaintiffs' and defendants' lawyers seek to get "their" kind of lawyers on the commissions. A few may be interested in patronage payoffs such as a nomination for a judicial post. But most appear to be concerned about "policy payoffs"; that is, "they want to get persons on the Bench who will be sympathetic, or at least not hostile, to their clients' interests."[78] This political-professional goal of lawyers illustrates the extent to which, particularly at the appellate level, judges shape the outcome of litigation by the way they develop and apply rules of law, and more importantly, lawyers know that this is so. The plan has clearly institutionalized the socio-economic cleavage in the bar and has politicized its organized associations.

This pluralistic model of the legal professions suggests a modification of the third hypothesis, as follows: 3a) *The cleavage in the bar between plaintiffs' lawyers and defendants' lawyers, between*

---

[77]Watson and Downing, *op. cit.*, pp. 20–21, 29. The authors recognize the fallibility of criteria for evaluating law schools, but on the basis of the legal literature cited and general reputation, identified Chicago, Columbia, Harvard, Michigan, and Yale as "prestigious national schools."

[78]*Ibid.*, pp. 22, 39.

small firms or solo practice and large firms, results in the representation of opposing interests in judicial endorsements by the bar.

The organizational base for such a legal-political sub-system appears to exist in Cuyahoga County, where by testimony of leaders of both groups, the Cuyahoga County Bar Association represents the plaintiffs' lawyer constellation of characteristics described by Watson and Downing, while the Cleveland Bar Association reflects the defendants'-corporation attorney syndrome. An unknown degree of overlapping membership exists between the two groups, mitigating the potentiality of conflict.

Mr. Woodle of the Cuyahoga County Bar Association reported that domination of the Cleveland Bar Association by a few large law firms was among the reasons for the founding of the Cuyahoga County bar in 1928. Support for the elective judiciary was written into the constitution of the new association at that time, a position similar to that of the plaintiffs' lawyers associations in St. Louis and Kansas City.

In spite of this reputed socio-economic cleavage in the Cleveland metropolitan bar, the judicial endorsements, as noted in Tables 16 and 17, do not differ significantly. Both groups have tended to endorse incumbents and Republicans. In fact the Cuyahoga County bar, purportedly representing the interests of less privileged groups in society, endorsed a higher proportion of Republican candidates in the 1960–1968 period (70.6%) than did the Cleveland Bar Association (65.5%). Investigation of rival bar associations in other Ohio metropolitan centers should be done to test the hypothesis of conflict representation among organized lawyers. If the role of the organized bar in judicial selection were to be institutionalized in Ohio, as proposed by the Ohio Bar Association, it is reasonable to predict that lawyers' associations would become politicized and that judicial politics would increase in salience for attorneys generally.

In New York City, a clear partisan cleavage exists between the Bronx and the Kings County Bar Associations, which have been charged with domination by Democrats, and the New York County Lawyers' Association, allegedly controlled by Republicans. Sayre and Kaufman have predicted that if the bar were given a formal role in judicial nominations, the change would result not in the removal of politics from the selection of judges, but in partisan domination of the bar.[79]

VII. THE OHIO BAR PLAN

Equipped with a modest amount of information about the Ohio judiciary, the electorate, and local bar advice on selection of judges, we are better prepared to evaluate the Ohio Bar Plan. The proposed alternative to nonpartisan election of judges clearly falls in the category of "invisible" means of selection. The governor would appoint the appellate judges of Ohio from a list of qualified persons submitted to him by a nominating commission. If they turn out to be incompetent judges, the governor cannot be held responsible; he was limited in his options by the choices of a body of low political visibility. Neither the governor's party nor the opposition party could be held responsible, since the nominating commission would be constitutionally bipartisan. A private occupational group (lawyers) would be given formal, institutionalized access to the selection of public officials (judges)[80] in whose decisions the lawyers have a vested interest. Such a public delegation of authority to a private body offends the principle of the accountability of public decision makers. Advocates of the judicial nominating commission stress the "completely confidential executive nature of the selection process." Secrecy is to be expected in appointment-selection processes; the vice here is in the combination of secrecy and official private group influence. Advocates of the plan also list among the desirable qualities of a judge "balanced and socially acceptable viewpoints."[81] Before giving a private group access to public selec-

[79]Wallace Sayre and Herbert Kaufman, "Courts and Politics in New York City," in Irwin N. Gertzog (ed.), *Readings on State and Local Government* (Englewood Cliffs, N.J.: Prentice-Hall, Inc., 1970), p. 321.

[80]Ohio, 108th General Assembly, Regular Session (1969–1970), H.J.R. No. 27, Sec. 6A (2); "not more than one-half of the commission shall be of the same political party. . . ."; "not less than one-half of the commission shall be members of the bar of Ohio." Sec. 6A (4).

[81]Elmo B. Hunter, "The Judicial Nomination Commission," *Judicature,* 52 (1969), 371, 373.

tion processes, the public should know to whom the judges' viewpoints should be "socially acceptable." This criterion implicitly recognizes the policy making function of the judge and, thereby, highlights the importance of the principle of accountability.

Since the Ohio Bar Association Plan leaves to the discretion of the legislature the means of selection of commission members, it is possible to make only a speculative evaluation of this feature. If lawyer elections were adopted for the selection of the lawyer members of the nominating commission as in Missouri, we would anticipate the politicization of the bar, and domination, as in Missouri, of the appellate nominating commission by defendants' lawyers in large law firms, oriented toward corporation interests. If the legislature adopted gubernatorial appointment of the lay members of the commission, then the politics of the governor's office would replace the politics of partisan county chairmen in the nominating process. In Missouri, the lay members have not articulated independent or "public" interests in the selection process, but those of the banks, insurance companies, realty firms, and public utilities by which they are employed. "Since most of (the laymen) turn to lawyers for advice on candidates, they also reflect the viewpoints of the Bar." Furthermore, in Missouri the lay members generally turned to the defendants' segment of the legal profession for advice on candidates, because they were best acquainted with the lawyers representing their own businesses or businesses like them.[82] After a year of experience with the judicial nominating commission in Utah, one observer called the commission "an anonymous and politically nonresponsible group controlled by vested interests within the various state bar associations."[83]

The work of the nominating commissions in Missouri has been exhaustively studied by Watson and Downing, who found that the state political culture—in Missouri a "cronyistic" friends and neighbors, one-party dominant type—shapes the nominating games

[82]Watson and Downing, *op. cit.*, pp. 337, 338.

[83]Ray M. Harding, "Case for Partisan Election of Judges," *American Bar Association Journal*, 55 (1969), 1163.

played by the commission. "Rigging," "loading," and "wiring" the panel are variants of the process by which the governor's ultimate choice is shaped or recognized by the nominating body.[84] It is clear that the institution of the nominating commission does not "eliminate" politics, but merely changes the kind of politics through which the selection is made.

The Ohio Bar Plan also contains a permissive feature which leaves to legislative discretion extension of the new method of selection to judges of the courts of common pleas.[85] Since the Ohio legislature has repeatedly expressed its objection to abandonment of the elective judiciary, legislative extension of the plan to the basic trial courts of the state seems improbable. In Missouri, the plan operates at both appellate and trial levels, with apparently more equal representation of the plaintiffs' lawyers' interests on the trial courts' nominating commissions than on the appellate commissions.[86] In view of the greater freedom of appellate judges to "make" law, an argument could be made for reversing the order of adoption.

The referendum in which a judge would run for re-election is not considered by the plan's sponsors to be an essential feature of the scheme. Under a system of "non-competitive elective tenure," the incumbent judge files a declaration of candidacy to succeed himself and is then entitled to submit his name to the voters without opposition for a vote on his continuation in office.[87] Glenn R. Winters, executive director of the American Judicature Society and principal nationwide sponsor of the plan, has written that the "chief role" of the referendum is "a reassurance to people who are steeped in the elective tradition that in adopting a merit plan they are not actually giving up everything but are still retaining an essential part of the elective system, and just getting some needed help in the hard part." Winters believes that the noncompetitive election will play a "diminishing role," presumably as voters become socialized to the

---

[84]Watson and Downing, *op. cit.*, pp. 107–108.
[85]H.J.R. No. 27, Sec. 6A (5).
[86]Watson and Downing, *op. cit.*, p. 337.
[87]H.J.R. No. 27, Sec. 6A (3).

new system, and that eventually the appointment will be for life or for good behavior.[88]

Such a referendum is similar in some respects to the uncontested judicial races in an elective system. It would constitute a major change for the voters of Ohio, since only a small proportion of Ohio judicial races from 1960 to 1968 were uncontested.[89] The experience with the referendum in other states suggests that it does not threaten a judge's tenure. In Missouri, on only 1 of 179 judicial ballots in twenty-five years have the voters rejected a sitting judge, and that was in the first election under the plan, surrounded by unusual circumstances. The participation of voters in Missouri Plan plebiscites tends to be very low; in 1964, voter participation for various judges ranged from 37 to 54% of those voting for state attorney general.[90] Only one other defeat of an incumbent judge has been reported in states using some form of the plan: In 1964, a supreme court justice in Alaska was rejected by the electorate.[91] Because of the record of negligible voter efficacy in unopposed races by incumbents, this type of election has been called "a device used by leaders in some nondemocratic countries to remain in office."[92]

Watson and Downing attempted to compare judges elected on the partisan ballot until 1940 and those selected under the Missouri Plan since that date. The two groups were found to have "more common than distinguishing characteristics." Both methods produced a judiciary of "locals" rather than "cosmopolitans;" plan judges did not tend to be elite types, as some critics of the plan had predicted. Differences were that more members of the majority party of the state were selected under the plan than prior to its use; the average age of judges increased; and the appellate judges chosen under the plan had more years of experience on the bench than

---

[88]"The Merit Plan for Judicial Selection and Tenure—Its Historical Development," *Duquesne Law Review*, 7 (1968–1969), 77.

[89]*Ibid.*, p. 22.

[90]Richard A. Watson, "Judging the Judges," *Judicature*, 53 (1970), 290.

[91]Alaska Judicial Council, 4th Report (Anchorage: Secretary to the Judicial Council, 1967), p. 16.

[92]Moran, *op. cit.*, p. 474. See also Thomas J. Stoval, Jr., "Judicial Babies and Constitutional Storks," *Texas Bar Journal*, 26 (1963), 256.

elective judges had, in contrast to trial judges selected under the plan, who had less experience.[93]

Evaluation of judicial decision making in the Missouri study was based on the opinions of a cross section of Missouri lawyers *about* decisions rather than an analysis of the decisions. A tendency was found among lawyers to believe that the plan resulted in putting "better" judges on the bench than those chosen by election. However, a socio-economic cleavage was apparent in attorneys' evaluations. Defendants' and corporation lawyers responded positively in most instances; plaintiffs' and criminal attorneys were more likely to see no improvement in the quality of the judiciary.[94]

A final note on the evaluation of Missouri's experience with the plan is that both the researchers and the lawyers they interviewed agreed that the plan had not eliminated "politics" from judicial selection, but had substituted the politics of the governor and the bar for the politics of county party organizations. Watson and Downing conclude:

> One might well argue that this new type of judicial selection politics is better than the old one because it is more pluralistic, or that the partisan considerations involved in it are likely to be broader and more enlightened because they emanate from the vantage point of the top man in the state political system rather than persons far down on the political ladder. But it is naive or misleading or both to suggest, as many of the Plan's supporters do, that it has taken the politics out of judicial selection.[95]

VIII. CONCLUSION AND PRESCRIPTION

Early in this investigation, the normative question was defined as: What system of selection best accommodates the necessary balance between accountability and independence?

We are now prepared to reject the Ohio Bar Association pro-

---

[93] Watson and Downing, *op. cit.*, pp. 344–345.
[94] *Ibid.*, pp. 345–347.
[95] *Ibid.*, p. 352.

posal for its failure to allow for the accountability of judges in the following ways:

1) The nominating commission provides for a combination of secrecy and private group influence which should not be legitimized in the selection process for public officials. Lawyers may indeed be specially qualified to evaluate judges; they also have a vested interest in the selection of judges potentially favorable to their clients. Bar associations should participate in judicial selection as any other private group in the political process; in an advisory capacity, giving advice to the voters in an elective system or advice to the governor in an appointive system. It is improper for the organized bar to dominate or to become a veto group within an official nominating commission.

2) The governor, although technically responsible for judicial appointments under the plan, cannot be held responsible by the voters for bad appointments, since his responsibility is shared with an anonymous group of decision makers.

3) The noncompetitive election for retention of the incumbent judge is a meaningless routine, admittedly built into the plan for the public relations purpose of reducing voter hostility to the adoption of the new method.

This research project was undertaken to provide a basis for evaluation of the Ohio Bar Association plan, not to make alternative recommendations. However, the challenge to the present system is strong. The analysis has normative implications which cannot easily be ignored. Hence a tentative prescription for reform follows.

The invisibility of the present method of selecting Ohio's judges also violates the criteria we have established in the following ways:

1) Although judicial candidates are nominated in partisan primaries, participation in those primaries is slight due to, among other things, the low salience of judicial politics to the voter.

2) In the election, the lack of party label deprives the voter of any aggregate information which would enable him to predict the policy predilections of a judicial candidate. This is particularly a serious deficiency at the appellate level, where judicial policy making is most common.

3) In the absence of a party label, the voter is guided by con-

siderations such as: a) familiarity of the name, which depends on the publicity the judge or other candidates with the same name have been able to secure in the media; and b) ethnic, religious, or racial identity, which may be meaningful to the voter entirely apart from the potential exercise of the judicial function.

4) Because of the advantage afforded by nonpartisan elections to the party of upper-status voters (in competitive states such as Ohio, the Republican party), the present system discriminates against those elements in society most in need of representation in the courts: lower-income, less-educated groups.

Of the two "visible" methods of judicial selection, a return to partisan elections is the less desirable for two reasons. Although such a change would meet the criterion of judicial accountability to the voters, it would diminish judicial independence, which is the other criterion to be met. That is, popular partisan election would make it more difficult for judges to be impartial and to resist pressure from interested parties to a case. Also, the politics of partisan elections tend to require judicial candidates to devote both time and concern to campaign and pre-campaign activities, including requesting money and assistance from people whose cases they may later have to decide. This is extractive politics, not politics in the large sense of policy making, of responding to the felt needs of the times. Extractive politics are indeed demeaning to judicial candidates and irrelevant to qualties of judicial (policy making) excellence.

The second visible method of judicial selection meets the criteria of independence and accountability. This method is gubernatorial appointment for life or until age seventy, with confirmation by the state senate, similar to the method of access to the federal judiciary except for the possible age limit on tenure. This method meets the criteria for three reasons. Accountability is provided through the political agent of appointment. The governor is a *singular* appointing power, the responsibility is clearly his, and the voters can hold him responsible for his judicial appointments. As in the federal judiciary, "in the long run, and with very few exceptions, 'good' appointments are good politics."[96] Secondly, inde-

[96]Grossman, *Lawyers and Judges, op. cit.*, p. 35.

pendence is provided by tenure (for life or until age seventy), which frees judges from pressure by parties to a case, such as individuals with money, utilities, banks, insurance companies, or labor unions, and from campaign necessities, such as money or votes.[97] As a popular check on tenure, it would be possible to provide a term of ten years, and then a noncompetitive election for tenure, although this feature has the disadvantages already discussed of the referendum under the Missouri Plan. Finally, if tenure is undesirable in the case of a particular judge because of mental or physical illness or incompetence, a removal procedure is presently available in the Ohio Constitution, after due notice and hearing, by concurrent resolution agreed to by two-thirds of both houses of the legislature. (Ohio Constitution, Art. II, sec. 38; Art. IV, sec. 17.)

The assumptions underlying executive appointment, like those of partisan election, are based on the realities of judicial decision making: because statutes and constitutions are susceptible to interpretation, judges make policy. Because their underlying values shape their decisions, judges' political qualifications are a necessary component of their ability to perform the judicial function. Such qualifications do not replace legal qualifications, but are important additions to them.[98] At the same time, judges need to be "free" to follow impartial norms (when they exist) in deciding cases. Selected by the visible means of executive appointment with confirmation by the senate, appellate judges could reflect the seemingly inconsistent but equally essential attributes of accountability and independence.

---

[97]Executive appointment for life had been used for the selection of the Massachusetts judiciary for 140 years when the federal Constitutional Convention in 1787 adopted this practice for the new nation's judges. Attempts to limit appointments to 10-year terms were defeated twice, once by the people of Massachusetts in 1853, and again in the state constitutional convention of 1917–1918. Although Massachusetts has experienced "at least the average amount of graft and corruption" in its legislative and executive branches, the judiciary has been unusually free of even the suspicion of partiality or corruption. Robert F. Drinan, S.J., "Judicial Appointments for Life by the Executive Branch of Government: Reflections on the Massachusetts Experience," *Texas Law Review*, 45 (1966), 1105 ff.

[98]Francis D. Wormuth and S. Grover Rich, Jr., "Politics, the Bar, and the Selection of Judges," *Utah Law Review*, 3 (1953), 463.

APPENDIX
OHIO STATE SUPREME COURT CONTESTS 1960–1968

		Candidates	
Year		*Republican*	*Democratic*
1960	(1)	Earl R. Hoover	*James F. Bell
	(2)	*Kingsley A. Taft	Joseph H. Ellison
	(3)	*C. William O'Neill	John W. Peck (unexpired term)
1962	(1-CJ)	*Kingsley A. Taft	C. J. Carl V. Weygandt
	(2)	*John M. Matthias	James J. Mayer
	(3)	*Paul M. Herbert	Richard T. Cole
1964	(1)	Francis B. Douglas	*Charles B. Zimmerman
	(2)	*C. William O'Neill	Joseph D. Bryan
	(3)	*Louis J. Schneider	Lynn B. Griffith (unexpired term)
	(4)	*Paul W. Brown	Rankin Gibson (unexpired term)
1966	(1)	*Louis J. Schneider	Clifford F. Brown
	(2)	*Paul W. Brown	Joseph D. Bryan
1968	(1-CJ)	*C. J. Kingsley Taft	John C. Duffy
	(2)	*John M. Matthias	No candidate
	(3)	*Thomas M. Herbert	Merrill D. Brothers

*Winner

The Politics of Public Higher Education in Ohio

Joseph B. Tucker

ALL OF HIGHER EDUCATION IS UNDOUBTEDLY UNDERGOING A REVOlution. While the cries of "relevance" and "involvement" have been reduced to cliches, universities are restructuring their decision making processes and redefining their goals. One problem unique to public higher education and of crucial importance in understanding the tensions, conflicts, and changes on public campuses has received little empirical study: the relationship between a state's political system and its institutions of public higher education.[1] As enrollments have soared, as competition for budget allocations has increased, and as pressures have mounted to involve the university more directly in social problems, the relationship of public higher education to state politics, always important, has become critical.

During this same period of great change and heightened tensions in higher education, efforts at modernizing and simplifying

---

[1]For a discussion of the concept "political system" see David Easton, *A Systems Analysis of Political Life* (New York: John Wiley and Sons, 1965). This study will use Easton's now famous definition of politics. Although open to some criticism, politics, he says, is the study of the "authoritative allocation of values for society."

state constitutions have been taking place at a rate unprecedented in the twentieth century. This has led two students of state politics to suggest that these "two important but seemingly unrelated areas of interest to students of American government appear to be converging. . . ." They are converging, they argue, because "those involved in higher education have begun to recognize the importance of state constitutional provisions and to lobby in constitutional conventions."[2] In the words of the former president of the State University of New York:

> With the tendency of the times toward more and more interest in public higher education by the people and their duly elected and appointed representatives, and a corresponding tendency to introduce political considerations into the process of educational planning; . . . with increasing pressures from business, industry, social agencies, or federal and state governments to shape the activities and curricula of the universities to their needs in research, training, and education and to give such needs the very highest priority; with the increase in abrasive challenges and charges inevitably hurled by both sides in any disagreement over the missions of universities—with all these factors and others, constitutional guarantees of university independence of action appear not only desirable but essential.[3]

Analyzing constitutional conventions over the past two decades and especially the recent ones in Hawaii, Michigan, New York, and Maryland, Gove states that the major discussion of public higher education has centered on university governance. The specific questions asked are:

> Should the constitution contain provisions on the method of selecting the governing board? If so, what kind? Should some degree of autonomy be granted to segments of the higher educational system? If so, how much and to what institutions? Should the constitution

---

[2]Samuel K. Gove and Susan Welch, "The Influence of State Constitutional Conventions on the Future of Higher Education," *Educational Record,* 50 (Spring, 1969), 206.

[3]Samuel B. Gould, "The University and the State: Fears and Realities," in W. John Minter (ed.), *Campus and Capitol; Higher Education and the State* (Boulder: Western Interstate Commission for Higher Education, 1966), p. 13.

provide for a state-wide coordinating board? If so, how much power should it have?[4]

Due primarily to the recent changes in the system of public higher education in Ohio, serious questions are now being raised in this state concerning institutional autonomy. During the 1960s Ohio's system of public higher education grew from six to eleven universities with over thirty branches and academic centers; witnessed the creation of a Board of Regents with certain statewide powers; increased its operating appropriations from $47,000,000 to $176,000,000; and felt increasing pressure for additional four-year institutions.[5] A recent management study of public higher education called for greater state centralization under the Board of Regents.[6]

Those concerned with institutional autonomy cannot look to the Ohio Constitution for protection; the present constitution says virtually nothing about public higher education. The only references deal with capital improvement programs (Art. VIII, Sec. 2e) and guaranteeing loans to residents attending institutions of higher education (Art. VI, Sec. 5). The current attention to constitutional change, coupled with recent developments in public higher education, suggests that the question of university autonomy might receive serious consideration in Ohio.[7]

This consideration should not take place in the abstract, however, but should be based on the empirical relationship between

---

[4]Gove and Welch, *op. cit.*, pp. 207–208. There is, of course, the question of whether higher education is so "basic" as to be included in the constitution. The position assumed in this paper, similar to the argument of Gove and Welch, is that the question will be determined by the political process in the state, not by abstract arguments.

[5]This material is taken from *Ohio Higher Education Basic Data Series* (Columbus: Ohio Board of Regents, 1969). The most recent data in this report covers 1968. The 1969–1971 biennium appropriations total $500,581,110.

[6]*Management Study and Analysis: Ohio Public Higher Education* (Chicago: Warren King and Associates, Inc., 1969).

[7]Earlier surveys of constitutional problem areas have ignored higher education. A recent report to the Stephen H. Wilder Foundation by W. Donald Heisel and Iola O. Hessler, *State Government for Our Times: A New Look at Ohio's Constitution* (Cincinnati: University of Cincinnati Institute of Governmental Research, 1970), also says nothing about higher education.

state politics and higher education policy making. Little or no research has been done in this area, either in Ohio or in other states.[8] This study attempts to outline the relationship between state politics and public higher education in Ohio; reviews the arguments concerning institutional autonomy in light of this relationship; and finally, offers certain recommendations concerning the constitutional status of public higher education.

I. THE OLD PATTERN: VOLUNTARY INSTITUTIONAL COOPERATION

To understand the current environment in which higher education functions in Ohio, as well as to understand what institutional autonomy has meant in the past, one must appreciate earlier institutional arrangements. Until the mid 1960s, public higher education in Ohio consisted of six state universities which cooperated through an Inter-University Council.[9] Formed in 1939, the I.U.C. represented an early effort at voluntary cooperation. It was the

---

[8]A recent bibliographic essay pointed out the dearth of research into the politics of public higher education—indeed, the lack of even one systematic study of the relationship between public higher education and state politics. See Samuel K. Gove and Barbara Whiteside Solomon, "The Politics of Higher Education: A Bibliographic Essay," *Journal of Higher Education,* 39 (April, 1968), 181–195. A few books, however, have made some significant contributions in this area: Malcolm Moos and Francis E. Rourke, *The Campus and the State* (Baltimore: The Johns Hopkins Press, 1959), and W. John Minter (ed.), *Campus and Capitol: Higher Education and the State* (Boulder: Western Interstate Commission for Higher Education, 1966). Although quite polemical, of considerable interest is James Ridgeway, *The Closed Corporation* (New York: Random House, 1968). The situation is, in fact, much better with regard to studies of the politics of public elementary and secondary education. Nicholas A. Masters, Robert H. Salisbury, and Thomas H. Eliot, *State Politics and the Public Schools* (New York: Alfred A. Knopf, 1964) and Stephen K. Bailey, Richard Frost, Paul E. Marsh, and Robert C. Wood, *Schoolmen and Politics: A Study of State Aid to Education in the Northeast* (Syracuse: Syracuse University Press, 1962).

[9]Actually there were only five institutions until 1951; in that year the state legislature created Central State College. Prior to that time it had existed as a part of Wilberforce University. The college had its origins in legislation passed in 1887 when the state, upon request of Wilberforce University, created a Normal and Industrial Department within Wilberforce to provide assistance in the education of Negro teachers.

key agency for some twenty years in the universities' relationships with state government. The major motivating force in the formation of the I.U.C. was the potentially harmful consequences that the existing laissez faire approach in higher education might produce.[10] The practice had been for each school to develop, submit, and lobby for its own programs and appropriations, with little regard for other institutions.

Ohio State University took the lead in calling the meeting which resulted in the formation of the I.U.C. OSU's central concern was apparent in a memorandum which accompanied the call for the meeting:

> The need is for a coordinated program of nurture and support which will strengthen each of the five state universities within the limits of its own best competence and reasonable public demand.
>
> At the same time the conclusion is inescapable and must be frankly faced by all concerned that the state cannot and should not embark upon the impossible purpose to build five equally large, highly specialized and all equivalent universities capable of comparison with such single outstanding institutions in surrounding states as the University of Michigan, University of Wisconsin, the University of Minnesota, the University of Illinois, and the like.[11]

The memorandum went on to suggest that Ohio State University was the logical place for all Ph.D. and professional work with

---

[10] M. M. Chambers not only suggests this reason but also cites another version of how the I.U.C. began. "Mr. Davey (Governor of Ohio) came from Kent and was very much interested in developing Kent State University. The other institutions felt that this interest was being evidenced at their expense. The result was an official agreement in 1939 to create the Inter-University Council." M. M. Chambers, *Voluntary Statewide Coordination in Public Higher Education* (Ann Arbor: The University of Michigan Press, 1961), p. 33. Former Governor John Bricker claims to have suggested to Ohio State that a council be formed, adding yet another factor. All of the versions, however, would appear to be compatible.

[11] Memorandum by The Ohio State University, January 7, 1939. Found in *Minutes of the Inter-University Council: Volume 1.* Volume 1 covers January, 1939, through December, 1960; Volume 2 reports the period January, 1961, through June, 1963. Reference to these volumes will be cited as Minutes. The volume, date, and page number of minutes will be listed whenever possible; since the minutes contain material other than records of regular meetings, this will not always be possible.

the other institutions foregoing these programs. This document was approved by the institutions and served more or less as a set of guiding principles. Even though the presidents had joined together, the I.U.C. was from the beginning an organization based on an uneasy truce.[12] The presidents realized that a cooperative effort in financial and other matters was to their self interest. What Banfield calls the "maintenance and enhancement needs of large formal organizations," however, would lead ultimately to the failure of this voluntary organization.[13]

An understanding of the modus operandi of the council is essential since, in some respects, it is still employed by the I.U.C.'s successor, the Ohio Board of Regents.[14]

Shortly after the I.U.C. was formed, the state finance director notified the group that the governor intended to recommend to the General Assembly an increase of one million dollars in the combined operations and maintenance appropriations for the five state universities. The finance director wanted the I.U.C. to assume the responsibility of fairly dividing the increase among the schools. In response, the council members drew up a proposal for the division of the total anticipated appropriation (increase included), which gave Ohio State University sixty percent of the funds. The remaining forty percent was apportioned among the other schools on the basis of enrollment.

Should the anticipated appropriation not materialize, each institution agreed to share the reduction at the same percentage rate as in the requests. If agreeing on a joint appropriations request became the cornerstone of the voluntary organization, the sharing of reductions on the same basis was the keystone. Failure in 1960 to agree on either of these two points signaled the impending demise of the I.U.C.

---

[12]The formal membership of the I.U.C. consisted not only of the presidents but also one trustee and the business manager from each institution.

[13]Edward C. Banfield, *Political Influence* (New York: The Free Press, 1961), p. 263. I came across the application of this concept to higher education in Allen Rosenbaum. "Competition in Public Higher Education: The Case of Illinois" (Unpublished manuscript, Institute of Government and Public Affairs, University of Illinios, no date).

[14]The following discussion is based on a reading of the Minutes: 1.

The central problem that was to plague the council throughout its important years was apparent at this first financial encounter: On what basis should the anticipated appropriation for higher education be divided? No cost analysis existed for any of the schools and, indeed, would not for many years. What resulted, and was to recur each biennium, was nothing more nor less than a protracted bargaining session among the university presidents. The preceding biennium percentage allocation was used as a starting point, and each institution's percentage of the upcoming biennial appropriations was adjusted slightly upward or downward. The ground rules stipulated, however, that Ohio State University would receive the lion's share of the appropriations due to its doctoral and professional programs. Even though the other institutions recognized Ohio State's need for higher levels of support, the administration of that institution was biennially fending off attempts to cut deeper into its percentage. In the latter years of the I.U.C., these efforts became even more vigorous and added to the tensions on the council.

Council members not only bargained among themselves but were in regular contact with the governor and director of finance attempting to increase their total appropriation. Minutes of the I.U.C. record numerous meetings with the governor and director of finance at which the university presidents sought higher levels of funding. The funding process, then, was not simply a matter of the presidents dividing a control figure handed down from the director of finance. Figures were often in a state of flux, and the final recommendations depended at times on such uncertainties as legislative approval of a proposed tax increase.

The universities were also actively involved in efforts to influence the legislature. While the presidents themselves occasionally testified at public hearings and met in private sessions with key legislative leaders and members of the finance committees, most of the lobbying was done by other university personnel. Quite often the individual most actively engaged from each institution was the business manager; at a few institutions an assistant to the president assumed major responsibility for legislative liaison.

Each university had one or two trustees who were quite useful politically. Reference in the I.U.C. minutes, interviews with university lobbyists from this period, and correspondence between presidents and trustees make clear the trustees' role. They could open political doors, as witnessed by this comment from a new university president to a trustee. "I appreciate deeply all the time which you gave me yesterday, as well as the arrangements which you made for me to meet Governor Lausche."[15] They intervened on behalf of the universities with the state bureaucracy. "I hopped on Deffenbacher (state director of finance) this morning about the dormitory architect's fees; the result should speak for itself. Also had a session this morning with Shively (another trustee) planning further pressure." When the opportunity arose, trustees attempted to promote the general interests of their institution. "You know how I hated to miss the doings . . . but companionship with that remarkable man named Lausche for a couple of days probably did more good than my presence at a board meeting."[16]

In addition to financial concerns, a continuing problem in the council was the issue of establishing additional institutions—particularly two-year campuses. It is worth considering this question in some detail since it highlights one of the weaknesses of the council as a planning agency and, at the same time, illustrates what the universities did in an area where they were quite autonomous.

As early as 1940, the Ohio College Association questioned the intentions of the state universities regarding the establishment of branch campuses. The I.U.C. minutes note that "Many of the private institutions in the state were opposed to certain extension and branch college activities of some of the state universities.[17] Although only two of the state unversities operated a total of four branches, the private colleges were well aware of the potential competition an expanded state system of higher education posed. Although it has not been a central concern of this study, it would

---

[15]Letter from John C. Baker to Arthur C. Johnson, February 10, 1945.

[16]Letters from Arthur C. Johnson to John C. Baker, November 12, 1945, and June 14, 1946. The latter letter concludes "Hope to see you on the 21st. Senator Adams will be getting a show degree; he is quite worth cultivating."

[17]Minutes: 1 (March 12, 1940), 3.

appear that private higher education in Ohio has not been a very strong political force.

The president of Ohio University, which operated two branches, encouraged the council to support the development of branches. In his words:

> The state universities should definitely undertake to organize such branch colleges in their respective regions in response to strong public demand in communities which are not now served by existing colleges or universities, or possibly even in communities which do have local institutions not offering those types of training which the state universities are competent to give.[18]

His enthusiasm was not shared by the other presidents; even the president of the university operating the other two branches was not sympathetic. Expressing a concern for the reaction of the private colleges, which would be amusing today, the majority of the council felt that "the private colleges in Ohio would be increasingly hostile to the state universities if the latter go into the 'branch college' business." It was therefore resolved that: "It be the sense of the Inter-University Council of Ohio that the establishment of "branch colleges" by the state universities be discouraged—and that this expression of joint judgment be communicated to the Boards of Trustees of the five state universities by their presidents."[19]

During the same period, the I.U.C. was very much opposed to the development of state-supported community colleges. When the American Council on Education encouraged such a development, the council responded:

> The proposal to encourage the establishment of Junior Colleges in larger communities, to be supported in part out of the general revenues of the state, is dangerous to the future welfare of state-supported institutions of higher learning.
>
> With public revenues now overburdened with growing demands for relief and pensions of all sorts, the continued support of existing institutions is seriously threatened. The proposal regarding state-supported Junior Colleges is a further distinct threat.

---

[18]Minutes: 1 (March 12, 1940), 4.
[19]*Ibid.*

> We, therefore, as institutional members of the American Council on Education, repudiate that suggestion, and protest against the support given to the proposal by the President of the American Council on Education. It is, in our opinion, not part of his function to advocate developments which are harmful to member institutions of that Council.[20]

Concern over competition for state tax dollars from other potential public institutions was a recurring theme in the minutes of the council. This is understandable in the light of economic conditions in 1940; the universities' continued opposition to junior or community colleges, however, reflected, among other things, the low level of public spending for higher education in Ohio. In the decades following World War II, whatever the needs for a rationally developed plan for expansion, the state universities attempted to pursue a course which would limit competition for educational monies and leave them in control of the system.

This course, contrary to the earlier position, was to support the establishment of branch campuses, which were basically self supporting until the 1960s. In order to accommodate the surge in enrollments following World War II, the council unanimously agreed that their earlier resolution should be "temporarily suspended until such time as in the judgment of the council the present emergency has passed."[21] The emergency, of course, did not pass. The issue surfaced again in 1956 when, in the face of another anticipated upsurge in college enrollments, the Ohio College Association called for a legislatively established Commission on Education Beyond the High School.

The concern over what such a commission might recommend was readily apparent. The long-time business manager and lobbyist for Ohio State was recorded as stating "we must be ready to exert leadership on this matter. There will be much agitation for community colleges and considerable pork-barrelling might result." The council's position on branches was never officially reversed, but it was clear at this meeting that the I.U.C. would favor expanded

---

[20]Minutes: 1 (April 24, 1940), 3.
[21]Minutes: 1 (May 15, 1946), 2.

branch operations. One of the presidents stated "we should move ahead with our branch campuses and . . . the problem might well be handled thereby."[22]

Inevitably, community colleges and other two-year institutions were established in Ohio. But a large number of students attending two-year programs are still enrolled at the university branches.[23] Branch campuses are, of course, a viable method of handling two-year programs. However, the branch system in Ohio cannot be counted a particular success. A recent consultant's report on the branch campuses submitted to the Ohio Board of Regents was especially damning. The report states at one point, "An all too common suspicion, adequately justified, is that the branches are run for the convenience of the home campuses rather than to meet the real needs of the community and clientele in which they exist."[24]

Discussing the great degree of centralized control the mother institution exerts over its branches the report continues:

> I am not persuaded that the controls presently exerted from afar are conducive to maintenance of standards or to sound education. I am certain that the controls delimit the kind of faculty, the students, and the administrative staff which join the branches. The passivity, the resignation through which impatience and frustration are occasionally revealed are inevitable in those who must perfunctorily perform without exerting either judgment or creativity.[25]

The consultant goes on to suggest that serious consideration be given to establishing the branches as autonomous community colleges. Only then, he argues, can the institutions meet the needs of the communities in which they exist. The question of how public higher

---

[22]Minutes: 1 (December 5, 1956), 3.

[23]21,208 students were enrolled at branches out of a total of 50,338 at community colleges, technical institutes, and branches (fall term, 1969). Of the enrollment at the four community colleges, Cuyahoga Community College alone accounted for 15,100 out of the 23,800. (*Ohio's Newly Developed System of Two-Year Colleges* [Columbus: Ohio Board of Regents, 1970], p. 8.)

[24]Paul Dressel, "A Report on Four Branch Campuses," prepared for the Ohio Board of Regents, June 20, 1970, p. 4.

[25]*Ibid.*, p. 10.

education should be structured will undoubtedly be a continuing political issue.[26]

Returning to the I.U.C., the foregoing illustrates how the council could not rise above the immediate self interest of the several institutions comprising it. I am not suggesting that the presidents of the state universities consciously developed a system of inferior education; on the contrary, the minutes reveal that the presidents believed that branch development was the best way to meet the growing needs in higher education. It is also true, however, given the financial constraints existing in Ohio, that the views of the I.U.C. presidents made the most sense politically.

The same concern for institutional autonomy is evident in the development of Ph.D. programs. In 1959 Ohio University entered the Ph.D. field, renouncing, in effect, the earlier agreement which gave Ohio State University sole jurisdiction over the doctorate. Most of the other state universities soon followed Ohio University's lead. Ohio and Miami Universities, due to the nature of their charters, have always had the power to grant the Ph.D. The legislature in 1959, in rather indirect language, gave Kent and Bowling Green State Universities the same power. Regardless of the "need" for additional Ph.D. programs, it is obvious that the expansion of doctoral work in Ohio was not well planned. Indeed, the president of one state university was recorded as saying "he entered into this area reluctantly but in self defense."[27] Supporting the conclusion reached here about the overriding concern for institutional autonomy, a 1963 study by the Legislative Service Commission stated, "This lack of effectiveness [of the I.U.C.] can be attributed primarily to the desire prevalent at most public universities to act independently, and to maintain institutional autonomy."[28]

Lyman A. Glenny was critical of the I.U.C. on broader grounds:

---

[26]In a recently released draft of the new master plan for the 1970s the Regents recommended that the branches be removed from the universities and designated community and technical colleges with independent governing boards. This recommendation met with opposition from many branch communities.

[27]Minutes: 2 (April 10, 1961), 5.

[28]Staff Research Report Number 53, *Coordination of Higher Education* (Columbus: Ohio Legislative Service Commission, 1963), p. 23.

> This study has come to the conclusion that the (Ohio) legislature's informal delegation of power to representatives of the existing institutions to make state-wide decisions does not promote the general welfare. In theory the voluntary agencies are not responsible for decisions on the important state-wide educational affairs, but in fact they do reach agreements on allocation of programs, graduate work, research emphasis, and functions. Institutions in the voluntary systems have often established sub-units of their own when new institutions would have been more appropriate and would have brought increased diversity. The fact that these decisions, which strike at the very core of educational policy, are not widely publicized to the legislature or to the citizenry makes them no less significant for the public interest.[29]

In other areas where one might reasonably expect autonomy, the state exercised rigid control over the universities. This was particularly true regarding custody and disbursement of university non-tax income. M. M. Chambers point out that the controls resulted from:

> A statute dating from the early years of this century, enacted as a result of the movement toward tight centralization of state financial control and abolishing the nineteenth-century abuses such as allowing some public officers to collect fees for services and keep them as their personal property, required that institutional and departmental income be promptly deposited in the state treasury and held there until appropriated by the legislature.[30]

Over the years the statute was amended, and the attorney general rendered several opinions attempting to clarify what the law required of universities. Chambers details the problems and confusion which resulted. Significant amendments in 1955 and 1961 greatly reduced the types of fees which had to be deposited in the state treasury and, in turn, increased the fiscal control of boards of trustees. Again citing Chambers:

> In the context of Ohio law and custom, this was a considerable step forward toward reasonable fiscal freedom for the universities. By the

[29]*Autonomy of Public Colleges* (New York: McGraw-Hill Book Company, 1959), p. 254.

[30]*Higher Education in the Fifty States* (Danville: The Interstate Printers and Publishers, 1970), p. 291.

> standards of Michigan and other states having constitutionally independent universities as well as other states whose legislatures have habitually respected the sphere of discretion properly belonging to university governing boards, Ohio's partial evolution just described was less than half a loaf.[31]

The universities' ability to control local non-academic personnel appointments was equally restricted. All hiring of such personnel had to go through the State Department of Personnel with the delays and bureaucratic snarls one would expect. These two examples serve to illuminate the other side of institutional autonomy in Ohio or, rather, the lack of it.

In assessing the period under consideration, the years of voluntary coordination, several conclusions are in order. As mentioned earlier, the universities attempted to establish close relationships with the political leaders of the state; as will be seen shortly, this is a pattern that has been followed by the Ohio Board of Regents. Without an organized constituency similar to many interest groups in the state, and lacking the financial resources of others, the spokesmen for public higher education had to cultivate and nurture support for their interests with modest resources. Despite this continuing political relationship, there is little evidence that there was political interference with the academic freedom of the universities. There were, of course, the previously mentioned controls, but these were becoming less rather than more restrictive. Whether or not one agrees with my assessment of the use of their autonomy, the universities did have considerable freedom of action in significant academic matters.

II. A STATUTORY STATEWIDE COORDINATING BOARD

Events leading to the creation of the Ohio Board of Regents are not presented here in great detail. Reference has already been made to the fact that tensions always existed within the I.U.C. Due

---

[31]*Ibid.*, pp. 291–295.

to the financial situation in Ohio in 1960, these tensions were particularly acute;[32] the presidents failed to agree on a joint percentage request for the 1961–1963 biennium, nor did they agree to a joint sharing of losses as in the past. The entrance of Ohio University into the Ph.D. field further added to the conflicts in the council. The capital appropriations for the same biennium are worth more attention because, in the words of one university president, the failure of the presidents to agree on this item meant that by the summer of 1961 the I.U.C. "had committed suicide."

Initially, the presidents had submitted through the I.U.C. a capital improvement request for the 1961–1963 biennium of twenty-five million dollars. Subsequently, the Speaker of the House, Representative Roger Cloud, developed his own proposal for capital improvements. Speaker Cloud had become interested in science and engineering education and their value for the economic growth of the state.[33] Introduced at his urging, H.J.R. 56 proposed the establishment at Ohio State University of a Technical Research Center and appropriated fifteen million dollars for its construction. The center was to be financed from the surpluses of a 1955 cigarette tax; this tax had been voted by a constitutional amendment to pay off a bond issue and in 1961 was producing revenue in excess of that needed to meet the obligations on the bonds. What happened thereafter is clearly stated in the following letter:

> It was suggested to me by an emissary on behalf of Speaker Cloud that if the universities would support House Joint Resolution No. 56, Cloud would be willing to have an understanding to the effect that all of the money available in the biennium 1963–65 would be shared by the four state universities and one state college other than Ohio State. It was estimated that somewhere between eight and ten million dollars would be available under the program in the two years 1963–65.

---

[32]This observation is based on an interview with a former university president. See also James Reichley, *States in Crisis* (Chapel Hill: The University of North Carolina Press, 1964), p. 136. Throughout this section I have relied on personal interviews with public officials and university personnel. In several cases individuals desired to remain anonymous.

[33]Proceedings of the Elections and Federal Relations Committee, Wednesday, June 21, 1961, found in Minutes: 2.

> I approached President Fawcett with this suggestion, and after considerable discussion he indicated his willingness to accept the proposal. This would mean that Ohio State would receive the first fifteen million dollars of surplus funds, but that these would be earmarked entirely for a Technological Research Center. It meant that the other five institutions would split all available funds in 1963–65. It meant further that beginning in 1965 the six institutions would share on a formula basis as determined by the Inter-University Council. President Fawcett recognized that this arrangement would work some difficulty with the orderly progress of the capital improvement program of the Ohio State University. In the interests of harmony among the state universities and in order to obtain an earmarked source of funds for capital improvements at the state universities, President Fawcett was willing to make this concession.
>
> Speaker Cloud further indicated that he hoped to have this agreement in writing so that it would be a matter of record and could be honored in the 1963 General Assembly regardless of the leadership personalities of the 105th General Assembly.
>
> I then approached President Baker to outline this compromise proposal. President Baker emphatically and quickly rejected the whole suggestion. I then reported back to the Speaker of the House that I was unable to arrange a compromise along the lines outlined to me. I wish to add for the record that I believe this compromise to have been a fair one under the circumstances and that I greatly regret the action of the officials of Ohio University in rejecting the proposal. I wish to emphasize again that I wish this matter to be made a matter of record of the Inter-University Council.[34]

Just one year later the Republican gubernatorial candidate, State Auditor James Rhodes, proposed the establishment of a statewide board for higher education. Following Rhodes's decisive victory over Governor Michael DiSalle, the council was informed by a university trustee with close political ties in the capital that:

> the establishment of a statutory board for higher education appears attractive from the legislative point of view. The pressure for a statutory board will be strong from the 105th General Assembly because of support from Speaker Cloud and because for the first time a

[34]Letter from President John Millett (Miami University) to Secretary of the I.U.C. July 7, 1961, found in Minutes: 2.

Governor elect has proposed a board as one of his specific legislative proposals.[35]

With the governor and legislative leadership committed to a state board, the basic issue, according to a former legislator was, "How much authority it should have?" The organizational patterns developed in other states offered several choices. The most basic was between a coordinating board or a consolidated governing board. The latter type of board, usually composed entirely of public members, supercedes individual governing boards and has power to administer the state system of higher education. Types of coordinating boards vary between those with a majority of institutional members with advisory powers to those composed entirely of public members with some policy-making powers. The Ohio Board of Regents created by the 105th General Assembly is a coordinating board of the latter type.

Composed of nine public members appointed by the governor with Senate confirmation, the board was given a long list of advisory and study making powers as well as some crucial policy making ones. Those policy making powers initially included the power to approve or disapprove the establishment of new branches, community colleges, technical institutes, and any other state institution of higher education; the same power was granted to the board over new degrees and degree programs. Probably its most significant advisory power is to review the appropriation requests of institutions and recommend the biennial higher education appropriations to the director of finance and the chairmen of the finance committees in each house of the legislature. The statute explicitly states, "The Board shall work in close cooperation with the director of

[35]Minutes: 2 (December 19, 1962), 3. Interviews with individuals on the scene in the 1963 legislature indicate the legislative mood was favorable to a state agency. The institutional lobbying in the 1961 session had been substantial and legislators were not happy with the situation. In the ensuing session, all but one university president opposed the regents bill. Aware that they could not block a statewide agency, they had introduced a bill providing for an agency which the universities could dominate. It is ironic that in the 1961 legislature the presidents had opposed and killed a bill much like the one they were now proposing.

finance in this respect and in all other matters concerning the expenditure of appropriated state funds by state colleges, universities, and other institutions of higher education."[36]

The creation of the Board of Regents quite obviously resulted in the loss of some autonomy for the individual institutions. Henceforth the board would determine when and where new institutions would be constructed and which universities could enter new Ph.D. fields. In what other ways the activities of the Board of Regents might impinge on the autonomy of the universities was of serious concern to the presidents.

In analyzing the operation of the Board of Regents, it is often difficult to separate substantive issues from the rhetoric which often seems to accompany a discussion of the board in the academic community. During its early years the board was faced with state university administrations, a major constituent group, which were hostile. All but one university president were opposed to the creation of the regents. With the board reviewing appropriation requests and making recommendations to the director of finance, the presidents were displaced as the major voice for higher education. In addition, the new Rhodes administration allegedly informed the university presidents that they were welcome in the state house only when invited.[37] While few individuals who were university presidents when the regents were created still serve in that capacity today, there is continuing conflict between the board and the university leadership.

Another factor clouding the issue of institutional autonomy is that of style.[38] This, in turn, is related to the general financial situation in Ohio. Had the state supported public higher education in a more generous manner during the decade of the 1960s, it is doubtful that there would have been the criticism of the board, whatever its style, which existed within the academic community. While the

---

[36]*Ohio Revised Code* Section 3333.04.J.

[37]Interview with university president, August 5, 1970.

[38]This discussion is based not only on interviews but also on my role as a participant in the Ohio Faculty Senate and, more importantly, as Ohio University's representative to the Faculty Advisory Committee. This faculty group meets monthly with the chancellor to discuss matters affecting higher education.

situation improved, particularly in the last biennium of the decade, Ohio continues to rank low in per capita support for higher education.[39] When the board was created, therefore, whatever concerns were held over institutional autonomy, university faculties and administrations generally expected the regents to be an outspoken champion for higher education. That is, the academic community had in mind a model of a board which would aggressively publicize the needs of higher education, attempt to educate the public to the need for higher levels of support, and consequently bring pressure to bear on the governor and legislature for action in that direction.

The Ohio Board of Regents, under the leadership of its appointed Chancellor John Millett, has not followed that mode of operation.* Indeed, the chancellor has repeatedly stated that the board is not a lobbyist for higher education, but rather a state agency created to provide certain supervision over public institutions and to recommend to the governor and legislature policies which are in the interest of the state. Not only has the role of the board developed in such a way as to cause resentment, but the way in which the chancellor defined his own role has further antagonized the academic community. The chancellor attempted to establish a close political relationship with key legislative leaders and especially the governor. So close was his relationship with the executive office that he was perceived by many as Governor Rhodes's higher education errand boy. This role, critics assert, failed to serve the unique interests of higher education.

A fundamental question is whether the chancellor's behavior with respect to the interests of higher education was consistent with either his publicly stated position or the unflattering perception held by his critics. One could look first to the appropriation levels for higher education over the past several years as a measure of successful leadership. Failure to improve significantly, however, is not proof that the chancellor has not been a strong spokesman for higher education, particularly in view of the history of public spend-

[39]Ohio currently ranks fourty-second in per capita appropriations for higher education, up from forty-sixth in 1959–1960.

*Early in 1972, Chancellor Millett announced his intention to retire. (Editors' Note.)

ing in Ohio. Similarly, great improvement is not necessarily proof of aggressive leadership; the improvement could be in spite of the role of the chancellor. In either case, appropriations are not necessarily conclusive. Depending on which indices one uses, the results are mixed. As indicated earlier, Ohio improved from forty-sixth to forty-second in per capita appropriations during the decade of the sixties; this is certainly not a startling increase. Tables 1 and 2 provide other measures of spending increases for higher education which suggest Ohio made significant improvement. It still has a long way to go to reach even the national average per capita appropriations of thirty-two dollars.

Regarding the leadership role of the chancellor, two individuals close to both state politics and the chancellor have some interesting observations. Obviously not impartial, these individuals claim that had the chancellor not played a highly political role, higher education would have suffered during the Rhodes administration. One

TABLE 1
APPROPRIATIONS FOR HIGHER EDUCATION, EIGHT-YEAR INCREASE, 1961-1962 TO 1969-1970, FIFTEEN LARGEST STATES

	First Four Years			*Second Four Years*	
Rank	*State*	*Increase*	*Rank*	*State*	*Increase*
(1)	New York	143%	(1)	OHIO	183%
(2)	Pennsylvania	121%	(2)	Massachusetts	166%
(3)	North Carolina	111%	(3)	New Jersey	148%
(4)	Massachusetts	110%	(4)	Pennsylvania	144%
(5)	Texas	95%	(5)	North Carolina	131%
(6)	Wisconsin	92%	(6)	New York	120%
(7)	Florida	86%	(7)	Wisconsin	111%
(8)	New Jersey	78%	(8)	Florida	108%
(9)	Illinois	76%	(9)	Texas	106%
(10)	Michigan	72%	(10)	Illinois	98%
(11)	California	67%	(11)	Minnesota	97%
(12)	OHIO	64%	(12)	California	81%
(13)	Indiana	63%	(13)	Michigan	73%
(14)	Iowa	54%	(14)	Indiana	71%
(15)	Minnesota	49%	(15)	Iowa	66%

SOURCE: ***Public Higher Education In Ohio During The Sixties*** **(Columbus: Ohio Board of Regents, 1970).**

TABLE 2
PER CAPITA APPROPRIATIONS FOR HIGHER EDUCATION
TEN-YEAR INCREASE, FIFTEEN LARGEST STATES

	1959–1960		*1969–1970*		*10-Year Gain*	
	Per Capita	*Rank*	*Per Capita*	*Rank*	*Percentage*	*Rank*
Iowa	$12.55	(1)	$36.55	(4)	191	(14)
Michigan	12.21	(2)	34.92	(5)	186	(15)
California	11.99	(3)	39.32	(1)	228	(11)
Minnesota	10.59	(4)	34.72	(6)	228	(12)
Indiana	9.75	(5)	30.20	(11)	210	(13)
Illinois	8.95	(6)	36.87	(3)	312	(9)
Wisconsin	8.81	(7)	39.21	(2)	345	(7)
Florida	8.15	(8)	31.72	(9)	289	(10)
Texas	7.41	(9)	30.94	(10)	318	(8)
North Carolina	6.23	(10)	34.65	(7)	456	(3)
New York	4.68	(11)	34.20	(8)	631	(1)
OHIO	4.46	(12)	22.38	(12)	402	(5)
Pennsylvania	3.84	(13)	21.22	(13)	453	(4)
New Jersey	3.62	(14)	17.83	(14)	393	(6)
Massachusetts	2.36	(15)	15.70	(15)	565	(2)

SOURCE: *Public Higher Education In Ohio During The Sixties* (Columbus: Ohio Board of Regents, 1970).

of these individuals, the former chief executive officer of the regents, says the chancellor "has used the political muscle of the governor to aid higher education" even though the governor was not basically sympathetic. This same source was not uncritical of the chancellor's tendency to be so quick to please the governor. There were a few occasions, he indicated, when the chancellor might have been well advised to oppose the chief executive. Such opposition would not have necessarily been public. This position holds, therefore, that while the chancellor might have been more independent at times, had he not adopted a style compatible with the incumbent administration, higher education would not have fared as well as it did.

Another observer, a former state legislator, one-time chairman of the Ohio Board of Regents, and currently one of the few active university lobbyists, is also laudatory of the role of the chancellor. According to him, the board is the prime lobbyist for higher education in the state and is doing a good job. While the chancellor and the current chairman of the board would not agree with his designation of them as lobbyists, he says, that is how they operate.

Some of the chancellor's own writing offers an insight on how he has defined his role. *Organization for the Public Service,* published in 1966, is particularly informative. The administrator in the public service, he says, must develop an awareness and appreciation of the political context in which he works; this is called the political perspective. It is imperative, according to Millett, that:

> the administrator begins his approach to organizational questions with this political perspective. He seeks to determine the political forces which may oppose change and those which may support change. He arrives at an estimate of the relative balance of power of these forces, including his own prestige, and then determines whether to proceed and how far to proceed.[40]

In a more recent volume the chancellor discusses the lack of political power attached to higher education. What influence higher education has

> depends in large measure upon the state's political leadership, reinforced by interested individuals among the political elite.
>
> It has been my experience that *the key person in the development of higher education policy in a state is the governor.*[41]

One need not agree with his approach, but in light of these observations, the chancellor's leadership of the board becomes more understandable. What to many appears to be a failure of leadership reflects his idea of the political perspective and his perception of the centrality of the governor in policy making for higher education. One final observation on the academic community's criticism of the chancellor is in order. The university presidents, through the

---

[40]John D. Millett, *Organization for the Public Service* (Princeton: D. Van Nostrand Company, 1966), p. 143.

[41]John D. Millett, "State Administration of Higher Education (The Perspective of Political Science)," in Clyde J. Wingfield (ed.), *The American University: A Public Administration Perspective* (Dallas: Southern Methodist University Press, 1970), p. 47. Emphasis added.

I.U.C., had never provided the outspoken leadership for higher education many expect of the chancellor. They had operated quietly and behind the scenes. Their style, collectively and individually, was much like the chancellor's.[42]

Returning to the question of university autonomy and the Board of Regents, we are fortunate to have available a document which lists several complaints of the university presidents. Early in the fall of 1969 a dinner was held in Columbus by the regents for the president and trustee representative of each institution. The group was presented with a document outlining the major issues which the board would consider in preparing the new master plan.[43] A number of presidents were upset that they had not been involved in the preparation of this document, and feared that they would not be seriously involved in the preparation of the new master plan. This had also been a complaint of university personnel about the preparation of the 1966 master plan.

This event triggered a critical response by the university presidents, a number of whom had grown more hostile to the regents as a result of what they saw as increasing centralization on the part of the board. The I.U.C. appointed a subcommittee of three presidents to draft a statement voicing their concerns and suggesting ways of achieving a better working relationship with the regents. The statement was circulated to the presidents and trustee members of the I.U.C. Following a discussion of the document, the I.U.C. members decided not to submit it to the chancellor. While the majority agreed with its contents, several presidents believed it would not be politic to be so critical of the Board of Regents. Subsequently, the statement, which never received formal I.U.C. approval, was leaked to the chancellor by one of the presidents. This was followed by a meeting at which several presidents presented the document to the chancellor and requested a meeting with the regents

---

[42]Such an observation, however, does not prove that the chancellor's style is "right" or "best." It does tend to support, I think, my earlier contention that the reaction of the presidents was due in part to their loss of status under a coordinating board.

[43]*Focus on the Future* (Columbus: Ohio Board of Regents, 1969).

to discuss its contents. The request was promptly denied by the chairman of the regents.[44]

The following excerpt from the document summarizes the I.U.C. criticisms:

> The state-assisted universities are genuinely troubled about the direction the Ohio system has been taking. To be sure, each institution has its own particular concerns, but there is general agreement that the most serious problems are these:
>
> 1. That there is little opportunity for consultation with the Regents staff and with the Regents on a range of issues vital to the institutions and to the welfare of the higher education enterprise.
> 2. That the Regents appear to be a political arm of state government —often to the neglect of the interests of the institutions.
> 3. That the special individual needs of individual institutions are frequently pushed aside in the constant pressure for a uniformity that necessarily neglects important differences.
> 4. That the Board of Regents neither serves as a strong spokesman for the cause of higher education nor does it encourage institutional leaders to speak in defense of their vital interests and their convictions.
> 5. That the Regents have over-emphasized the quantitative expansion of educational opportunity at the expense of the qualitative strengthening of established institutions.
> 6. That the operating style of the Regents is frequently authoritarian, with little serious effort made to enlist genuine participation in the solution of common problems.
> 7. That local institutional initiative is steadily diminished as a result of an ever-thickening web of reports, instructions, procedures, clearances, etc. As an example, the great effort expended in preparation of budget estimates often is waste motion since these appear not to figure in the subsidy formulae which the Regents rely upon.
> 8. That the communication gap between the institutions and the Regents is widening. This is not a matter of personality conflicts; it is simply that arrangements are not made to encourage, or even permit, cooperative action on the part of the presidents and the

---

[44]Interview with John Marshall Briley, Chairman of the Ohio Board of Regents, August 7, 1970. Chairman Briley indicated that he wrote a letter to President Fawcett specifically rebutting the complaints listed in the memorandum. He decided against mailing it, however, and, instead, sent a letter stating that no useful purpose could be served by a meeting.

Chancellor. At best the regular monthly meeting is informational —with a one-way flow of information; at worst the meetings become unstructured adversary proceedings in which impromptu concessions are made on points where opposition is too great.

9. That initiative is throttled as institutions are pressed into a standard bureaucratic mold. As never before the universities are on the defensive. It is as if there were something intrinsically wrong in making the case for expansion of programs and capacity—this at a time when the educational system plainly lags in the production of trained manpower and much-needed research and service.[45]

If one is looking for evidence that the board has eroded university autonomy by assuming powers not legislatively granted to it, the list is not very helpful. A number of the complaints, not unexpected in light of the earlier discussion, deal with the style of operation of the regents. It is quite apparent that the presidents resent what they see as a lack of consultation. Item seven is the only one which suggests a heavy handed bureaucracy further limiting the autonomy legally retained by the universities. Whether these "procedures, clearances, etc." actually pose serious restrictions is questionable, however, as the following, more detailed statement should indicate:

> The stated objective of the Chancellor is to enhance institutional initiative through the subsidy budget system, leaving internal allocation of funds in the hands of the institution. This is all to the good. However, with respect to the capital fund budget the judgment of the Regents now supercedes that of the institution. In some instances, the institution has learned about the amount and proposed distribution of the capital budget only as the recommended budget appears in the formal submission, whether to the Finance Department or the General Assembly. The newly revised Standard Operating Procedure relating to capital budget enlarges the review authority of the Regents over capital programming. At virtually every step, the power of the Regents is joined with the power of other state offices (the State Architect, the Director of Public Works, the Director of Finance, and the Controlling Board) in a review of institutional decisions. The new

[45] "*Role of the Ohio Board of Regents and of the Several Institutions of Higher Learning in the Coordination and Management of the Educational Enterprise*" (confidential memorandum prepared by a special committee of the I.U.C.), pp. 14–16.

> six-page procedure itemizes forty separate steps in the design, funding, and construction of a new facility. At no time were the institutions given the opportunity to participate in the development of procedures which affect their vital interests. The new procedures have been presented as a *fait accompli*.[46]

The one decision of the regents which caused the greatest critical reaction from the faculties of several state universities is not mentioned in the above document. It concerned the choice of academic calendar. Traditionally, each state institution had selected its own calendar; in 1967, however, the chancellor requested state support per F.T.E. student based on a quarter calendar. There was and is no requirement that each institution adopt the quarter calendar, but for a school to have refused to do so would have resulted in a loss of operating subsidy. Consequently, all state institutions are now on the quarter calendar.

In summary, two major observations are in order. The statutory power of the regents to review university budgets and recommend operating and capital improvement support for the system is one of the major sources of conflict with the universities. The Board of Regents, in attempting to develop a more rational basis for requesting legislative appropriations, has required detailed information from the universities in a standardized format. Indeed, one of the stated goals of the chancellor is to have the regents establish budgetary consistency within the system of public higher education.[47] Further, the legislature has given the board the power to oversee in a general way the release of state monies to the universities. That these powers have resulted in standardization and a loss of autonomy for local boards of trustees is incontestable.

Second, the universities, according to the I.U.C. memorandum, are apparently unable to point to specific examples of board restrictions on academic freedom or, for that matter, interference in

---

[46] *Ibid.*, pp. 7–8.

[47] The chancellor's most recent effort in this direction is his *Planning, Programming and Budgeting for Ohio's Public Institutions of Higher Education* (Columbus: Ohio Board of Regents, 1970).

strictly internal academic matters.[48] As indicated, the criticism appears to stem from the political displacement of the university presidents by the regents and chancellor and from the subsequent styles they have adopted. I am not so naive as to suggest that the "ever-thickening web of reports, instructions, procedures, clearances, etc." can affect only the management or operational autonomy of a university. Within an institution the very fact that certain data must be collected may shape academic policy in subtle ways. On the other hand, the availability of the data can lead to a more rational, internal policy making process.

It is important to note that in other areas the board's actions have resulted in less centralization, a fact often overlooked. Lack of institutional control of fees and centralized personnel policies were mentioned earlier as sources of irritation to the universities. Under the leadership of the Board of Regents, the 106th General Assembly enacted legislation giving the trustees of each institution control over all types of fees and income, completing the reform begun in 1961. The same legislature granted to each university the power to control its own personnel policies, within the limits of state civil service legislation and review by the department of personnel.[49] In addition, the 108th General Assembly passed legislation, again at the urging of the regents, to exempt state institutions of higher education from state travel regulations; the trustees of each institution are permitted to set up their own rules subject to approval of the state emergency board. Such legislation may not appear particularly significant but, collectively, it grants greater autonomy to each university in its day-to-day operation.

Behind the scenes, the board has also defended the autonomy of the universities against what it considers unwarranted legislative interference. This may take the form of attempting quietly to kill legislation in committee or to eliminate particularly restrictive provisions of pending bills. The efforts of the Board of Regents

[48]By internal academic matters, I have in mind such things as course offerings, credit hours, reduced teaching loads, size of classes, etc.

[49]It is interesting to note that the chancellor's efforts led to resentment on the part of the director of personnel. In the next legislative session he unsuccessfully attempted to remove this power from the universities.

may well go unnoticed in the latter case, since legislation may pass which the universities still find objectionable. One example of such activity involved H.B. 1219, which was passed by the 108th General Assembly. H.B. 1219, growing out of the Ohio campus disorders of 1970, provides that if university students, faculty, and personnel are charged with specific acts listed in the law, they may be suspended by a regents-appointed lawyer referee prior to actual trial.

The law is much more extensive and complex than the above might suggest and serious questions of its constitutionality have been raised. The point here, however, is that an earlier version of the bill provided that any state university forced to close would immediately lose its state operating subsidy. Opposed to such a drastic step, the chancellor agreed to rewrite the board's rule which defined full-time equivalent student. Actually, one sentence was added to the rule:

> Recognizing minor variations in academic calendar planning, these procedures for determining full-time equivalent student enrollment assume an academic year of thirty-three weeks including thirty weeks of regular course instruction, and a summer term of eleven weeks including ten weeks of regular course instruction.[50]

By including the number of weeks in the academic calendar, not previously specified, the rule could now be used to cut off state funds if that minimum were not met. At the same time, since it was to be administered by the board, it left room for administrative discretion. The chancellor intended that if institutions were forced to close they could indicate plans to make up the lost time and not lose state support. Such activity is in keeping with the role of the Board of Regents as defined by the chancellor. He has stated that one of the major roles of the regents is to act as a political intermediary, putting the board between the governor and legislature, and the individual schools.

The 108th Ohio General Assembly saw an increasing number of bills introduced which, from the universities' point of view, called

---

[50]*Minutes of Meeting of Ohio Board of Regents,* June 19, 1970, p. 1.

for a very active political intermediary. In fact, it can be argued that the legislature, rather than the regents, poses the greatest threat to the remaining autonomy of the universities.

In 1967 the General Assembly gave the regents, as a part of the appropriations act, the final power to approve tuition and fee increases requested by the institutions of higher learning. In 1967 and again in 1970, several bills were introduced which would have added to the centralization of educational policy making. While they did not pass, these bills suggest a growing legislative mood for greater control over the universities.

H.B. 251 produced the greatest reaction on the part of the universities. This bill would have legislated a forty-hour work week for the faculty, including fifteen hours of "student class contact" per week. It is interesting to note that on this issue, not willing to leave the role of political intermediary to the chancellor, the university presidents took the initiative. This was the same period when the university presidents were growing increasingly unhappy with the chancellor, culminating in the memo mentioned earlier. A meeting was arranged between Representative Schinnerer, Chairman of the House Education Committee and a co-sponsor of the bill, and the presidents. It was agreed that no action would be taken on the bill until the presidents had undertaken a study of faculty work loads. Although not the subject of pending legislation, the presidents agreed also to study the question of administrative salaries and staffing. The studies were conducted at Ohio State University and in early February, 1970, the I.U.C. met with the sponsors of the bill, the Speaker and Majority Leader of the House, and one member of the Senate to discuss the studies.[51]

Sponsors of the legislation were not particularly happy with the contents or tone of the studies, and they sent a letter to the Chairman of the I.U.C. which stated:

> In effect, the Committee said that legislators don't know about universities and, hence, should make no value judgments concerning

---

[51]*Faculty Load Study*, An Inter-University Council of Ohio Study, 1970; and *A Study of Administrative Salaries and Staffing at the Twelve State-Assisted Universities in Ohio*, An Inter-University Council of Ohio Study, 1970.

> them. We should be limited to making the appropriations, followed by complete silence. You might be surprised to learn how nervous and unhappy the stockholders (taxpayers) are becoming about the state universities.[52]

H.B. 1111 and H.B. 955 were the other bills from the 108th General Assembly with the greatest implications for institutional autonomy. The former bill would have established a salary schedule based on credit hours taught for all state university faculty. In addition, a Faculty Salary Evaluation Board was called for to review each research or community service project proposed by any faculty member and supported in any way by state funds. The board would have to approve the budget for such projects and the hours to be supported from state funds.

Based on a management consultant's report to the Joint Legislative Committee to Review the Administration of Education in Ohio, H.B. 955 called for sweeping standardization within the system of higher education.[53] The Ohio Board of Regents was required to develop uniform systems and procedures for all state-assisted institutions of higher education in connection with: budget preparation and administration; student data systems; student registration; admissions procedures; curriculum, student, faculty, and facility scheduling; library acquisition, cataloging, and circulation control; management reporting systems; inventory control; purchasing procedures; personnel records and payrolls.

The sponsors of these bills were unable to generate sufficient support to call them out of committee. In all likelihood, however, the universities can expect increasing legislative interest in their internal operations. Chancellor Millett has interpreted these bills as a form of legislative needling and has stated that university administrations and faculties can ignore them at their peril.[54]

---

[52]Letter from Representative Hadley Schinnerer to President Novice Fawcett, February 23, 1970.

[53]See *Management Study and Analysis: Ohio Public Higher Education, op. cit.*

[54]The Joint Legislative Committee to Review the Administration of Education in Ohio met in the fall of 1970 with representatives from Warren King.

III. CONSTITUTIONAL STATUS FOR PUBLIC HIGHER EDUCATION AND INSTITUTIONAL AUTONOMY

While reference has been made throughout this study to institutional autonomy, the concept has not been carefully discussed. An analysis of this concept and its implications for the quality of higher education can now be pursued with the general overview of the relationship between higher education and state politics completed.

The literature on institutional autonomy and state control is quite extensive and not at all in agreement on a definition of the concept of autonomy.[55] The position taken here is that the concept is a relative one. In a recent paper, Lyman A. Glenny states that if one takes such a position, then one must ask relative to what?

> Relative to the position from which one examines autonomy as student, faculty member, president, board member, director for statewide coordination, state budget officer, governor or legislator? Relative to academic freedom, administrative independence, or policy control? Relative to the time frame of reference—past history, present practice, or future concerns? Relative to experience and reasonable expectation or to imagination and unbridled aspiration? Relative to institutional interests or the public interest?[56]

Glenny suggests that the discussion can best be delt with by eliminating "two conceptual variants—academic freedom and administrative independence—which have tended to confuse most analyses of autonomy."[57] The most recent evidence indicates that concern over academic freedom is not the basis for opposition to statewide planning and coordination. Academic freedom as used here means the freedom of faculty and students to pursue knowledge, to publicize their findings, and to engage in the teaching-

---

[55]See Moos and Rourke, *op. cit.;* M. M. Chambers, ***Voluntary Statewide Coordination***, *op. cit.;* Lyman Glenny, *op. cit.;* and Minter, *op. cit.*

[56]Lyman A. Glenny, "Institutional Autonomy for Whom?" (Paper read at the 25th National Conference on Higher Education, Chicago, Illinois, March 2, 1970), p. 2. The following discussion relies heavily on the ideas in Glenny's paper.

[57]*Ibid.*

learning process. In a similar vein "recent studies agree that many of the atrocity stories about autonomy concern judgments by extra-institutional bureaucrats on the discretionary powers of in-college bureaucrats about administrative details."[58] The core of any discussion of autonomy should center on questions of educational policy:

> Who makes policy? Toward what objectives? For which segments of college clientele? By what educational means? These are questions at the heart of the matter. Should each institution have absolute autonomy without regard for answers which other autonomous institutions provide? Does the state (society) have a stake which might rightfully exceed the collective desires and interests of autonomous institutions? Should that stake be recognized and means taken to provide for it? Should the state allow institutions to engage in wasteful duplication of programs, roles, and functions? Should the state attempt to obtain optimum service for scarce resources?[59]

Glenny concludes that societal interests must prevail over institutional interests; most state legislatures have apparently reached the same conclusion since forty-seven statewide boards for higher education have been established to date. It is obvious that such agencies curtail the autonomy of state universities. Based on this study of Ohio, I would agree with Glenny that "these impositions are substantive and are not only defensible but also desirable."[60] The reasons for this position should be clear by now, but perhaps it would be helpful to review the consequences of institutional autonomy in Ohio.

The opposition of Ohio's state universities to new, independent public two-year colleges or four-year institutions was a common theme throughout most of the period surveyed in this study. The universities wanted branch campuses which they could control and often make in their own image. As Glenny points out, the autonomy

---

[58]Glenny refers to three important studies dealing with this issue which were discussed at a two-day workshop in St. Louis in January, 1970, *op. cit.*, p. 2.

[59]*Ibid.*, p. 3.

[60]*Ibid.* Such a position does not, quite obviously, commit one to agreeing with each and every policy a statewide board may recommend or adopt.

of the universities in such matters actually leads to a limitation of diversity and opportunity.

The unplanned and uncoordinated movement of a number of state universities into Ph.D. programs was another example of the need for some central control. While public institutions of higher education plead for autonomy to develop their own uniqueness, experience shows that, if left alone, teachers colleges and state colleges attempt to become comprehensive universities, emulating the state university. Such developments inevitably lessen diversity and lead to a waste of resources. An increase in the number of institutions granting the Ph.D. in Ohio may have been needed when Ohio University broke the I.U.C. agreement; its action and the defensive reaction of other institutions, however, were not calculated to best serve public higher education in the state.

Glenny cites other examples of how the exercise of institutional autonomy has resulted in questionable educational policy. In a number of states the universities, faced with growing numbers of applicants, have become increasingly selective. This raises the question of the fate of the student with modest abilities if all the universities are allowed to set high admission standards. Glenny asks, "Does the board have a duty to maintain diversity in program and student opportunity although it means control in substantive educational policy?"[61] Public universities in Ohio have not become so selective as to raise serious problems in this area. Despite Ohio's open admissions law, however, they all attempt to be selective. Miami University has been the most successful; its freshman class S.A.T. scores are comparable to those of the better private schools in the state.[62] Increased selectivity by Ohio's public universities could, in time, lead to action by the Board of Regents.

The results of autonomy in Ohio lead me strongly to support a statewide coordinating agency. The issue of constitutional status

[61] *Ibid.*, p. 5.

[62] H.B. 1014, introduced in the 108th General Assembly, was directed specifically at Miami's selectivity. The bill stated that preference may be given students graduating in the upper forty percent of their high school graduating class in assigning them to dormitories. "Within the above such group, no basis of selection other than chronological order of application or lottery may be used."

for the state universities still remains. After all, the basic argument favoring constitutional status is that it promotes institutional autonomy. However, it is possible that constitutional status may also relate significantly to the issue of academic freedom. If that is the case, then there might be compelling reason to support such status even in light of the obvious problems posed by institutional autonomy.

M. M. Chambers states that constitutional status for state universities "means a number of crucial freedoms":

1. The university governing board has custody and control of the university funds, and none must be deposited in the state treasury.
2. The board is not required to accept the state treasurer as its ex officio treasurer, or to depend on the attorney general for legal services, or to have its financial affairs audited by the state auditor (for the essential post-audit it may employ a private accounting firm) or pre-audited by any state officer.
3. The legislature does not make "line-item" appropriations to the board, but instead makes "lump-sum" appropriations and leaves the allocations to specific items of university operating expenditure to the discretion of the board.
4. No employees of the university are subject to the regulations of the state civil service system for classified state employees.
5. The university is not required to make purchases through a state purchasing office.
6. No state editor or state printer or other similar functionary has any voice whatever in determining what the university shall print and publish.
7. The university governing board has sole authority to fix the fees to be charged for tuition and other services, and the salaries and wages and perquisites of all university employees, including president, faculty members and all others.[63]

With the exception of item six, none of the above relate directly to questions of academic freedom. This is not to say that some of the other advantages of constitutional status may not be related indirectly to that issue. Items two, three, and five list areas which, if restricted by legislative or central bureaucratic action, could seriously erode academic freedom. Moos and Rourke cite examples

[63]*Higher Education in the Fifty States, op. cit.,* pp. 50–51.

where pre-auditing, legislative appropriations, and central purchasing led to an infringement on academic freedom. Their examples, however, tend to be isolated.

It is also important to note that, even among those universities enjoying constitutional status, most do not exercise all of the freedoms listed by Chambers. Even in Michigan, where the universities are considered to have an exalted constitutional position, there is a serious question of how much protection such status actually provides. Moos and Rourke state that, "striking examples of the manner in which the fiscal power of the legislature can penetrate the constitutional barrier have occurred in Michigan, the state in which the precedent of the Constitutional university was first established."[64]

The most recent example of this "penetration" is the 1970 appropriations act for Michigan universities. The Michigan legislature, as a condition on the appropriations, specified limits on out-of-state enrollments; forfeiture of state scholarship aid for conviction of certain offenses; loss of faculty salary for other specified acts; and mandated minimum classroom contact ranging from fifteen hours at community colleges to ten hours at graduate institutions.[65] While this example and the examples of Moos and Rourke have more to do with institutional autonomy than academic freedom, one can assume that if the legislature is able to curtail institutional autonomy in spite of the constitution, it could also restrict academic freedom.

By law and tradition the universities in Ohio exercise several of the freedoms cited by Chambers. In those areas where they do not (pre and post audit by the state, civil service status for non-contract personnel, regents' approval of fee and tuition increases) there is little evidence that academic freedom is threatened. This is not to say the universities do not experience inconvenience on occasion.

Constitutional status may provide some protection against

---

[64]*op. cit.*, p. 30.

[65]Excerpts from Enrolled Senate Bill No. 1179, Ohio Board of Regents, mimeo.

state encroachment on academic freedom, but the evidence suggests it is marginal. Indeed, one student of state politics has suggested that constitutional status for state universities is similar to home rule for cities as a supposed panacea. Each has come to represent a highly desired status, but the advantages are more symbolic than real.[66] Not only can the legislature "penetrate" the constitutional barrier, but, should a university challenge such action in court, "it risks a Pyrrhic victory in which its legal autonomy would be upheld at considerable cost to its relations with the community."[67]

It is useful to examine the reaction of others involved in higher education to the question of constitutional status. The Chancellor of the Ohio Board of Regents sees little advantage to such a provision for state universities; further, he cites the Michigan experience as prohibiting the development of a coordinated system of higher education. The chancellor's unfavorable view of a constitutional provision which would undermine the state coordinating agency is not surprising. Citing the California system, he is not interested in the Board of Regents obtaining constitutional status, either.[68] At the most he would favor a general statement, similar to that recommended in the Model State Constitution, that "a system of higher education should be provided." The chairman of the Board of Regents is of a similar opinion; he believes the constitution should be as brief and flexible as possible.[69]

The views of state university trustees on the issue were obtained by means of a mailed questionnaire. Trustees were asked two questions involving constitutional status for state universities. The first asked their opinions about raising the constitutional status question before the Constitutional Revision Commission or a con-

[66]The comparison is that of Professor Samuel K. Gove, Director, Institute of Government and Public Affairs, University of Illinois.

[67]Moos and Rourke, *op. cit.*, p. 32.

[68]Interview, July 22, 1970. Although the Board of Regents of the multi-campus University of California system has constitutional status, this has not prohibited periodic political interference. Given the position of the chancellor and the attitude of most college presidents toward the board, the possibility of constitutional status for the Ohio Board of Regents was not seriously investigated.

[69]Interview, August 7, 1970.

vention, if it is called. The other question was aimed at determining how many trustees actually favored granting state universities constitutional status. Their responses are reported in Tables 3 and 4.[70]

TABLE 3
TRUSTEE RESPONSE TO RAISING QUESTION OF CONSTITUTIONAL STATUS FOR STATE UNIVERSITIES BEFORE CONSTITUTIONAL CONVENTION OR COMMISSION

	Yes	*No*	*No Opinion*	*Total*
Number	17	11	12	40
Percentage	42.5	27.5	30.0	100.0

TABLE 4
TRUSTEE RESPONSE TO WHETHER STATE UNIVERSITIES SHOULD BE GRANTED CONSTITUTIONAL STATUS

	Yes	*No*	*No Opinion*	*Total*
Number	12	13	15	40
Percentage	30.0	32.5	37.5	100.0

Even trustees do not appear to represent a reservoir of support for state universities obtaining constitutional status. The results should be viewed with some caution, however. Since the questionnaire could not go into great detail in explaining the issue, the results might have been different if the trustees had been more fully informed. Nonetheless, given the negative and no opinion responses, it is obvious that it is not a significant issue.

The preceding discussion leads me to conclude that constitutional status for Ohio's state universities is not a compelling item

[70]Questionnaires were mailed to all trustees of the eleven state universities. (Actually, questionnaires were sent to University of Cincinnati trustees as well, but since it is still a municipal institution, the responses were excluded here.) At the time of the mailing, seven positions out of a total of ninety-nine were vacant due to deaths or resignations. Forty-three questionnaires were returned from the ninety-two trustees receiving them; three did not answer the questions being considered here. The response, then, was 43.4% (40 out of 92).

for the agenda of constitutional revision. Such status would inevitably weaken the coordinating power of the Ohio Board of Regents. The evidence does not suggest that academic freedom has been severely threatened by the current practices of the state and, further, constitutional status for universities appears to be of limited value in defending it. Undoubtedly the greatest guarantee against unwarranted state interference in the intellectual life of the university is to encourage greater public support and understanding of public higher education. In the final analysis, "The freedom that public colleges and universities have traditionally enjoyed in American society has always been dependent upon public awareness that free institutions of higher learning are essential to the welfare and progress of the community."[71]

[71]Moos and Rourke, *op. cit.*, p. 318.

PART IV

State Government and Urban Problems

Editors' Introduction

The backdrop for this section is the continuing urbanization of Ohio. The Advance Report of the 1970 Census classified 75.3% of the total population as "urban." In addition, the Census Bureau defines thirteen Standard Metropolitan Statistical Areas whose central cities are in Ohio (see map on endleaf). Three interstate SMSA's have central cities in other states, but suburban counties in Ohio. Except for the Toledo and Lima areas, the urban concentrations form a southwest-northeast belt of metropolitan areas from Cincinnati through Dayton, Columbus, Mansfield, and Akron to Cleveland.

In the most recent decade, six of the central cities of over 100,000 lost population, and only two gained. The gains of Toledo and Columbus were attributable to annexation. The most dramatic losses were Youngstown (−16.1%), Cleveland (−14.3%), and Cincinnati (−10.0%). Even smaller cities, such as Hamilton, Springfield, and Canton, lost population between 1960 and 1970. Population growth in the suburbs offset the central city losses, so that the proportion of the state's population in SMSA's slightly increased (see Table 1).

In summary, suburban areas grew so rapidly that 90.3% of the state's population increase took place within the thirty-one

TABLE 1
DISTRIBUTION OF OHIO POPULATION
1960 AND 1970

	1960		*1970*	
State population	9,706,397	100.0%	10,652,017	100.0%
SMSA central cities	3,501,333	36.1	3,429,005	32.2
Remainder of SMSA's	3,884,590	40.0	4,810,528	45.2
Remainder of state	2,320,474	23.9	2,412,484	22.6

SOURCE. 1970 Census of Population Advance Report DC(V1)-37.

counties comprising the sixteen Standard Metropolitan Statistical Areas, despite a decline of 72,328 in total central city populations. The total increase for the remaining fifty-seven counties of the state was 92,010. The number of cities of over 25,000 population grew from twenty-six in 1940 to forty-eight in 1970. The distribution of cities in broad population groups is shown in Table 2.

TABLE 2
LARGE CITIES IN OHIO
1940, 1960, AND 1970

	Number of Cities		
Population Range	*1940*	*1960*	*1970*
25,000–49,999	14	22	28
50,000–99,999	4	10	11
100,000 or more	8	8	9
TOTAL	26	40	48

SOURCE. 1940, 1960, and 1970 Census of Population.

The following two chapters evaluate the capacity of the Ohio political system to deal with issues raised by urbanization. Although one is written from the local government perspective and the other from the state's, both come to a similar conclusion. They agree that an urban policy that simply leaves all options to unfettered local choice is likely to produce inaction.

Bowden and Hamilton examine an unsuccessful charter reform movement for Summit County. They point out that the success of the municipal reform movement at the beginning of the twentieth century had unforeseen consequences fifty years later. The home rule guarantees of the Ohio Constitution, which once preserved municipal integrity from the depredations of the legislature, now keep the state from acting in order to break local stalemates. In the authors' phrase, home rule is not a gateway for adapting local government structure to metropolitan conditions, but a dead end.

Another conclusion is implied in the Bowden and Hamilton study. The referendum provision of Article X means that any county charter proposal that shifts municipal or township powers to the county level must receive four separate majorities if it is to pass. This hurdle places charter commissions in a dilemma. If they propose a plan that produces a genuine metropolitan government, the concurrent majorities requirement dooms the plan to failure. If they opt to maximize the chances of referendum success, the charter must be so limited in scope that it will arouse little popular interest. In either case the plan loses, but for different reasons.

Coke's paper on urban policy in Ohio state government presents some reasons why there has been as much inaction at the state level as among local governments. He concludes that state government needs some clearing of the decks simply as a prelude to the determination of an appropriate state role. In late 1971 and early 1972 some of the necessary actions were taken. The passage of the first state personal income tax in December, 1971, opened up a revenue source through which the state could provide meaningful financial aid to cities. A month later a Department of Economic and Community Development was created by an administrative merger of the Department of Development and the Department of Urban Affairs. As Coke observes, the two agencies had been in conflict since 1967. The new department was to contain four divisions: development planning, housing and community assistance, economic development, and administration of justice. Finally, the governor announced the creation of the Ohio Commission on Local Government Services. Among the early tasks of the commission is to be an examination of comprehensive subdistricting schemes, through which district development agencies could begin to coordinate state programs and local planning objectives.

Some Notes on Metropolitics in Ohio

John H. Bowden and Howard D. Hamilton

NONE OF THE RELATIVELY FEW COMMUNITIES WHICH HAVE established some species of metropolitan government are within the borders of Ohio, although it is one of the most urban states. Ohio contains all or parts of sixteen Standard Metropolitan Statistical Areas, seven of which exceed half a million population and two over a million. In most states any "metro" scheme requires specific enabling legislation, but that formidable obstacle is absent in Ohio. It is one of the few states with a county home rule provision in its constitution, adopted by a popularly initiated amendment in 1933. Article X confers on counties all the prerogatives of home rule cities. A county charter may revise the structure of county government in any manner that its citizens wish, and any municipal functions and powers may be vested in the county exclusively or jointly with its municipalities. Not only is local discretion plenary, but also the county is feasible geographically. In eight SMSA's, more than 80% of the population is entirely within one county.

Thus, since 1933 the citizens of any county have had the authority to remodel their county government and/or to make it an instrument for metropolitan government. But four decades have elapsed without a single successful use of Article X. Attempts have occurred in Cuyahoga (thrice), Franklin, Hamilton, Lucas (twice), Montgomery, and Summit counties; all have failed.[1] Article X was initiated because the legislature had been unresponsive to pleas for "modernizing" county structures. Its proponents assumed that home rule would be the gateway to reform, as it had been for city government, but that premise proved erroneous. Some explanations for the failure can be gleaned from the literature of metropolitics, from an examination of the repeated efforts in Cleveland, and from the data gathered in our investigation of the proposed Summit County Charter of 1970.

I. ARTICLE X: MECHANICS OF COUNTY CHARTERS

The procedures for a county charter are similar to those for city charters except for the referenda requirements. A proposal to establish a drafting commission may be placed on the ballot either by resolution of the county commissioners or by petition of ten percent of the electorate. The referendum occurs simultaneously with an election of the commission members, who acquire authority if the proposition is endorsed by a majority of those voting on it.

The commissioners, usually local notables, secure nomination by petition. While the election is nonpartisan, most candidates are likely to run on some slate. Thus, for example, the 1958 Cleveland election was won by a Democratic party slate running against a Republican and several minor slates;[2] in the 1969 Akron election there was a black slate and a chamber of commerce slate.[3] The charter commission, elected countywide, consists of the top fifteen vote-getters. Since only seven may be residents of the same city, the core city must be content with less than a majority of the seats. The commission has ten months to complete its work and is re-

[1]Francis R. Aumann and Harvey Walker, *The Government and Administration of Ohio* (New York: Crowell, 1958), p. 424. Subsequent to the attempts described in Aumann and Walker, futile efforts have occurred in Cuyahoga (1959), Lucas, (1959), and Summit (1970).

[2]Scott Greer, *Metropolitics* (New York: Wiley, 1963), p. 95.

[3]John Bowden, *The Summit County Charter Debacle* (unpublished M.A. thesis, Kent State University, 1971), pp. 21–23.

quired to place its product on the ballot at the next general election, one year after the election of the commission.

Ohio voters appear generally to favor county reform as a concept but not as a reality. Although they occasionally reject a call for a charter commission, the usual pattern is that the proposal carries (sometimes by a comfortable margin), the commissioners formulate a charter, and their handiwork is voted down. As a case in point, 60% of the Summit electorate voted for the charter commission and 60% voted against the charter.

One root of this anomaly is to be found in the referendum requirement of Article X. Adoption of a charter that only revises the structure of county government requires approval by a simple majority. A charter which invests the county with any municipal powers must be approved by three or four concurrent majorities: in the largest city, the balance of the county, the entire county, and (in counties of less than 500,000 population) a majority of the municipalities and townships.[4] The rationale for these "four hurdles" is that they protect the city from being swallowed by the county and, reciprocally, protect the suburbs from being swallowed by the city.

This latter-day application of Calhoun's concurrent majority doctrine virtually guarantees that there will be no metropolitan charters in Ohio. Even when a plan is favored by a majority of the county electorate, as was the 1935 Cuyahoga charter, it can be vetoed by the electorate of the core city, or the outlying county, or a combination of villages and townships. The root of the difficulty is the ambiguity of the notion of home rule in such situations. What should be the unit, the metropolis or the existing municipalities? Article X tilts the scales decisively in favor of the existing units. Indeed, Article X is less a home rule article than a mirage.

This is a critical instance of one of the perennial issues of popular sovereignty. Policy should be the will of the majority, but which majority? The geographically and numerically largest majority or a smaller, more local majority? Article X has the appear-

---

[4]The fourth hurdle applied to all counties before a 1957 amendment, which apparently was intended to facilitate efforts in Cuyahoga.

ance of being a reasonable compromise: the decision shall be by concurrent majorities, but the appearance is specious. As Calhoun knew, the concurrent majority doctrine gives each local majority a veto power—it is a mask for minority rule. That was the issue at the Philadelphia Convention in 1787, and the decision was unequivocal. The will of the national majority should prevail over the preferences of local majorities. That formula is reversed by Article X. The dogma of the "right of local self-government" thereby becomes the prerogative of existing local units to retain their identities and powers and to veto metropolitan schemes. Consequently home rule is not a gateway to metropolitan reorganization, and such proposals usually fail. They succeed only in extraordinary circumstances with tremendous effort. The price of success is likely to be an anemic metro.

II. THE CLEVELAND EXPERIENCE

Cleveland perhaps holds the national record for futile attempts to fashion a metropolitan government. The Cuyahoga electorate voted on this matter ten times between 1933 and 1959, twice for facilitating amendments of the state constitution, five times on whether to write a charter, and three times on charters. The overall county vote was affirmative six times. The 1935 charter was endorsed by a majority but failed (barely) to carry outside Cleveland and in a majority of the fifty-four municipalities. The 1950 charter lost by small margins in both Cleveland and the county, and the 1959 charter received even less support, particularly in Cleveland.[5]

A familiar generalization of metropolitics is that, in the past, metropolitan government plans were supported by the central city and torpedoed by suburban residents who sought to preserve their isolation in miniature republics, to escape taxes, and to shirk re-

[5]The source of data for this section, unless otherwise cited, is Richard A. Watson and John H. Romani, "Metropolitan Government for Metropolitan Cleveland," *Midwest Journal of Political Science,* 5 (November, 1961), 365–390.

TABLE 1
PERCENT POSITIVE VOTE IN CLEVELAND AND SUBURBS OF CUYAHOGA COUNTY ON METROPOLITAN ISSUES

	Issue	*Cleveland*	*Suburbs*
1933	Const. amendment	69.5	58.8
1934	Charter commission	58.5	61.5
1935	County charter	54.0	49.8
1936	Charter commission	48.2	51.8
1941	Charter commission	42.8	46.9
1949	Charter commission	57.4	67.7
1950	County charter	47.1	48.7
1957	Const. amendment	58.1	55.6
1958	Charter commission	61.0	68.7
1959	County charter	42.4	46.7

SOURCE: Watson and Romani, "Metropolitan Government for Metropolitan Cleveland."

sponsibility for the problems of the city. But now the tables are turning, as businessmen realize that they have left hostages in the city and disfranchised themselves, while control of the city polity slips from the hands of the WASP bourgeoisie into the hands of working class and ethnic politicians. Now metro schemes are rejected by the city blue collar and ethnic voters, who wish to retain full control of affairs in "their city." The pattern of racial and class segregation between the city and suburbia makes the achievement of a metro by plebiscite increasingly less likely. The very economic and social trends which intensify the need for political integration of the metropolis also make it politically unfeasible.[6]

Cleveland's experience fits the model. The 1935 charter was supported by Cleveland voters and defeated by the suburbs. Suburban support slipped slightly for each of the subsequent charters, but Cleveland support dropped sharply, to 42% in 1959. The 1959 defeat was principally due to opposition from black leaders, the mayor, and other central city officials, who resisted loss of functions to a county metro, even though the charter was written by a commission of organization Democrats and was endorsed by

[6]Cf. Edward Banfield, "The Politics of Metropolitan Organization," *Midwest Journal of Political Science,* 1 (May, 1957), 77–91.

TABLE 2
BLACK POLITICAL STRENGTH AND VOTE FOR METROPOLITAN ISSUES IN CLEVELAND

Year	*Number of Black Wards**	*Pct. of City Vote Cast in Black Wards*	*Pct. Positive Vote Black Wards*	*Pct. Positive Vote White Wards*
1935	3	7.9	77.0	52.1
1949	3	5.8	72.1	56.5
1950	3	5.2	64.8	46.2
1957	4	6.0	72.1	57.2
1958	7	15.0	50.2	62.7
1959	8	21.2	29.3	45.9

*Wards with black councilmen.
SOURCE: Watson and Romani, "Metropolitan Government for Metropolitan Cleveland."

the AFL-CIO, as well as the chamber of commerce.[7] A metro has scant chance against the opposition of the central city mayor and the "machine of the incumbents."[8]

In 1959, as previously, the charter was promoted and liberally financed by affluent businessmen, many of whom surely were only daylight residents of Cleveland. By that date the fate of their planning was more in the hands of black leaders than the business elite. Black voters had given overwhelming support to the previous charters, but gave only 29% in 1959. Had they voted as before, the charter would have carried in Cleveland. There were some particular reasons for the black opposition—reportedly the leadership was approached maladroitly by the charterites, and the charter lacked a civil service provision—but the data of Table 2 indicate that the more fundamental reason was the expanded stake of blacks, with eight councilmen, in the City of Cleveland.

Now that blacks have acquired considerably more political clout in Cleveland, and elsewhere, simultaneously with a desire for self-determination, the prospects for metro plans under the referen-

[7]Greer, *op. cit.*, pp. 93–95.

[8]During the preceding year, a metro sponsored by the St. Louis "establishment" was defeated 2 to 1 in the city and 3 to 1 in the county. What did the city and county voters know about the matter? Very little, except that Mayor Tucker was against it. Greer, *op. cit.*, pp. 97–133, 171–173.

dum requirements of Article X are hardly auspicious. It has been speculated that actual experience with power and the struggle to operate and sustain the decaying cities without a tax base could produce second thoughts about metropolitanism. But even if black city officials should come to see merit in a metro, that view would not necessarily extend to the rest of the leadership and the rank and file. Recognition and power have singular importance for a minority that has had the experience of blacks in America. And "where else in our society are the segregated, the insulted, and the injured as fairly represented as in *their* municipality?"[9] Furthermore, black city officials may not be obliged to seize one horn of the dilemma of bankruptcy or a metro, if Congress continues to bail out the cities by grants for housing, urban renewal, public works, expressways, mass transit, education, and welfare. There is more than one way to siphon dollars from suburbia to the city.

III. THE SUMMIT COUNTY FIASCO

The Calhounism of Article X is by no means the exclusive barrier to metropolitan reorganization efforts. The 1950 and 1959 Cuyahoga charters and one in Lucas County in 1959 lost both inside and outside the central city. The Summit charter lost uniformly, except in one Akron silk stocking ward. The concurrent majorities requirement is an insuperable barrier, but usually the barrier itself is not reached. The nemesis of most county charters is simply the referendum process.

The 1970 Summit County experience furnishes some explanation for why county charters lose in referenda. They are opposed strenuously by local officialdom and perhaps a local party organization. The machine of the incumbents has intense motivation because of high personal stakes. It has a network of contacts for mobilizing an opposition. Its propaganda is likely to be effective since most voters have little or no interest in the matter. With a paucity of information, the voters have little comprehension of the

[9]Scott Greer, *Governing the Metropolis* (New York: Wiley, 1967), p. 148.

rationale of a metro or the esoteric concepts of the reform model of local government. Any reorganization plan imposes tangible personal costs on incumbents, who may be able to convince some interest groups and numerous voters that they also would incur personal costs. On the other hand, the proposed scheme offers distinct personal benefits to few voters and only the possibility of some vague collective benefits. Hence, those against the proposal have more motivation and resolution than the "good government" coalition. They also have the organization for grass roots campaigning, whereas the charterites are obliged to campaign in the mass media, which is an unsatisfactory means for selling their product. It is hardly surprising that some interest groups and numerous voters opt for perceived personal benefits (real or fictitious), instead of unperceived or uncertain and insubstantial collective benefits, or that many bewildered voters adhere to the prudential maxims, "better the evil that is known" and "when in doubt, vote no."

The Summit charter from genesis to demise was a paradigm of metropolitics, although it was not a metro charter. It was initiated by the Akron Chamber of Commerce's Urban Services Study Committee, which perceived some critical metropolitan needs and viewed the Jacksonian structure of county government as woefully defective. The publication of its report coincided with a county deficit and other events damaging to the county's image. Consequently, the hour seemed propitious for reform, and the county commissioners readily agreed to move the question. All but four of the charter commissioners were elected from the chamber's slate and the officers had been members of the chamber's urban services study committee. The enlightened businessmen arranged to coopt support by slating members of other elites, including a black schoolman and two union officials, and they had the enthusiastic support of the Akron daily paper. However, two elites, the local officials and party leaders, were excluded from the commission. The reformers preferred the image of a nonpartisan citizens' body, which they hoped would not only facilitate deliberations but also foster public confidence and keep the matter "out of politics." That strategy failed on both scores.

The manner of the commission's genesis enabled it to operate smoothly and on schedule, because its officers were dedicated, its distinguished members were knowledgeable and experienced in collective decision making, and the body enjoyed high ideological consensus. These were archetype civic reformers imbued with the National Municipal League ideology, but not blindly so; their product contained some significant deviations from the reform model of local government.

The commission's neighborhood hearings were very poorly attended. Did that indicate public confidence or indifference? Most of the testimony was by township and county officials defending their respective interests. The chairman of the county Democratic committee was for a metro, "real change," but not this "half baked" plan. The only official's testimony endorsing the charter's principles unequivocally was by the mayor of Akron. Some other officials were known to be sympathetic, but when the campaign arrived, the charter commission was not supported by a single voice in the courthouse or city hall, except the president of the county employees union.

It was abundantly clear from the testimony that a metro charter would be futile; consequently, the commission proposed merely to supplant the venerable Jacksonian model of county government with the city reform model. It presented a strong mayor rather than the council-manager form. An elected chief executive would be invested with plenary administrative authority and would appoint all officials except the judges and auditor. All but three of the thirteen councilmen would be elected by districts in partisan elections. Appointment of board and commission members would entail council confirmation, but not for department heads. Patronage would be replaced by a civil service system, and arrangements were prescribed for accounting, budgeting, and auditing. To appease township and village officials, the charter explicitly denied the county any municipal powers. The Akron reformers chose the half-a-loaf strategy strictly for tactical reasons, and they displayed a Fabian outlook, harboring the thought that a "modern" county government might be a foundation for the evolution of metropolitan government.

The charterites anticipated opposition from some county officials, but they could hardly have anticipated some of the tactics which the county officials employed. During September and October much of the charterites' energy was diverted from the campaign to coping with successive obstacles erected by the incumbents, who were adroitly exploiting legalisms and litigation.

Two of the harassing tactics involved printing and distribution of a pamphlet edition of the charter. The county auditor discovered that the three advertisements of the printing contract were spread over fifteen days rather than the three weeks required by statute. Thereupon he compelled readvertising, which delayed the printing. Then, as the pamphlets were being mailed, the Board of Elections objected to the use of the board office as the return address. The charterites spent the next few days intercepting the pamphlets at the post office, blacking out the return address, and rebundling. As a result, the pamphlets reached the voters only a week before election day.

A taxpayer suit was filed, seeking removal of the charter question from the ballot due to alleged procedural errors. As is usual in taxpayer suits, whose purpose is often obstructionism, a host of errors was claimed. The plaintiffs appeared to be acting with the approval of some county officials and Democratic party

TABLE 3
CONTRIBUTIONS TO THE RIGHT TO VOTE COMMITTEE

Summit County Sheriff's Association	$5,027
Ladies Auxiliary of the Sheriff's Dept.	1,000
Democratic Office Holders Association	1,000
Springfield Twp. Democratic Club	20
Summit Co. Assn. of Township Trustees	211
Township trustees and clerks (6)	701
Leo Berg, chairman	200
Arnold Rosenfeld, co-chairman	200
A bail bondsman	100
Other individuals (8)	926
Miscellaneous, anonymous	35
TOTAL	$9,419

SOURCE: Financial statement filed with Board of Elections.

leaders. The court dismissed the complaint, but the charter was under a cloud of uncertainty until five days before election day.

The identity of the charter opposition was unknown to the public, because a strategy of the opponents was concealment. That was accomplished effectively by twin tactics. There were no public pronouncements by the officials, and their propaganda was issued under the label of the "Right to Vote Committee." The identity of the opposition is, however, quite visible in the financial statement filed after the election by the RVC: a numerically small alliance of professional Democrats and county and township officials, most notably the sheriff (see Table 3).

The campaign budgets of the opposing forces were of equal size. Both used billboards and newspaper advertisements for their principal propaganda. The opposition had considerably more insertions and space. The procharter advertising was unimaginative, pedestrian, and too little, too late—partially because their energy was diverted by the harassment. The RVC advertising drummed three themes: "Don't Lose Your Right to Vote," "Stop Inflationary Taxes," and the County Executive would appoint "these officials: sheriff, prosecutor . . . ." The advertising did not mention that the county executive would be elected nor that the charter provided for the election of fourteen officials instead of the existing eleven. The RVC effectively used time-tested propaganda devices: slogans and symbols, repetition, half-truths, confusion, and accusation. "Have They Been Telling It Like It Is? No!" The campaign, as usual, generated some heat but no light. The absence of solid information and reasoning perhaps is indicative of the defectiveness of a plebiscite on such technical subjects. In the propaganda battle, the charterites inherently were at a disadvantage. Public understanding of the concepts and principles of the charter and their rationale could not be achieved instantly by advertisements.

The contest was close until a week before the balloting, when the Akron Labor Council passed a resolution condemning the charter. The influence of the sheriff was again visible:

> The charter form will take away the friends we need in county government. Sheriff Robert Campbell is our friend, as are others, and it is the sheriff who could enforce injunctions against us during a strike.

The council's executive-secretary, one of the unionist members of the charter commission, and the president of the county employees union were unable to check the stampede. That was the *coup de grace* for the Summit County Charter.

IV. THE MINDS OF THE VOTERS

Immediately after the election, a survey was conducted of the electorate's interest, perceptions, substantive information and misinformation, the volume of successful communication, the credibility and influence of campaign themes, and correlates of voting on the issue. The sample was every one-thousandth dwelling unit in Akron, Cuyahoga Falls, and Tallmadge. The sample was small, 112 interviews, but it appears to have been accurate.[10]

Voting was phenomenally heavy in 1970, but a fifth of the voters did not mark the charter ballot. The most vivid picture in the survey data is massive apathy. Three-fourths of the sample stated that they had little or no interest in the charter referendum and one-third said "none." The apathy was so pervasive that less than half of the respondents discussed the charter with anyone and less than one-fourth with anyone outside the home. Obviously, governmental reorganization is an esoteric subject without salience for the public. An archaic and fragmented polity is not perceived as a problem in the absence of some dramatic crisis. Thus, a given

[10]Confidence in the sample is fortified by the sampling method, the 99% completion rate, and the correspondence of voting data to the official vote in some selected homogeneous precincts:

	Percent Vote for Charter	
Character of Precincts	*Selected Precincts*	*Survey Sample*
White, blue collar (8)	31	31
Black (11)	33	42
High income (26)	64	56
Entire county	40	40

of metropolitics is inertia, a rock on which charter movements may founder.

Despite the substantial volume of publicity, absolutely no messages were received by about a third of the public. Apathy and selective perception combined to make the charter a non-event for them. Some respondents mentioned that their first inkling of the matter was their confrontation with the ballot. One-third said that they looked at the charter pamphlet and about two-thirds recalled that there had been some newspaper advertisements. Thus the campaign furnished no information to a third of the public, and the principal communication medium was the superficial, and considerably misleading, slogans and newspaper advertising.

Aside from the *Beacon-Journal* feature articles, which few people read, the only source of comprehensive and unbiased information was the pamphlet copy of the charter. The herculean labor of the charter commission was largely in vain. Two-fifths of the sample were unaware of the pamphlet's existence. When asked "What was in the pamphlet?" only a fourth of the sample and a third of the voters replied correctly that it contained the charter text. This is eloquent testimony to the ineffectiveness of official pamphlets. The impression of Table 4 that the pamphlet was quite influential for the minority that examined it is probably misleading because voting on this issue correlated sharply with both occupation and education. Half of the respondents who knew

TABLE 4

KNOWLEDGE OF CHARTER PAMPHLET CONTENTS

"What was in the pamphlet?"	*Voters* *For*	*Voters* *Against*	*Nonvoters*	*Percent of Sample*
It was a copy of the charter	16	13	0	26
Couldn't understand it.	0	3	0	3
Didn't read it.	5	5	4	12
No recall of its contents	5	11	6	19
Subtotal	26	32	10	61
Unaware of the pamphlet	10	22	12	39
TOTAL	36	54	22	100

that the pamphlet was the charter had attended college and a fourth were professionals or business executives. Consequently, it appears that the only substantial effect of the pamphlet was to enable a third of the electorate to know more about what they voted on.

The reputed "power of the press" seems to be nonexistent in this case. It is said that although newspapers may not be influential for national elections, their influence may be substantial in local elections and particularly for referenda. The county's only daily published feature articles "explaining" the charter, numerous news items, and an editorial lauding the charter. Only a fifth of the sample reported seeing anything about the charter in newspapers except campaign advertisements. When asked "What people or groups were for the charter?" only 6% mentioned the *Beacon-Journal.*[11]

In view of the preceding data, the level of public knowledge could not have been high, and some rough measurements demonstrate that there was more public ignorance than knowledge. The sample was asked "Now recalling what you read and heard, what were the arguments for the charter?" "What were the arguments against the charter?" With a generous coding of the responses, 39% stated a pro argument and 44% a con argument, and 29% knew both a pro and con argument (Table 5).

Here is evidence of the effectiveness of the opposition cam-

TABLE 5
KNOWLEDGE OF CHARTER ARGUMENTS

	Voters			*Percent of*
	For	*Against*	*Nonvoter*	*Sample*
Knew some:				
Pro argument only	4	5	2	10
Con argument only	2	15	0	15
Both	18	15	0	29
Knew no arguments	12	19	20	46
TOTAL	36	54	22	100

[11]The overwhelmingly defeated St. Louis charter was supported by both dailies, and the press has supported the repeated efforts in Cleveland. Greer, *Metropolitics*, pp. 67–70, 93.

TABLE 6
RECOGNITION OF PROTAGONISTS

What people or groups were . . . For the charter		Against the charter	
Beacon Journal	7	The sheriff	7
Charter Commission	2	County officials	3
Public officials and/or employees	8	Right to Vote Com.	1
Politicians	6	Union leaders	1
Businessmen	6	Labor	18
Upper class people and organizations	5	Taxpayers	3
*Miscellaneous	10	*Miscellaneous	10
SUB-TOTAL	44	SUB-TOTAL	43
Don't know	68	Don't know	69

*Most of dubious validity.

paign. Con arguments were heard more widely. The disparity was greater than is evident in Table 5, because most of the reported con arguments were playbacks of the opposition propaganda themes, whereas the stated pro arguments included such generalities as "more efficiency" or "it would be a better government." The anti propaganda had simple themes and potent symbols; the pro propaganda themes were hazy and the symbols were pallid. An honest case for the charter could not be packaged in simple slogans and stirring symbols.

The identity of the protagonists is one of the most useful benchmarks for appraising the validity of any propaganda (see Table 6). In this instance, however, such identity was not a voting cue for the bulk of the electorate; two-thirds of the sample had no perception of who was for or against the charter, and several replies were erroneous. Only 9% knew that the opposition kingpins were county officials, and no one mentioned the Democratic party.

An indirect method was used to make an interesting set of measurements of substantive information. Respondents were asked if they agreed with the propositions listed in Table 7. How can one explain the contradiction between Table 7 and the election tally, other than by assuming that most voters did not know what they were voting on? It would be possible, of course, for an informed

TABLE 7
AGREEMENT WITH MAJOR CHARTER PROVISIONS
(percent of sample)

	Agree	*Disagree*	*No Opinion*
For making laws, Summit County should have a large elected council.	73	20	7
Summit County should have a chief executive, elected by the people.	62	28	11
County employees should be hired on a civil service system.	89	4	6

voter to decide that election of the traditional county officers is more important than those three provisions of the charter combined, but few voters engaged in that calculus.

The data of Table 7 do not fit the election returns, but they do match all our measurements of interest, communication, and information; they also match the findings of a study of the St. Louis charter referendum:

> It is clear that neither the protagonists nor the antagonists "got through to the voter." . . . only ten percent of the voters had roughly correct notions of three most important provisions of the plan. Only about twenty percent could state any of these major provisions correctly. Thus the ordinary voters were not even voting on the plan; nobody knows what they were voting on.[12]

What were the Summit County voters voting on? Some were voting on the caricature of the charter manufactured by the opposition, many were voting on a single provision with no knowledge of the other provisions, many were voting against taxes, some were voting on the advice of their union leaders, some were voting for the Democratic party, some were voting to save townships, some were voting to assist their political cronies or to keep patronage jobs, some were voting on faith, more were voting on fear—the instinctive apprehension of change that was cultivated by opposition propaganda—some were voting against a nefarious plot by the

[12]Greer, *Governing the Metropolis*, p. 125.

"politicians" and "they" who were trying to put something over on the people. As in St. Louis, few were voting on the charter.

The evidence is overwhelming that the charterites communicated with few voters but that the opposition was more successful. "How did you decide how to vote?" Most responses were enigmatic or meaningless; there was, however, a contrast in the responses of the pro and con voters. Most pro voters gave hazy, nonexplicit reasons, but anti voters usually gave explicit ones—the opposition propaganda themes: taxes, right to vote, or too much power for one man. How much credence did the public attach to the propaganda slogans "Stop Inflationary Taxes" and "Don't Lose Your Right to Vote"? A very considerable amount. Only a third of the sample denied the validity of the former and only half denied the latter. Table 8 shows that the credibility of those slogans was far and away the strongest correlate of the voting.

That a majority of the naysayers were voting against taxes is corroborated by the voting on three simultaneous property tax levies (Table 9) and by the demographic correlates data (Table 10). Virtually all of the votes against the three picayune levies for long established health programs were cast by persons who rejected the charter. Impressive evidence has been marshalled for the proposition that "public-regarding" and "private-regarding" attitudes are important in referenda voting.[13] The opposition

TABLE 8

CREDIBILITY OF PROPAGANDA SLOGANS AND VOTING

Perceptions of the Charter	*Voters For*	*Voters Against*
Charter would raise taxes (only)	8	12
Take away the right to vote (only)	2	9
Agreed with both themes	3	19
No opinion on one or both themes	4	8
Disagreed with both themes	19	6
TOTAL	36	54

[13]James Q. Wilson and Edward C. Banfield, "Public-Regardingness as a Value Premise in Voting Behavior," *American Political Science Review,* 58 (December, 1964), 876–887.

TABLE 9
ASSOCIATION OF VOTING ON CHARTER AND PROPERTY TAX LEVIES

Levy support rate of:	*Pro-Charter Voters*	*Anti-Charter Voters*
Mental Health Renewal	95%	71%
New Mental Health Levy	95	68
New County Hospital Levy	86	52

leaders were distinctly private-regarding; evidently many of their supporters were also private-regarding folk.

The demographic correlates of the charter vote contain few surprises. Nay voting was greatest among senior citizens and skilled, unionized workers. The voting correlated with each of the social status variables, and the charter received majority support only from businessmen (modestly) and professionals (markedly). The bourgeois charter project was supported by the bourgeoisie. Although the Democratic party waged covert opposition, the Re-

TABLE 10
DEMOGRAPHIC CORRELATES OF CHARTER VOTE

	Voters in Sample	*Per-cent for*		*Voters in Sample*	*Per-cent for*
Education			Union affiliation		
Less than 12 years	16	44	Member	36	31
High school graduate	40	25	Nonmember	54	45
Some college	34	56	Party identification		
Income			Democrat	63	38
Less than $5000	14	36	Republican	20	45
$5000 to $9999	34	41	Independent	7	57
$10000 to $14999	26	46	Age		
$15000 and up	9	56	21 to 39	30	37
Occupation			40 to 59	42	45
Unskilled worker	27	37	60 and up	18	33
Skilled worker	27	26	Race		
White collar worker	13	38	White	78	40
Business executive	11	55	Black	12	42
Professional	11	73			

publican party sat out the dance. The hapless charter commission found itself in neither a nonpartisan nor a fully partisan situation. The battle was half-partisan, the worst of all worlds.

V. HOME RULE: GATEWAY OR CUL-DE-SAC?

In the Progressive era the municipal reform movement raised the banner of home rule as a strategy for restructuring local government. Home rule was a successful strategy for its initial purpose, but for the post-World War II goal of metropolitan reorganization, it has been conspicuously unsuccessful. Home rule has not been the gateway to metropolitan reform in Ohio; it has been a *cul-de-sac*. The principal reasons why Article X has been a magnificent failure are: (1) the concurrent majorities ratification requirements, (2) our segregated residential patterns—segregation by the pocketbook and race—(3) the resistance of entrenched local officialdom with numerous allies possessing vested interests in the regime, and (4) the use of the referendum as the decision-making institution.

The combination of the latter two alone, as in the Summit County affair, can defeat reorganization attempts. Any referendum is hazardous for a metropolitan charter, because the public has so little knowledge for evaluating it, and also little competence in evaluting the credentials of clashing information and advice on the matter. "Some people say it is a good thing, but others say. . . ." Even if anyone were listening, it would be impossible to achieve mass understanding of the principles and rationale of a metro or the reform model of local government instantly by billboard. The popular knowledge and apathy which handicap the proponents of change are advantageous for the propaganda issued by the machine of the incumbents. A reorganization might win at the polls despite the apathy and knowledge deficit if the community elites were fully united, but how frequently will any substantial reorganization of the polity of a metropolis not beget potent opposition elites?[14]

[14]One instance was Miami. Cf. Edward Sofen, *The Miami Metropolitan Experiment* (Bloomington: Indiana University Press, 1963).

The survey data indicate that the Summit County referendum was a game of roulette. Is the referendum the most sensible mechanism for making policy decisions of such complexity? That may be thinking the impossible, but we asked the Summit sample's opinion of two statements. "The people did not have sufficient information for voting on the charter." Two-thirds agreed. ("The people," one may infer, actually was "me.") And "The county charter matter is too technical and complicated for voters; it should be decided some other way." A third disagreed, but 54% assented.

For revising the constitution of the local polity, American political theory provides only two mechanisms and legitimizers, the legislature by statute or the local electorate by plebiscite. Legislatures are understandably loath to "impose" charters, and the existence of a home rule article in the constitution is a convenient justification for avoiding it. Simultaneously the referendum makes the alternative route hazardous to say the least. Both roads to metropolitan reorganization appear to be closed in Ohio. There is scant prospect for metropolitan reorganization unless the legislature ventures to engage in some "dictatorship" or "enlightened despotism."

Curiously, the municipal reform movement appears to have contributed to its present predicament. Hoisting the home rule banner, it succeeded in stripping the legislature of the authority to design the constitution of the local polity. Very possibly the benighted legislatures would have more understanding of these matters than local electorates, but they were divested of the necessary authority by the civic reform movement.

The Development of Urban Policies in Ohio State Government

James G. Coke

AN OBSERVER WITH A LIVELY SENSE OF IRONY MIGHT BE tempted to overstress the state's lack of response to the problems found in urban Ohio. He could compare the expanding industrial wealth of the state with the growing poverty of school districts, some of which have been forced to close until higher property taxes were approved by the voters. In a state that ranked among the top five recipients of federal grants, he could observe that 1968 AFDC payments to an urban family of four were 69% of the U.S. poverty line standard, and 83% of the minimums that the state itself had defined. He might even point out that in the state that produced a pioneer in urban planning and land use control like Alfred Bettman, local governments show little interest in modern zoning innovations, and a state court of appeals recently declared airport approach zoning unconstitutional.[1]

The author acknowledges with gratitude the financial assistance of the Rutgers Center for Urban Studies (now the Center for Urban Social Science Research), which in 1969 supported field interviews concerning state urban programs in Ohio.

[1]On February 2, 1972, the Ohio Supreme Court reversed the decision of the lower court and upheld the constitutionality of the airport zoning authorization in Ohio Revised Code Ch. 4563. 29 *Ohio State 2d* 39.

I. THE MAINTENANCE OF A TRADITIONAL ROLE

Ohio's posture toward its urban areas has such strongly ironic aspects that the state might seem unique for the extent of its non-involvement. But, in truth, the track record of Ohio state government is not materially different from the performance of the rest of the states. As Alan K. Campbell has observed, "Federal and local governments have undergone many reforms in attempting to adjust to the increasing metropolitanization of the nation. State governments have not kept pace."[2] A report of the Advisory Commission on Intergovernmental Relations was more explicit: "As the road to the present urban hell was paved, many major sins of omission and commission can be ascribed to the States."[3] Since its inception in 1959, the Advisory Commission has urged the states to assume a much greater burden of responsibility for urban problem-solving.

At the beginning of the 1960s, the national norm for state urban policy was essentially non-involvement. Writing about Michigan, VerBurg and Press summarized the content of what we might term the "traditional" state approach: "The state provided enabling legislation, financing alternatives, and even financial assistance through state-collected, locally-shared revenues. Essentially, however, the posture of state government, in its perceived role, provided little direction and assumed little responsibility for urban conditions."[4] Urban problems, in this view, are not conditions that affect groups of people; instead they are procedural and substantive constraints on a class of local governments. Dealing with stress on local government is nothing new for the states. It requires only "a little rechanneling of tax funds here, a bit of expert assist-

---

[2]Alan K. Campbell, "Breakthrough or Stalemate? State Politics," in Alan K. Campbell (ed.), *The States and the Urban Crisis* (Englewood Cliffs, N.J.: Prentice-Hall, Inc. 1970), p. 196.

[3]*Urban America and the Federal System,* prepared by Allan D. Manvel for the Advisory Commission on Intergovernmental Relations, Report M-47 (Washington, D.C., October, 1969), p. 2.

[4]Kenneth VerBurg and O. Charles Press, "Role of the State in Solving Michigan's Urban Crisis" (1971, mimeo., 39 pp.), p. 36.

ance there, a dash of home rule for one place and a jigger of regional coordination in another."[5]

During the 1960s, in some states and in some urban issues, there began an uneven development of other policies. A few states imitated, in a limited way, the federal government's grants-plus-standards approach. Some set new standards for local performance, but did not provide financial assistance. A very few experimented with direct action in urban development. None of these approaches was at all well-developed in Ohio by the end of the decade. The traditional posture was still the rule, and concessions to the new approaches were frequently a matter of style, rather than substance.

It is certainly not the lack of urban populations that inhibited Ohio from moving beyond the traditional role. By 1970, thirty-one of the eighty-eight counties were within the boundaries of Standard Metropolitan Statistical Areas; the state contained twenty cities of over 50,000 population; and there had been a substantial migration of blacks and low-income Appalachian whites into the major urban centers. The components of 1970 state policy can be summarized and compared with other states, as follows.

State Administrative Organization

During the decade, the most common organizational responses at the state level were the creation of agencies for local affairs and the reorganization of state planning. New York established the first agency to assist local government in 1959, and at least half the states had followed suit by 1970. About two-thirds of these units postdated 1966, when the Demonstration Cities and Metropolitan Development Act authorized grants to the states to provide technical assistance to small communities.

Ohio's Department of Urban Affairs was created in 1967. Its special limitations will be described later; it is sufficient to observe here that the department's urban programs did not progress beyond the strictly advisory approach, in contrast to the innovative op-

[5]John N. Kolesar, "The States and Urban Planning and Development," in Campbell (ed.), *op. cit.,* p. 114.

erating responsibilities of similar departments in Connecticut, New Jersey, Rhode Island, and Pennsylvania.[6]

Unlike departments of local affairs, state planning agencies were familiar units in state administrative structures. They first appeared in the mid-1930s. After 1960, most states reorganized the planning function. The predominant trend was to remove state planning from the usual location within the commerce or development department and to make it a staff arm of the governor. At the beginning of the decade, thirty-seven states had planning agencies: twenty-three in development departments and three in the governor's office. In 1969, all states had planning agencies, with twenty attached to the governor and only thirteen remaining in development departments.[7]

Ohio did not participate in these trends. A State Planning Division was created in 1963 in the Department of Development, and it stayed there. The governor had no staff group in his office whose mission was urban program development or state planning, nor did he request staff assistance until 1969, when, in the Condition of the State message, Governor James A. Rhodes asked the General Assembly to create an Ohio State Planning Office in the Office of the Governor. The proposed legislation was not passed.[8]

State-Local Coordination

The rapid increase in the number of federal categorical grants and the comprehensive planning-areawide review requirements of the Demonstration Cities and Metropolitan Development Act of 1966 and the Intergovernmental Cooperation Act of 1968 have stimulated many states to encourage the establishment of regional

---

[6]Joseph F. Zimmerman, "A Growing Trend: State Agencies for Local Affairs Moving from Advisory to Coordinating and Operating Roles," *National Civic Review*, 58 (November, 1969), 462–468.

[7]Thad L. Beyle, Sureva Seligson, and Deil S. Wright, "New Directions in State Planning," *Journal of the American Institute of Planners*, 35 (September, 1969), 335. The remaining state planning agencies (eleven in 1960, and seventeen in 1969) were either independent boards or located in a variety of other parent departments.

[8]S.B. No. 163, 108th General Assembly, Regular Session, 1969–1970.

organizations of local governments. Federal requirements provided the initial impetus, but it has been found that the local delivery of state services needs as much coordination as federal grants. The fragmentation of state functions is illustrated in Ohio by the fact that twenty state agencies have twenty-eight separate arrangements, which result in 332 regions. Of the twenty-eight regional schemes, no two have identical boundaries.[9]

Comprehensive subdistricting of a state requires complementary actions by several decision-making centers. First, there is strong gubernatorial support, usually expressed through an executive order that authorizes the drawing of district boundaries, directs state agencies to use them, and recognizes district organizations as the coordinating mechanisms for both federal and state programs. Second, the legislature passes the enabling legislation and makes financial support available. Finally, program development and day-to-day administration are carried out through a policy staff in the governor's office and an operations staff in a community affairs agency.[10]

By the end of the decade, thirty-three states had delineated substate districts that would be suitable for regional planning and state program coordination, but only twenty had officially designated them.[11] About a dozen states were providing direct financial assistance to substate district organizations, usually on a matching basis.[12] The most extensive programs were those of Texas, Connecticut, Virginia, and Georgia. The twenty-one regional commissions in Texas are designated by law as political subdivisions, and they are expected to operate as "umbrella" agencies for law en-

---

[9]*The Regional Dilemma: A Preliminary Study,* prepared by the Division of Intergovernmental Services, Ohio Department of Urban Affairs (January, 1969, mimeo., 74 pp. plus appendices), p. 2.

[10]For a full statement of a recommended state strategy, see ***Regional Councils and the States,*** Special Report No. 8 of the National Service to Regional Councils (Washington, D. C., November, 1968).

[11]*Ibid.,* p. 6, and George S. Blair, "State-Local Relations in 1968–1969," *The Book of the States 1970–71* (Lexington, Ky.: The Council of State Governments, 1970), p. 275.

[12]National Service to Regional Councils, "State Financial Assistance to Regional Councils" (August, 1970, mimeo., 3 pp.).

forcement planning, comprehensive health planning, and areawide review of local government applications for federal grants.[13] The state provides $500,000 annually in general support funds, disbursed on a per capita basis.

In Ohio, subdistricting has not been a subject of either gubernatorial or legislative concern. The Department of Development designated eight "regions" in 1965, and a report was prepared on the general characteristics of each. The only area of the state where district organizations have been created is the Ohio Appalachian Region. Three development agencies were established in 1967 and 1968, but only one has boundaries that coincide with the regional definitions of the Department of Development.

State Financial Assistance

Despite growing federal grants, cities find their financial situation deteriorating. In a survey of 838 cities conducted by the International City Management Association, 57% of the respondents ranked "inadequate financial resources" as their number one problem.[14] Nevertheless, the "effectiveness of state government in contributing to resolution of the great fiscal difficulties which accompany urban growth has been, on the whole, woefully poor."[15] Some states have assumed either total or partial responsibility for functions that had previously been financed at the local level. For example, public education is primarily state-financed in North Carolina; public health is a state responsibility in Rhode Island; and Massachusetts has assumed the full burden of welfare, including general relief.

A few states have adopted another approach; they provide part of the local share of federal urban grant programs. The Advisory Commission on Intergovernmental Relations has gathered

[13]Areawide review is required by Title IV of the Intergovernment Cooperation Act of 1968. Federal requirements and guidelines are contained in OMB Circular A–95.

[14]"Federal, State, Local Relationships," *Urban Data Service Report,* Vol. 1, No. 12 (International City Management Association, December, 1969), p. 6.

[15]Roy W. Bahl, "State Taxes, Expenditures and the Fiscal Plight of the Cities," in Campbell (ed.), *op. cit.,* p. 85.

1967 data about the extent of this practice in six basically urban programs.[16] Thirty-six states provided aid for airport construction, and twenty supplemented local participation in the cost of sewage treatment facilities. Eleven states assisted in the local share of urban renewal, ten in urban mass transit, seven in water and sewer projects, and only four in hospital and medical facility construction. Few states were extensively committed to supplementary aid; seven made grants in four or more of the six programs listed above.

Ohio neither transferred local burdens to the state level nor embarked on expanded grant-in-aid programs during the 1960s. In fact, there was a reverse tendency to shift state burdens to the localities. State government did not "buy into" any of the federal programs; it has provided no Model Cities supplementary funds, no grants for mass transportation services or equipment, and no money for the non-federal share in urban renewal projects. Although the state gives financial aid to localities in the traditional health-education-welfare fields, urban and rural jurisdictions have equal access to these grants.

The only state grant that seems specially applicable to urban areas is the Disadvantaged Youth Program, commonly referred to as the "ADC Program."[17] A local school district containing at least one-hundred children aged 5–17 who receive AFDC, or in which at least five percent of the total school enrollment is composed of such children, is eligible to receive $175 for every AFDC pupil. The Division of School Finance notifies each eligible school district of the availability of these funds. The school district then proposes a program for their use, following a set of state guidelines that stipulate nineteen acceptable program categories.

State Direct Action

Late in the decade some states moved toward direct action that challenged long-established routines in state-local relations.

---

[16]ACIR, *Fiscal Balance in the American Federal System, Vol. 1,* Report A-31 (Washington, D.C., October, 1967), pp. 250–253.

[17]Ohio Revised Code 3317.06.

These activities raised the possibility that the states could take the initiative in setting their own urban program priorities, rather than responding to outside stimuli. Some direct action programs suggested a state role that goes beyond the lowest common denominator of local government acceptance, on the one hand, and the facilitation of federal programs, on the other. The states, at last, could be more than middlemen.

Examples of direct action include New York's Urban Development Corporation and New Jersey's Hackensack Meadowlands Development Commission.[18] The Maine and Oregon legislatures placed the exercise of certain zoning controls at the state level in 1969. A prelude to direct action was the creation of transportation departments, which existed in thirteen states by 1970. Maryland's establishment of a comprehensive transportation trust fund is especially noteworthy. The unification of all user fees and taxes in order to finance highways, mass transit, ports, and airports offers the opportunity to coordinate all transportation modes in a statewide development plan. If coordination of this type occurs, the states will have broken some ancient ground rules about the separate treatment of modes and the preferential position of highways.[19]

No comparable initiatives occurred in Ohio in the 1960s. Direct action was as unexplored as subdistricting and urban financial aid. Only in the establishment of a Department of Urban Affairs did Ohio keep pace with new developments in state government, and, in operation, DUA was to suffer serious limitations.

In view of this record, it is not surprising that Ohio municipal officials, especially in the larger cities, display considerable skepticism about state government capabilities. Many see a wide gap between the pretensions of state agencies and their actual perform-

---

[18]Kolesar, *op. cit.*, pp. 124–126. The UDC could override local zoning in accomplishing its objectives in housing, urban renewal, and industrial development. The Meadowlands Commission was created to develop twenty-eight square miles of marshes located in fourteen municipalities; it, too, could override local vetoes.

[19]Norman Beckman, "Development of National Urban Growth Policy: Legislative Review 1970," *Journal of the American Institute of Planners, 37* (May, 1971), 159, 149.

ance. Several of the largest cities prefer a direct federal-city partnership, because it is felt that Ohio's fiscal policies work to the disadvantage of the large metropolitan areas.[20]

These attitudes are corroborated by survey data that rank the states according to the percent of cities whose chief administrative officers believe that their state government provides significant help in the solution of city problems (Table 1). Among the fourteen states from which twenty or more cities responded, Ohio ranks next to last as a source of assistance. By contrast, two

TABLE 1
CITY OPINIONS OF THE EXTENT OF HELP FROM STATE AND FEDERAL GOVERNMENTS, BY STATE

	Percent of Reporting Cities Indicating Significant Help From	
State	*State Government*	*Federal Government*
Pennsylvania	59	41
New York	57	56
Connecticut	54	70
Michigan	51	65
Illinois	45	42
Massachusetts	40	48
Texas	39	46
California	35	51
North Carolina	30	77
New Jersey	27	36
Missouri	23	71
Kansas	20	47
OHIO	20	54
Florida	3	67

SOURCE: "Federal, State, Local Relationships," ***op. cit.,*** **Tables 8 and 9, pp. 15–16.**

[20]There is research support for their view. Frederick Stocker has studied the impact in the Cleveland area of the three major state aids: the highway fund, the local government fund, and the school foundation program. He concludes that "none appears . . . to have operated in such a way as to accomplish any significant equalization within the Cleveland metropolitan area or between the counties in the Cleveland SMSA and the balance of the state." Frederick Stocker, "Fiscal Disparities in the Cleveland, Ohio, Metropolitan Area," in ACIR, *Fiscal Balance in the American Federal System, Vol. 2*, Report A–31 (Washington, D.C., October, 1967), p. 266.

and a half times as many Ohio city officials report that the federal government provides significant help.

II. STEPS TOWARD URBAN POLICY DEVELOPMENT

To explain the persistence in Ohio of the "traditional" state posture toward urban areas, we will describe the actions of major decision-making centers that were involved in urban policy. These include the legislature, the governor's office, state planning and development agencies, and local government agencies. An overview indicates that during the 1960s a state concern about urban problems developed, but the actual steps taken toward solutions were minimal and uncoordinated.

The Legislature

At the first session after the 1966 reapportionment, the legislature organized itself to deal with urban issues through the House Local Government and Urban Affairs Committee and the Senate Urban and Highway Affairs Committee. These committees have been mainly concerned with the facilitating and enabling functions of state legislation. In this regard, the legislature reflects a widespread uncertainty as to whether the State of Ohio is in fact a state, or merely a fortuitous collection of eighty-eight counties. Since problems are viewed as applicable to classes of local governments, the typical response of the legislature has been to enable the concerned local units to organize in an appropriate way and to finance their own activities. The legislature, in effect, has patted the localities on the back, handed them a set of procedural and financial tools, and wished them the best of luck.

This pattern of response changed somewhat in the late 1960s. The major concern for an active state role came from a few members of the Senate, which in 1967 took the initiative in creating a Joint Committee on the Role of the State in Urban Problems. The Legislative Service Commission undertook several staff studies of housing, transportation, and poverty programs for the joint committee.[21] Although the committee's report resulted in several legislative proposals, the actual results of the 1969 and 1970 legislative sessions were quite limited. The bills that became law were in the familiar mold of simple facilitation. Included were a law that called for the State Board of Building Standards to issue a model building code for one-, two-, and three-family dwellings, which cities can adopt by reference, and a law requiring the board to develop performance standards that will allow modular and prefabricated housing. In 1970, an Ohio Housing Development Board was created with the authority to make interest-free loans to nonprofit sponsors in order to conduct design and market feasibility studies and to acquire options on land.

The Governor's Office

James A. Rhodes's two terms as governor (1963–1971) were characterized by a strong emphasis on the economic development of the state as a whole. Concentrating state energies on attracting new industry and expanding jobs in the private sector, the governor's policies made it extremely difficult for the state to develop funding for urban aid programs.

In 1964, Ohio ranked forty-sixth in state tax collections per capita and twenty-third in local tax collections per capita. To the "development"-minded, these rankings were a source of state pride, not a matter of state concern. When the Advisory Commission on Intergovernmental Relations published 1967 data on the amount taken by state and local taxes per thousand dollars of personal income, joy was unrestrained. The Ohio Development Department immediately placed an advertisement in *The Wall Street Journal* headed "Ohio's State and Local Taxes are the Lowest in the Nation!"[22] The ad reproduced the ACIR data and declared, "Ohio understands that state and local taxes must be treated as a cost of production. . . . When these low taxes . . . and Ohio's

---

[21]Two of the studies were published, *The Role of the State in Urban Affairs,* Report No. 99 (March, 1969), and *Programs Affecting the Urban Poor,* Information Bulletin 1969–2 (June, 1969).

[22]*The Wall Street Journal,* March 11, 1969.

ideal business climate are combined, . . . you have an ideal industrial location." For the convenience of industrial prospects in Brussels, Caracas, and Tokyo, local telephone numbers were listed. The toll-free numbers for the hard-pressed mayors of Ohio cities were not published so widely.

In the last two years of his second term, Governor Rhodes showed greater interest in urban-related problems. His 1969 message on the Condition of the State placed high priority on the creation of an Ohio State Planning Office in the Office of the Governor, on financing for low- and middle-income housing, and on additional money for pollution control and abatement to be spent by the Ohio Water Development Authority. It should be noted, however, that the proposals made by the governor were to be financed by revenue bonds; this method is evidence of the power of the low-tax ideology.

State Agencies

In 1970, two state agencies were directly responsible for planning and urban policy. The older was the Development Department, established in 1963. The department contained six divisions, one of which carried out state planning and administered the distribution of federal "701" planning assistance funds to local governments. The Planning Division was not as well-staffed as the divisions that promoted the economic development of the state. In line with gubernatorial priorities, the state planning function remained subservient to the other missions of the department. A statement of departmental functions made planning's subordinate role clear:

> The Development Department was created in the words of the enabling legislation, to "develop and promote programs designed to make the best use of the resources of the state so as to assure a balanced economy and continued economic growth for Ohio." From the standpoint of the expansion-minded executive, this objective boils down to two practical programs. The first is the encouragement and assistance offered to industry to locate manufacturing facilities in Ohio . . . ***The second is encouraging and assisting local communities in Ohio to properly plan and prepare for incoming industry.*** (emphasis supplied)

The younger department, the Department of Urban Affairs, was established in October, 1967. It had four divisions: the Intergovernmental Service Division, with four field offices; a Division of Legal Services, which provided assistance in drafting ordinances and state legislation; the Division of Urban Development, to aid local communities in federal grantsmanship; and a Division of Finance, which gave localities help in setting up appropriate accounting systems, particularly in federally-assisted programs.

The historical origins of DUA are unusual. It was an elevation to departmental status of the Ohio Office of Opportunity, which was created in 1965 to monitor local, federally funded anti-poverty programs and to involve Ohio in the work of the Appalachian Regional Commission. The first director of DUA served as director of O.O.O. Thus, the urban affairs functions were grafted onto existing programs concerned with the Appalachia and anti-poverty programs. In early 1967, Governor Rhodes transformed O.O.O. by executive order into the Bureau of Urban Affairs. Several months later, the legislature changed the bureau to a department.

The relationships between the Development Department and the Department of Urban Affairs were not harmonious. The pattern of conflict began in the fall of 1967 in the debate over the enabling legislation. When the acting director of the Bureau of Urban Affairs drafted the DUA legislation, he proposed that the administration of "701" planning grants be transferred from the Development Department to the new department. The Development Department subsequently claimed that it had not been consulted on the matter. In an atmosphere of acrimony, the legislature chose to leave "701" where it was, but the conflict between the two departments was not ended. The underlying issue was which department was to obtain recognition as the final authority over state urban programs.

The Planning Division of the Development Department continued to act as the state planning agency and to administer "701" planning assistance. Its natural constituency group at the local government level consisted of the county and regional planning commissions, which have a history of extensive activity in Ohio. In 1971, there were twenty-five county planning commissions and fifty-three regional planning commissions, covering eighty-three of the state's eighty-eight counties.[23] The Development Department had strong links to these agencies and protected their interests in the legislature.

The Department of Urban Affairs, on the other hand, originally had no ready-made constituency among local governments. However, it soon became responsible for the law enforcement planning process required under the Omnibus Crime Control and Safe Streets Act of 1968. DUA used the planning requirements of the legislation to divide the state into fifteen districts and stimulate the establishment of new agencies in eleven of them. Most were named "council of governments."[24] Although thirteen restricted themselves to law enforcement planning, DUA seems to have hoped that they would become multi-purpose COGs. The councils have legislative authorization through a 1967 enabling act that drew heavily on the ACIR model and was promoted in the legislature by the Department of Urban Affairs.[25]

DUA envisioned the COGs as its natural constituency group, which would grow in power as they added other responsibilities to the law enforcement planning foundation. Thus, the conflict between the Development Department and the Department of Urban Affairs at the state capital had a mirror image at the local level in suspicions between regional planning commissions and COGs.

The governor's office was unwilling to make basic decisions about the respective roles of Development and DUA. In addition to keeping the inter-agency rivalry alive, gubernatorial indecision had other consequences. A primary reason for the legislature's failure to act on the 1969 request for a new State Planning Office was the governor's silence on his preference of agency philosophy and style between DUA and Development. Furthermore, the governor postponed as long as possible a decision on naming the state clearinghouse required under the federal Office of Management and

[23]*Directory of Ohio Planning Organizations – 1971* (Planning Division, Ohio Development Department, 1971), pp. 5 and 9.

[24]*Ibid.*, p. 19.

[25]Ohio Revised Code 167.01–167.08.

Budget Circular A–95. The state clearinghouse was to perform the review and comment function for federal grant applications coming from agencies outside the jurisdiction of metropolitan clearinghouses, as required under Title IV of the Intergovernmental Cooperation Act of 1968. Since the jurisdiction of the state clearinghouse was to include sixty counties and the state government itself, the designation of one department would have been a telling blow to the aspirations of the other. After a long delay, the governor solved his dilemma by designating neither department. In September, 1969, he named his own office as the Ohio Planning and Development Clearinghouse.

Under the most favorable conditions (meaning gubernatorial support, strong staff leadership, direct operating responsibilities, and adequate financing, including state grants to local units), state departments of urban affairs have experienced difficulties when they attempted to develop and implement state urban policies. They run afoul of both bureaucratic norms in state agencies and home rule sentiments in local government. As Kolesar concludes, "Operating on the urban frontier, without a clear product to advertise, with no consensus strategy to provide cover, treading across levels and lines of government, challenging dearly held views on race, home rule and even motherhood, such departments could not achieve safety without surrender."[26]

The Ohio Department of Urban Affairs did not operate under favorable conditions. Among the principal factors creating difficulties was the unwillingness of the governor and the legislature to provide state grants-in-aid for urban purposes. In the absence of financial leverage, DUA had only technical assistance to offer. This was not a very saleable commodity in the largest cities, which are perfectly capable of preparing their own federal grant applications and running their own programs. The many smaller cities needed technical assistance, but DUAs small staff prevented the scope and level of assistance that would have convinced the smaller cities of DUAs usefulness.

The ICMA survey data support this assessment. Only 5% of

[26]Kolesar, in Campbell (ed.), *op. cit.*, p. 119.

Ohio cities reported contacting DUA once a week or more often than once a week. The comparable data for Connecticut, Rhode Island, New Jersey, and Pennsylvania are 54%, 33%, 30%, and 8%. At the other end of the scale, 43% of Ohio cities contacted DUA less frequently than once every six months. By contrast, the data for the other four states are 9%, 0%, 16%, and 25%.[27]

Agencies at the Local Level

The structure of planning and development agencies at the local level reflects the fragmentation of effort at the state level. Fragmentation prevents a synoptic view of urban problems at both levels. The county and regional planning commissions are, by and large, dedicated to traditional land-use planning activities, with an emphasis on zoning and subdivision regulations as the major public control over urban development. In addition to the law enforcement planning councils of governments, there are three interstate planning commissions, three multi-purpose COGs, and one interstate regional planning authority set up as a non-profit corporation. Most of the COGs and other multi-county agencies are hothouse growths. They are engaged primarily in activities mandated by federal grant requirements, such as comprehensive transportation planning, A–95 metropolitan clearinghouse review, and law enforcement planning. It is highly unlikely that COGs would have taken root in the Ohio local political culture without such outside stimuli.

Anti-poverty programs are carried on by forty-nine community action agencies, of which twenty-seven cover a single county and twenty-two cover two or more counties.[28] Only two counties do not have community action programs. These agencies have few linkages to other planning efforts at the local level and relate at the state level to the Ohio Office of Opportunity in DUA. The Development Department, in its thrust for economic expansion, has spawned a number of local and county Community Improve-

---

[27] "Federal, State, Local Relationships," *op. cit.*, Table 33, pp. 49–50.
[28] *Directory of Ohio Planning Organizations—1971*, pp. 111–116.

ment Corporations. The CICs are usually public extensions of the local chambers of commerce. The eleven 314 (b) comprehensive health planning agencies cover eighty-one counties.[29] These non-profit organizations are linked to the state Department of Health. They go their own way, quite separate from the planning activities carried on by the COGs or the regional planning commissions.

III. REASONS FOR STATE INACTION

At the end of the 1960s, Ohio state government was playing a minimal role in the solution of urban problems, as compared with some other states with similar urban and economic characteristics. In accounting for the maintenance of a traditional posture, one cannot attribute much influence to the formal structure of the state and local governments. No important constraints are imposed by the state constitution. The governor possesses relatively strong powers. With the advice and consent of two-thirds of the Senate, he appoints twenty of the twenty-two department heads, who then serve at his pleasure. A reapportioned legislature has brought to the statehouse a number of competent senators and representatives from the urban areas.

At the local level, government is not especially complex or unwieldy. The urban areas contain relatively few special districts. Ohio's cities have extensive home rule power, which gives them flexibility in organizational forms and procedures, as well as some substantive powers. Although townships abound, the counties are not hampered by township powers. The county commissioners have the authority to provide several urban-type services, as well as to employ a county administrator.

What seems to have occurred during the 1960s is that three basic tendencies, common to all state governments, operated with particularly strong impact in Ohio. These universal tendencies, which we may call informal "decision rules," explain much of the

---

[29] *Ibid.*, p. 17.

slow development of state urban policy in Ohio during the decade. Briefly, the decision rules are as follows:

Decision Rule 1: *A pre-eminent objective of state policy should be to maximize the state's attractions, vis-a-vis all other states, in the competition for as large a share as possible of the nation's economic and industrial growth.* In this national competition for scarce jobs, it is widely believed that state tax policy is an important factor in the calculus of industrial location decisions. Therefore, low state taxes are desirable.

Table 2 provides information about revenue effort and tax burdens in selected Midwest and Atlantic industrial states. Ohio seems to have applied Decision Rule 1 with a vengeance through its tax policies.

If the 1966–1967 total revenue effort (local government general revenue, plus state taxes, per $1,000 of personal income) for Ohio's 13 SMSA's is examined, it is found that they rank among the lowest of the nation's 216 metropolitan areas. The range is

TABLE 2
STATE AND LOCAL TAX EFFORT AND TAXPAYER BURDENS, 1968
(Tax Items Related To Total State Personal Income)

State	*All Taxes*		*Direct Personal Taxes*		*"Big Three" Personal Taxes***	
	State Percent of Personal Income, Related to U.S. Avg.	*State Rank*	*State Percent of Personal Income, Related to U.S. Avg.*	*State Rank*	*State Percent of Personal Income, Related to U.S. Avg.*	*State Rank*
New York	122	4	121	6	135	2
Wisconsin	114	11	115	11	123	6
Michigan	102	21	104	21	109	16
Indiana	90	38	82*	45	100	19
Pennsylvania	87	42	90	38	86	37
Illinois	82	50	88	43	86	32
OHIO	81	51	76	49	74	45

***Excludes Indiana's general gross receipts tax on business firms.**
****Personal income, general retail sales, and estimated non-business property taxes.**
SOURCE: Advisory Commission on Intergovernmental Relations, *State and Local Finances, Significant Features, 1967 to 1970,* M-50 (Washington, D.C., November, 1969), Tables 1-A and 1-B, pp. 7–10.

from Canton's 73.1% of the national SMSA average (rank 213) to Cincinnati's 89.6% (rank 137). Yet it is the low *state* tax effort that produces this result. Considering only local government general revenue per $1,000 of personal income, one finds that Ohio's SMSA's are making an average revenue effort from their own sources. The Ohio SMSA median is $57.80 of local government general revenue per $1,000 personal income, and the median for all SMSA's in the country is $57.40.[30]

Ohio state government was so geared to the quest for industry in the 1960s that the development of new tax sources became extraordinarily difficult. The state indeed kept taxes down, but among the costs of the policy were the absence of state grants for urban programs and an over-emphasis on state-aided public improvements that can be financed by revenue bonds. In his 1969 message, the governor proposed non-tax supported revenue bond financing for no less than six new state programs: low- and middle-income housing, five industrial research and development centers and an international trade center, interceptor sewers and treatment plants, mental health facilities, technical training schools, and the expansion of medical school facilities.

Decision Rule 2: *The local government units that constitute the basic units for organizing state-wide electoral politics should all be on an equal footing in laying claim to a share of state services. In each functional area of state responsibility, state services should be disaggregated so that the smallest jurisdiction can receive a unit of each service.*

Ohio provides two examples of the application of this decision rule. One is the state airport program. Under the terms of a bond issue approved by the voters in 1964, $5 million was made available for state aid for airports. The funds were divided so that each county could lay claim to $100,000 for constructing a 4,000-foot airstrip capable of handling business jets. The disaggregation of airport aid to the county level tied in with the theme of jobs and progress for all Ohioans, because industrial growth would presumably be facilitated by having a small airport in each county. To

[30]ACIR, *op. cit.,* Table 2, pp. 13–20.

illustrate how difficult it would have been to devote such funds to urban aviation development, one need only reflect on the fact that $5 million would construct less than one-half of one modern jet runway.

The other example is the distribution of a $250 million bond issue to correct "urban traffic bottlenecks." When the money was distributed in 1969, each county received a share, regardless of its urban character. The distribution formula worked so that the eleven counties that received the largest amounts per motor vehicle registered in the county (a range of $55–$88 per vehicle) contained only five cities over 25,000 population, the largest of which had 35,000 people. By contrast, the eleven counties that received the smallest amounts per vehicle (a range of $40-$45 per vehicle) contained all nine of the state's cities of over 100,000 population.

Decision Rule 3: *State legislation should facilitate, rather than mandate, action at the local level.*

As noted earlier, the Ohio legislature tended to deal with urban problems by giving local governments options that they are free to accept or reject. The 1970 legislative approach to the crisis in urban mass transportation, for example, was to broaden the powers that could be exercised by regional transit authorities. If localities fail to take advantage of enabling legislation, they have no cause to complain about lack of state initiative. In justifying a budget that did not propose increases in state welfare payments, the governor observed, "Two years ago a plan was offered to counties to make possible increased aid payments. Only four counties have acted."[31]

IV. CONCLUSION

The effect of the three "decision rules" in Ohio has been to postpone the development of statewide, state-financed urban development programs. But, beyond this, it is worthwhile noting that the logic of the decision rules is to strengthen the tendency toward

[31] "The Condition of the State," James A. Rhodes, Governor (February 5, 1969, mimeo., 26 pp.), p. 7.

functional fragmentation in the federal system as a whole. When there is no state urban program money independent of categorical federal grants, state agencies simply have no leverage to develop a set of statewide urban development priorities. They must divert their energies to the cultivation of constituencies that will support them in bargaining with other autonomous bureaucracies at the state capital. In Ohio, this has been one of the principal difficulties faced by the Department of Urban Affairs.

To predict how long Ohio will retain its traditional posture would be hazardous. Based upon the arguments of this paper, the conditions likely to result in change would include the development of new state tax sources and a reorganization of the state agencies with urban policy responsibilities. The former would liberate the state from its restricted role as a passive conduit of federal money; the latter would give some long-range program development capabilities to the governor and the legislature.

These, however, are necessary, not sufficient conditions. In Ohio's political culture, the second decision rule is likely to be especially persistent, and, as the suburbanization of population continues, a redistributive urban policy will be increasingly difficult to implement. James Reichley's suggestion seems appropriate in the Ohio situation: "To achieve any genuine reconstruction of the cities, it will be necessary . . . to include the needs of the cities in some *total program* for the reconstruction of our entire society. In this way, the interest as well as the moral sympathy of the suburban and outstate majority could be touched."[32] To embark on such a task will test the political leadership and administrative resources of any state.

---

[32]A. James Reichley, "The Political Containment of the Cities," in Campbell (ed.), *op. cit.*, p. 195.

PART V

The Politics of Constitutional Revision

Editors' Introduction

Reflecting on the American penchant for constitution writing, Albert Sturm has noted that "American states have probably had more experience in constitution-making and revision than all other governments of the world combined until the accession of new countries to nationhood during the last decade."* Despite this experience (or perhaps because of it), the constitutions of many states continue to be subject to claims of inadequacy. Critics note that the existing documents often place undue restrictions on the legislature, fragment power among quasi-autonomous executives, restrict unduly the initiative of local governments, and contain masses of unnecessary and antiquated detail. In brief, it is argued, state constitutions leave much to be desired as fundamental documents.

In considering the "adequacy" of a state constitution, the analyst should keep two factors in mind. One is the obvious point that constitutions are political documents, allocating benefits to certain elements of society and defining constraints on state decision making centers. The other is entirely unrelated to the particu-

*Albert L. Sturm, *Thirty Years of State Constitution Making, 1938–1968*, (New York: National Municipal League, 1970), p. 10.

lars of substance, e.g., which groups are especially benefited, what limits are placed on taxing, spending, and borrowing, etc. It is simply the ease or difficulty of changing the document itself. To the extent that change is relatively simple, the rules can be periodically redefined to reflect new social-political conditions. When constitutional change is inordinately difficult, the public costs may be very high; emerging problems come to be defined as "insoluble" because of constitutional restrictions, or, if the problem proves pressing, significant amounts of time and energy will be spent seeking means of circumventing troublesome provisions.

Whatever its substantive weaknesses, the Ohio Constitution is readily changeable. Indeed, Ohio is one of only fourteen states with constitutions providing for all the three basic methods of change. More specifically, under Article XVI of the Ohio Constitution, changes may be originated by joint resolution of the legislature, initiative petitions from the electorate, and proposals from a constitutional convention. Regardless of the source, all proposed amendments must be approved by referendum.

Throughout Ohio's history the methods of change have been used with unequal frequency. Constitutional conventions, for example, were held in 1802, 1850–1851, 1873, and 1912. Article XVI provides two mechanisms for the calling of a convention. A two-thirds vote in each house of the General Assembly favoring the question of calling a convention places the issue on the ballot. Alternatively, Section 3 of Article XVI requires that the question be automatically presented to the electorate every twenty years. Public support for constitutional conventions has, to date, been lacking. In both 1932 and 1952 the question was defeated by the voters.

The initiative petition device has become less important over time. Between 1913 and 1970, thirty-one proposed amendments have been placed on the ballot by initiative petition; nine were approved. In the more recent past, 1951–1969, the device was used to submit only two amendments to the public; both were defeated.

A new approach to constitutional revision was adopted by the Ohio legislature in 1969. At that time, legislation creating the Ohio Constitutional Revision Commission was passed. Composed of twelve legislators and twenty other members chosen by the legislature, the commission is mandated to report biennially to the General Assembly. The assembly then has discretionary power to submit commission propositions to the electorate. Since its inception the commission has organized into three major subject matter committees—legislative-executive, local government, and taxation and finance. The staff of the commission has produced a series of research papers on selected constitutional problems; these have served as background materials for public hearings held by the commission. Throughout the next decade the Constitutional Revision Commission will undoubtedly serve as an important adjunct to the legislature in identifying and proposing solutions to constitutional problems.

The most frequently employed method of constitutional change in Ohio is the legislative joint resolution. Involved are two decisions—that of the General Assembly to approve the resolution and place it on the ballot, and that by the electorate to accept or reject the proposal. The chapters in this section analyze both types of decisions. William Spratley provides a comprehensive study of General Assembly voting behavior on joint resolutions over three decades. To provide comparative groups, legislators are divided into categories of party, constituency type, occupation, and region. Spratley's major conclusion is that, over the past thirty years, political parties emerge as the categoric groups usually in conflict and often the most cohesive in voting.

Carl Lieberman's study deals with the electoral response to legislative joint resolutions. By correlating county level voting and demographic data, Lieberman finds that, unlike patterns in the legislature, party is apparently irrelevant in explaining variations in referendum voting. A set of variables associated with urbanization seems to be the most salient predictor of referendum success. particularly on non-fiscal issues. Contrary to conventional wisdom, Lieberman shows that the electorate has not been reluctant to support referendums of all types. In fact, over a twenty-year period, financial referendums have received greater voter support than nonfinancial referendums in all but two Ohio counties.

An Analysis of General Assembly Voting on Ohio Constitutional Issues, 1941–1970

William A. Spratley

THE 1912 OHIO CONSTITUTIONAL CONVENTION, IN A BURST OF Progressive enthusiasm, proposed 41 amendments to the 1851 Constitution; 33 were approved by the electorate. Since then, constitutional amendments have been submitted to referendum at a rate of 2 per year. Most are placed on the ballot through legislative action. This study examines the General Assembly voting patterns on constitutional amendment proposals over the last thirty years. The range of constitutional issues examined and screened by the legislature is more extensive than many would imagine. Between 1941 and 1970, a total of 711 changes in various articles of the Ohio Constitution were introduced in the General Assembly. From this universe of proposals, a set of roll calls was selected for analysis.

The methodology of roll-call measurement follows closely the techniques described recently by three students of legislative behavior.[1] Using measures of intra-group cohesion and inter-group

The author is indebted to Professor Bradlee Karan, Director of the College of Wooster Institute of Politics, and Carl Zimmerman, Director of the College of Wooster Computer Center, for their advice on problems of methodology and analysis. The complete selection of the Ohio legislative source material was made available to this grateful researcher by the Library of the Ohio State University College of Law. Computer and other research facilities were provided by the College of Wooster.

[1]Lee Anderson, Meredith Watts, and Allen Wilcox, *Legislative Roll-Call Analysis* (Evanston, Illinois: Northwestern University Press, 1966).

conflict, Senate and House voting patterns are presented by the cumulative roll calls on each constitutional article and by session-to-session longitudinal comparison on all constitutional roll calls. The basic finding is that political parties are the source of the most cohesion and conflict in legislative voting on constitutional issues.

I. THREE DECADES OF GENERAL ASSEMBLY JOINT RESOLUTIONS

Constitutional Authority For Change

Under Article XVI of the Ohio Constitution, amendments may be initiated in three ways: joint resolution of the legislature, constitutional convention mandated by election, or initiative petition signed by at least ten percent of the electors who voted in the last gubernatorial election. Joint resolutions of the Ohio General Assembly have been the most frequently utilized and most successful method of proposing constitutional change. Like other bills, a joint resolution is introduced by one or more legislators and then referred to committee. Approval by a three-fifths vote in each chamber is required. Upon passage, the joint resolution is filed with the Secretary of State for submission on a separate ballot, without party designation, to be voted upon at either a general or primary election. It is exempt from gubernatorial veto. The amendment must be published once a week for five consecutive weeks prior to the election in at least one newspaper in each county. If a majority of those casting ballots on the question approve, the measure becomes part of the constitution.

Since 1912, 109 amendments have been presented to the Ohio electorate, with 61 approved and 48 rejected.[2] The General Assembly initiated 78 of the 109 amendments, while 31 attempts resulted from initiative petitions. Only 9 of the 31 changes proposed by initiative petitions were approved by the electorate, while 52 of the 78 propositions of the General Assembly received popular majorities.

---

[2]Arthur A. Schwartz and Ted W. Brown, "Voter Participation in Constitutional Amendment and Legislation" (Columbus, 1968, mimeo.).

Increase in Proposed Constitutional Amendments

Fifty-nine of the 109 amendments since 1912 were submitted to the electorate in the 1941–1970 period (see Table 1). Fifty-five

TABLE 1
OHIO CONSTITUTIONAL AMENDMENTS PROPOSED
TO ELECTORATE, 1941–1970

Year	*Total Submitted*	*Passed*	*Failed*	*Proposed By General Assem.*	*Proposed By Initiative*
1941	—	—	—	—	—
1942	1	1	—	1	—
1943	—	—	—	—	—
1944	2	2	—	2	—
1945	—	—	—	—	—
1946	—	—	—	—	—
1947	4	4	—	3	1
1948	—	—	—	—	—
1949	2	1	1	1	1
1950	—	—	—	—	—
1951	1	1	—	1	—
1952	—	—	—	—	—
1953	9	9	—	9	—
1954	2	1	1	2	—
1955	3	1	2	3	—
1956	2	2	—	2	—
1957	3	2	1	3	—
1958	2	—	2	1	1
1959	2	2	—	2	—
1960	—	—	—	—	—
1961	4	4	—	4	—
1962	1	—	1	—	1
1963	1	1	—	1	—
1964	1	1	—	1	—
1965	6	4	2	6	—
1966	—	—	—	—	—
1967	3	1	2	3	—
1968	5	4	1	5	—
1969	2	1	1	2	—
1970	3	3	—	3	—
TOTALS	59	45	14	55	4

SOURCE: Arthur A. Schwartz and Ted W. Brown, "Voter Participation in Constitutional Amendment and Legislation, 1912 through 1968" (Columbus, 1968, mimeo.).

TABLE 2
JOINT RESOLUTIONS APPEARING ON OHIO BALLOT AS PROPOSED CONSTITUTIONAL AMENDMENTS, ELECTION DATE, ARTICLE AMENDED, FINAL ROLL-CALL VOTE, AND ELECTION VOTE, 1941–1970

No.	*Election Date*	*Article(s) Amended*	*House Yes*	*House No*	*Senate Yes*	*Senate No*	*Election Vote Total Yes*	*Election Vote Total No*
1)	11-3-42	IV	117	0	29	0	954,704	448,981
2)	11-7-44	IV	116	5	28	0	1,429,635	611,276
3)	11-7-44	IV	127	0	28	3	1,279,216	633,843
4)	11-4-47	VIII			33	0	1,497,804	478,701
5)	11-4-47	IV,XVII	108	4	26	0	855,106	692,061
6)	11-4-47	VIII	103	18	28	3	782,158	762,129
7)	11-8-49	IV	113	2	21	4	874,291	876,647
8)	11-6-51	IV	114	6	27	0	875,083	696,672
9)	11-4-52	Con-Con	—	—	—	—	1,020,235	1,977,313
10)	11-3-53	VIII	100	18	26	0	1,035,869	676,496
11)	11-3-53	VI	87	20	28	2	913,134	693,624
12)	11-3-53	IX	112	0	30	0	755,725	622,245
13)	11-3-53	IX	111	4	30	0	905,059	650,567
14)	11-3-53	II	111	4	30	0	1,004,862	405,210
15)	11-3-53	XV	111	4	30	0	1,092,268	500,830
16)	11-3-53	XIV	111	4	30	0	789,511	541,477
17)	11-3-53	VIII	111	4	30	0	948,014	616,113
18)	11-3-53	XVII	111	4	30	0	835,195	493,099
19)	11-2-54	III,XVII	101	20	28	4	1,165,650	933,716
20)	11-2-54	XI	—	—	—	—	945,373	1,081,099
21)	11-8-55	VIII	109	24	21	12	1,154,976	909,030
22)	11-8-55	II	101	10	27	3	793,384	1,142,738
23)	11-8-55	IV	98	22	29	1	849,677	1,107,646
24)	11-6-56	VIII	119	1	30	0	2,202,510	889,245
25)	11-6-56	II,XI	83	42	20	11	1,636,449	1,214,643
26)	11-5-57	XV	84	16	27	3	696,372	1,040,638
27)	11-5-57	V	103	0	32	0	1,072,396	658,244
28)	11-5-57	X	111	24	29	0	832,912	799,094
29)	11-4-58	X	91	36	30	0	1,108,383	1,410,277
30)	11-3-59	XVIII	118	3	29	0	1,085,378	775,610
31)	11-3-59	IV	111	5	29	0	1,028,914	809,957
32)	11-7-61	II	122	8	33	0	1,251,105	650,064
33)	11-7-61	II	122	5	33	1	1,394,429	516,992
34)	11-7-61	IX	115	0	36	0	947,130	944,705
35)	11-7-61	III	120	0	27	11	1,168,831	642,512
36)	11-5-63	VIII	92	38	30	2	1,397,971	922,687

No.	Election Date	Article(s) Amended	House Yes	House No	Senate Yes	Senate No	Election Vote Total Yes	Election Vote Total No
37)	5-5-64	VIII	118	5	29	3	1,011,817	538,684
38)	5-4-65	VI	114	0	32	0	847,927	438,945
39)	5-4-65	VIII	97	15	27	4	715,642	548,557
40)	5-4-65	XI	84	41	20	12	595,288	681,823
41)	5-4-65	VIII	110	8	31	1	711,031	542,802
42)	11-2-65	IV	108	10	27	1	1,194,966	1,073,671
43)	11-2-65	X	98	35	23	9	892,657	1,346,597
44)	5-2-67	VIII	70	27	27	6	508,364	1,022,078
45)	5-2-67	II,XI	77	21	23	10	699,021	850,068
46)	11-7-67	II,XI	80	9	23	9	1,315,736	908,010
47)	5-7-68	VI	62	1	29	0	847,861	695,368
48)	5-7-68	II	80	9	23	9	1,020,500	487,938
49)	5-7-68	IV	77	17	33	0	925,481	556,530
50)	11-5-68	VIII	77	16	29	1	1,732,512	1,550,959
51)	11-5-68	XII	86	0	33	0	1,382,016	1,825,615
52)	11-4-69	V	83	12	30	3	1,226,592	1,274,334
53)	11-4-69	III,XVII	86	3	29	0	1,432,960	795,813
54)	11-3-70	XII	88	2	29	2	2,115,557	711,761
55)	11-3-70	XVIII	64	14	25	2	1,326,818	1,212,814
56)	11-3-70	V	85	6	25	1	1,702,600	1,073,058

TABLE 3

JOINT RESOLUTIONS OFFERED, PASSED, OR DEFEATED BY EACH LEGISLATIVE CHAMBER AND APPROVED BY BOTH HOUSES, 1941–1970

Session	Years	No. Offered Senate	No. Passed or Defeated in Senate	No. Offered House	No. Passed or Defeated in House	No. Off. Both	No. Approv. Both
94	41-42	6	1P	21	1P 1D	27	1
95	43-44	5	2P	12	2P 1D	17	2
96	45-46	3	2P	18	–	21	–
97	47-48	10	5P	22	4P	32	3
98	49-50	11	2P	22	2P 2D	33	1
99	51-52	1	1P	13	1P	14	1
100	53-54	23	11P	36	11P 2D	59	11
101	55-56	16	5P 1D	25	7P 1D	41	5
102	57-58	26	4P 2D	13	4P	39	4
103	59-60	30	3P 1D	24	3P	54	2
104	61-62	32	4P 1D	25	5P	57	4
105	63-64	23	2P	28	2P 2D	51	2
106	65-66	28	8P 2D	43	6P 3D	71	6
107	67-68	18	8P	41	9P	59	8
108	69-70	21	5P	30	5P	51	5
TOTALS		253	63P 7D	373	62P 12D	626	55

TABLE 4

PROPOSED CHANGES TO ARTICLES OF THE OHIO CONSTITUTION, BY LEGISLATIVE SESSION, 1941–1970

	Number of Changes Proposed for Each Article																
	I	*II*	*III*	*IV*	*V*	*VI*	*VII*	*VIII*	*IX*	*X*	*XI*	*XII*	*XV*	*XVI*	*XVII*	*XVIII*	*Total*
1941–42	1	3	4	4	4	1	1	2	—	—	2	4	2	2	1	—	31
1943–44	—	3	—	4	2	—	—	3	—	—	1	3	—	—	—	—	16
1945–46	—	4	3	—	3	1	—	4	—	—	1	4	—	—	—	1	21
1947–47	1	4	4	1	1	1	—	11	—	1	4	4	—	1	—	—	33
1949–50	3	9	7	2	2	1	—	3	—	—	1	2	3	—	7	1	41
SUB. TOT.	5	23	18	11	12	4	1	23	0	1	9	17	5	3	8	2	142
1951–52	—	2	2	2	1	1	—	—	—	—	2	—	4	—	2	—	16
1953–54	1	15	13	4	2	2	1	7	3	1	5	3	5	—	7	2	71
1955–56	—	11	4	3	5	—	—	6	—	—	5	4	4	—	—	—	42
1957–58	2	9	4	6	4	—	—	1	—	3	3	3	3	—	—	2	40
1959–60	6	15	2	8	8	—	—	1	—	1	3	3	4	—	1	2	64
SUB. TOT.	9	52	25	23	20	3	1	15	3	5	18	13	20	0	10	6	233
1961–62	1	18	7	6	7	—	—	2	1	2	7	7	3	—	—	—	61
1963–64	4	12	3	4	4	—	—	7	—	2	6	11	3	—	3	—	59
1965–66	5	24	3	11	4	1	—	—	—	2	22	11	3	3	—	—	89
1967–68	1	23	2	2	7	1	—	5	—	1	9	9	5	1	—	1	67
1969–70	2	5	4	2	16	—	—	5	—	—	—	13	7	2	1	1	58
SUB. TOT.	13	82	19	25	38	2	0	19	1	7	44	52	21	6	4	2	335
	Bill of Rights	Legislative	Executive	Judicial	Elective Franch.	Education	Pub. Institutions	Pub. Debt & Works	Militia	Co. & Twp. Organ.	Apportionment	Finance & Taxation	Miscellaneous	Amendments	Elections	Municipal Corps.	Total Number of Proposed Changes to Articles
TOTALS	27	157	62	59	70	9	2	57	4	13	71	82	46	9	22	10	711

originated in the legislature as joint resolutions. By decade, there were 7 such proposals from 1941–1950, 23 from 1951–1960, and 25 from 1961–1970. Table 2 lists the final roll-call votes in the legislature and the election results for the 55 issues, plus the 1952 mandatory referendum on a convention.

The volume of proposed amendments in the General Assembly indicates growing concern for constitutional revision. In the decade of the 1940s, just before the unsuccessful call for an Ohio Constitutional Convention in 1952, legislators introduced 130 joint resolutions as constitutional amendments (see Table 3). These 95 House and 35 Senate joint resolutions proposed a total of 142 changes in separate articles of the constitution (see Table 4). Only 8 resolutions received legislative approval and appeared on the ballot in the forties.

The past twenty years have produced a substantial increase in the total number of joint resolutions introduced in the legislature and a doubling of the number of changes proposed to separate articles of the constitution, compared with the decade of the 1940s. In the 1960s, 289 legislative joint resolutions (167 in the House and 122 in the Senate) have been offered. Since a resolution sometimes changes more than one article, the sum of the articles modified by these 289 joint resolutions is 335.

Changes to Article II, the Legislative section of the constitution, have dominated the joint resolutions, particularly during the last decade (see Table 4). The legislative reapportionment issue undoubtedly accounts for some of the increase, but this research does not provide a definitive explanation for the large number of proposals to change the legislative article.

A final observation concerning the history of joint resolutions is the comparison of those introduced in the General Assembly with those receiving the approval of both chambers in Table 5. Constitutional articles for which changes have most often been proposed are not the articles most frequently subject to referendum (see Table 5). Only 8 out of 157 joint resolutions concerning the Legislative article were approved by the General Assembly and appeared on the ballot. Proposed amendments to the articles concerning Public Debt & Public Works, Judicial, and Elections had the great-

TABLE 5
CONSTITUTIONAL CHANGES PROPOSED IN LEGISLATURE COMPARED TO NUMBER OF AMENDMENTS APPEARING ON BALLOT, BY ARTICLE AND ISSUE, 1941–1970

		Number of Changes Proposed in General Assembly				*No. Changes on Ballot as*
Article	*Issue Area*	*1941–50*	*1951–60*	*1961–70*	*Total*	*Amendments*
I	Bill of Rights	5	9	13	27	0
II	Legislature	23	52	82	157	8
III	Executive	18	25	19	62	3
IV	Judicial	11	23	25	59	10
V	Elective Franchise	12	20	38	70	3
VI	Education	4	3	2	9	2
VII	Public Institutions	1	1	0	2	0
VIII	Pub. Debt & Pub. Works	23	15	19	57	12
IX	Militia	0	3	1	4	3
X	Co. & Twp. Organ.	1	5	7	13	3
XI	Apportionment	9	18	44	71	5
XII	Finance & Taxation	17	13	52	82	2
XV	Miscellaneous	5	20	21	46	2
XVI	Amendment	3	0	6	9	0
XVII	Elections	8	10	4	22	4
XVIII	Municipal Corporations	2	6	2	10	2
	TOTALS	142	233	335	711	59

est chance of success in the last thirty years. While many resolutions were introduced to modify the articles on Finance & Taxation, Elective Franchise, Executive, and Apportionment, relatively few were passed by the legislature.

II. COHESION, CONFLICT, PARTICIPATION, AND CONTEST AMONG LEGISLATIVE GROUPS

Roll-Call Analysis Research Design

The methodology utilized in this study measures variations in the voting behavior of groups of Ohio legislators. Four categoric groups are identified by characteristics of party, constituency, occupation, and region. Voting behavior has been compared among the categoric groups for the period of the last three decades by roll calls on each constitutional article and by all constitutional roll calls for each two-year legislative session.

It is important to note some limitations of roll-call analysis. First, it is not assumed that the observation of a roll-call vote will allow the observer to determine the cause of the legislator's vote. All the indices of party, constituency, occupation, and region taken together must be cautiously applied. Second, roll-call analysis is not a description of the entire legislative process. Many other influences, even on the voting act, are present.

Selection of Roll Calls and Issues

Many roll-call votes taken in the Ohio legislature are unanimous or nearly so. Some minimum level of dissenting votes is needed in order to measure inter-group conflict. In this study, only those roll calls are included in which at least ten percent of the legislators voted in opposition to the majority.

All roll calls in this study are votes on either substantive or procedural aspects of proposed constitutional amendments. Substantive roll calls refer to votes to adopt or amend the body of the joint resolution, while procedural roll calls are matters of ending debate, referring to committee, etc. Some roll calls, such as a motion to lay on the table, are procedural by definition, yet may have the substantive effect of defeating passage of the legislation. The "issue areas" of this study are the articles of the Ohio Constitution which the joint resolution seeks to change. Of the eighteen articles (issue areas), the roll calls included in this study affect thirteen articles in the House of Representatives and nine in the Senate.

Table 6 shows the number of roll calls examined by article and the years of each vote. While only 92 roll calls were gathered in the House and only 55 in the Senate, the joint resolutions would often amend more than one article. This was especially true in Senate joint resolutions. As a result, the 147 total roll calls in the

TABLE 6
NUMBER OF ROLL CALLS EXAMINED BY ISSUE AREA, 1941–1970

Article	*Issue Area*	*No. of Roll Calls Analyzed* *House*	*Senate*	*Total*	*Years of Legislative Votes*
I	Bill of Rights	4	0	4	47* 49* 65*
II	Legislative	16	20	36	43* 53 55 57⁺ 59⁺ 65 67
III	Executive	1	6	7	53 55⁺ 61⁺
IV	Judicial	7	5	12	49⁺ 55 62⁺ 65 67*
V	Elective Franchise	10	2	12	55* 59* 63* 65 67⁺ 69*
VI	Education	1	0	1	53*
VIII	Pub. Debt & Pub. Works	29	14	43	47* 53* 55 61* 63 67
X	Co. & Twp. Organ.	14	9	23	57 59 65
XI	Apportionment	8	15	23	53 55 63* 65* 67⁺
XII	Finance & Taxation	1	0	1	68*
XV	Miscellaneous	5	0	5	41* 49* 57*
XVII	Elections	1	3	4	53
XVIII	Municipal Corporations	1	1	2	57⁺ 70*
	TOTAL	98	75	173	

*Indicates House vote only
⁺Indicates Senate vote only
Year number alone indicates vote in both chambers

General Assembly from 1941 to 1970 provide 173 proposed constitutional changes to thirteen of the eighteen articles or issue areas.

Categoric Group Characteristics of Party, Constituency, Occupation and Region

> The distinguishing mark of research on voting behavior of categoric groups is that the analysis begins with the classification of legislators into certain categories or groups. These categories originate in the mind of the researcher, and presumably, will be related to his theoretical concerns and substantive interests.[3]

In the research design, four categories were utilized that have

[3]Anderson, Watts, and Wilcox, *op. cit.*, p. 29.

been of interest in previous studies of legislative behavior. These classifications were political party, urban-rural constituency, region, and occupation.

The political party affiliation of each legislator presents an obvious basis for grouping senators and representatives. The Republican Party has been dominant in almost all of the last fifteen legislative sessions (see Table 7). Democratic Party majorities in both chambers of the General Assembly existed only in 1949–1950 and again in 1959–1960. The equal number of the Republican and Democratic senators in 1965–1966 can be treated as a Republican majority, since the Republican lieutenant governor could cast a tie-breaking vote as presiding officer.

To operationalize the urban-rural category, the U.S. Census Bureau's definition of Standard Metropolitan Statistical Areas (SMSA) was correlated with Ohio legislative district boundaries. An "urban" district was defined as one inside an SMSA. All others were "rural." In 1949 a total of eighteen Ohio counties were included within metropolitan area boundaries. This increased to twenty-seven counties in 1967. Up-dated listings of metropolitan areas were published in 1952, 1956, and 1962. Legislators were categorized as having a rural or urban constituency by the Standard Metropolitan Statistical Area list released nearest their term in the General Assembly.

Although Ohio's natural geographic and geologic divisions do not split the state into north-south regions, the old National Road (now Route 40) provides a convenient, state-wide Mason-Dixon line. The third category is, therefore, composed of a northern and a southern legislative group.

The fourth and only personal characteristic used for defining a categoric group is occupation. As law is the predominant occupational background for Ohio legislators, as elsewhere in the nation, the voting behavior of lawyers is compared with non-lawyers.

Table 7 shows the composition of all four categoric groups in each of the fifteen sessions of the General Assembly between 1941 and 1970. The 1851 Ohio Constitution set up an apportionment formula that resulted in frequent changes in the number of mem-

TABLE 7

COMPOSITION OF CATEGORIC VOTING GROUPS, 1941–1970

Gen. Assem. No.	Years	Party		Constituency		Occupation		Region		Total Legislators	
		House	*Senate*	*House*	*Senate*	*House*	*Senate*	*House*	*Senate*	*House*	*Senate*
94	1941–42	78R 60D	19R 17D	65U 73R	25U 11R	101N 37L	23N 12L	88N 50S	27N 9S	138	36
95	1943–44	111R 25D	28R 5D	66U 70R	24U 9R	98N 38L	20N 13L	86N 50S	24N 9S	136	33
96	1945–46	89R 47D	20R 13D	66U 70R	24U 9R	107N 29L	23N 10L	83N 53S	23N 10S	136	33
97	1947–48	123R 16D	32R 4D	70U 69R	26U 10R	96N 43L	19N 17L	89N 50S	26N 10S	139	36
98	1949–50	66R 69D	14R 19D	65U 70R	23U 10R	99N 36L	21N 12L	86N 49S	22N 11S	135	33
99	1951–52	99R 36D	26R 7D	62U 73R	23U 10R	87N 48L	22N 11L	84N 51S	22N 11S	135	33
100	1953–54	102R 34D	23R 10D	66U 70R	24U 9R	93N 43L	20N 13L	86N 50S	22N 11S	136	33
101	1955–56	89R 47D	21R 12D	66U 70R	24U 9R	93N 43L	23N 10L	84N 52S	22N 11S	136	33
102	1957–58	97R 42D	22R 12D	69U 70R	24U 10R	86N 53L	23N 11L	86N 53S	24N 10S	139	34
103	1959–60	61R 78D	13R 20D	70U 69R	23U 10R	91N 48L	24N 9L	86N 53S	22N 11S	139	33
104	1961–62	84R 55D	20R 18D	70U 69R	28U 10R	88N 51L	29N 9L	85N 54S	26N 12S	139	38
105	1963–64	88R 49D	20R 13D	68U 69R	25U 8R	87N 50L	21N 12L	83N 54S	23N 10S	137	33
106	1965–66	75R 62D	16R 16D	77U 60R	25U 7R	90N 47L	21N 11L	83N 54S	22N 10S	137	32
107	1967–68	62R 37D	23R 10D	76U 23R	25U 8R	61N 38L	22N 11L	63N 36S	21N 12S	99	33
108	1969–70	64R 35D	21R 12D	76U 23R	25U 8R	63N 36L	19N 14L	63N 36S	21N 12S	99	33

Abbreviations:

Under Party:
D = Democrat
R = Republican

Under Constituency:
U = Urban
R = Rural

Under Occupation:
N = Non-Lawyer
L = Lawyer

Under Region:
N = Northern
S = Southern

bers of the House and Senate. Until the 1966 redistricting, Ohio was the only state in which the number of members in each chamber often varied from session to session.

Methods of Measuring Behavior of Categoric Groups

The basic roll-call data were collected from a total universe of all House and Senate Joint Resolutions, which are listed in the General Assembly *Bulletin* for each session. The votes on all joint resolutions reaching the House or Senate floor were then examined in the House and Senate *Journals*. Those votes which had a 10% dissent level or more were recorded for each legislator and later coded and placed on punch cards.

By means of ACCUM,[4] a Fortran computer program designed to provide a profile of each legislative vote, three statistical measures (Rice Index of Cohesion, Rice Index of Likeness, and Riker Coefficient of Significance) were derived. The program's output also listed the division of the vote by each categoric subgroup (e.g., total "yeas" and "nays" for Democrats and Republicans) and a total division of the vote.

The Rice Index of Cohesion, while the simplest of intra-group behavior measures, is the most widely utilized measurement. It is the only intra-group index used in this study. The range of the index is from zero, which would occur when equal numbers of a group vote on opposite sides, to one hundred, which is the value when all members of a group vote on the same side.[5]

It is important to note that this index measures only intragroup cohesion, and in no way indicates whether party, constituency, occupation, or regional groups are voting against one another. The analyst must find some other device to assess intergroup conflict. The Rice Index of Likeness is used to measure the

---

[4]*Ibid.*, p. 176. The output of the ACCUM program prints out consecutively numbered roll calls. The data were arranged chronologically with a punch card provided for each legislator in every House and Senate session where a roll call received more than ten percent of the dissenting vote.

[5]*Ibid.*, p. 43, and Stuart A. Rice., *Quantitave Methods in Politics* (New York: Alfred A. Knopf, 1928), and "The Behavior of Legislative Groups," *Political Science Quarterly*, 40 (1925), 60–72.

difference between any two groups in their response to a roll call. The higher the index value, the less difference there is between voting groups. If two categoric groups vote totally in opposition to one another, the Index of Likeness value is zero.[6]

To measure the significance of the total vote on a roll call and to determine whether a categoric group contains opposing subgroups, William H. Riker has developed a coefficient of significance. This "significance value":

> represents a numerical index mathematically derived from (1) the number of members present and voting on a particular measure, and (2) the degree to which the outcome of the issue is contested. "Significance," defined in this manner, is actually a composite index of "participation" and "conflict." The most significant roll call is one in which all members of the legislature are present and voting and in which there is the maximum possible division of responses (maximum participation, maximum conflict). The least significant roll call is one in which only a quoroum is present and all vote together (minimum participation, minimum conflict).[7]

The higher the numerical value, the greater the "significance" of the roll call in terms of participation and conflict. Since the coefficient of significance does not involve categoric groups, but measures participation and conflict generally, each roll call has only one coefficient. These coefficients can be averaged to obtain a mean coefficient of significance for each issue area.

III. ROLL CALL VOTING ANALYSIS OF CONSTITUTIONAL ISSUES IN THE OHIO HOUSE OF REPRESENTATIVES, 1941–1970

The House of Representatives has been the chamber most productive of proposed changes to the Ohio Constitution during the last three decades. A total of 373 House Joint Resolutions were

---

[6]Anderson, Watts, and Wilcox, *op. cit.*, p. 44.

[7]William H. Riker, "A Method for Determining the Significance of Roll Calls in Voting Bodies," in Wahlke and Eulau (eds.), *Legislative Behavior* (Glencoe, Ill.: Free Press, 1959), pp. 379–380.

offered, with 95 in the forties, 111 in the fifties, and 167 in the sixties. As shown in Table 3, the House has passed 62.

Excluding those votes in which less than ten percent of the representatives voted in opposition to the majority, a total of 92 roll calls were examined. Thirty-five originated in the 107th session of 1967–1968. Only the 96th session of 1945–1946, and the 99th session of 1951–1952 did not provide a single roll call. Table 6 lists the distribution of roll calls among constitutional articles.

Two levels of analysis of the roll-call measurements are employed. First, the mean values of each measurement are grouped by constitutional issues and compared by categoric groups for the entire thirty-year period. Secondly, a longitudinal view is secured by grouping mean values of the measurements on all constitutional issues during each General Assembly and comparing categoric groups by the chronological order of the legislative sessions.

TABLE 9
PARTY: HOUSE REPUBLICANS VS. DEMOCRATS IN RANK ORDER OF MEAN COHESION INDICES, BY CONSTITUTIONAL ARTICLE

Republicans			*Democrats*		
Rank	*Mean Cohesion Index*	*Roll-Call Issues & Constitutional Articles*	*Rank*	*Mean Cohesion Index*	*Roll-Call Issues & Constitutional Articles*
1)	81.8	Finance & Taxation XII	1)	72.8	Apportionment XI
2)	80.4	Executive III	2)	68.4	Pub. Debt & Pub. Works VIII
3)	80.4	Elections XVII	3)	64.8	Miscellaneous XV
4)	78.6	Education VI	4)	64.3	Municipal Corps. XVIII
5)	65.8	Legislative II	5)	58.1	Elective Franchise V
6)	64.5	Pub. Debt & Pub. Works VIII	6)	51.8	Judicial IV
7)	64.0	Municipal Corps. XVIII	7)	49.4	Legislative II
8)	57.7	Apportionment XI	8)	48.1	Bill of Rights I
9)	53.5	Judicial IV	9)	42.9	Co. & Twp. Organ. X
10)	46.4	Miscellaneous XV	10)	33.3	Finance & Taxation XII
11)	32.8	Co. & Twp. Organ. X	11)	28.6	Executive III
12)	32.5	Bill of Rights I	12)	28.6	Elections XVII
13)	27.1	Elective Franchise V	13)	4.3	Education VI

House Intra-Group Cohesion

On nine of the thirteen constitutional articles, party was the most cohesive voting factor when the mean indices of cohesion for party, constituency, occupation, and region are compared. Tables 9, 10, 11, and 12 show each of these categoric groups in rank order of mean indices by constitutional article, over the three decades.

The nine issue areas of the constitution where party was the most cohesive voting factor were: Bill of Rights, Legislative, Executive, Elective Franchise, Education, Public Debt and Public Works, Apportionment, Miscellaneous, and Elections.

Republican legislators showed a good deal more cohesion than Democrats on amendments affecting Finance & Taxation, Executive, Elections, Education, and Legislative. However, all these issues involved only one roll call, except for Article II (Legislative),

TABLE 10
CONSTITUENCY: HOUSE URBAN VS. RURAL MEMBERS IN RANK ORDER OF MEAN COHESION INDICES, BY CONSTITUTIONAL ARTICLE

Urban			*Rural*		
Rank	*Mean Cohesion Index*	*Roll-Call Issues & Constitutional Articles*	*Rank*	*Mean Cohesion Index*	*Roll-Call Issues & Constitutional Articles*
1)	72.4	Municipal Corps. XVIII	1)	73.9	Finance & Taxation XII
2)	68.4	Executive III	2)	69.0	Education VI
3)	68.4	Elections XVII	3)	68.3	Executive III
4)	67.2	Finance & Taxation XII	4)	68.3	Elections XVII
			5)	50.8	Judicial IV
5)	56.7	Co. & Twp. Organ. X	6)	47.9	Pub. Debt & Pub. Works VIII
6)	55.1	Education VI			
7)	53.1	Judicial IV	7)	47.8	Legislative II
8)	47.1	Miscellaneous XV	8)	45.7	Apportionment XI
9)	41.2	Elective Franchise V	9)	42.4	Bill of Rights I
10)	37.3	Legislative II	10)	40.0	Municipal Corps. XVIII
11)	32.9	Pub. Debt & Pub. Works VIII	11)	36.2	Miscellaneous XV
12)	24.4	Apportionment XI	12)	35.5	Co. & Twp. Organ. X
13)	23.6	Bill of Rights I	13)	27.4	Elective Franchise V

TABLE 11

OCCUPATION: HOUSE LAWYERS V. NON-LAWYERS IN RANK ORDER OF MEAN COHESION INDICES, BY CONSTITUTIONAL ARTICLE

Lawyers			*Non-Lawyers*		
Rank	*Mean Cohesion Index*	*Roll-Call Issues & Constitutional Articles*	*Rank*	*Mean Cohesion Index*	*Roll-Call Issues & Constitutional Articles*
1)	79.3	Finance & Taxation XII	1)	70.8	Municipal Corps. XVIII
2)	77.8	Executive III	2)	70.7	Education VI
3)	77.8	Elections XVII	3)	64.3	Executive III
4)	62.8	Judicial IV	4)	64.3	Elections XVII
5)	53.3	Municipal Corps. XVIII	5)	63.9	Finance & Taxation XII
6)	52.4	Legislative II	6)	51.6	Judicial IV
7)	46.2	Pub. Debt & Pub. Works VIII	7)	35.3	Co. & Twp. Organ. X
8)	43.8	Education VI	8)	34.5	Elective Franchise V
9)	41.9	Co. & Twp. Organ. X	9)	34.3	Pub. Debt & Pub. Works VIII
10)	36.4	Miscellaneous XV	10)	33.2	Legislative II
11)	30.8	Apportionment XI	11)	31.6	Miscellaneous XV
12)	29.1	Elective Franchise V	12)	26.2	Apportionment XI
13)	18.5	Bill of Rights I	13)	24.3	Bill of Rights I

TABLE 12

REGION: HOUSE NORTH VS. SOUTH MEMBERS IN RANK ORDER OF MEAN COHESION INDICES, BY CONSTITUTIONAL ARTICLE

North			*South*		
Rank	*Mean Cohesion Index*	*Roll-Call Issues & Constitutional Articles*	*Rank*	*Mean Cohesion Index*	*Roll-Call Issues & Constitutional Articles*
1)	61.1	Executive III	1)	88.2	Finance & Taxation XII
2)	61.1	Elections XVII	2)	85.7	Municipal Corps. XVIII
3)	57.1	Finance & Taxation XII	3)	79.2	Executive III
4)	53.1	Education VI	4)	79.2	Elections XVII
5)	52.2	Judicial IV	5)	76.7	Education VI
6)	52.0	Municipal Corps. XVIII	6)	58.2	Pub. Debt & Pub. Works VIII
7)	41.6	Miscellaneous XV	7)	54.4	Legislative II
8)	39.8	Co. & Twp. Organ. X	8)	52.6	Judicial IV
9)	35.9	Legislative II	9)	43.6	Apportionment XI
10)	29.7	Elective Franchise V	10)	42.3	Elective Franchise V
11)	27.7	Pub. Debt & Pub. Works VIII	11)	32.8	Co. & Twp. Organ. X
12)	25.1	Apportionment XI	12)	27.4	Miscellaneous XV
13)	10.2	Bill of Rights I	13)	21.1	Bill of Rights I

TABLE 13
MEAN RICE INDICES OF COHESION ON ALL HOUSE ROLL CALLS, BY CATEGORIC GROUP

Years	*No. of Roll Calls*	*Party*		*Constituency*		*Region*		*Occupation*	
		Rep.	*Dem.*	*Urban*	*Rural*	*North*	*South*	*Lawyers*	*Non-Law.*
1941–42	2	58.2	96.4	58.2	25.9	32.5	18.0	21.8	12.2
1943–44	1	18.7	38.5	41.4	6.3	35.9	0.0	58.8	9.1
1947–48	3	49.6	67.0	36.7	58.3	33.8	46.5	42.1	37.2
1949–50	3	30.3	43.8	35.2	36.1	26.8	13.8	24.9	22.0
1953–54	6	68.3	53.9	36.0	50.0	32.3	59.4	46.4	40.1
1955–56	9	67.1	57.8	50.0	58.8	43.7	62.2	57.0	49.8
1957–58	9	35.4	31.2	44.6	46.3	33.2	30.7	42.1	34.3
1959–60	10	19.4	55.1	51.2	13.4	30.1	33.8	38.2	27.6
1961–62	1	97.5	33.3	30.3	62.5	35.1	62.3	48.9	44.6
1963–64	4	48.9	56.7	22.9	44.8	26.3	36.0	28.1	31.5
1965–66	7	49.0	47.5	42.4	34.9	34.6	40.6	36.9	34.1
1967–68	35	62.1	71.1	33.6	50.2	26.7	57.6	49.0	32.2
1969–70	2	63.9	94.1	72.3	61.3	64.5	78.1	45.2	83.7

which included sixteen roll-call votes. On the other hand, Democrats were noticeably more cohesive on the average when voting on articles relating to Apportionment, County and Township Organization, Miscellaneous, Bill of Rights, and Elective Franchise.

On the two areas of Finance & Taxation and Municipal Corporations (Articles XII and XVIII), the regional categoric group of southern Ohio legislators formed the most cohesive voting bloc. The northern Ohio legislators were the least cohesive of any categoric group.

On the single issue of County and Township Organization (Article X), urban legislators displayed the most cohesion of any categoric group. Urban House members exhibited a noticeably higher cohesion on Article XVIII (Municipal Corporations) than rural members. On Article IV, the Judicial issue, the lawyers had the highest cohesion of any group.

The mean Rice indices on all constitutional issues, when viewed chronologically by sessions, show that usually during each session one or both of the parties exhibited the highest cohesion of any group.

House Inter-Group Conflict

On eleven of the thirteen constitutional articles, the index of likeness values for the parties in the House were the lowest of the four categoric groups. This indicates that the highest conflict on constitutional issues in the House occurs mainly between Democrats and Republicans. As shown in Table 14, a high level of conflict exists between partisans on the issues of Apportionment, Public Debt & Public Works, Legislative, and Miscellaneous (Articles XI, VIII, II, and XV).

On Article X, concerning County and Township Organization, conflict is the greatest between rural and urban legislators. On the issue of Municipal Corporations (Article XVIII), the regional group of northern versus southern legislators produced the highest conflict measurement, only slightly above the constituency category. Generally, the occupational categoric group of lawyers versus non-lawyers showed the least conflict of the four variables.

The mean indices of likeness comparing each group on issues during each session shows the chronological dominance of party conflict (Table 15). Conflict between rural and urban House members was slightly higher during the 94th session of 1941–1942 and most noticeably highest in the 102nd session of 1957–1958. The occupational categoric group exhibited the highest conflict in the 95th session of 1943–1944 and the 108th session of 1969–1970.

House Participation and Contest

Those constitutional issues in the House which commanded the most participation and contest were Bill of Rights, Public Debt & Public Works, Apportionment, and Elective Franchise (Articles I, VIII, XI, and II), as shown in the rank order of mean coefficients of significance in Table 16.

As a measure of floor participation and contest of House members over the thirteen sessions chronologically arranged (Table 17), the mean coefficient of significance fluctuates from year to year. The differing coefficient values do not appear related to the presence or absence of any particular roll-call issue. The number of

TABLE 14
HOUSE MEAN INDICES OF LIKENESS IN ASCENDING ORDER OF PARTY LIKENESS, BY CATEGORIC GROUP

Roll-Call Issue and Constitutional Article	*No. of Roll Calls*	*Party R vs. D*	*Const. U vs. R*	*Region N vs. S*	*Occup. L vs. NL*
Apportionment XI	8	38	76	85	91
Pub. Debt & Pub. Works VIII	29	43	90	81	85
Legislative II	16	53	91	78	88
Miscellaneous XV	5	57	81	85	92
Bill of Rights I	4	60	69	92	91
Education VI	1	63	93	88	87
Elective Franchise V	10	72	86	89	93
Elections XVII	1	74	100	91	93
Executive III	1	74	100	91	93
Finance & Taxation XII	1	76	97	84	92
Co. & Twp. Organ. X	14	84	71	94	84
Judicial IV	7	88	93	95	88
Municipal Corps. XVIII	1	100	84	83	91

TABLE 15
MEAN INDICES OF LIKENESS ON ALL HOUSE ROLL CALLS, BY CATEGORIC GROUP AND SESSION

Years	*Session*	*No. of Roll Calls*	*Mean Indices of Likeness*			
			Party D vs. R	*Constituency U vs. R*	*Occupation L vs. NL*	*Region N vs. S*
1941–42	94	2	61	59	95	75
1943–44	95	1	90	82	75	82
1947–48	97	3	42	77	91	92
1949–50	98	3	70	80	90	90
1953–54	100	6	45	90	91	86
1955–56	101	9	65	85	89	90
1957–58	102	9	85	72	81	95
1959–60	103	10	73	80	93	91
1961–62	104	1	35	84	98	86
1963–64	105	4	54	80	92	84
1965–66	106	7	77	82	93	90
1967–68	107	35	44	90	86	81
1969–70	108	2	92	90	80	90

TABLE 16
RANK ORDER OF MEAN COEFFICIENTS OF SIGNIFICANCE ON HOUSE ROLL CALLS, BY CONSTITUTIONAL ARTICLE

Rank	*Roll-Call Issue and Article*	*Mean Coefficient of Significance*	*No. of Roll Calls*
1)	Bill of Rights I	.7506	4
2)	Public Debt & Public Works VIII	.7189	29
3)	Apportionment XI	.7168	8
4)	Elective Franchise V	.6965	10
5)	Legislative II	.6680	16
6)	County and Township Organization X	.6569	14
7)	Miscellaneous XV	.5689	5
8)	Judicial IV	.5496	7
9)	Finances & Taxation XII	.4703	1
10)	Executive III	.4486	1
11)	Elections XVII	.4486	1
12)	Education VI	.3879	1
13)	Municipal Corporations XVIII	.3860	1

TABLE 17
MEAN COEFFICIENT OF SIGNIFICANCE OF HOUSE AND SENATE ROLL CALLS, BY CONSTITUTIONAL ISSUE, 1941–1970

Years	*Session*	*No. of House Roll Calls*	*Mean Coefficient of Significance*	*No. of Senate Roll Calls*	*Mean Coefficient of Significance*
1941–42	94	2	.7328	—	—
1943–44	95	1	.7333	—	—
1945–46	96	—	—	—	—
1947–48	97	3	.4744	—	—
1949–50	98	3	.5728	1	.3393
1951–52	99	—	—	—	—
1953–54	100	6	.5822	3	.4546
1955–56	101	9	.5677	9	.7556
1957–58	102	9	.6838	5	.7699
1959–60	103	10	.6731	6	.7887
1961–62	104	1	.6368	2	.8599
1963–64	105	4	.7119	2	.8549
1965–66	106	7	.7107	8	.4033
1967–68	107	35	.6969	22	.7054
1969–70	108	2	.4288	—	—

members participating and the degree of their contest on issues seems to be generally less in the House than in the Senate.

IV. ROLL-CALL VOTING ANALYSIS OF CONSTITUTIONAL ISSUES IN THE OHIO SENATE, 1949–1968

A total of 253 Senate Joint Resolutions were introduced during the last three decades: 35 in the forties, 96 in the fifties, and 122 in the sixties. Sixty-three were passed.

Only 55 roll calls on constitutional issues with the minimum ten percent level of dissent are available for our analysis of the Senate. These roll-call votes occurred in nine of the fifteen sessions. The Senate sessions with no roll calls were the 94th, 95th, 96th, and 97th during the period 1941–1948, the 99th session of 1951–1952, and the 108th session of 1969–1970. As in the House voting, a sizeable portion of the Senate roll calls (22) derive from the single session of 1967–1968.

Senate Intra-Group Cohesion

In contrast to the House, the constituency categoric group is the most cohesive voting group on constitutional issues in the Senate. Tables 18, 19, 20, and 21 present the groups in rank order of mean Rice indices on all roll calls, by constitutional article, over the nine sessions between 1949 and 1968.

On five of the nine constitutional articles or issue areas, cohesion is the greatest within the rural group. The five issues of high rural cohesiveness are Public Debt & Public Works, Apportionment, Elections, Legislative, and Executive (Articles VIII, XI, II, and III). It should be noted in comparing Tables 18 and 19 that the rural legislators are only slightly more cohesive than Republicans on the three issues of Public Debt & Public Works, Apportionment, and Legislative. Comparing all categoric groups, the urban legislators in the Senate are the least cohesive on constitutional issues.

Party is the basis for the most cohesion on three issues. Demo-

TABLE 18
PARTY: SENATE REPUBLICANS VS. DEMOCRATS IN RANK ORDER OF MEAN COHESION INDICES, BY CONSTITUTIONAL ARTICLE

Republicans			*Democrats*		
Rank	*Mean Cohesion Index*	*Roll-Call Issues & Constitutional Articles*	*Rank*	*Mean Cohesion Index*	*Roll-Call Issues & Constitutional Articles*
1)	98.3	Pub. Debt & Pub. Works VIII	1)	100.0	Elective Franchise V
2)	93.6	Apportionment XI	2)	87.8	Judicial IV
3)	87.9	Legislative II	3)	82.5	Executive III
4)	83.5	Judicial IV	4)	69.4	Legislative II
5)	75.6	Executive III	5)	66.7	Municipal Corps. XVIII
6)	71.2	Elections XVII	6)	65.4	Pub. Debt & Pub. Works VIII
7)	60.1	Co. & Twp. Organ. X	7)	64.3	Elections XVII
8)	48.3	Elective Franchise V	8)	61.6	Apportionment XI
9)	42.9	Municipal Corps. XVIII	9)	38.2	Co. & Twp. Organ. X

TABLE 19
CONSTITUENCY: SENATE URBAN VS. RURAL MEMBERS IN RANK ORDER OF MEAN COHESION INDICES, BY CONSTITUTIONAL ARTICLE

Urban			*Rural*		
Rank	*Mean Cohesion Index*	*Roll-Call Issues & Constitutional Articles*	*Rank*	*Mean Cohesion Index*	*Roll-Call Issues & Constitutional Articles*
1)	60.8	Elections XVII	1)	100.0	Pub. Debt & Pub. Works VIII
2)	44.9	Elective Franchise V	2)	93.8	Apportionment XI
3)	44.2	Co. & Twp. Organ. X	3)	91.7	Elections XVII
4)	40.6	Executive III	4)	88.9	Legislative II
5)	39.8	Legislative II	5)	88.8	Executive III
6)	37.6	Judicial IV	6)	63.5	Judicial IV
7)	36.0	Apportionment XI	7)	60.0	Municipal Corps. XVIII
8)	25.3	Pub. Debt & Pub. Works VIII	8)	47.5	Elective Franchise V
9)	21.7	Municipal Corps. XVIII	9)	26.5	Co. & Twp. Organ. X

TABLE 20
OCCUPATION: SENATE LAWYERS V. NON-LAWYERS IN RANK ORDER OF MEAN COHESION INDICES, BY CONSTITUTIONAL ARTICLE

Lawyers			*Non-lawyers*		
Rank	*Mean Cohesion Index*	*Roll-Call Issues & Constitutional Articles*	*Rank*	*Mean Cohesion Index*	*Roll-Call Issues & Constitutional Articles*
1)	62.1	Co. & Twp. Organ. X	1)	85.5	Elections XVII
2)	61.0	Apportionment XI	2)	51.5	Executive III
3)	60.3	Elective Franchise V	3)	50.9	Elective Franchise V
4)	59.3	Pub. Debt & Pub. Works VIII	4)	47.0	Apportionment XI
			5)	46.4	Legislative II
5)	55.6	Judicial IV	6)	37.7	Co. & Twp. Organ. X
6)	52.4	Legislative II	7)	37.7	Judicial IV
7)	43.7	Executive III	8)	31.3	Pub. Debt & Pub. Works VIII
8)	42.2	Elections XVII			
9)	0.0	Municipal Corps. XVIII	9)	4.3	Municipal Corps. XVIII

TABLE 21
REGION: SENATE NORTH V. SOUTH MEMBERS IN RANK ORDER OF MEAN COHESION INDICES, BY CONSTITUTIONAL ARTICLE

North			*South*		
Rank	*Mean Cohesion Index*	*Roll-Call Issues & Constitutional Articles*	*Rank*	*Mean Cohesion Index*	*Roll-Call Issues & Constitutional Articles*
1)	74.1	Elections XVII	1)	82.4	Pub. Debt & Pub. Works VIII
2)	61.4	Elective Franchise V			
3)	46.0	Executive III	2)	78.6	Apportionment XI
4)	42.1	Judicial IV	3)	67.6	Legislative II
5)	38.7	Legislative II	4)	64.7	Judicial IV
6)	35.5	Apportionment XI	5)	56.1	Elections XVII
7)	32.0	Co. & Twp. Organ. X	6)	55.6	Municipal Corps. XVIII
8)	22.2	Pub. Debt & Pub. Works VIII			
			7)	55.0	Co. & Twp. Organ. X
9)	16.7	Municipal Corps. XVIII	8)	51.5	Executive III
			9)	39.4	Elective Franchise V

crats form the most cohesive group on the roll calls involving Elective Franchise, Judicial, and Municipal Corporations (Articles V, IV, and XVIII). Republicans are noticeably less cohesive than Democrats on the issues of Elective Franchise and Municipal Corporations, while exhibiting more cohesion on the Apportionment issue.

On the single issue of County & Township Organization (Article X), the occupational sub-group of lawyers was the most cohesive, although only slightly higher than Republicans. On no Senate roll-call issue was the regional categoric group the most cohesive. As a whole, the southern legislators were more cohesive than the northern senators, as illustrated in Table 21. This finding is similar to the House of Representatives (see Table 12).

The mean Rice indices, when arrayed chronologically by sessions, do not indicate the party group as the dominant cohesion factor, as Table 13 displays for House voting (see Table 22). Party was most cohesive in four sessions, constituency type in three sessions, and region in two.

Senate Inter-Group Conflict

On eight of the nine constitutional articles and issues, the index of likeness values for the parties in the Senate were the lowest of

TABLE 22
MEAN RICE INDICES OF COHESION ON ALL SENATE ROLL CALLS BY CATEGORIC GROUP

	No. of Roll	*Party*		*Constituency*		*Region*		*Occupation*	
Years	*Calls*	*Rep.*	*Dem.*	*Urban*	*Rural*	*North*	*South*	*Lawyers*	*Non-Law.*
1949–50	1	50.0	76.5	68.4	66.7	86.7	40.0	60.0	73.3
1953–54	3	71.2	64.3	60.8	91.6	74.1	56.1	42.2	85.5
1955–56	6	88.4	92.9	19.6	92.6	19.3	69.4	49.3	26.0
1957–58	5	30.7	72.7	22.3	56.7	78.6	39.4	33.5	42.5
1959–60	6	63.5	75.9	50.7	43.2	39.7	25.6	23.2	34.5
1961–62	2	94.7	61.1	29.7	80.0	30.8	55.0	49.3	24.1
1963–64	2	88.2	78.5	12.5	100.0	13.6	77.8	27.3	10.0
1965–66	8	81.7	43.7	42.8	26.6	31.7	63.9	64.3	31.1
1967–68	22	97.0	64.2	29.9	98.9	20.0	82.3	66.6	36.5

the four categoric groups. As in the House, this shows a conflict pattern in the Senate primarily of Democrats versus Republicans, except that there is less cohesion within the Senate parties, as we have just seen.

Table 23 lists the Senate mean indices of likeness arranged in ascending order. A comparison of Table 23 and Table 14 shows that party conflict is greater in the Senate than the House. Like the House, the Senate issues exhibiting the most party conflict were Public Debt & Public Works, Apportionment, and Legislative. The issues of Articles IV, XVIII, and V (Judicial, Municipal Corporations, and Elective Franchise), produced more party conflict in the Senate than the House. In general, constituency conflict was less than party conflict, yet a rural versus urban conflict was more evident than regional or occupational divisions.

When compared by sessions, the mean indices of likeness for each categoric group shows party conflict dominant (Table 24). Except for the 98th session of 1949–1950 with regional conflict the highest and the 100th session of 1953–1954 where occupational conflict is emphasized, the remaining seven consecutive sessions of the Ohio Senate feature high party conflict on constitutional issues.

Senate Participation and Contest

The constitutional issues in which senators showed high participation and contest were Municipal Corporations, Elective Fran-

TABLE 23
SENATE MEAN INDICES OF LIKENESS IN ASCENDING ORDER OF PARTY LIKENESS, BY CATEGORIC GROUP

Roll-Call Issue and Constitutional Article	*No. of Roll Calls*	*Party R vs. D*	*Const. U vs. R*	*Region N vs. S*	*Occup. L vs. NL*
Pub. Debt & Pub. Works VIII	14	18	61	68	86
Apportionment XI	15	35	69	75	83
Legislative II	20	35	67	74	83
Judicial IV	5	37	72	69	81
Municipal Corps. XVIII	1	45	59	64	98
Elective Franchise V	2	47	82	67	71
Executive III	6	56	70	86	81
Co. & Twp. Organ. X	9	60	75	76	70
Elections XVII	8	85	91	78	78

TABLE 24
MEAN INDICES OF LIKENESS ON ALL SENATE ROLL CALLS, BY CATEGORIC GROUP AND SESSION

Years	*Session*	*No. of Roll Calls*	*Party D vs. R*	*Constituency U vs. R*	*Occupation L vs. NL*	*Region N vs. S*
1949–50	98	1	87	99	93	77
1953–54	100	3	85	85	78	91
1955–56	101	6	22	58	83	72
1957–58	102	5	59	76	69	61
1959–60	103	6	38	55	85	78
1961–62	104	2	22	59	82	76
1963–64	105	2	16	44	88	54
1965–66	106	8	48	79	74	75
1967–68	107	22	22	65	85	71

chise, and Public Debt & Public Works (Articles XVIII, V, and VIII). The nine constitutional issues examined in the Senate are shown in rank order of descending mean coefficient of significance (Table 25).

The Municipal Corporations issue, which ranks first in the Senate list, is at the bottom of the similar House ranking (see Table 16). While Public Debt & Public Works issues commanded high coefficients of significance in both the House and Senate, senators

TABLE 25
RANK ORDER OF MEAN COEFFICIENTS OF SIGNIFICANCE ON SENATE ROLL CALLS, BY CONSTITUTIONAL ARTICLE

Rank	*Roll-Call Issue and Article*	*Mean Coefficient of Significance*	*No. of Roll Calls*
1)	Municipal Corporations XVIII	.9593	1
2)	Elective Franchise V	.7390	2
3)	Public Debt & Public Works VIII	.7351	14
4)	Legislative II	.6565	20
5)	Judicial IV	.6526	5
6)	Apportionment XI	.6457	15
7)	Executive III	.6315	6
8)	Elections XVII	.4546	3
9)	County and Township Organization X	.4493	9

exhibited noticeably less participation and contest over the Apportionment issue (Article XI), than did representatives in the House.

As noted earlier in Table 17, the significance values are generally higher in the Senate. However, the mean coefficient of significance varied from session to session in the Senate as in the House.

V. CONCLUSION

Party Cohesion and Conflict in Ohio Constitutional Amendment Legislative Voting

In summary, political parties emerge as the categoric groups usually in conflict and often the most cohesive in voting. This is not to say that personal, constituency, occupational, or regional forces do not influence Ohio legislators at some juncture in the consideration of constitutional amendments. Indeed, we have not considered other influences, such as the committee structure, lobbyists, or legislators' perception of the constitution.

TABLE 26
MOST COHESIVE CATEGORIC SUB-GROUPS, BY CONSTITUTIONAL ROLL-CALL ISSUE IN OHIO HOUSE AND SENATE

Roll-Call Issue & Constitutional Article	*House 1941–1970*	*Senate 1949–1968*
Bill of Rights I	Democrat	—
Legislative II	Republican	Rural
Executive III	Republican	Rural
Judicial IV	Lawyers	Democrat
Elective Franchise V	Democrat	Democrat
Education VI	Republican	—
Public Debt & Public Works VIII	Democrat	Rural
County & Township Organization X	Urban	Lawyers
Apportionment XI	Democrat	Rural
Finance & Taxation XII	Southern	—
Miscellaneous XV	Democrat	—
Elections XVII	Republican	Rural
Municipal Corporations XVIII	Southern	Democrat

The listing of the most cohesive sub-groups in Table 26 illustrates the dominance of the parties. Although the rural sub-group appears the most cohesive in the Senate, Republican cohesion was only slightly less. When the two chambers are compared, cohesion among partisans on constitutional issues is higher in the House than the Senate.

While party cohesion varies on issues and between the two legislative chambers, conflict between the parties on constitutional issues is the most common basis of inter-group conflict in both chambers (see Table 27). The patchwork process of amending the Ohio Constitution over the last thirty years is a highly partisan procedure on most issues. The increased volume of constitutional joint resolutions in recent years mobilizes unified parties as the most frequent voting coalitions.

Party Behavior on Other Legislative Issues

Is high party cohesion and conflict on constitutional issues typical for other legislative issues? After analyzing voting patterns in the Ohio Senate and House of Representatives for the years 1935,

TABLE 27
CATEGORIC GROUPS IN MOST CONFLICT ON CONSTITUTIONAL ROLL-CALL ISSUES IN OHIO HOUSE AND SENATE

Roll-Call Issue & Constitutional Article	*House 1941–1970*	*Senate 1949–1968*
Bill of Rights I	Party	—
Legislative II	Party	Party
Executive III	Party	Party
Judicial IV	Party-Occupation	Party
Elective Franchise V	Party	Party
Education VI	Party	—
Public Debt & Public Works VIII	Party	Party
County & Township Organization X	Constituency	Party
Apportionment XI	Party	Party
Finance & Taxation XII	Party	—
Miscellaneous XV	Party	—
Elections XVII	Party	Region-Occupation
Municipal Corporation XVIII	Region	Party

1949, 1955, and 1957, Thomas Flinn concluded that "the parties are reasonably cohesive, and come into conflict with each other fairly often."[8]

More recently a study of 228 roll-call votes on twenty-one issue areas of state policy was completed for the Ohio House of Representatives, 108th Ohio General Assembly.[9] The same categoric groups were compared through similar roll-call measurements. High party cohesion and conflict were reflected in voting behavior on nearly all issues.

Among the twenty-one issue areas, Appropriations, Highways, and Financial Institutions & Loans provided the most significant partisan conflict, while least associated with party conflict were issues concerning Higher Education, County Government, and Liquor Control (see Table 28).[10] Constituency differences were important in explaining only Liquor Control voting patterns. Occupational and regional groups were not important as voting blocs.

While party conflict thus would seem evident during most of the last three decades of Ohio legislative history, the legislators themselves do not share this view. The following question was asked of all Ohio legislators in 1957 and 1969: "There are always conflicting opinions in a legislature. How do you rank these particular conflicts of opinion in the order of their importance in Ohio?" When responses from a sample of Ohio legislators in 1957 were compared with samples of the California, New Jersey, and Tennessee legislatures, it was observed that:

> The surprising finding involves Ohio. Though Ohio has a reasonably competitive party system on the state legislative level, and though in fact party divisions are significant in legislative voting, there is a good deal of perceptual confusion in regard to the importance of party conflict. In the House, conflict crystallization is very poor—49 per

---

[8]Thomas A. Flinn, "The Outline of Ohio Politics," *Western Political Quarterly,* 13 (1960), 721.

[9]William A. Spratley, "Legislative Politics: Party and Constituency in the 108th Ohio General Assembly" (unpublished senior independent study, The College of Wooster Institute of Politics, 1970).

[10]The percentage of roll calls in each issue area for which a Chi Square test indicated party was a statistically significant variable is reported in Table 28.

TABLE 28
RANK ORDER OF PARTY ROLL CALLS, BY PERCENTAGE OF CHI-SQUARE SIGNIFICANCE LEVEL, 1969 OHIO HOUSE, 108TH GENERAL ASSEMBLY

Rank	*Issue*	*Roll Calls (N)*	*Percentages* X^2 *.01*	X^2 *.05*
1)	Appropriations	25	100%	100%
2)	Highways	6	83	83
3)	Financial Institutions & Loans	6	83	83
4)	Occupations & Professions	4	75	75
5)	Natural Resources & Parks	17	65	82
6)	Health & Safety	14	64	79
7)	Motor Vehicles	11	64	64
8)	Taxation	10	60	60
9)	Civil Rights	5	60	80
10)	Courts & Procedures	23	52	61
11)	Crimes & Law Enforcement	8	50	63
12)	Elections	4	50	75
13)	Schools & Libraries	19	47	58
14)	State Government	16	47	53
15)	Public Officials & Employees	13	46	46
16)	Industry, Commerce & Labor	11	40	80
17)	Agriculture	7	29	57
18)	Political Subdivisions	14	14	36
19)	Liquor Control	12	8	15
20)	County Government	7	0	0
21)	Higher Education	3	0	0

> cent considering party conflict important and, correspondingly, 51 per cent considering it not important. In the Senate, party conflict is deemed important by 59 per cent, indicative of little consensus. Evidently, the majority's grip on the legislative situation was so firm in 1957 that legislators could not see effective minority opposition.[11]

In 1969 a mail questionnaire replicating the same question about legislative conflict was answered by forty-two percent of the

[11] John C. Wahlke, William Buchanan, Heinz Eulau, and Leroy Ferguson, *The Legislative System: Explorations in Legislative Behavior* (New York: John Wiley & Sons, 1962).

members of the Ohio legislature.[12] The self-perception of party conflict remained at virtually the same level for both 1957 and 1969, perhaps because the majority party position was strong both times (see Table 29).

In summary, the evidence of party cohesion and conflict appears characteristic of voting on most issues, including the area of constitutional change in the legislature. The legislators, however, do not perceive of party as the most important basis of conflict.

Ohio Constitutional Convention: Alternative to a Party Constitution?

The substantial increase in the piecemeal amendment process in Ohio demonstrates the need for change of the state constitution. Noting a similar national increase in legislative referral of amendments, John E. Bebout declares the products of this process "clearly reflect the accelerating obsolescence of many parts of state constitutions."[13] Yet, important areas of constitutional reform have been neglected by the legislative referral of amendments process. A more comprehensive approach may be needed, such as a convention. In Ohio, as nationally:

> State constitutional revision should have highest priority in restructuring state governments to meet modern needs. Stress should be placed on repealing limitations that prevent constructive legislative and executive action, on clarifying the roles and relationships of the three branches of government, on permitting thorough modernization of local government in both rural and urban areas, and on eliminating matters more appropriate for legislative and executive action.[14]

Should a constitutional convention convene in Ohio, two important questions are raised by the present research. First, will a

[12]Spratley, *op. cit.*, p. 48.

[13]John E. Bebout, "State Constitutions and Constitutional Revision, 1965–67," *The Book of the States, 1968–1969,* The Council of State Governments (Chicago: 1968) p. 4.

[14]*Modernizing State Government*, Committee for Economic Development, A Statement by the Research and Policy Committee, July, 1967, pp. 19–20.

TABLE 29
LEGISLATORS' SELF PERCEPTION OF CONFLICT IN THE OHIO GENERAL ASSEMBLY, 1957 AND 1969

1957[a]			
House *N=121*		*Senate* *N=29*	
Type of Conflict	*% Important*	*Type of Conflict*	*% Important*
Urban-rural	79	Urban-rural	65
Labor	61	Liberal-conservative	59
Liberal-conservative	52	Party	59
Party	49	Labor	55
Governor	36	Governor	38
Regional	17	Regional	10

1969[b]			
House *N=37*		*Senate* *N=15*	
Type of Conflict	*% Important*	*Type of Conflict*	*% Important*
Liberal-conservative	73	Liberal-conservative	84
Urban-rural	67	Party	59
Party	47	Urban-rural	51
Governor	47	Regional	46
Labor	33	Governor	43
Regional	13	Labor	35

SOURCES: [a]Wahlke, Eulau, Buchanan, Ferguson, *The Legislative System,* p. 425.
[b]Spratley, *Legislative Politics,* p. 79, Questions Nos. 55 thru 60 on 1969 Institute of Politics Legislator Questionnaire.

convention be dominated by the same party conflicts found in the voting process of constitutional amendment in the Ohio General Assembly? If an Ohio Constitutional Convention provides an effective means of curtailing partisan considerations in molding needed constitutional reform, the second question then arises: Can there be a reasonable chance for passage of a new constitution or amendments offered by a convention which did not permit the overt participation of Ohio political parties?

Without political party support in 1952, the call for a convention was decisively defeated at the polls. Yet education of the public to the highly partisan nature of the piecemeal amendment process might achieve a widespread recognition of the need for a constitutional convention. An awareness of reform at the grass roots was successful in securing public approval of most of the constitutional amendments offered by the 1912 Ohio Constitutional Convention, a body of "distinctly liberal mood."[15] Whatever the approach to comprehensive reform, it would be appropriate to conclude that:

> while a constitution is a *political document* in the highest sense of the word, it should not be a party document or a document to serve the immediate interest of particular persons. It should, rather, provide a setting in which future party battles can be fought and future political issues faced under rules that are fair to all.[16]

[15]Eugene Roseboom and Francis P. Weisenburger, *A History of Ohio* (New York: Prentice-Hall, 1953), p. 454.

[16]John E. Bebout, *Contemporary Approaches To State Constitutional Revision*, Alan L. Clem, (ed.), Report No. 58, Governmental Research Bureau, The University of South Dakota (Sioux Falls, S. D.: Modern Press, 1970), p. 25.

Voting Patterns in Constitutional Referendums in Ohio

Carl Lieberman

ALTHOUGH MANY STUDIES HAVE BEEN MADE OF REFERENDUMS IN the United States, few have focused in recent years on proposed constitutional amendments. Fewer still have sought to examine intrastate differences in voting behavior on these referendums over a period of time.[1] Most research on referendums falls into one of three

---

This article is a revised version of a paper presented at the annual meeting of the Ohio Association of Economists and Political Scientists in Dayton, Ohio, on April 2, 1971. The author wishes to express his gratitude to the Research (Faculty Projects) Committee of The University of Akron for its financial support of this study during the academic year 1969–1970. He would also like to thank the following persons for their assistance and useful suggestions: Priscilla Van Doros; John K. Henderson; Dr. Yong H. Cho, Associate Professor of Urban Studies and Political Science at The University of Akron; Dr. Paul A. Weidner, Professor of Political Science at The University of Akron; Mrs. Judy Hanson; and Robert Seeman and the staff of The University of Akron Computer Center.

[1]See Hugh A. Bone, "State Constitutional Revision: A Review and New Strategy," *State Government*, 42 (Winter, 1969), 49. Among the recent studies of referendums on statewide constitutional questions are Allan H. Lammers and David Kenney, "Correlates of Constitutional Change in Illinois," *Public Affairs Bulletin* (Southern Illinois University), 3 (September–October, 1970), pages unnumbered; John E. Mueller, "Voting on the Propositions: Ballot Patterns and Historical Trends in California," *American Political Science Review*, 63 (December, 1969), 1197–1212; Joseph P. Pisciotte, "How Illinois Did It," *National Civic Review*, 58 (July, 1969), 291–296; Raymond E. Wolfinger and Fred I. Greenstein, "The Repeal of Fair Housing in California: An Analysis of Referendum Voting," *American Political Science Review*, 62 (September, 1968), 753–769; Norman C. Thomas, "The Electorate and State Constitutional Revision: An Analysis of Four Michigan Referenda," *Midwest Journal of Political Science*, 12 (February, 1968), 115–129; and I. Ridgeway Davis, "Connecticut Con-Con," *National Civic Review*, 56(April, 1967), 194–201.

categories: (1) works dealing with the introduction of the referendum and its early use within the United States;[2] (2) longitudinal studies of statewide referendums, which often do not distinguish clearly between statutory and constitutional referenda nor always provide extensive information about electoral differences among counties in the same state;[3] and (3) examinations of local referendums.[4]

---

[2]See Ellis Paxson Oberholtzer, *The Referendum in America: A Discussion of Law-Making by Popular Vote* (Reprint; Freeport, N. J.: Books for Libraries Press, 1970); and James D. Barnett, *The Operations of the Initiative and Referendum in Oregon* (New York: Macmillan Company, 1915); and William B. Munro (ed.), *The Initiative, Referendum and Recall* (New York: Macmillan Company, 1913).

[3]See James K. Pollock, *The Initiative and Referendum in Michigan* (University of Michigan, Michigan Governmental Studies, No. 6; Ann Arbor: University of Michigan Press, 1940); V. O. Key, Jr. and Winston W. Crouch, *The Initiative and Referendum in California* (Berkeley: University of California Press, 1939); Winston W. Crouch, *The Initiative and Referendum in California* (Los Angeles: The Haynes Foundation, 1950); Lawrence Lee Pelletier, *The Initiative and Referendum in Maine* (Brunswick, Maine: Bureau for Research in Municipal Government, Bowdoin College, 1951); Joseph G. LaPalombara, *The Initiative and Referendum in Oregon: 1938–1948* (Corvallis, Oregon: Oregon State College, 1950), and Raymond V. Anderson, *Adoption and Operation of Initiative and Referendum in North Dakota* (unpublished doctoral thesis, Faculty of the Graduate School, University of Minnesota, 1962).

[4]See, for example, Alvin Boskoff and Harmon Zeigler, *Voting Patterns in a Local Election* (Philadelphia and New York: J. B. Lippincott Company, 1964); Richard W. Brandsma, *Direct Democracy and Water Policy: A Preliminary Examination of a Special District Election* (California Government Series No. 10; University of California, 1966); James S. Gionocchio, *Fiscal Policy-Making by Plebiscite: Local Tax and Bond Referenda in Ohio* (M.A. thesis, Department of Political Science, Bowling Green State University, 1970); Gilbert Y. Steiner, "Municipal Tax Referenda and the Political Process," *Current Economic Comment,* 15 (February, 1953), 3–16; Thomas F. A. Plaut, "Analysis of Voting Behavior on a Fluoridation Referendum," *Public Opinion Quarterly,* 23 (Summer, 1959), 213–222; Walter C. Kaufman and Scott Greer, "Voting in a Metropolitan Area: An Application of Social Area Analysis," *Social Forces,* 38 (March, 1960), 196–204; John E. Horton and Wayne E. Thompson, "Powerlessness and Political Negativism: A Study of Defeated Local Referendums," *American Journal of Sociology,* 67 (March, 1962), 485–493; Edward L. McDill and Jeane Clare Ridley, "Status, Anomia, Political Alienation and Political Participation," *American Journal of Sociology,* 68 (September, 1962), 205–213; James A. Norton, "Referenda Voting in a Metropolitan Area," *Western Political Quarterly,* 16 (March, 1963), 195–212; James Q. Wilson and Edward C. Banfield, "Public Regardingness as a Value Premise in Voting Behavior," *American Political*

This study seeks to provide information about electoral behavior in recent constitutional referendums in Ohio in order to determine statewide and county patterns of voting. Dealing with constitutional referendums submitted to the voters of Ohio between 1951 and 1969, it examines forty-five proposed constitutional amendments referred to the voters by the General Assembly. There were no referendums on constitutional questions in Ohio in 1950. Thus, all referendums during a twenty-year period have been examined. Though the time period selected was somewhat arbitrary, it did have two advantages. It was long enough to permit the formulation of some generalizations and recent enough to demonstrate contemporary patterns of electoral behavior.

The two proposed amendments submitted to the people by initiative petition during this period, as well as the question of calling a convention to revise the state constitution,[5] have been omitted from this analysis. Voting patterns in the state as a whole and in each of the eighty-eight counties have been analyzed with reference to six questions: (1) What effect does the timing of a referendum have upon its likelihood of passage? (2) How does the extent of voter participation influence approval levels for constitutional referendums? (3) Do referendums which call for floating bonds or spending state moneys have a better or worse chance of passage than other constitutional questions? (4) Do levels of approval for constitutional referendums vary very much from one part of the state to another? (5) Are levels of approval for constitutional referendums positively or negatively related to levels of support for Republican

---

Science Review, 58 (December, 1964), 876–887; Clarence N. Stone, "Local Referendums: An Alternative to the Alienated Voter Model," *Public Opinion Quarterly*, 29 (Summer, 1965), 213–222; Harlan Hahn, "Northern Referenda on Fair Housing: The Response of White Voters," *Western Political Quarterly*, 21 (September, 1968), 483–495; Howard D. Hamilton, "Direct Legislation: Some Implications of Open Housing Referenda," *American Political Science Review*, 64 (March, 1970), 124–137; and Harlan Hahn, "Correlates of Public Sentiments About War," *American Political Science Review*, 64 (December, 1970), 1186–1198.

[5]Article XVI, Section 3, of the Constitution of Ohio provides that in 1932 "and in each twentieth year thereafter, the question: 'Shall there be a convention to revise, alter, or amend the constitution,' shall be submitted to the electors of the state."

candidates? (6) How do patterns of approval for constitutional referendums within each county correlate with such socio economic characteristics as urbanization, education, income, percentage of foreign-born residents, and percentage of owner-occupied housing units?

I. CONSTITUTIONAL REFERENDUMS IN OHIO: AN OVERVIEW

If one examines the questions submitted to the people of Ohio after they had approved the bulk of the amendments proposed by the Constitutional Convention of 1912, he will find that constitutional propositions in this state are usually accepted by the voters. Indeed, since 1940, more than three-fourths of these referendums have been acted upon favorably by the electors (see Table 1). Between 1951 and 1969, thirty-four of the forty-five constitutional questions (75.5%) were passed by the people.

Two important qualifications, however, must be made to the

TABLE 1
CONSTITUTIONAL REFERENDUMS IN OHIO, 1913–1970*

Time Period	*No. of Referendums*	*Referendums Approved by Voters*	*Percentage of Referendums Approved by Voters*
1913–1919	7	2	28.6
1920–1929	11	4	36.4
1930–1939	5	3	60.0
1940–1949	7	6	85.7
1950–1959	23	18	78.3
1960–1969	22	16	72.7
1970	3	3	100.0
TOTALS	78	52	66.7

*Does not include thirty-one amendments proposed through the initiative process or the mandatory question for calling a constitutional convention, which was submitted to the voters in 1932 and 1952.

SOURCE: Arthur A. Schwartz and Ted W. Brown, "Voter Participation in Constitutional Amendment and Legislation: Proposed Constitutional Amendments, Initiated Legislation, and Elections 1912 Through 1968," mimeo. (Columbus: Secretary of State, n.d.); Secretary of State, "Number of Precincts, County Vote for Constitutional Amendments, and Number of Electors Voting—General Election, November 4, 1969," mimeo., and *Ohio Almanac 1971* (Lorain, Ohio: The Lorain Journal Company, 1970), p. 14.

general statement that voters in Ohio have been favorably disposed to constitutional propositions. Those amendments which were submitted through the use of initiative petition[6] have generally failed of passage. Between 1913 and 1970, only nine of thirty-one initiated amendments (29%) were approved. During the period 1951–1969, there were two amendments submitted to the people by means of the initiative process; both were defeated.[7]

The mandatory referenda calling for a convention to revise the state constitution have also failed by substantial margins. In 1932, 44.7% of the voters approved the calling of a state constitutional convention. The 1952 referendum was defeated by an even greater majority. Sixty-six percent of the electors who voted on this question rejected it, and it failed to pass in any county in the state.

II. TIMING AND VOTER PARTICIPATION

An analysis of the approval of constitutional questions during the period 1951–1969 suggests that the timing of the referendums has only a limited effect on their chance of passage. Of the thirty-five questions submitted to the voters in November elections, twenty-seven (77.1%) were approved, while seven of the ten amendments (70.0%) submitted in the May elections were also adopted. Furthermore, dividing the referendums into two additional categories—those submitted in gubernatorial or presidential election years and those voted upon in off-year elections—shows

[6]Article II (Sections la, lb, le, lf, and lg) of the Constitution of Ohio provides for the use of the initiative at the state and municipal level. A petition signed by three percent of the electors is needed for submitting proposed legislation to the General Assembly for prompt action. If the legislature does not pass the proposed bill or approves it in amended form, the legislation may be submitted to the voters by the filing of a supplementary petition signed by at least three percent of the electors in addition to those signing the original petition.

[7]The first proposed constitutional amendment, which was submitted to the people by the initiative process in 1958, would have forbidden labor contracts which establish union membership as a condition for continuing employment. The second, which was submitted to the people in 1962, would have limited the power of the state to forbid the sale of certain goods and services on Sunday.

that there is little difference in approval levels. Of the eleven questions proposed in gubernatorial and presidential election years, eight (72.7%) were approved, while twenty-six (76.5%) of the thirty-four amendments submitted in odd-numbered years were acted upon favorably by the voters. It is only when referendums in presidential and gubernatorial election years are divided between those held in May and those conducted in November that one discovers a noticeable difference in the rate of approval. All four of the amendments submitted in the May primaries were adopted, but only four of the seven amendments (57.1%) proposed in the general elections of even-numbered years were approved.

It is a well-known fact that the number of people voting on issues is generally smaller than the number voting for candidates for public office.[8] An examination of the forty-five constitutional questions under consideration also indicates that the success of referendums is inversely related to the level of voter participation. The average number of electors participating in each of the thirty-four referendums which were approved was 1,822,056, while the mean number voting in the eleven referendums where issues were defeated was 2,043,640. It is possible that the difference in the number of voters participating in successful and unsuccessful referendums is merely a reflection of the more controversial nature of those issues that fail. It is also possible that the heightened passions and increased turnout which characterize a major partisan race lead to a larger negative vote. Certainly, it is true that turnout is generally greatest in the November elections of the even numbered years, when we elect a governor or a president. The mean number of participants in the constitutional referendums that failed in the November elections of the even numbered years under con-

---

[8]Sturm and Key both point out the relatively small number of electors who generally vote on constitutional questions. Albert Sturm, *Methods of State Constitutional Reform* (Michigan Governmental Studies No. 28; Ann Arbor: University of Michigan Press, 1954), p. 48; and V. O. Key, Jr., *Politics, Parties and Pressure Groups* (5th ed.; New York: Thomas Y. Crowell Company, 1964), pp. 582–583. Although occasionally, 90% or more of those electors voting in Ohio's general elections in even numbered years have voted on constitutional questions, more often about four-fifths of the total number of voters have participated in this manner.

sideration was 2,584,254; the average number of voters in those referendums that passed was 2,831,421. A third explanation—one advanced by some scholars—is that an increase in voter participation usually leads to an increase in the number of electors who are alienated from the political process and who express their feelings of powerlessness by voting against issues.[9]

III. FINANCIAL REFERENDUMS

In light of the recent defeats of new tax levies and bond issues throughout Ohio,[10] it is interesting to note that the voters have been prepared to increase the public debt of the state and to extend its financial obligations. During the period under examination, seven constitutional amendments providing for an increase in the public debt or for the floating of bonds were submitted to the people by the legislature; all were passed.[11] In 1965, two amendments were referred to the people by the legislature and were approved. One amendment authorized the state to guarantee loans to residents attending institutions of higher education and the other permitted the state to guarantee loans for industrial development.[12] Four of the seven amendments specifically authorizing increased expenditures by the state or granting the state the power to incur additional debt were approved by more than 60% of the voters; more than three-fifths of the electors also approved the amendment guaranteeing loans to residents attending institutions of higher learning. Indeed, twenty-two counties approved all of the "financial" referendums to which reference has been made. Only

---

[9]See, for example, Horton and Thompson, *op. cit.*, pp. 487–488.

[10]In 1969, only 44% of new school levies and 33% of the school bond issues were approved by voters in Ohio. Gionocchio, *op. cit.*, pp. 94–95.

[11]One amendment provided a bonus for Korean War veterans, while the other six dealt with increasing the public debt for highways and other public works, and for economic development.

[12]In 1955 and 1965, two proposed laws were submitted to the voters by initiative petition which would have increased state expenditures; both were defeated. The first would have increased unemployment compensation, and the second would have amended the school foundation program and raised taxes to support it.

rural Holmes and Putnam counties rejected as many as five of the nine questions.

Why have financial referendums, which have increased state expenditures, led to the floating of bonds, and caused the state to extend its financial obligations, been so favorably received by the voters? One can only make some educated guesses as to the reasons for electoral acceptance. Perhaps the uses for which authorization of moneys have been requested are popular. The bonus for Korean War veterans, for example, won overwhelming approval in 1956 and received a majority in every county in the state. Moreover, the referendums generally have not been directly tied to increasing unpopular taxes.[13]

IV. GEOGRAPHICAL DISTRIBUTION OF REFERENDUMS APPROVALS

While there is generally a high level of acceptance for financial referendums, there is great variance in the level of support for constitutional change among Ohio's eighty-eight counties. Between 1951 and 1969, the mean number of questions approved was 27.3 (60.7%). However, the range was great, varying from a low of fourteen approvals (31.1%) in Noble County to a high of thirty-nine approvals (86.7%) in Geauga County. It is also true that the range of votes in favor of referendums during this period was substantial. Only 45.0% of all the votes cast in Putnam County were in favor of the forty-five constitutional questions which were submitted, while 60.0% of the votes in Erie County approved these referendums.[14]

---

[13]The bonds for highways have been secured by a pledge of moneys received from fees, licenses, and taxes relating to motor vehicles and the fuel for such vehicles. Two bond issues were secured by a tax on cigarettes. No bond issue or loan guarantee was directly backed by an income tax or an increase in the general sales tax. Only the Korean War veteran's bonus provided that "The Commissioners of the Sinking Fund shall, on or before the first day of July in each calendar year, levy and certify to the auditor of the state of Ohio a state tax on all taxable property subject to taxation on the general tax lists of all counties in the state of Ohio for such year at such rate as it shall determine to be necessary . . ." to meet the cost of the debt. (Article VIII, Section 2d of the Constitution of Ohio).

[14]A summary of voting patterns and a complete list of the number of referendums approved in each county are found in the Appendix.

Although a completely clear geographical pattern does not emerge, a disproportionate number of high-approval counties seem to be found in the northeastern part of the state. While thirty-four constitutional referendums were approved in the state as a whole during the period under consideration, only ten counties approved thirty-four or more of these questions. Six of those counties—Ashtabula, Cuyahoga, Geauga, Lake, Medina, and Wayne—are in northeastern Ohio. Five of the ten counties with the highest percentage of favorable votes—Ashtabula, Cuyahoga, Geauga, Summit, and Wayne—are also found in the northeastern region.

V. REFERENDUMS AND REPUBLICAN VOTING

In addition to the factors of timing, rates of voter participation, subject matter, and geographical bases, the relationships between partisan voting patterns and levels of approval for constitutional referendums have been examined. It was hypothesized that there would be an inverse relationship between level of support for Republican candidates and level of approval for constitutional questions. This was based upon the assumption that the Republican Party gains its highest level of support from conservative rural voters. To test this hypothesis, an Index of Republican Support was calculated for each county. The index is based upon the average percentages of voter support from 1950 to 1968 for three key offices—president, governor, and county commissioner. It was computed by adding the Republican percentages of the total two-party vote for each office between 1950 and 1968 and dividing the sum by three.[15]

---

[15]In Adams County, for example, 56.2% of the two-party vote for president was Republican. During the time period under examination, 55.4% of the two-party vote for governor was Republican, as was 52.6% of the vote for county commissioner. Thus, the Index of Republican Support for Adams County was 54.7 ($\frac{56.2 + 55.4 + 52.6}{3} = \frac{164.2}{3} = 54.7$). In all cases the percentages used to calculate the Index of Republican Support were derived from data published in *Ohio Election Statistics,* the biannual publication of Ohio's Secretary of State.

The seventeen Democratic counties (those with an Index of Republican Support of under 50) approved an average of 26.3 referendums as compared to an average of 27.6 referendums approved in Republican counties. The mean approval rate for Republican counties was slightly higher than that for Democratic counties, but as Table 2 shows, the level of Republican support explains very little of the variance in their willingness to ratify constitutional propositions.

The relationship between the Index of Republican Support and the approval of constitutional questions appears to be negligible. Is there, however, a strong relationship between partisan voting patterns and "close" or "safe" voting within each county? To provide a partial answer to the question, a measure of the closeness of votes was devised. Referendum votes were classified as "safe" if at least 60% of the electors voted either for or against. All other votes were categorized as "competitive." Affirmative safe votes are those in which 60% or more of the voters approved a referendum; negative safe votes are those in which 60% or more of the electors rejected a proposition.[16]

As Table 3 indicates, Republican counties have more safe affirmative votes than Democratic counties. Analysis also shows that the most competitive counties—those with an index of Republican support between 45.0 and 55.0—have the largest total number of competitive votes. The most Republican counties, on the other

TABLE 2
CORRELATIONS BETWEEN LEVELS OF APPROVAL FOR CONSTITUTIONAL REFERENDUMS IN OHIO, 1951–1969, AND THE INDEX OF REPUBLICAN SUPPORT

Variable	*Simple Coefficients of Correlation with Index of Republican Support*
Percent of refs. approved	.0447
Percent of all votes approving refs.	.0885
Percent of votes approving financial refs.	.1191
Percent of votes approving nonfinancial refs.	.1501

[16]See the Appendix for a complete tally of safe votes in each county.

TABLE 3
VOTING PATTERNS ON CONSTITUTIONAL QUESTIONS IN OHIO, 1951–1969, IN DEMOCRATIC AND REPUBLICAN COUNTIES

Type of County	*No. of Counties*	*Type of Vote*			
		Competitive		*Safe*	
		Approve	*Disapprove*	*Affirm*	*Neg*
Democratic	17	14.8	12.4	11.5	6.4
Republican	71	14.0	10.6	13.6	6.8

hand, have the largest average number of safe votes (Table 4). Clearly, the evidence fails to support the initial hypothesis concerning the relationship between the level of support for the Republican Party and the degree of support for constitutional questions. Indeed, it suggests, instead, that Republican counties are somewhat more likely to support constitutional change than their Democratic counterparts. Only the most Democratic counties (those with an index of Republican support below 45.0) have a higher overall rate of approval than do the Republican counties.

VI. CONSTITUTIONAL REFERENDUMS AND SOCIO-ECONOMIC CHARACTERISTICS

Voting behavior in partisan races and in referendums has been shown to be related to certain socio-economic characteristics. Among the more important are the level of urbanization within a political unit, the average income of its people, the educational level of its inhabitants, the percentage of dwelling units that are owner-occupied, and the proportion of foreign-born residents.

TABLE 4
INDEX OF REPUBLICAN SUPPORT AND VOTING PATTERNS ON CONSTITUTIONAL QUESTIONS IN OHIO, 1951–1969

Index of Rep. Support	*No. of Counties*	*Type of Vote*			
		Competitive		*Safe*	
		Approve	*Disapprove*	*Affirm*	*Neg*
Below 45.0	7	13.4	11.6	14.9	5.1
45.0–55.0	35	14.9	11.2	12.3	6.5
Over 55.0	46	13.6	10.7	13.6	7.1

The influence of urbanization upon voting behavior in constitutional referendums has been discussed by several scholars. On the one hand, Froman and Garcia have found that constitutional change occurs most frequently in states with stronger interest groups and in those which are dominated by one party; these states tend to be less urban.[17] However, studies in several states indicate that support for constitutional change is greatest among urban voters.[18]

Lammers and Kenney report a high correlation between income, education, and affirmative voting in the 1968 referendum to call a constitutional convention in Illinois.[19] In his study of referenda voting in Cuyahoga County, Norton has shown that there is a positive relationship between pro-metropolitan voting and education and wealth.[20]

Owner-occupancy rates are often good indicators of wealth and social status. Banfield and Wilson have considered the proportion of owner-occupied housing units and the percentage of persons of foreign stock in their study of local bond referenda.[21]

---

[17]Lewis A. Froman, Jr., "Some Effects of Interest Group Strength in State Politics," *American Political Science Review,* 60 (December, 1966), 954–955, 957–958; and Thomas V. Garcia, *Inter-Party Competition, Direct Legislation and Electoral Participation in the American States, 1950–1960* (unpublished Ph. D. dissertation, University of Massachusetts, 1967), p. 35.

[18]George P. Mather, *Effects of the Use of Voting Machines on Total Votes Cast: Iowa — 1920–1960* (Iowa City: University of Iowa, Institute of Public Affairs, 1964), pp. 48, 53–54; G. Theodore Mitau, *State and Local Government: Politics and Processes* (New York: Charles Scribner's Sons, 1966), p. 41.

[19]Lammers and Kenney, *loc. cit.*

[20]Norton, *op. cit.,* p. 211.

[21]Wilson and Banfield, *loc. cit.* In their study of thirty-five expenditure proposals in seven cities, Professors Wilson and Banfield examined the relationship between affirmative voting and a variety of factors, including the proportion of dwelling units which are owner-occupied and the percentage of persons of foreign stock (i.e., those persons born abroad or who have at least one parent who was born in a foreign country). In fact they even considered the national origin of persons in selected wards and precincts. Unfortunately, information concerning national origin and the total number of persons of foreign stock within all of Ohio's counties is not available from Census Bureau reports. Hence, I have considered instead the percentage of persons of foreign birth within each county. Statistics have been computed from data found in U.S. Bureau of the Census, *U. S. Census of Population: 1960.* Vol. I, *Characteristics of the Population,* Part 37, Ohio (Washington, D. C.: U. S. Government Printing Office, 1963), pp. 37-363–37-371.

To examine the impact of socio-economic characteristics on constitutional voting in Ohio's counties, simple and multiple coefficients of correlation have been computed between four dependent variables—the percentage of referendums approved, the percentage of all votes approving constitutional referendums, the percentage of votes approving financial referendums, and the percentage of votes approving nonfinancial referendums—and five independent variables: the percentage of persons living in urban areas, household income,[22] the median years of education for residents twenty-five years of age and over, the percentage of housing units which are owner-occupied,[23] and the percentage of residents who are foreign born. Multiple correlations have also been computed between the dependent variables and the five socio-economic variables,[24] together with a political factor, the Index of Republican Support.

Certain conclusions can be drawn from Table 5 concerning electoral support for constitutional amendments. All socio-economic characteristics, except percentage of owner-occupied housing units, are significantly related to the following dependent variables: percentage of referendums approved, percentage of all votes approving referendums, and percentage of votes approving nonfinancial referendums. The strongest simple correlations are between household income and each dependent variable. The socio-economic char-

[22]Household income refers to per household effective buying income in 1960. See *Statistical Abstract of Ohio 1969* (Columbus: Economic Research Division, Development Department, 1969), pp. 260–261.

[23]The percentage of housing units which are owner-occupied is based on the percentage of all occupied housing units which fall into the category. Vacant housing units have been omitted from consideration. See *Statistical Abstract of Ohio, 1969,* p. 121.

[24]To insure uniformity, the socio-economic characteristics are based on 1960 data. Because levels of urbanization, income, and education are constantly changing, data gathered in any year are subject to criticism when related to behavior occurring in preceding or subsequent years. Nevertheless, because accurate data are not always available on an annual basis and averaging information gathered from several statistical periods is cumbersome and of questionable value, a year often must be selected. Nineteen hundred and sixty was used because it was a census year and the midpoint of the period under examination. Twenty-three of the forty-five referendums fell within the period 1955–1965, five years preceding and five years following the collection of this information.

TABLE 5

CORRELATIONS BETWEEN SUPPORT FOR CONSTITUTIONAL REFERENDUMS IN OHIO COUNTIES AND CERTAIN SOCIO-ECONOMIC AND POLITICAL INDICATORS

	Urbanization Simple r	*Household Income Simple r*	*Median Years Education Simple r*	*Percent Owner-Occupied Housing Units Simple r*	*Percent Foreign-Born Simple r*	*Multiple Correlation (All Socio-Economic Indicators)* R	R^2	*Multiple Correlation (All Socio-Economic Indicators, Together with the Index of Republican Support)* R	R^2
Percentage of referendums approved	.61*	.71*	.59*	−.11	.48*	.75	.56	.78	.61
Percentage of all votes approving referendums	.48*	.58*	.50*	−.14	.41*	.63	.40	.67	.45
Percentage of votes approving financial referendums	.10	.07	.01	.02	.12	.14	.02	.34	.12
Percentage of votes approving nonfinancial referendums	.53*	.68*	.63*	−.15	.44*	.75	.56	.79	.62

*Significance Level: .001

acteristics in combination explain between 39% and 56% of the variance for each of the three indicators of support for constitutional change.

It is possible that the percentage of owner-occupied housing units explains so little of the variance because at the county level it is an inadequate indicator of wealth or social status. However, urbanization, income, and education, which are usually related to social status, all correlate strongly and positively with the dependent variables under consideration.

Though urbanization is related to each of the dependent variables, important exceptions to this pattern can be found. For example, Geauga County, with its high level of approval, has a proportionately small urban population. Such exceptions might be explained by their proximity to heavily urbanized areas. Geauga County adjoins Cuyahoga County and, since 1963, has been part of the Cleveland Standard Metropolitan Statistical Area. Counties that are part of metropolitan areas have a higher average approval rate than nonmetropolitan counties. The seventeen counties that were part of an SMSA in 1960 approved an average of 31.9 constitutional propositions, while the nonmetropolitan counties had a mean approval rate of 26.2.

None of the socio-economic variables shows a strong positive relationship to the percentage of favorable votes cast in financial referendum elections. This suggests that socio-economic factors may be less important than political or "psychological" factors, such as popular perceptions of the questions on the ballot. Such perceptions might be the product in large measure of the support or opposition of news media and interest groups. Under any circumstance, it is interesting that the socio-economic factors together explain only 2% of the variance, while these same factors in combination with the Index of Republican Support can explain almost 12%.

VII. SUMMARY OF FINDINGS AND SUGGESTIONS FOR FURTHER RESEARCH

This study has examined county and statewide voting patterns on forty-five constitutional questions submitted to the voters of

Ohio between 1951 and 1969. The major findings are summarized below:

1. The voters generally approve constitutional referendums.
2. Voters show about the same willingness to support questions submitted in even numbered and odd numbered election years. Aside from even numbered years, when constitutional referendums are more likely to be approved in May than in November, electors are as likely to support questions in the primaries as in the general elections.
3. The average number of participants in elections in which questions were defeated was greater than for successful referendums.
4. Financial referendums increasing the public debt or extending the financial obligations of the state have been overwhelmingly supported by the electorate. All proposed constitutional amendments dealing with financial matters have passed during the last twenty years.
5. A disproportionately large number of high-approval counties are found in the northeastern region of the state.
6. Although the mean number of constitutional questions approved by Republican counties is somewhat higher, the relationship between the level of support for major Republican candidates and the level of approval for constitutional referendums is statistically weak. However, Republican counties have more "safe" votes than do Democratic counties. They are somewhat more likely to give overwhelming support to those questions which they approve.
7. The more politically competitive counties have a higher average number of competitive referendum votes than do strong Democratic or Republican counties.
8. Four socio-economic characteristics—urbanization, household income, education, and the percent of foreign-born residents—are positively related to the following dependent variables: the percentage of referendums approved, the percentage of all votes approving referendums, and the percentage of votes approving nonfinancial referendums. The

percent of owner-occupied housing units is only weakly related to levels of support for constitutional change.

9. Socio-economic characteristics are weakly related to the percentage of affirmative voting on financial referendums.

A study of voting patterns at the statewide or county level may be useful in alerting scholars to the trends within large political units. It may also identify counties where the most sympathy for constitutional change is likely to be found, thus helping advocates of change to focus their efforts most effectively. Nevertheless, such a study tells us little or nothing about individual electoral behavior. Future longitudinal studies of constitutional referendums might well include interviews with a carefully selected sample of voters prior to, or immediately following, each election. Such interviews should focus upon knowledge of the questions, sources of voter information about issues on the ballot, and the factors motivating individuals to vote for or against propositions. Specifically, we should try to determine if newspapers or political parties exert a powerful influence upon voters, as some scholars have suggested.[25]

Additional longitudinal studies are also needed on campaign techniques in constitutional referendum elections. These studies might include interviews with political leaders, as well as an examination of journalistic reports within counties and an analysis of political propaganda supporting or opposing constitutional questions. Scholars might well examine patterns of expenditures, trends in advertising techniques, and the impact of campaigning as reflected in turnout rates and affirmative or negative voting.

Both intrastate and interstate comparative studies are needed if we are to better understand the factors influencing individual and group behavior. Although time-consuming and potentially expensive, an examination of these topics may well expand our knowledge of political behavior and state politics.

---

[25] In his study of referendums in California, Mueller found little evidence to support the proposition that newspaper recommendations substantially influenced individual electoral choice. Mueller, *op. cit.*, pp. 1204–1206. Professors Mueller and Thomas both suggest that parties can affect the voting preferences of electors when they choose to take a position on specific referendums. See Mueller, *op. cit.*, pp. 1206–1207; and Thomas, *op. cit.*, pp. 126, 129.

APPENDIX

Table A1 classifies the votes on constitutional referendums for each of the eighty-eight counties in Ohio. Safe votes are those in which 60% or more of the electors voted either for or against a question. Safe affirmative votes are those in which at least 60% of the voters have approved a question; safe negative votes are those in which a like percentage of the electors opposed a question on the ballot. Competitive votes are those in which less than 60% of the electors have voted in favor of, or in opposition to, a proposition.

TABLE A1
PATTERNS OF VOTING IN CONSTITUTIONAL REFERENDUMS IN OHIO, 1951–1969, CLASSIFIED BY TYPE OF VOTE AND COUNTY

Counties	*Referendums Approved*	*Referendums Percent of All Approved*	*Competitive Votes Approve*	*Competitive Votes Disapprove*	*Safe Votes Affirmative*	*Safe Votes Negative*
Adams	16	35.6	12	15	4	14
Allen	31	68.9	18	11	13	3
Ashland	31	68.9	15	10	16	4
Ashtabula	34	75.6	9	9	25	2
Athens	24	53.3	13	15	11	6
Auglaize	28	62.2	17	9	11	8
Belmont	29	64.4	18	10	11	6
Brown	24	53.3	17	11	7	10
Butler	29	64.4	15	9	14	7
Carroll	25	55.6	16	13	9	7
Champaign	27	60.0	15	9	12	9
Clark	27	60.0	17	10	10	8
Clermont	31	68.9	16	7	15	7
Clinton	25	55.6	10	15	15	5
Columbiana	29	64.4	17	11	12	5
Coshocton	21	46.7	10	15	11	9
Crawford	27	60.0	15	12	12	6
Cuyahoga	38	84.4	12	6	26	1
Darke	18	40.0	12	14	6	13
Defiance	28	62.2	12	10	16	7
Delaware	31	68.9	13	9	18	5
Erie	37	82.2	7	6	30	2
Fairfield	25	55.6	15	11	10	9

TABLE A1 Continued

Counties	Referendums Approved	Percent of All Referendums Approved	Competitive Votes Approve	Competitive Votes Disapprove	Safe Votes Affirmative	Safe Votes Negative
Fayette	28	62.2	19	8	9	9
Franklin	36	80.0	13	8	23	1
Fulton	29	64.4	10	11	19	5
Gallia	25	55.6	13	12	12	8
Geauga	39	86.7	12	6	27	0
Greene	34	75.6	12	9	22	2
Guernsey	21	46.7	15	11	6	13
Hamilton	34	75.6	12	8	22	3
Hancock	35	77.8	11	7	24	3
Hardin	20	44.4	15	14	5	11
Harrison	26	57.8	18	13	8	6
Henry	28	62.2	12	12	16	5
Highland	20	44.4	9	16	11	9
Hocking	25	55.6	21	10	4	10
Holmes	15	33.3	12	20	3	10
Huron	32	71.1	13	7	19	6
Jackson	26	57.8	13	11	13	8
Jefferson	30	66.7	14	12	16	3
Knox	24	53.3	11	13	13	8
Lake	35	77.8	12	5	23	5
Lawrence	25	55.6	19	10	6	10
Licking	28	62.2	19	10	9	7
Logan	27	60.0	13	12	14	6
Lorain	29	64.4	21	8	8	8
Lucas	33	73.3	11	10	22	2
Madison	29	64.4	12	12	17	4
Mahoning	29	64.4	14	9	15	7
Marion	26	57.8	16	14	10	5
Medina	34	75.6	13	10	21	1
Meigs	22	48.9	12	6	10	17
Mercer	19	42.2	15	14	4	12
Miami	36	80.0	11	7	25	2
Monroe	19	42.2	10	15	9	11
Montgomery	32	71.1	18	9	14	4
Morgan	20	44.4	9	12	11	13
Morrow	22	48.9	16	11	6	12
Muskingum	31	68.9	17	8	14	6
Noble	14	31.1	8	16	6	15
Ottawa	33	73.3	8	9	25	3

TABLE A1 Continued

Counties	Referendums Approved	Percent of All Referendums Approved	Competitive Votes Approve/Disapprove		Safe Votes Affirmative/Negative	
Paulding	17	37.8	12	13	5	15
Perry	26	57.8	19	8	7	11
Pickaway	25	55.6	16	14	9	6
Pike	20	44.4	14	20	6	5
Portage	32	71.1	17	11	15	2
Preble	28	62.2	13	10	15	7
Putnam	15	33.3	12	18	3	12
Richland	32	71.1	17	8	15	5
Ross	33	73.3	20	8	13	4
Sandusky	32	71.1	16	9	16	4
Scioto	30	66.7	20	11	10	4
Seneca	32	71.1	16	9	16	4
Shelby	22	48.9	14	15	8	8
Stark	29	64.4	17	10	12	6
Summit	33	73.3	12	9	21	3
Trumbull	27	60.0	22	12	5	6
Tuscarawas	23	51.1	7	18	16	4
Union	25	55.6	13	11	12	9
Van Wert	24	53.3	13	11	11	10
Vinton	17	37.8	9	17	8	11
Warren	33	73.3	15	9	18	3
Washington	29	64.4	17	10	12	6
Wayne	34	75.6	13	8	21	3
Williams	31	68.9	15	7	16	7
Wood	33	73.3	13	10	20	2
Wyandot	24	53.3	16	13	8	8

Table A2 classifies the percentage of favorable votes on all constitutional questions referred to the people by the legislature. The percentage of favorable votes is shown for all constitutional referenda, for financial questions (i.e., those propositions providing for an increase in the debt or a guarantee of loans by the state), and for nonfinancial referenda.

TABLE A2
PERCENTAGE OF VOTES APPROVING CONSTITUTIONAL REFERENDUMS IN OHIO, 1951–1969

Counties	*Votes Approving All Referendums*	*Votes Approving Financial Referendums*	*Votes Approving Nonfinancial Referendums*
Adams	48.7%	59.1%	45.6%
Allen	54.7	60.7	53.1
Ashland	54.5	61.5	52.5
Ashtabula	58.3	64.1	56.7
Athens	53.3	63.7	50.3
Auglaize	51.2	60.4	48.6
Belmont	53.4	62.6	50.8
Brown	49.7	58.4	47.3
Butler	52.9	58.4	51.5
Carroll	49.5	66.1	45.5
Champaign	51.5	57.1	49.2
Clark	50.8	55.5	49.6
Clermont	52.8	58.5	51.3
Clinton	53.3	59.4	51.6
Columbiana	55.7	62.1	53.8
Coshocton	49.3	60.0	46.3
Crawford	51.8	58.6	50.0
Cuyahoga	59.1	62.6	58.2
Darke	46.3	45.8	46.5
Defiance	53.5	62.8	51.1
Delaware	55.5	62.4	53.6
Erie	60.0	65.6	58.2
Fairfield	50.8	57.5	48.8
Fayette	50.7	58.1	48.5
Franklin	58.3	62.7	56.9
Fulton	56.8	65.3	54.1
Gallia	53.7	66.5	49.2
Geauga	59.5	64.8	58.0

TABLE A2 Continued

Counties	*Votes Approving All Referendums*	*Votes Approving Financial Referendums*	*Votes Approving Nonfinancial Referendums*
Greene	56.0	60.1	54.8
Guernsey	48.7	58.2	45.6
Hamilton	56.8	56.6	56.8
Hancock	58.3	65.8	56.1
Hardin	48.5	54.8	46.7
Harrison	51.0	61.5	47.8
Henry	55.1	61.2	53.1
Highland	50.2	59.2	47.5
Hocking	50.0	60.2	46.8
Holmes	46.5	49.6	45.3
Huron	55.3	60.0	53.3
Jackson	53.9	67.9	49.4
Jefferson	56.2	65.5	53.4
Knox	51.5	57.6	49.7
Lake	54.9	60.4	53.2
Lawrence	49.9	59.6	47.0
Licking	51.5	57.1	49.7
Logan	53.3	58.9	51.6
Lorain	50.3	51.5	50.0
Lucas	57.0	64.3	55.1
Madison	54.9	63.1	52.4
Mahoning	52.7	61.7	50.0
Marion	52.6	59.0	50.7
Medina	57.8	62.6	56.4
Meigs	51.0	64.5	46.2
Mercer	48.3	56.1	45.8
Miami	58.9	66.4	56.6
Monroe	50.1	62.4	45.8
Montgomery	54.6	58.5	53.3
Morgan	50.0	60.7	46.4
Morrow	47.8	53.8	45.8
Muskingum	54.5	64.1	51.2
Noble	45.6	59.9	40.9
Ottawa	58.5	65.6	56.5
Paulding	46.4	52.6	44.7
Perry	50.5	61.8	47.1
Pickaway	52.0	59.1	49.6
Pike	52.2	60.4	40.9

TABLE A2 Continued

Counties	*Votes Approving All Referendums*	*Votes Approving Financial Referendums*	*Votes Approving Nonfinancial Referendums*
Portage	55.8	58.5	55.0
Preble	51.5	54.0	50.7
Putnam	45.0	51.9	42.9
Richland	53.3	55.0	52.9
Ross	54.8	63.0	52.3
Sandusky	55.6	61.1	54.0
Scioto	53.3	61.4	50.6
Seneca	53.8	62.4	51.3
Shelby	50.8	59.0	48.2
Stark	52.4	57.4	50.9
Summit	58.2	62.7	57.0
Trumbull	50.2	56.7	48.2
Tuscarawas	49.7	55.7	47.2
Union	51.8	57.5	56.7
Van Wert	50.6	58.9	48.1
Vinton	49.5	62.9	44.4
Warren	54.5	60.4	53.7
Washington	53.6	65.2	49.8
Wayne	58.6	63.8	57.2
Williams	56.4	64.1	54.0
Wood	57.5	64.9	55.4
Wyandot	50.7	55.8	49.1

PART VI

A Bibliographic Note

A Bibliographic Note

THE STUDENT OF POLITICS LOOKING FOR CONTEMPORARY ANALYSES of the Ohio political system will find the quantity of available literature meager. With the exception of the works of a few authors, the orientation of most writings is primarily historical or legal-institutional.

By far the most astute political analyses are found in studies by Thomas A. Flinn, John H. Fenton, and Howard D. Hamilton. Taken as a group, these studies are the foundation for understanding state politics. In his articles, "The Outline of Ohio Politics," *Western Political Quarterly,* 13 (September, 1960), 702–721, and "Continuity and Change in Ohio Politics," *Journal of Politics,* 24 (August, 1964), 521–544, Flinn uses state and county election results to determine the bases of party support, as well as to trace the evolution of party followings. An article by Flinn and Frederick M. Wirt, "Local Party Leaders; Groups of Like Minded Men," *Midwest Journal of Political Science,* 9 (February, 1965), 77–98, utilizes survey data about the attitudes of county party leaders toward selected state and national issues.

John H. Fenton's contribution is a comparative study of partisan politics in six midwestern states. In the book *Midwest Politics* (New York: Holt, Rinehart and Winston, 1966), Fenton identifies three state party systems as "issue-oriented" and three as "job-oriented." He discusses the causes and consequences of each orientation. Ohio parties are categorized as job-oriented and its politics as issueless.

The work edited by Howard D. Hamilton, *Reapportioning Legislatures* (Columbus: Charles E. Merrill Books, Inc., 1966), deals with the criteria for reapportionment. Hamilton's chapter, "Some Observations in Ohio: Single-Member Districts, Multi-Member Districts and the Floating Fraction," offers a history and analysis of the effects of various methods of apportioning state legislative seats in Ohio. Flinn also has a section entitled "The Election System and the Party System."

Several works by historians contribute to an understanding of contemporary political structures and culture in Ohio. Two of the most comprehensive are the five volumes of Emilius Randall and Daniel J. Ryan entitled *History of Ohio* (New York: The Century History Co., 1912) and the six volumes edited by Carl Wittke, *The History of the State of Ohio* (Columbus: Ohio State Archaeological and Historical Society, 1941–1942). The former concentrates heavily on political and economic history. Wittke's volumes, on the other hand, are of broader scope, including settlement patterns and the religious, cultural, scientific, and economic aspects of state development.

In addition to these comprehensive studies, a large number of books and articles deal with particular eras or substantive aspects of Ohio history. Robert E. Chaddock, for example, has included a detailed description of early Ohio settlement patterns in *Ohio Before 1850* (New York: Columbia University, 1908).

Chronicles of early nineteenth-century political parties include William Utter's "Saint Tammany in Ohio: A Study of Frontier Politics," *Mississippi Valley Historical Review,* 15 (1928–1929), 321–341 and H. J. Webster's "History of the Democratic Party Organization in the Northwest," *Ohio State Archaeological and Historical Society Quarterly,* 37 (1928), 439–591, and 38 (1929), 47–182. Politics in the latter half of the nineteenth century is covered by Harold C. Davis in "The Economic Basis of Ohio Politics (1820–1940)," *The Ohio State Archaeological and Historical*

Society Quarterly, 47 (1938), 288–318, and by George H. Porter in "Ohio Politics During the Civil War Period," *Studies in History, Economics and Public Law*, Vol. 40, No. 2 (1911), 5–255, and "Ohio in National Politics, 1865–1896," *The Ohio State Archaeological and Historical Quarterly*, 37 (1928), 220–427.

Among the more legal-institutional descriptions of Ohio government, the two most comprehensive general works are *The Government and Administration of Ohio*, by Francis R. Aumann and Harvey Walker (New York: Thomas Y. Crowell Co., 1956), and *Ohio Government*, by Albert H. Rose (St. Louis: Educational Publishers, Inc., 1953). The latter was revised and published in 1960 by the University of Dayton Press as *The State and Local Government of Ohio*.

Studies of the state constitution include two prepared prior to mandatory referenda on the calling of a state constitutional convention. W. Donald Heisel and Iola O. Hessler, *State Government for Our Times* (Cincinnati: The Stephen H. Wilder Foundation, 1970), and Harvey Walker (ed.), *An Analysis and Appraisal of the Ohio State Constitution, 1851–1951* (Cincinnati: The Stephen H. Wilder Foundation, 1951) provide complete coverage of problem areas in the constitution. Concerning the Ohio judiciary, three studies deserve some mention. Francis Aumann, in "The Development of the Judicial System in Ohio," *The Ohio State Archaeological and Historical Society Quarterly*, 41 (1932), 195–236, discusses the constitutional evolution of the courts. A more recent critique of the judicial system may be found in two Staff Research Reports (Nos. 35 and 75, 1959 and 1965) by the Ohio Legislative Service Commission.

Other Sources

History

Croly, Herbert, *Marcus Alonzo Hanna — His Life and Work* (New York: The Macmillan Co., 1919).

Russell, Francis, *The Shadow of Blooming Grove* (New York: McGraw-Hill Book Co., 1968).

Warner, Hoyt Landon, *Progressivism in Ohio, 1897–1917* (Columbus: Ohio State University Press, 1964).

Parties, Interest Groups, and Electoral Behavior

Bindley, Joe H., "An Analysis of Voting Behavior in Ohio," (Unpublished Ph.D. dissertation, University of Pittsburgh, 1959).

Bliss, Ray C., "The Role of the State Chairman," in James M. Cannon (ed.), *Politics U.S.A.* (Garden City: Doubleday and Co., 1960), pp. 159–170.

Brazier, Gary P., "The Ohio Architect's Guild," in Richard P. Frost (ed.), *Cases in State and Local Government* (Englewood Cliffs, N.J.: Prentice-Hall, Inc., 1961), pp. 41–49.

Eulau, Heinz, "The Ecological Basis of Party Systems: The Case of Ohio," *Midwest Journal of Political Science,* 1 (August, 1957), 125–135.

Fenton, John H., "The Right to Work Vote in Ohio," *Midwest Journal of Political Science,* 3 (August, 1959), 241–253.

Flinn, Thomas A., "How Mr. Nixon Took Ohio: A Short Reply to Senator Kennedy's Question," *Western Political Quarterly,* 15 (June, 1962), 274–279.

———, "Party Responsibility in the States: Some Causal Factors," *American Political Science Review,* 58 (March, 1964), 60–71.

———, "State Politics and the 1968 Election in Ohio" (A paper prepared for delivery at the 1971 meeting of the Midwest Political Science Association, Chicago, April 29–May 1, dittoed.)

Glantz, Oscar, "The Negro Voter in Northern Industrial Cities," *Western Political Quarterly,* 13 (December, 1960), 999–1010.

Gump, W. Robert, "The Functions of Patronage in American Party Politics: An Empirical Reappraisal," *Midwest Journal of Political Science,* 15 (February, 1971), 87–107.

Jauchius, Rollin D., "Gubernatorial Roles: An Assessment by Five Ohio Governors" (Unpublished Ph.D. dissertation, Ohio State University, 1971).

Klein, Bernard W., "Political Partisanship in Four State Legislatures," 1967, Ph.D. (order No. 66–8472) 229 pp., Micro. $3.00, Xerox $10.35 (Political Science).

Peirce, Neal R., *The Megastates of America: People, Politics, and Power in the Ten Great States* (New York: W. W. Norton & Company, 1972).

The State Legislature

Barber, Kathleen Lucas, "Reapportionment in Ohio and Michigan: Political Revolution Reconsidered," 1969, Ph.D. (order No. 69–9332) 242 pp., Micro. $3.15, Xerox $11.05 (Political Science).

Hale, Myron Q., "The Ohio Fair Housing Law," in Lynn W. Eley and Thomas W. Casstevens (eds.), *The Politics of Fair Housing Legislation* (San Francisco: Chandler Publishing Company, 1968).

LeBlanc, Hugh L., "Voting in State Senates: Party and Constituency Influences," *Midwest Journal of Political Science,* 13 (February, 1969), 33–57.

Masotti, Louis, and Kathleen Barber, "'Better Men' Running? Effects of the Change to Single-Member from Multi-Member Legislature Districts in Ohio are Obscure," *National Civic Review,* 56 (October, 1967), 504–511.

Ohio Legislative Service Commission, *Legislative Services, Facilities and Procedures,* Staff Report No. 81 (Columbus: 1966).

Wahlke, John, *et al., The Legislative System* (New York: Wiley, 1962).

Waltzer, Herbert, "Apportionment and Districting in Ohio: Components of

Deadlock," in Malcolm E. Jewell (ed.), *The Politics of Reapportionment* (New York: Atherton Press, 1962), pp. 173–188.

Fiscal Policies

Bowman, John H., *et al., Local Government Tax Revision in Ohio* (Columbus, Ohio: Battelle Memorial Institute, 1968).
Burke, John F., Jr., and Edric A. Weld, Jr., *A Profile of State Government Taxation and Revenue for Ohio, 1968,* Working Paper in Economics No. 23 (Revised), Department of Economics, Cleveland State University, April 3, 1970.
Gotherman, John, Jr., "Development of The Income Tax in Ohio," *Ohio Cities and Villages,* 14 (March, 1966), 11–13.
———, "Municipal Income Taxation . . . The Changing Ohio Scene," *Ohio Cities and Villages,* 15 (March, 1967) 11–13.
Ohio Legislative Service Commission, *The Ohio School Foundation Program,* Staff Research Report No. 94, (Columbus, 1969).
Ohio Tax Study Commission, *The State and Local Tax Structure of Ohio* (Columbus, 1967).
Sacks, Seymour, *et al., Financing Government in a Metropolitan Area* (Glencoe: Free Press, 1961).
Starner, George Frederich, "Variation In the Level of Taxes on Property, An Ohio Case," 1970, Ph.D. (order No. 70–19,366) 156 pp., Micro. $4.00, Xerox $7.40 (Economics).
Stocker, Frederick D., *The Rough Road to Tax Reform — The Ohio Experience,* Working Paper in Public Policy No. 1, College of Administrative Science, Ohio State University, March, 1972.

Local Government and Politics

Bremner, Robert H., "The Civic Revival in Ohio," *American Journal of Economics and Sociology,* 8 (October, 1948), 61–68.
———, "Reformed Businessman: Tom L. Johnson," *American Journal of Economics and Sociology,* 8 (April, 1949), 299–309.
———, "Municipal Ownership and Economic Privilege," *American Journal of Economics and Sociology,* 9 (July, 1950), 477–482.
———, "The Street Railway Controversy in Cleveland," *American Journal of Economics and Sociology,* 10 (January, 1951), 185–206.
———, "How Privilege Fights," *American Journal of Economics and Sociology,* 11 (January, 1952), 203–214.
———, "The Political Techniques of the Progressives," *American Journal of Economics and Sociology,* 12 (January, 1952), 189–200.
———, "Humanizing Cleveland and Toledo," *American Journal of Economics and Sociology,* 13 (January, 1953), 179–190.
———, "Harris R. Cooley and Cooley Farms," *American Journal of Economics and Sociology,* 14 (October, 1954), 71–75.
———, "Police, Penal and Parole Policies in Cleveland and Toledo," *American Journal of Economics and Sociology,* 14 (July, 1955), 387–398.
Derthick, Martha, *Cleveland* (Cambridge, Mass.: Joint Center for Urban Studies of MIT and Harvard University, 1963).

Gotherman, John, Jr., "Municipal Charters in Ohio," *Ohio Cities and Villages,* 12 (October, 1964), 10–22.

Gray, Kenneth E., *A Report on Politics in Cincinnati,* (Cambridge, Mass.: Joint Center for Urban Studies of MIT and Harvard University, 1959).

Hamilton, Howard D., "Direct Legislation: Some Implications of Open Housing Referenda," *American Political Science Review,* 64 (March, 1970), 124–137.

Holden, Matthew, *County Government in Ohio* (Cleveland: Cleveland Metropolitan Services Commission, 1958).

Howe, Frederick, C., *The Confessions of a Reformer* (Chicago: Quadrangle Books, 1967).

Key, V. O., Jr., "Partisanship and County Office," *American Political Science Review,* 47 (June, 1953), 525–532.

Mitler, Z. L. "Boss Cox's Cincinnati: A Study in Urbanization and Politics, 1880–1914," *Journal of American History,* 54 (March, 1968), 23–38.

Norton, James A., "Referenda Voting in a Metropolitan Area," *Western Political Quarterly,* 16 (March, 1963), 195–213.

Ohio Legislative Service Commission, *County Budget Commissions,* Staff Research Report No. 91, (Columbus, 1969).

Walker, Harvey, "Municipal Government in Ohio Before 1912," *Ohio State Law Journal,* 9 (Winter, 1948), 1–17.

Watson, Richard A., and John H. Romani, "Metropolitan Government for Metropolitan Cleveland," *Midwest Journal of Political Science,* 5 (November, 1961), 365–390.

Index

STANDARD METROPOLITAN STATISTICAL AREAS
IN OHIO